Law *of* Sale of Goods

LAW
of
Sale of Goods

Akhileshwar Pathak

OXFORD
UNIVERSITY PRESS

OXFORD
UNIVERSITY PRESS

Oxford University Press is a department of the University of Oxford.
It furthers the University's objective of excellence in research, scholarship,
and education by publishing worldwide. Oxford is a registered trademark of
Oxford University Press in the UK and in certain other countries

Published in India by
Oxford University Press
YMCA Library Building, 1 Jai Singh Road, New Delhi 110 001, India

ISBN-13: 978-0-19-809222-3
ISBN-10: 0-19-809222-9

Typeset in 10.5/13.1 Minion Pro
by Excellent Laser Typesetters, Pitampura, Delhi 110 034
Printed in India by G.H. Prints Pvt Ltd, New Delhi 110 020

To
Talin and Sanvi

Contents

Introduction

It is a popular myth, which lawyers do little to dispel, that the law is a highly technical matter with mysterious rules leading to results which are contrary to commonsense. Nothing could be further from the truth, both in general and in the particular instance of the law relating to the repudiation of contracts.

Justice Donaldson in *Warinco A.G. v. Samor S.P.A.*[1]

This book makes a departure from the conventional way law books are written: organized in sections, briefly summarizing every court judgment on the subject. Often, the summaries are just a line or two taken from the head notes of the reported cases. This is not a method that is conducive for an understanding of the law, especially a common-law-based subject like the sale of goods. In the following pages, we will explore the evolution of the law of sale of goods. This will guide us in developing a method for understanding the subject.

[1] *Warinco A.G. v. Samor S.P.A.*, (1977) 2 Lloyd's Rep. 582.

DEVELOPMENT OF THE LAW OF SALE OF GOODS

Trade and traders have existed for centuries. Governing institutions came up with laws to settle disputes among the traders. Thus, commercial law developed wherever there was trade. However, it is the British experience through colonial expansion that was propagated to most parts of the world. Thus, we locate the law with reference to its evolution in England. English judges decided cases on the basis of usage and customs of the community, and the prevailing notions of reason and justice. The courts relied heavily upon prior judgments. As similar cases were similarly decided, certain kinds of reasoning and principles came to be formulated. The courts thereafter followed these principles as the law. Through this process of precedence, a body of judge-made law gradually developed that came to be called common law. The development took place in several fields, including in issues connected with contracts, sale of goods, carriage and transportation, negotiable instruments, banking, and trademarks.

Contract was the general name used for different kinds of business relations, which included sales, leasing of land and premises, transportation of goods through rail and ship, and money lending and pawning. The essential elements of this were offer, acceptance, and consideration. Every dispute on a contract was thus also a dispute in the particular field to which it was related. Therefore, alongside contract law, the courts also, through their decisions, formulated rules and principles to be followed while deciding disputes in those specific fields. With the development of trade, commerce, and industry, the law for each such field became elaborate and specialized. One of the specialized laws to emerge was the law of sale of goods.

The law of sale of goods, thus, built itself on the foundation of contract law. It took contract law as given and provided further details in relation to the specific nature of the contract. The rules and principles common law courts had formulated in relation to the sale of goods were codified as the Sale of Goods Act, 1893. This was widely adopted in the commonwealth countries and the United States of America. In India, the act was adopted with minor changes in the Sale of Goods Act, 1930. The Contract Act, 1872, had contained the law of sale of goods. This was deleted with the enactment of the Sale of Goods Act, 1930.

The Sale of Goods Act, 1893, was not the only common law to be codified. Towards the end of the nineteenth century, several fields of common law were codified. Common law was a precedence-based system. Over a period of time, the cases became numerous and the load cumbersome. At times, the court cases could present conflicting views. Thus, codification was undertaken to extract the principles formulated by the courts and present them in a systematic manner. One approach in interpreting the codified common law was to treat the act like any other

enactment. The courts thus attempted to interpret the text of its sections without reference to prior court cases. The approach did not work. Unlike other statutory provisions, these were not the texts authored by the legislature, but was drawn from the principles formulated by prior court judgments. The provisions were best understood with reference to their source. Thus, the courts continued to rely on the prior cases. The act thus became a part of common law.

Following this, the text of the Sale of Goods Act, 1930, is an expression of the trade practices of late nineteenth century England. The law of sale of goods, like the Contract Act, 1872, as it derives from everyday practices is common sense, generalized over a long period of time. If one takes up a contemporary case on the sale of goods, it would refer to the cases decided in the past century for the principles. The referred cases in turn refer to cases decided in the prior decades and century. The chain can be tracked up to the 1700s, but these cases are not readily accessible. Thus, it is not that one case or one judge has set the principles. The principles have been reiterated and refined over the centuries. At each stage, with the development of trade and commerce, the courts were presented with new contexts for the application of the principles. Through this process, the principles as well as the link between them were elaborated and refined. Thus, the law of sale of goods is generalized common sense.

We can discern five distinct themes in the clustering of the principles on the sale of goods. First, a sale is a contract where ownership in goods is transferred for a price. The nature of the contract had posed specific disputes that common law courts had to resolve. An example of this is when and how ownership is transferred from the buyer to the seller. Ownership is a concept on which the entire social order rests. The overarching principle was composed of a network of principles on specific goods, non-specific goods, delivery of goods, possession, ascertainment, and risk. One part of the Sale of Goods Act, 1930, is codification of these principles.

Second, as a sale is a contract of a specific kind, some principles can be simply derived from contract law. For example, the general principle for compensation for breach of contract is to put the party in the position they would be if the contract were not breached. As a contract for sale is for a price, the compensation becomes the difference in the price the innocent party would get for the same goods in the market. Some parts of the Sale of Goods Act, 1930, are simply derived from contract law.

Third, sale is a special form of contract, and thus the general principles of contract law would undoubtedly apply. However, as the law of sale of goods was being made as an act, it also needed to be self-contained. Thus, some provisions in the act are merely codification of contract law. An example of this is the provision that a sale contract can be made through express or implied communication.

Fourth, the concept of ownership is as old as the law on contract and sale, and no person could deprive another of his ownership. Any benefit drawn from another's property has to be restored as unjust enrichment. Compromising the concept of ownership would collapse the social order. Thus, law has always been firm and rigid on protecting the owner. As a sale was a contract for transfer of ownership towards the performance of the contract, whether the ownership had transferred to the buyer or not became a central question. If the ownership had transferred, the seller could not have the ownership re-vested in him. He could only claim the price. The protection of ownership runs through the act.

Fifth, ordinarily only an owner can transfer ownership in goods. With the development of trade and commerce, a conflict developed between two demands. On the one hand, only the owner should be able to transfer the ownership. On the other hand, a bona fide buyer should not be deprived of the benefit of ownership even if the seller had no authority to transfer the goods. Rejecting this would hold trade and commerce back, but it will also erode the very foundation of society based on ownership. The law naturally sided with the owner. However, there were some exceptions, admitted through statutory enactments called the Factors Acts. The provisions of the Factors Acts were assimilated in the Sale of Goods Act, 1930.

Thus, instead of seeing the provisions as random principles put in the act, we will try to understand their basis.

ORGANIZATION OF THIS BOOK

Passing of ownership has several implications. Chapter 1 explores the nature and formation of a contract of sale. In Chapters 2 to 4, we will explore the point of time at which the buyer becomes the owner of goods. The passing of ownership depends on whether the contract of sale was for specific goods or unascertained goods. Both the types of contracts privilege the intention of the parties. If the contract is silent on the passing of property, the law provides the default option. Chapter 5 deals with sale by persons other than the owner. Ordinarily, only an owner can transfer ownership in goods. The law makes some exceptions to this principle.

A crucial concern for the buyer is the quality of goods. In the past, there was no remedy for the buyer against the seller as there was no knowing who sold what to whom. Thus, the principle was essentially 'buyer beware'; that is, the buyer purchases at his own risk. With the development of trade and commerce, to give stability to trade and commerce, the courts came to give better protection to buyers, expressed in the language of conditions and warranties implied by the law. By the time the law came to be codified, several exceptions to the principle of the buyer beware had developed. As contracts are voluntarily formed, the parties are free to omit the conditions and warranties implied by the law, and often do. Chapter 6 is on quality of goods.

Chapters 9 to 11 are on the duties and rights of the buyer and seller. The buyer has to pay money to the seller, and the law specifies when this takes place. This section will also explore the manner in which delivery of goods is made by the seller. The buyer has the right to examine the goods after delivery. The law gives authorization to an unpaid seller—one who ought to have been paid, but hasn't—in retaining possession of the goods even if the ownership is transferred to the buyer.

If the contract was foundational to the sale of goods, the sale of goods was to become foundational for the subsequent develop-ment of law. Laws imposing tax and regulating trade, commerce, or business practices used the terms used in the Sale of Goods Act, 1930, for their scope and application. As the sales tax laws were worded, the tax could apply only on the 'sale' of goods. There was much litigation on the meaning of 'sale' in the sales tax laws until the courts finally concluded that it had to be given the meaning specified in the Sale of Goods Act, 1930. The Parliament later amended the Constitution to neutralize the judgments, and there have been further court judgments exploring the scope of the constitutional amendment. As intangible forms of property have developed, such as computer software, the question has arisen as to whether these are goods. With the imposition of the service tax, another question has arisen distinguishing a contract of sale from service. These areas have been at the forefront of the evolution of law. We explore this towards the end of the book.

Before starting out, let us note that a reference to the Sale of Goods Act, 1893, would mean reference to the English law, and the Sale of Goods Act, 1930, would refer to the law in India. As the Indian law is derived from the English one, the two acts will be interchangeably used through the book.

Nature and Formation of Contract of Sale

The sale as a form of transaction has existed for centuries. The laws, contracts, and sale of goods developed simultaneously. Several principles of contract emerged from disputes on sale of goods, and in the organization and systematization of the law, the sale was recognized as a specific form of contract. Let us explore the nature of a sale contract by assigning a name to the following contracts:

Contract 1: X contracts to give away for good his washing machine to Y in exchange for a television.

Contract 2: M contracts to give away for good his washing machine to Z for a payment of Rs 10,000.

Contract 3: B contracts to allow C to use his washing machine for a payment of Rs 2,000. The machine has to be returned after a year.

Contract 4: D contracts to give P his washing machine for a loan of Rs 10,000. P is required to give back the machine in the same condition when the loan is repaid with interest.

The transaction in Contract 1 is barter; in Contract 2, sale; Contract 3, hire; and Contract 4, pledge. What distinguishes a contract of sale from the others?

NATURE OF CONTRACT OF SALE

A sale is a contract where the ownership of goods is transferred for a price in cash. In the language of contract law, in a contract of sale, the consideration for the buyer is the transfer of ownership in goods, and that for the seller is a price in cash. The common law courts had developed this branch of law for the transfer of ownership in goods, that is, tangible movable property, while the land laws dealt with immovable property. We will explore the scope of goods later in the chapter. For the time being, we shall assume that tangible movable properties are certainly goods. Consider the following transactions:

Transaction 1: The government compulsorily acquired a truck owned by B, evaluated it at Rs 6 lakhs, and paid the amount to B.

Transaction 2: X gifted a laptop to A.

Transaction 3: A shop sold a laptop to X for Rs 40,000.

Are these transactions sales? We would recognize only the third as one. In all these transactions, there is a transfer of owner-ship of goods. However, in the first case, as the truck is compulsorily acquired, is not a contract, and thus not a sale. The second case, as it is a gift, is not a contract and thus, not a sale. Sections 4 and 5 express these principles. Section 5 reads:

5. Contract of sale how made:

(1) A contract of sale is made by an offer to buy or sell goods for a price and the acceptance of such offer. The contract may provide for the immediate delivery of the goods or immediate payment of the price or both, or for the delivery or payment by instalments, or that the delivery or payment or both shall be postponed.

(2) Subject to the provisions of any law for the time being in force, a contract of sale may be made in writing or by word of mouth, or partly in writing and partly by word of mouth or may be implied from the conduct of the parties.

A sale is first and foremost a contract, and can be formed only if it meets the requisites of one. Section 4 supports Section 5:

4. Sale and agreement to sell:

(1) A contract of sale of goods is a contract whereby the seller transfers or agrees to transfer the property in goods to the buyer for a price. There may be a contract of sale between one part-owner and another.

(2) A contract of sale may be absolute or conditional.

(3) Where under a contract of sale the property in the goods is transferred from the seller to the buyer, the contract is called a sale, but where the transfer of the property in the goods is to take place at a future time or subject to some condition thereafter to be fulfilled, the contract is called an agreement to sell.

(4) An agreement to sell becomes a sale when the time elapses or the conditions are fulfilled subject to which the property in the goods is to be transferred.

A contract is a voluntary, consensual activity. Thus, it is for the parties to decide when the considerations would transact. Similarly, in a contract of sale, it is for the parties to decide when the ownership will transfer and the buyer will pay the price. The buyer may be required to pay immediately, on creation of the contract, on delivery, or even pay in instalments. Similarly, the ownership can transfer any time, from the very moment the contract is made to a point of time in the future. The transfer of ownership, however, creates a significant effect. Only owners can divest themselves of the exclusive use and enjoyment of the goods. Once the ownership is transferred, the buyer becomes the owner, and no fetters should be imposed on the buyer. Thus, once ownership is transferred, even if the buyer is in breach of his obligations, the ownership cannot be re-vested in the seller. For this reason, the law of sale of goods makes a distinction between a sale and an agreement to sell. In the latter, the owner has a contractual obligation to transfer the ownership but has not done it yet. He can refuse to transfer the ownership. This will only be a breach of his contractual obligation, for which he will have to pay damages. However, once the seller performs his contractual obligation and transfers the ownership, he can only claim the price. The ownership cannot be restored to him, even if the buyer is in default. In a sale, the maturation of an agreement to sell represents the transition in the rights and obligations of the buyer and the seller. A sale cannot take place without an agreement to sell. However, the ownership may transfer with the formation of agreement itself. The offer may specify that the ownership would transfer the moment the offer is accepted. Section 5 uses the term 'contract of sale' to represent formation of a contract for sale of goods, whether the ownership is transferred or will be transferred.

FORMATION OF A CONTRACT OF SALE

A contract of sale can be made through acceptance of an offer. The offer must be clear, definite, and unambiguous. An offer should be distinguished from an invitation to offer. The communication between the parties can be express or implied; that is, the parties can communicate in writing or orally, or the communication between the parties can be discerned from their conduct. The parties must have the capacity to contract. A contract of sale entered into with a minor is void. It can also be void on the grounds of illegality, mistake, or impossibility. Similarly, a contract of sale caused by coercion, misrepresentation, fraud, or undue influence is voidable and can be set aside by the aggrieved party. A contract of sale must be made by the free consent of the contracting parties. This aspect has been relevant in relation to the application of sales tax.

The state makes laws regulating and curtailing economic activity. The extent of regulation can range from the state compulsorily acquiring goods to significant control that diminishes the freedom of individuals. Let us examine this further with a review of court judgments.

Kirkness v. John Hudson and Co. Ltd

Railway Wagons owned by John Hudson and Co. were requisitioned by the Minister of Transport in the UK. The wagons were subsequently acquired by the British Transport Commission without its assent under the Transport Act, 1947.[1] Section 29 of the act made provision for compulsory taking of property with appropriate compensation. The amount paid by the Commission as compensation was substantially higher than the written down value of the wagons for income tax purposes.

Within the Income Tax Act, a gain made from the sale of a capital asset was taxable. The tax authorities claimed that the difference between the written down value and the amount received from the government was income and taxed it. The dispute before the court was whether the acquisition was a sale. Viscount Simonds for the House of Lords observed:

My Lords, in my opinion the company's wagons were not sold, and it would be a grave misuse of language to say that they were sold. To say of a man who has had his property taken from him against his will and been awarded compensation in the settlement of which he has had no voice, to say of such a man that he has sold his property appears to me to be as far from the truth as to say of a man who has been deprived of his property without compensation that he has given it away. Alike in the ordinary use of language and in its legal concept a sale connotes the mutual assent of two parties. So far as the ordinary use of language is concerned it is difficult to avoid being dogmatic, but for my part I can only echo what Singleton L.J. said in his admirably clear judgments 'What would anyone accustomed to the use of the words "sale" or "sold" answer'? It seems to me that everyone must say 'Hudsons did not sell'. I am content to march in step with everyone and say 'Hudsons did not sell'. Nor is a different result reached by an attempt to analyse the legal concept.

---

[1] *Kirkness* v. *John Hudson and Co. Ltd*, (1955) AC 696.

In *New India Sugar Mills Ltd, M/s* v. *Commissioner of Sales Tax, Bihar*[2] the government had complete control over the acquisition of sugar from the mill owners. The Supreme Court ruled that the procurement was not a sale. In post-Independence India, transactions in several commodities came to be regulated under the Essential Commodities Act. Several cases came before the courts contending that sales tax would not apply as transactions were not voluntary and therefore, not sales. The high courts had taken conflicting view of the matter. The Supreme Court reviewed the law in *Vishnu Agencies (Pvt.) Ltd, M/s* v. *Commercial Tax Officer.*

Vishnu Agencies (Pvt.) Ltd, M/s v. Commercial Tax Officer

Under the Essential Commodities Act, West Bengal regulated the production, supply, and distribution of cement, and stocking it required a licence.[3] Under the conditions of the licence, a named permit holder was to be supplied the quantity and price mentioned in the permit, which was generally valid for fifteen days. The dispute was whether the transaction was a sale. The Supreme Court ruled:

In order ... to determine whether there was any agreement or consensuality between the parties, we must have regard to their conduct at or about the time when the goods changed hands. In the first place, it is not obligatory on a trader to deal in cement nor on any one to acquire it. The primary fact, therefore, is that the decision of the trader to deal in an essential commodity is volitional. Such volition carries with it the willingness to trade in the commodity strictly on the terms of Control Orders. The consumer too, who is under no legal compulsion to acquire or possess cement, decides as a matter of his volition to obtain it on the terms of the permit or the order of allotment issued in his favour. That brings the two parties together, one of whom is willing to supply the essential commodity and the other to receive it. When the allottee presents his permit to the dealer, he signifies his willingness to obtain the commodity from the dealer on the terms stated in the permit. His conduct reflects his consent. And when, upon the presentation of the permit, the dealer acts upon it, he impliedly agrees to supply the commodity to the allottee on the terms by which he has voluntarily bound himself to trade in the commodity. His conduct too reflects his consent. Thus, though both parties are bound to comply with the legal requirements governing the transaction, they agree as between themselves to enter into the transaction on statutory terms, one agreeing to supply the commodity to the other on those terms and the other agreeing to accept it from him on the very terms. It is therefore not correct to say that the transactions between the appellant and the allottees are not consensual. They, with their free consent, agreed to enter into the transactions.

We are also of the opinion that though the terms of the transaction are mostly predetermined by law, it cannot be said that there is no area at all in which there is not scope for the parties to bargain.

The court also declared, 'The true position in law is as stated above, namely, that so long as mutual assent, express or implied, is not totally excluded the transaction will amount to a sale.'

SALE DISTINGUISHED FROM OTHER CONTRACTS

There are two reasons for distinguishing a contract of sale from other kinds of contract. The Sale of Goods Act, 1930, applies to only the contract of sale. If a contract is for sale

---

[2] *New India Sugar Mills Ltd, M/s* v. *Commissioner of Sales Tax, Bihar*, AIR (1963) SC 1207.

[3] *Vishnu Agencies (Pvt.) Ltd, M/s* v. *Commercial Tax Officer*, AIR (1978) SC 449.

of goods, both the Sale of Goods Act, 1930, and the Contract Act, 1872, will apply. If the contract is not for sale of goods, only the Contract Act, 1872, will apply. The Sale of Goods Act, 1930, as we will see, gives several rights to the parties. The distinction becomes important for availing these additional rights. Another relevance of the distinction is the application of sales tax. The Constitution of India demarcates the legislative domains of the Centre and states. The latter have the legislative competence to impose sales tax. The states' enactments in this area took the concept of sale from the law on the sale of goods. This was inevitable as the sale was a well-established concept. As a result, the concept of sale is integral to the sales tax laws. Let us begin by exploring the distinction between sale and exchange.

Sale and Exchange

A contract of sale is for transfer of ownership of goods for a price. Thus, a barter or exchange is not a contract of sale. Let us examine whether the following are sale contracts:

Contract 1: A and B entered into a contract where A transferred the ownership in a book to B and in return, received a pen from B.

Contract 2: D paid a shop Rs 14,000 and received the ownership and delivery of a new refrigerator.

Contract 3: A and B entered into a contract where A transferred the ownership in a book to B and in return, received a pen and Rs 50 from B.

Contract 4: In an 'exchange programme', a shop valued X's old refrigerator at Rs 3,000. X selected a new fridge priced at Rs 12,000. At the end of it, X gave the shop Rs 9,000 and an old working fridge and received a new fridge.

The first contract is an exchange, and thus not a sale. The second is indeed a sale. In the third contract, the entire consideration is not in cash, so it is an exchange. The fourth appears to be an exchange, but the parties have put a price for the old fridge. Effectively, the contract is two separate but related contracts, one for the sale of an old fridge and the other for a purchase of a new fridge. This example is based on *Aldridge* v. *Johnson*.[4] Aldridge had entered into an agreement to exchange a hundred quarters of barley for thirty-two bullocks and £ 23. The bullocks were evaluated at £ 6 each and the barley at a total of £ 215 on the basis of a fixed per quarter rate. The court affirmed that the exchange was a sale.

Sale and Hire Purchase

Let us examine the following contracts and decide whether they are contracts of sale.

Contract 1: B paid the price for a washing machine and received delivery. Ownership transferred to the buyer on delivery.

Contract 2: X transferred the ownership in a washing machine to B. B was to pay the price in 10 instalments, one each month.

Contract 3: Y gave a washing machine to C. The machine was priced at Rs 12,000. C was to pay Rs 1,000 each month to Y. On paying the last instalment, the ownership of the washing machine was to transfer to C.

Contract 4: Z gave a television to D to use. D was to pay Z Rs 100 each month and to return the television at the end of six months.

Contract 5: M gave a washing machine to D, who was to pay M Rs 200 each month. After 36 months, D has the option to pay Rs 2,000 and get the ownership of the machine.

---

[4] *James Wilsher Aldridge* v. *Patrick Johnson*, (1857) 7 Ellis and Blackburn 885.

Contract 1 is a contract of sale as the ownership has transferred. Contract 2 is also a contract of sale; the only difference is that the seller is to be paid in instalments. Contract 3 is a sale as well. The ownership is to transfer to the buyer on the payment of the last instalment. However, as the ownership has not transferred as yet, there is an agreement to sell but no sale as yet. Contract 4 is not a contract of sale but a contract to hire a television. Neither is Contract 5, as there is no agreement between the parties on transfer of ownership. It is a contract of hire with an option for the hirer to purchase the washing machine. If the hirer opts to purchase the washing machine, a contract of sale will be formed. Let us examine the distinction between a sale and hire purchase with a review of court judgments.

Helby v. Matthews

Helby hired his piano to Brewster for three years at a stipulated rent to be paid every month.[5] The agreement included the following provisions:

A. That the hirer may terminate the hiring by delivering up to the owner the said instrument.

B. If the hirer shall punctually pay the full sum of £18 18s. by 10s. 6d. at date of signing, and by 36 monthly instalments of 10&S 6d. in advance as aforesaid, the said instrument shall become the sole and absolute property of the hirer.

C. Unless and until the full sum of £18 18s. be paid, the said instrument shall be and continue to be the sole property of the owner.

After four months, Brewster pledged the piano without the consent of the owner. The terms of hire had prohibited creating any rights on the piano or moving the piano from the premises. The owner demanded that the piano be restored to him, but the person to whom the piano was pawned claimed that as Brewster had 'bought or agreed to buy' the piano, he had the right to pawn it. The Court of Appeal held it to be a conditional sale. The case came before the House of Lords. Lord Herschell delivered the following judgment:

My Lords, I cannot, with all respect, concur in the view of the Court of Appeal, that upon the true construction of the agreement Brewster had 'agreed to buy' the piano. An agreement to buy imports a legal obligation to buy. If there was no such legal obligation, there cannot, in my opinion, properly be said to have been an agreement to buy. Where is any such legal obligation to be found? Brewster might buy or not just as he pleased. He did not agree to make thirty-six or any number of monthly payments. All that he undertook was to make the monthly payment of 10s. 6d. so long as he kept the piano. He had an option no doubt to buy it by continuing the stipulated payments for a sufficient length of time. If he had exercised that option he would have become the purchaser. I cannot see under these circumstances how he can be said either to have bought or agreed to buy the piano. The terms of the contract did not upon its execution bind him to buy, but left him free to do so or not as he pleased, and nothing happened after the contract was made to impose that obligation.

Thus, the difference between a contract of sale and hire purchase is that in a contract of sale, the parties have an obligation to transfer the ownership, whereas in a hire purchase there is no obligation to transfer the ownership but an option for the hirer to opt to buy the hired goods. The following is a case from the Supreme Court bringing out the distinction between a sale and hire purchase.

K.L. Johar and Co., M/s v. Deputy Commercial Tax Officer, Coimbatore III

The Seventh Schedule of the Constitution of India creates three lists: the Union List, State

---

[5] *Helby* v. *Matthews, House of Lords*, (1895) AC 471.

List, and Concurrent List. This Lists delineate the legislative powers of the Centre and states. Entry 48 of the State List gave the power to the states to impose tax on 'sale of goods'. The act imposing sales tax in Tamil Nadu defined a 'sale' and added the following explanation: 'A transfer of goods on the hire-purchase or other instalment system of payment shall, notwithstanding the fact that the seller retains the title in the goods as security for payment of the price, be deemed to be a sale.'[6]

Following these provisions, the sales tax department was taxing motor cars given on hire purchase contracts. It was contested that Entry 48 in List II in the Seventh Schedule limited the power of the state legislature to tax only sales. The term has to be given the meaning as in the Sale of Goods Act, 1930: a contract where the property in the goods passes to the buyer. A hire purchase agreement thus cannot be deemed to be a 'sale'. The Supreme Court noted:

It is necessary in this connection to understand the nature of a typical hire-purchase agreement as distinct from a sale in which the price is to be paid later by instalments. In the case of a sale in which the price is to be paid by instalments, the property passes as soon as the sale is made, even though the price has not been fully paid and may later be paid in instalments. This follows from the definition of sale in S. 4 of the Indian Sale of Goods Act as distinguished from (an agreement to sell) which requires that the seller transfers the property in the goods to the buyer for a price. The essence of a sale is that the property is transferred from the seller to the buyer for a price, whether paid at once or paid later in instalments. On the other hand, a hire-purchase agreement, as its very name implies, has two aspects. There is first an aspect of bailment of the goods subjected to the hire-purchase agreement, and there is next an element of sale which fructifies when the option to purchase, which is usually a term of hire-purchase agreements, is exercised by the intending purchaser. Thus the intending purchaser is known as the hirer so long as the option to purchase is not exercised, and the essence of a hire-purchase agreement properly so called is that the property in the goods does not pass at the time of the agreement but remains in the intending seller, and only passes later when the option is exercised by the intending purchaser. The distinguishing feature of a typical hire-purchase agreement therefore is that the property does not pass when the agreement is made but only passes when the options is finally exercised after complying with all the terms of the agreement.

It is clear therefore that the State legislature when it proceeds to legislate … under Entry 54 of List II of the Seventh Schedule to the Constitution, can only tax sale within the meaning of that word as defined in the Sale of Goods Act. The essence of sale under the Sale of Goods Act is that the property should pass from the seller to the buyer when a contract of sale is made except in a case of conditional sale. Hire purchase agreements are not conditional sales. Therefore, any legislation by the State legislature making any agreement or transaction in which the property does not pass from the seller to the buyer a sale would be beyond its legislative competence. What Explanation I does is to lay down that a hire purchase agreement shall be deemed to be a sale in spite of the fact that the property does not pass at the time of such agreement from the seller to the buyer. Therefore, Explanation I as it stands is beyond the legislative competence of the State legislature.

Sale and Bailment

In a bailment, the owner delivers the goods to another person under a contract. The bailee delivers the goods back to the owner or to another person at his instructions. The ownership does not transfer to the bailee. The following is an interesting case in this regard. United Breweries Limited, a manufacturer of

---

[6] *K.L. Johar and Co., M/s* v. *Deputy Commercial Tax Officer*, Coimbatore III, AIR (1965) SC 1082.

beer, had elaborate practices to retrieve glass bottles from buyers for refilling. A customer was refunded Rs 1 on returning a bottle. A similar mechanism was put in place in the entire distribution chain. The company paid taxes only on the content, not on the refund price of the bottle. The sale tax authorities charged tax on the total amount paid by the customer while buying the bottle. The Supreme Court concluded that the intention of the parties was only to sell the content. The buyer was a bailee of the bottle, whose ownership continued to be with the company. It noted:

… the customers clearly know the price they will have to pay for the beer. They are required to pay an additional amount by way of deposit for taking away the bottle which is refunded if the bottle is returned. If the bottle is not returned, the deposit is retained as liquidated damages for the loss of the bottle. There is a clear intention not to sell the bottle. Hence, we are of the view that the deposits cannot be considered as price of the bottles.

Ordinarily, there would be no confusion between sale and bailment.

Sale, Work, and Service Contract

A contract of sale is different from a service contract. In a contract of sale, the ownership would transfer to the buyer for a consideration. Some contracts, however, include both aspects; the person may become the owner of the goods and also receive a service. The question will then be whether the contract is for sale of goods, provision of service, or both. Let us first examine the concept of divisibility of a contract with the following illustration. A car owner took his car to an authorized service station. The charges displayed by the service station were as follows:

1. Servicing: Rs 600
2. RTO approved sun filter (Price): Rs 800

3. Putting up of sun filter on the car windows: Rs 200

The customer asked the station for all the three. This is a single offer leading to formation of a contract where the station was to service the car and install sun filters. The intention of the parties was to sell the sun filter to the customer. They wanted it to be three separate contracts, one for servicing of the car, the second for the sale of the sun filter, and the third for installing the sun filter. Contrast this division of a contract with the case of a technician who serviced a washing machine. The charges for servicing the washing machine were Rs 200. The technician had a small role of tape whose maximum retail sale price was Rs 10. He exhausted the entire roll of tape on the joints of the water pipes. It is possible to separate Rs 190 as the consideration for the service from Rs 10 for supplying the tape. However, the parties did not intend two separate contracts but a single non-divisible one. Thus, whether a contract is divisible is not a question of whether it can be broken into its constituents, but depends on the intention of the parties. Taking the contract as a whole, is it a contract for sale or service? The contract was for the provision of a service, in the course of which the tape was consumed. The essence of the contract was service; the tape was incidental. Thus, it is a contract of service. In contrast, where a retailer contracts to supply and configure a laptop for Rs 30,000, this is a contract of sale, even if it has an element of service. The following is a landmark case on the two concepts of divisibility of contract and essence or core of the contract.

Robinson v. Graves

A person verbally commissioned an artist to paint a portrait of a lady and agreed to pay a specified amount.[7] After the painter had finished the portrait, the customer repudiated the contract. The parties were in dispute on the claims of the painter. The customer claimed that this was a sale of goods. Section 4 of the Sale of Goods Act, 1893, provided that a sale contract for a value larger than £ 10 was binding only if there was a note or memorandum in writing. The painter contested that the contract was not for sale of a painting but for his work and labour. The damages payable to the painter for the breach depended on whether the contract was one of sale of goods. The court noted:

The question to be decided is this: Whether when a person goes to an artist to have a portrait painted, it may be his own portrait or the portrait of some friend (as for instance his wife), and the commission is accepted by the artist, they are making a bargain for the manufacture of future goods to be delivered when those goods come into existence in circumstances which make it a sale of goods within the meaning of s. 4 of the Sale of Goods Act, 1893 ... I can imagine that nothing would be more surprising to a client going to a portrait painter to have his portrait painted and to the artist who was accepting the commission than to be told that they were making a bargain about the sale of goods. It is, of course, possible that a picture may be ordered in such circumstances as will make it an order for goods to be supplied in the future, but it does not follow that that is the inference to be drawn in every case as between the client and the artist. Looking at the propositions involved from the point of view of interpreting the words in the English language it seems to me that the painting of a portrait in these circumstances would not, in the ordinary use of the English language, be deemed to be the purchase and sale of that which is produced by the artist. It would, on the contrary, be held to be an undertaking by the artist to exercise such skill as he was possessed of in order to produce for

reward a thing which would ultimately have to be accepted by the client. If that is so, the contract in this case was not a contract for the sale of goods within the meaning of s. 4 of the Sale of Goods Act, 1893.

...

If you find ... that the substance of the contract was the production of something to be sold ... then that is a sale of goods. But if the substance of the contract, on the other hand, is that skill and labour have to be exercised for the production of the article and that it is only ancillary to that there will pass from the artist to his client or customer some materials in addition to the skill involved in the production of the portrait, that does not make any difference to the result, because the substance of the contract is the skill and experience of the artist in producing the picture.

For these reasons I am of opinion that in this case the substance of the matter was an agreement for the exercise of skill and it was only incidental that some materials would have to pass from the artist to the gentleman who commissioned the portrait. For these reasons I think that this was not a contract for the sale of goods within the meaning of s. 4 of the Sale of Goods Act, 1893, but it was a contract for work and labour and materials.

Thus, in each case, a judgment has to be made whether the core of the contract is the sale of the material or provision of skill and labour. The following cases from the Supreme Court distinguish between sale and service.

Union of India v. Central India Machinery Manufacturing Co. Ltd

The Indian Railways commissioned the Central India Machinery Manufacturing Co. Ltd to manufacture wagons.[8] The sales tax authorities taxed the transaction, regarding it as a sale of wagons. The company, however, contended that it was a contract for work and

---

[7] *Robinson* v. *Graves*, (1935) 1 KB 579.

[8] *Union of India* v. *Central India Machinery Manufacturing Co. Ltd,* AIR (1977) SC 1537.

labour. The case came before the Supreme Court. The Supreme Court noted:

… transfer of property in goods for a price is the linchpin of the definition. Under Section 4 the Sale of Goods Act, 1930, also, in the definition of the term 'sale' stress is laid on the element of transfer of property in the goods. According to the Roman jurists, also, the purport of a contract of sale is that the seller divests himself of all proprietary right in the thing sold in favour of the buyer. It is this requisite which often distinguishes a contract of sale of goods from a contract for work and services. Even so, the difficulty of distinguishing between these two types of contracts is an age-old one.

The Supreme Court drew its position from Halsbury's Laws of England:

A contract of sale of goods must be distinguished from a contract for work and labour. The distinction is often a fine one. A contract of sale is a contract whose main object is the transfer of the property in and the delivery of the possession of a chattel as a chattel to the buyer. Where the main object of work undertaken by the payee of the price is not the transfer of a chattel *qua* chattel, the contract is one for work and labour. The test is whether or not the work and labour bestowed end in anything that can properly become the subject of sale; neither the ownership of materials, nor the value of the skill and labour as compared with the value of the materials is conclusive, although such matters may be taken into consideration in determining in the circumstances of a particular case, whether the contract is in substance, one for work and labour or one for the sale of a chattel.

The Court applied the above formulation in appraising the specific contract for the delivery of railway wagons. In this case, almost all the raw material for the construction of the wagon came from the company. Despite this, applying the above principle, the court concluded that the contract was for sale of wagons.

Vanguard Rolling Shutters v. Commissioner of Sales Tax

Vanguard Rolling Shutters and Steel Works were in the business of fabricating and installing iron shutters to the specific requirements of their customers.[9] Vanguard Ltd made its customers sign a contract, which included the following clauses:

Please erect at our premises … Nos of … of the following dimensions against the contract price of Rs …

1. Full payment against delivery prior to despatch or documents by Bank. It is clearly understood that there will be no such thing as to make payment after fixing.

2. Material will be carried to the site of work at cost of the party. Our responsibility ceases when the same leaves our premises.

…

4. We do not hold ourselves responsible for any structural damage or dispute with the landlord. Masonry work will be done by the party at his cost according to our instructions.

…

6. No responsibilities for non-delivery or late dispatch of goods due to any reason beyond our control.

The sales tax authority took the transaction as a sale of iron shutters, while Vanguard Ltd argued that it was a work contract. The Supreme Court noted:

It is well settled that a work contract is a contract for construction of bridges, buildings etc., and includes contracts which combine labour, skill and materials executed for a lump sum. The question as to under what circumstances a contract can be said to be a work contact is not free from difficulty and has to depend on the facts of each case. It is difficult to lay down any rule of universal

[9] *Vanguard Rolling Shutters and Steel Works, M/s v. Commissioner of Sales Tax*, AIR (1977) SC 1505.

application, but there are some well recognised tests which are laid down by decided cases of this Court which afford guidelines for determining as to whether a contract in question is a work contract or a contract for supply of goods. One of the important tests is to find out whether the contract is primarily a contract for supply of materials at a price agreed to between the parties for the materials so supplied and the work or service rendered is incidental to the execution of the contract. If so, the contract is one for sale of materials and the sale proceeds would be exigible to sales tax. On the other hand, where the contract is primarily a contact for work and labour and materials are supplied in execution of such contract, there is no contract for sale of materials but it is a work contract. The circumstance that the materials have no separate identity as a commercial article and it is only by bestowing work and labour upon them, as for example, by affixing them to the building in case of window-leaves or wooden doors and windows that they acquire commercial identity, would be prima facie indicative of a work contract. So also, where certain materials are not merely supplied but fixed to an immovable property so as to become a permanent fixture and an accretion to the said property, the contract prima facie would be a work contract. This is exactly what has happened in the present case.

The process involved in the fabrication of a rolling shutter and its actual installation on the premises was a continuous one. It would be completed only when the shutters were put up with masonry work. What was created at the end was a firmly fixed, immovable property. The price charged was a lump-sum amount, without reference to material and work. These were important considerations in the court decision that the transaction was a composite, consolidated contract of work.

In that regard, does a hotel sell food or provide a dining service? The following two cases examine this.

State of H.P. v. M/s Associated Hotels of India Ltd

Associated Hotels of India have several hotels, including the Cecil Hotel at Shimla.[10] Like any hotel, it provided several facilities to its guests, including furnished boarding, running hot and cold water, and linen. The bill was an all inclusive one, charging on the basis of per day and night of stay in the hotel. The hotel also ran a restaurant, which served meals to the guests, who could order food from the price list. They paid a bill for the various food items that they consumed at a definite rate mentioned in the menu. The sales tax authority claimed that food was being sold, and proceeded to charge sales tax on the food served by the restaurant to the guests. Associated Hotels contested this and claimed it to be a contract of service for the provision of hospitality. The case came before the Supreme Court. The court first commented on the distinction between a sale and a work contract, which we have already reviewed in the earlier cases. The court proceeded thus:

… in considering whether a transaction falls within the purview of sales tax, it becomes necessary at the threshold, to determine the nature of the contract involved in such a transaction, for the purpose of ascertaining whether it constitutes a contract of sale or a contract of work or service. If it is of the latter kind, it obviously would not attract the tax. … such determination depends in each case, upon its facts and circumstances. Mere passing of property in an article or commodity during the course of the performance of the transaction in question does not render it a transaction of sale. For, even in a contract purely of work or service, it is possible that articles may have to be used by the person executing the work and property in such articles or materials may pass to the other party. That would not necessarily convert

[10] State of H.P. v. M/s Associated Hotels of India Ltd, AIR (1972) SC 1131.

the contract into one of sale of those materials. In every case, the Court would have to find out what was the primary object of the transaction and the intention of the parties while entering into it. It may in some cases be that even while entering into a contract of work or even service, parties might enter into separate agreements, one of work and service and the other of sale and purchase of materials to be used in the course of executing the work or performing the service. But then, in such cases, the transaction would not be one and indivisible, but would fall into two separate agreements, one of work or service and the other of sale.

The Court then turned to exploring the nature of a contract between a hotel and its guests:

What precisely then, is the nature of the transaction and the intention of the parties when a hotelier receives a guest in his hotel? Is there in that transaction an intention to sell him food contained in the meals served to him during his stay in the hotel? It stands to reason that during such stay, a well equipped hotel would have to furnish a number of amenities to render the customer's stay comfortable. In the supply of such amenities, do the hotelier and his customer enter into several contracts every time an amenity is furnished? When a traveller, by plane or by steamship, purchases his passage-ticket, the transaction is one for the passage from one place to another. If, in the course of carrying out that transaction, the traveller is supplied with drinks or meals or cigarettes, no one would think that the transaction involves separate sales each time any of those things is supplied. The transaction is essentially one of carrying the passenger to his destination and if in performance of the contract of carriage, something is supplied to him, such supply is only incidental to that service, not changing either the pattern or the nature of the contract. Similarly, when clothes are given for washing to a laundry, there is a transaction which essentially involves work or service, and if the laundryman stitches a button to a garment which has fallen off, there is no sale of the button or the thread. A number of such cases involving incidental uses of materials

can be cited, none of which can be said to involve a sale as part of the main transaction.

The transaction in question is essentially one and indivisible, namely, one of receiving a customer in the hotel to stay. Even if the transaction is to be disintegrated, there is no question of the supply of meals during such stay constituting a separate contract of sale, since no intention on the part of the parties to sell and purchase food stuff supplied during meal times can be realistically spelt out. No doubt, the customer, during his stay, consumes a number of food stuffs. It may be possible to say that the property in those food stuffs passes from the hotelier to the customer at least to the extent of the food stuffs consumed by him. Even if that be so, mere transfer of property, as aforesaid, is not conclusive and does not render the event of such supply and consumption a sale, since there is no intention to sell and purchase. The transaction essentially, is one of service by the hotelier in the performance of which meals are served as part of and incidental to that service, such amenities being regarded as essential in all well conducted modern hotels. The bill prepared by the hotelier is one and indivisible, not being capable by approximation of being split up into one for residence and the other for meals. No doubt, such a bill would be prepared after consideration of the costs of meals, but that would be so for all the other amenities given to the customer. For example, when the customer uses a fan in the room allotted to him, there is surely no sale of electricity, nor a hire of the fan. Such amenities, including that of meals, are part and parcel of the service which is in reality, the transaction between the parties.

The Court relied on the law in England:

In England, a hotel under the Hotel Proprietors Act, 1956 is an establishment held out by the proprietor as offering food, drink, and if so required, sleeping accommodation, without special contract, to any traveller presenting himself and who appears able and willing to pay a reasonable sum for the services and facilities provided. This definition, which is also the definition of an inn, still excludes, as formerly, boarding houses, lodging houses and public houses, which are merely alehouses and in none of which there is the obligation to receive and entertain guests. An inn-keeper, that is to say, in the present days, a hotel proprietor, in his capacity as an innkeeper is, on the other hand, bound by the common law or the custom of the realm to receive and lodge in his inn, all comers who are travellers and to entertain them at reasonable prices without any special or previous contract unless he has some reasonable ground of refusal. ... The rights and obligations of hotel proprietors are governed by a statute which has more or less incorporated the common law. The contract between such a hotel proprietor and a traveller presenting himself to him for lodging is one which is essentially a contract of service and facilities provided at reasonable price.

The Supreme Court, thus, concluded:

The transaction between a hotelier and a visitor to his hotel is thus, one essentially of service in the performance of which and as part of the amenities incidental to that service, the hotelier serves meals at stated hours. The Revenue, therefore, was not entitled to split up the transaction into two parts, one of service and the other of sale of food stuffs and to split up also the bill charged by the hotelier as consisting of charges for lodging and charges for food stuffs served to him with a view to bring the latter under the Act.

Northern India Caterers v. Lt Governor of Delhi

The question of the serving of food in a res-taurant was further examined in *Northern India Caterers* v. *Lt Governor of Delhi*. The question raised was whether the food eaten in a restaurant by non-residents was a sale.[11] Should sales tax be charged on this? We could say that a restaurant provides the service of supplying food. Restaurants offer a certain décor, lighting, air conditioning, special

crockery, and service by waiters. Thus, it offers a service, not a sale of food. The Supreme Court reiterated the position taken in *State of HP* v. *M/s Associated Hotels of India Ltd.*[12] The Supreme Court ruled that the case was no different from the case of residents eating at the restaurant:

It has already been noticed that in regard to ho-tels, this Court has, in Associated Hotels of India Limited, ... adopted the concept of the English law that there is no sale when food and drink are supplied to guests residing in the hotel. The court pointed out that the supply of meals was essen-tially in the nature of a service provided to them and could not be identified as a transaction of sale. The Court declined to accept the proposition that the Revenue was entitled to split up the transac-tion into two parts, one of service and the other of sale of foodstuffs. If that be true in respect of hotels, a similar approach seems to be called for on principle in the case of restaurants. No reason has been shown to us for preferring any other. The classical legal view being that a number of services are concomitantly provided by way of hospitality, the supply of meals must be regarded as minis-tering to a bodily want or to the satisfaction of a human need.

The Court, thus, held that it was not amenable to be taxed. The government took the case back to the Supreme Court in review.[13] The apprehension of the states was that even food vendors—in whose case there was only a sale of food across the counter—would take advantage of the ruling. The Supreme Court clarified:

... we have no hesitation in saying that where food is supplied in an eating-house or restaurant, and it is established upon the facts that the substance of

---

[11] *Northern India Caterers, M/s (India)* v. *Lt Governor of Delhi*, AIR (1978) SC 1591.

[12] *State of H.P.* v. *M/s Associated Hotels of India Ltd*, AIR (1972) SC 1131.

[13] *Northern India Caterers (India)* v. *Lt Governor of Delhi*, AIR (1980) SC 674.

the transaction, evidenced by its dominant object, is a sale of food and the rendering of services is merely incidental, the transaction would undoubtedly be exigible to sales-tax. In every case, it will be for the taxing authority to ascertain the facts when making an assessment under the relevant sales tax law and to determine upon those facts, whether a sale of the food supplied is intended.

The Parliament neutralized the Supreme Court rulings through the forty-sixth amendment to the Constitution of India to deem hire purchase, works contract, and provision of food to be sales and thus taxable. Since then, disputes have shifted to making a distinction between sale and other contracts with reference to the constitutional provisions. Further, the Parliament introduced service tax on three services in 1994. Over the years, service tax has been extended to a large number of services. The distinction between a contract for sale and for provision of service has become important for the application of the two taxes. In the concluding chapter, we will review the development of the law on sale and taxation.

Scope of Goods

In a contract of sale, the consideration for the buyer is transfer of ownership in goods, and the law applies only in relation to goods. The law, as it emerged, treated land and building as one class of property. The State was interested in collecting agricultural revenue from land, and so it maintained a record of the landholders. This was extended to include ownership of houses and buildings. Further, as the land property was limited and immovable, the State had to play a central role in ascertaining and fixing ownership and interest on it. For this reason, immovable property came to be treated separately by the land laws. In contrast to this were

movable property like horses, grain, ploughs, and carriages. These came to be called goods. The law of sale of goods was for the movable property.

Cash is also a property and movable. Should it be goods? Money is the very medium for exchange; it cannot be exchanged with itself, and further, it will readily get mixed up with other money to lose its distinctiveness. Thus, money should not be taken to be goods. However, an antique coin or currency note is valued in itself and not as a medium of exchange. An antique piece will retain its distinctiveness and not get mixed up with money in circulation.[14] Thus, these would be goods.

Suppose a person felled a tree standing on his plot of land and had an agreement with a person to sell it for Rs 5,000. Is this a contract of sale? The tree was attached to immovable property and is thus not movable. However, once it has been separated from the land, it has become movable, so the contract is a contract of sale. Consider a contract where a landowner enters in an agreement where a buyer will pay him Rs 5,000 and fell a tree standing on his land and take it away. Can a standing timber be goods? The point is whether the interest in the timber standing on land relates primarily to an interest in the land or timber. The following case, dating from before codification, examines the point.

Marshall v. Green

A person purchased certain growing trees on a plot of land to be removed at the earliest. The question was whether this was a sale of goods. Grove J. noted:

It seems to me that, in determining the question whether there was a contract for an interest in

---

[14] *Moss* v. *Hancock*, (1899) 2 QB 111.

land, we must look to what the parties intended to contract for.... Here the trees were to be cut as soon as possible, but even assuming that they were not to be cut for a month, I think that the test would be whether the parties really looked to their deriving benefit from the land, or merely intended that the land should be in the nature of a warehouse for the trees during that period. Here the parties clearly never contemplated that the purchaser should have anything in the nature of an interest in the land; he was only to have so much timber, which happened to be affixed to the land at the time, but was to be removed as soon as possible, and was to derive no benefit from the soil. If the contract had been for the sale of a young plantation of some rapidly-growing timber, which was not to be cut down until it had become substantially changed and had derived benefit from the land, there might have been an interest in land, but this is not such a case.[15]

A thing attached to the ground was counted as goods if it was agreed that it would be removed. Thus, in the evolution of the economy, there emerged two kinds of property: immovable and movable. Immovable property, as it was attached to land, was treated as an interest in land with the land laws. Other properties were movable property. Both were physical, tangible properties. Thus, Section 3(36) of the General Clauses Act, 1893, defines movable property as 'property of every description, except immovable property'. This begs the question of what immovable property is. Section 3(26) defines it as that which 'shall include land, benefits to arise out of land, and things attached to the earth, or permanently fastened to anything attached to the earth'.

The law of sale of goods was created to deal with disputes arising from tangible movable property. As the economy developed, intangible forms of property came into being.

For example, A loans money to B and has a right to be paid back. A has a right over B, and this right is itself a property. It could be claimed that these properties were movable properties and therefore goods. However, the law had developed with and was organized around tangible movable property, and the emergent form of property was excluded by common law courts. 'Goods' in the English law, the Sales of Goods Act, 1893, was defined to 'include all chattels personal other than things in action and money.'

In common law, 'personal property' was distinguished from 'real property'. Real property was immovable property, and any other was personal property.[16] Movable property could be tangible or intangible. However, intangible property was excluded by the phrase 'other than things in action', which was another expression for 'chose in action', or a right to sue, an intangible right protected by the law. It had no existence other than the recognition given by the law. Thus, common law limited the application of the law of sale of goods to tangible movable property. Following the English law, Section 2(7) of the Sale of Goods Act, 1930, states that '"goods" means every kind of movable property other than actionable claims and money; and includes stock and shares, growing crops, grass, and things attached to or forming part of the land which are agreed to be severed before sale or under the contract of sale'. The term 'actionable claim' was intended to be the equivalent of chose in action; however, it has become quite different.

Actionable Claim

The chapter on sale of goods in the Indian Contract Act, 1872, defined goods to be 'every kind of movable property' other than

---

[15] *Marshall* v. *Green*, (1875–76) LR 1 CPD 35.

[16] Chattel was another name for personal property.

'actionable claims and money'. 'Actionable claim' was not defined in the Contract Act, 1872. The term, however, was defined in the Transfer of Property Act, 1882. The meaning of the term was the same as chose in action. The definition, however, was amended in 1900 to give it a narrower meaning. The definition of goods in the Sale of Goods Act, 1930, was reproduced from the Contract Act, 1872. Section 3 of the Transfer of Property Act, 1882 defined actionable claim as 'A claim which the civil courts recognise as affording grounds of relief is actionable, whether a suit for its enforcement is or is not actually pending or likely to become necessary.' The definition was very close to 'thing in action', that is, the right to sue. The definition was amended in 1900 to read:

A claim to any debt, other than a debt secured by mortgage of immovable property or by hypothecation or pledge of movable property or to any beneficial interest in movable property not in the possession, either actual or constructive, of the claimant, which the Civil Courts recognize as affording grounds for reliefs, whether such debt or beneficial interest be existent, accruing, conditional or contingent.

This was a much narrower scope of actionable claim, limiting it to the claim to debt and beneficial interest. A debt can be secured or unsecured. It can be secured by mortgage of immovable property or by hypothecation or pledge of movable property. Only a claim to a debt that is not secured is an actionable claim. A beneficial interest arises when a trust is created; that is, when an owner transfers a property to another person to hold it and manage it for the benefit of the named persons. The person in whom the property is vested is the trustee and the persons to benefit from the trust are the beneficiaries. The right of the beneficiaries against the trustee

to derive the benefit of the property is the beneficial interest. The definition recognizes a claim to a beneficial interest in a movable property that is not in the possession of the person to be an actionable claim. The amendment limited the scope of actionable claim and thus expanded the scope of goods. Following the definition, in the case of a breach of a contractual term, the court will decide the claims of the parties and award damages. It is only a right to sue and not an actionable claim. However, a claim for arrear of rents, as the rent is owed, is actionable. The Supreme Court in *Sunrise Associates, M/s* v. *Govt of NCT of Delhi* noted:

An actionable claim is of course as its nomenclature suggests, only a claim. A claim might connote a demand, but in the context of the definition it is right, albeit an incorporeal one. Every claim is not an actionable claim. It must be a claim either to a debt or to a beneficial interest in movable property. The beneficial interest is not the movable property itself, and may be existent, accruing, conditional or contingent. The movable property in which such beneficial interest is claimed, must not be in the possession of the claimant.

...

An actionable claim would include a right to recover insurance money or a partner's right to sue for an account of a dissolved partnership ... A claim for arrears of rent has also been held to be an actionable claim (State of Bihar v. Maharajadhiraja Sir Kameshwar Singh, 1952 SCR 889, 910). A right to the credit in a provident fund account has also been held to an actionable claim. (Official Trustee, Bengal v. L. Chippendale, AIR 1944 Cal 335; Bhupati Mohan Das. v. Phanindra Chandra Chakravarty and another, AIR 1935 Cal 756).[17]

The following case is on whether a lottery ticket is goods, and relates to the nature of the

[17] *H. Anraj* v. *Government of Tamil Nadu*, AIR (1986) SC 63.

property and beneficial interest the holder has in the ticket.

Sunrise Associates, M/s v. Govt of NCT of Delhi

In *H. Anraj* v. *Government of Tamil Nadu*[18] the question before the Supreme Court was whether lottery tickets were goods for the levy of sales tax. The court noted that the lottery ticket per se had no innate value. It was merely evidence of two rights for the buyer, the right to participate in the draw and the right to claim a prize. A right is a property and thus both were movable property. As the second right was a beneficial interest in the prize money, it was an actionable claim. Thus, this was not counted as goods. However, the right to participate in the draw was not an actionable claim. Following this, the court held the ticket to be goods and taxable. Several high courts understood the ratio of the case differently. Thus, the question was referred to a constitutional bench in *Sunrise Associates, M/s* v. *Govt of NCT of Delhi*.[19] The Supreme Court resolved the issue thus:

A lottery ticket has no value in itself. It is a mere piece of paper. Its value lies in the fact that it represents a chance or a right to a conditional benefit of winning a prize of a greater value than the consideration paid for the transfer of that chance. It is nothing more than a token or evidence of this right.

...

The sale of a ticket does not necessarily involve the sale of goods. For example the purchase of a railway ticket gives the right to a person to travel by railway. It is nothing other than a contract of carriage. The actual ticket is merely evidence of the right to travel. ... Like railway tickets, a ticket to see a cinema or a pawn brokers ticket are memoranda or contracts between the vendors of the ticket and the purchasers. Cases on whether the terms specified on such tickets bind the purchaser are legion. It is sufficient for our purposes to note that tickets are themselves, normally evidence of and in some cases the contract between the buyer of the ticket and its seller. Therefore a lottery ticket can be held to be goods if at all only because it evidences the transfer of a right.

The question is, what is this right which the ticket represents? There can be no doubt that on purchasing a lottery ticket, the purchaser would have a claim to a conditional interest in the prize money which is not in the purchaser's possession. The right would fall squarely within the definition of an actionable claim and would therefore, be excluded from the definition of 'goods' under the Sale of Goods Act and the Sales Tax statutes. This was also accepted in H. Anraj when the Court said that to the extent that the sale of a lottery ticket involved a transfer of the right to claim a prize depending on chance, it was an assignment of an actionable claim.

...

The further distinction sought to be drawn in H. Anraj between the chance to win and the right to participate in the draw was in our opinion unwarranted. A lottery having been held to be in essence a chance for a prize, the sale of a lottery ticket can only be a sale of that chance. There is no other element. Every right can be sub-divided into lesser rights. When these lesser rights culminate in a legally recognizable right, it is the latter which defines the right. The right to participate in the draw is a part of the composite right of the chance to win and it does not feature separately in the definition of the word 'lottery'. It is an implicit part of the chance to win. It is not a different right. The separation is specious since neither of the rights can stand without the other. A draw without a chance to win is meaningless and one cannot claim a prize without participating in the draw. In fact the transfer of the chance to win assumes participation in the draw.

...

---

[18] Ibid.
[19] *Sunrise Associates, M/s* v. *Govt of NCT of Delhi*, AIR (2006) SC 1908.

There is no value in the mere right to participate in the draw and the purchaser does not pay for the right to participate. The consideration is paid for the chance to win. There is therefore no distinction between the two rights. The right to participate being an inseparable part of the chance to win is therefore part of an actionable claim.

...

We are therefore of the view that the decision in H. Anraj incorrectly held that a sale of a lottery ticket involved a sale of goods. There was no sale of goods within the meaning of Sales Tax Acts of the different States but at the highest a transfer of an actionable claim. The decision to the extent that it held otherwise is accordingly overruled though prospectively with effect from the date of this judgment.

The lottery ticket created a contingent interest; the holder of the lottery ticket would have received the prize in the event that he had won it. Note that the definition of actionable claim ends with 'whether such debt or beneficial interest be existent, accruing, conditional or contingent'. Thus, the contingent interest in the prize was held to be an actionable claim. As the court brought out, there was only one composite interest, a contingent interest in the prize.

Thus, the law of sale of goods, which started out by covering tangible movable property, has come to cover all movable property other than actionable claims. This, on the face of it, qualifies several forms of intangible property as goods. However, not all of them do qualify as such. As we will see in subsequent chapters, possession and delivery are integral to a contract of sale. Thus, in addition to being a movable property, the property must be capable of being utilized, possessed, and delivered. We will visit this aspect in another chapter after learning the concept of possession and delivery. As the law has developed around tangible movable property, the landmark court judgments bringing out the principles are all on tangible movable property.

Share as Goods

A share is an intangible form of property and was not considered goods in the English law. However, it was explicitly included in the definition of goods in the Indian law to give protection to the buyers of shares. In *R.D. Goyal* v. *Reliance Industries Limited*,[20] Reliance Industries Limited had invited offers from the public for issue of shares and debentures. R.D. Goyal contested that the invitation itself was an unfair trade practice within the now-repealed Monopolies and Restrictive Trade Practices Act, 1969. The practice would be unfair if it related to promotion of 'goods'. 'Goods' had the same definition within the act as in the Sale of Goods Act, 1930. The questions then were whether, first, debentures were goods; and second, a share could be considered goods before allotment. The Supreme Court ruled: 'Debentures, as ordinarily understood, in our considered view, would not come within the purview of definition of goods as it is simply an instrument of acknowledgement of debt by the company whereby it undertakes to pay the amount covered by it and till then it undertakes further to pay interest thereon to the debenture-holders.' The court further noted: 'Debentures having regard to the definition of "actionable claim" as defined in Section 3 of the Transfer of Property Act would constitute actionable claims except where they are secured by mortgage or immovable property or hypothecation or pledge of immovable property.'

Thus, a debenture secured by mortgage, hypothecation, or pledge of immovable

[20] *R.D. Goyal* v. *Reliance Industries Limited*, (2003) (1) SCC 81.

property would be considered as goods. A share is specifically included in the definition of goods; the question in this case was whether a share was goods before it was issued. The Supreme Court noted:

Shares before their allotment, in our opinion, are not goods. In Sri Gopal Jalan & Co. vs Calcutta Stock Exchange Association Ltd. 1964 AIR(SC) 250), it has been held that in Company law 'allotment' means the appropriation out of the previously unappropriated capital of a company, of a certain number of shares to a person. Till allotment is made, shares do not exist as such. It is only on allotment in this sense that the shares come into existence. Therefore, till the shares are actually issued, the question of the company having issued shares as transferable property would not arise and thus there cannot be any doubt whatsoever that the shares before their allotment would not come into existence and they cannot be regarded as goods. Debentures would also not come within the purview of the definition of stock.

GOODS, OWNERSHIP, POSSESSION, AND DELIVERY

A sale is a contract where the ownership in goods is transferred for a price in cash. Ownership is an important concern for the buyer as well as the seller. The owner is entitled to an exclusive enjoyment of the goods. If the goods are lost, get damaged, or perish, the loss falls on the owner. Thus, risk passes with ownership. Only the owner can transfer property in the goods. Thus, in the course of a sales transaction, once the ownership is transferred to the buyer, even if the buyer were in complete breach of contract, the ownership would not re-vest in the seller. The seller will have only the right to claim the price of the goods, not the right to regain ownership. For these two reasons, the point of transfer of ownership is so important that the law makes a distinction between a sale and an agreement to sell. So, how and when is the ownership transferred

from the seller to the buyer in a sale contract? There are several principles governing the transfer of ownership from the seller to the buyer. We will be exploring these in the following chapters. The principles build on concepts like delivery, possession, and ascertained and unascertained goods.

Specific, Unascertained, and Future Goods

Let us try and identify whether the following are contracts of sale, and the nature of goods to be sold.

Contract 1: X contracted with Y to sell him his only study desk, the one in his study, for Rs 12,000.

Contract 2: A customer entered in a contract with a retailer to buy a Maruti Zen, specifically of the 'metal pearl' colour for Rs 5 lakhs.

Contract 3: A carpenter entered in a contract to make and supply 50 tables. The parties had settled on the material and dimensions of the table.

Contract 4: A shopkeeper had packed tomatoes in one-kilogram packs. A customer pointed at a particular bag and asked the shopkeeper to give it to him.

Contract 5: A customer examined the tomatoes kept in a basket and requested the shopkeeper to sell him one kilogram. The shopkeeper accepted the offer.

Are the goods identifiable? In the first contract, the parties have settled on a specific table. The seller cannot supply a similar table instead. In the second contract, the description of the goods is given but the agreement is not on a particular car. The seller can supply any car that meets the description. To perform the contract, the retailer would need to settle on a particular car and deliver it to the buyer. In this case, the goods are not ascertained at the time of the agreement. In the third case, the goods have yet to come into existence; the seller must create the goods and deliver it to the buyer. These are called future goods. In the fourth case, the buyer has asked for a particular pack of tomatoes. The goods are specific. In contrast, in the last case, the parties are settled on the lot from which the buyer is to be given the tomatoes, but there is no agreement on selling specific tomatoes. The seller will separate one kilogram of tomatoes to deliver it to the buyer. The goods would become ascertained only on its separation from the bulk.

All of the above are valid sale contracts. Whether the sale is for specific goods or unascertained goods is relevant to the performance of the contract and transfer of ownership. Goods that are identifiable are specific goods or ascertained goods. Goods that are not specific and unascertained goods include goods yet to be made, goods with general descriptions, and goods not separated from bulk.

Ownership, Delivery, and Possession

A person can be the owner of only specific or identified goods. Let us try to identify the owner and the person who physically has the goods in the following situations:

1. B gave his car to a garage for repairing.
2. Z borrowed a book from his college library.
3. A transport company is carrying the goods belonging to Rubicon Ltd from one factory location to another.
4. A construction company hired a crane from a leasing company.

The owner of certain goods is the person to whom those goods 'belong' or who has the

exclusive right over them. Ownership and possession are different. A person may have the custody of the goods, like the garage or the transporter in the above illustrations, but not own it, and the owner may not have the possession of the goods. In these cases, how did one party come to be in possession of the goods? Simply put, the owner had delivered the goods. Let us explore the concept of delivery.

1. X gave his jacket to a drycleaner for drycleaning.
2. The self-service store gave a customer the items purchased by her in a bag after she paid the bill.
3. Y bought a washing machine from a store. The store brought the machine to the customer's house the next day from their warehouse and installed it.
4. A thief walked away with the laptop of another person.
5. A thug intimidated a person and made him part with his camera.

In all these cases, the person has come to be in possession of the goods. But not all of it is delivered by the owner. In 4 and 5, possession was acquired with force. Thus, delivery is voluntarily giving possession of goods to another. Delivery of goods is an integral part of sale. If ownership vests the owner with the physical control over the goods, delivery is acquiring that physical control. For a sale contract to be complete, not only should the ownership transfer to the buyer, the seller must also deliver the goods to the buyer. Section 2(2) of the Act defines it thus: '"delivery" means voluntary transfer of possession from one person to another'. The term possession has not been defined, but is given the general common law concept. Section 33 elaborates different modes by which delivery can be made in a sale contract: 'Delivery of goods sold may be made by doing anything which the parties agree shall be treated as delivery or which has the effect of putting the goods in the possession of the buyer or of any person authorised to hold them on his behalf.'

Let us try to understand the section with the following cases:

1. The self-service store gave a customer the items purchased by her in a bag after she paid the bill.

2. Y bought a laptop from a store on Sunday. Y sent his driver the next day to bring the laptop. The store delivered the laptop to him.

3. The seller gave the key of a car to its buyer.

4. The seller gave the buyer the key to the warehouse in which the sold goods were kept.

The first case counts as a delivery as the store has given the possession of the bought goods to the buyer. In the second case, the possession has been given to a person authorized by the buyer. In the third and fourth, the sellers have not been given the possession of the goods by actually putting it in the hands of the buyers. However, giving the car key has the 'effect of putting the goods in the possession of the buyer'. The definition of delivery is broader than just physically handing over the goods, though it is the most obvious one. Giving the key to a warehouse or the ignition key of an automobile is also delivery, as it gives physical access to the goods.[21] Let us look at the following transactions between the parties:

1. The newspaper vendor leaves the newspaper at the door of the house.

2. B bought a bench. Under the contract, the seller was to put the bench at a designated place in a public park.

In the first case, the seller has not given possession of the goods to the buyer. However, the parties have an agreement that leaving the newspaper at the door would be taken to be delivering the goods. If the newspaper is stolen or gets wet or is torn apart by a dog, the buyer cannot claim that the goods were not delivered to him. Similarly, in the second case, the seller has not given the possession of the bench to the buyer. However, the parties have agreed that leaving the bench abandoned in a public park would be taken to be delivery. The first part of Section 33 covers this: 'anything [to] which the parties agree shall be treated as delivery.'

Another aspect we need to become familiar with is goods being in a deliverable state. According to Section 2, 'goods are said to be in a "deliverable state" when they are in such state that the buyer would under the contract be bound to take delivery of them'. Thus, if the seller is yet to do something to the goods under the contract, the goods would not be in a deliverable state.

What must the parties do once the goods have been made in a deliverable state? Section 31 provides: 'It is the duty of the seller to deliver the goods and of the buyer to accept and pay for them, in accordance with the terms of the contract of sale.' The section is self-explanatory. What if the contract does not provide the time of delivering the goods? Section 32 provides the answer:

32. Payment and delivery are concurrent conditions: Unless otherwise agreed, delivery of the goods and payment of the price are concurrent

---

[21] There is yet another kind, called a constructive delivery. We will become familiar with it in another chapter.

conditions, that is to say, the seller shall be ready and willing to give possession of the goods to the buyer in exchange for the price, and the buyer shall be ready and willing to pay the price in exchange for possession of the goods.

The section is ambiguous as to who should move first. The seller could claim that he was willing and ready to deliver but the buyer did not come forward with the money. And the buyer could claim that he was ready with the money but the seller did not come forward. Section 35 clarifies this: 'Apart from any express contract, the seller of goods is not bound to deliver them until the buyer applies for delivery.'

If the contract does not mention the time of delivery, the buyer should inform the seller that he is ready to take delivery and that the goods should be delivered to him. Thereafter, the delivery and payment are concurrent conditions. If the seller is unwilling to pay, the buyer can refuse delivery and vice versa. Thus, a sale involves ownership, delivery, payment, and possession. A sale contract can be for specific goods or unascertained goods. The principles for transfer of ownership for ascertained goods and unascertained goods are grouped separately. In the following chapter we will examine transfer of ownership in ascertained goods.

Transfer of Ownership
Specific Goods

A contract of sale can be for specific goods or unascertained goods. In this chapter, we will look at the transfer of ownership in specific goods. A sale is a special form of contract where the consideration for the buyer is transfer of ownership in goods, and for the seller, the price in cash. Taking this as the basic principle, let us examine the passing of the ownership to the buyer in the following contracts:

Contract 1: According to the terms of a signed agreement between the parties for the sale of a second-hand laptop, the ownership of the laptop would pass to the buyer on Monday and the buyer would pay the price on Friday.

Contract 2: According to the terms of a signed agreement between the parties for the sale of a second-hand laptop, the buyer would pay the entire price the next Monday and the ownership would transfer the subsequent Monday.

Contract 3: A self-service store had paintings by new artists put on display. The customer brought a painting to the counter, the billing was done and he paid the money. The clerk then put the painting in a polythene bag and handed it over to the customer.

Contracts are voluntary agreements between parties. As a sale contract is about the buyer getting the ownership, the parties should specify when the ownership will pass to the buyer. A contract can be express or implied; the parties can provide for the passing of the property in precise terms or it can be inferred from their conduct. In the first and second cases, the goods are specific, and the parties have provided for the transfer of ownership in express terms. The ownership will transfer as provided in the contract. In the third case too, the painting is a specific item.[1] The communication between the

[1] There is a reason for choosing a painting and not a mass-produced commodity, like a box of washing powder, in the illustration. We will see in Chapter 6 that the sale of generic goods would still be a sale by description and not of the specific box the customer had in his trolley. This is because the intent of the parties is to sell goods of that description. A painting

parties in most self-service store transactions is implied. Thus, the manner in which transactions in a self-service store are done determines if there is an implied term on transfer of ownership. An agreement in a self-service store is made when the store accepts the offer of the customer. No store will let the customer take away the goods without paying. And a store gives the goods to the customer immediately on paying. Thus, it is implied that the ownership transfers immediately on paying the price.

OWNERSHIP TRANSFER AS INTENDED BY THE PARTIES

We have seen that as a sale is a contract, effect has to be given to the intention of the parties. Thus, ownership is transferred as intended by the parties. Section 19 states the principle we have formulated:

Section 19. Property passes when intended to pass:

(1) Where there is a contract for the sale of specific or ascertained goods, the property in them is transferred to the buyer at such time as the parties to the contract intend it to be transferred.

(2) For the purpose of ascertaining the intention of the parties, regard shall be had to the terms of the contract, the conduct of the parties and the circumstances of the case.

In a written contract, the courts usually restrict themselves to the written terms and assume that the parties intended the written terms alone to govern the contract. Section 19(2) makes an important addition in relation to sale contracts. The courts can also supplement the terms of the contract with the conduct of the parties and the circumstances of the case to ascertain the parties' intent on

transfer of ownership.[2] The following case illustrates the scope of Section 19(2).

Re Anchor Line (Henderson Brothers) Ltd

The Anchor Line took over a berth at Yorkhill Basin, Glasgow, from the Ocean Steamship Co. Ltd.[3] The Ocean Company owned an electric crane, and the parties entered into the following agreement over it:

(1) We agree that you take over the crane ... for a deferred purchase price of £4,000.

(2) Until the completion of the purchase you agree to pay us for interest and depreciation at the rate of £350 per annum for the first two years after taking over, £450 per annum for the second two years, and £400 per annum thereafter.

(3) Of these sums, a proportion amounting to £240, or 6 per cent of the purchase price of the crane, is to be regarded as depreciation, and the total of these annual payments for depreciation is to be deducted from the above-mentioned amount of £4,000 in order to arrive at the balance actually to be paid by you on completion of the purchase, whenever that may take place.

(4) In the meantime you will have entire charge of and responsibility for the crane in every respect.

We suggest that the payments be made quarterly, and that the date for your taking over the crane be fixed as from Sept. 5, 1931.

No date for completion of the purchase was made. However, following the above terms, the price would have been fully paid off after seventeen years. The Anchor Line Ltd made regular quarterly payments for about four years. The company then underwent voluntary liquidation. The question before the court was whether the crane was the property of Anchor Line Ltd or Ocean Steamship Co. Ltd. The lower court had concluded that the

---

by an artist are specific goods, as each painting is distinct.

[2] *R. v. Ward Ltd. v. Bignall*, (1967) 1 QB 534.
[3] *Re Anchor Line (Henderson Brothers) Ltd*, (1936) 2 All ER 941.

contract was silent on the time of passing of the ownership in the crane. The Court of Appeal noted that the contract was 'not happily' drafted. However, it concluded on examining all the clauses of the contract, 'I find, in the contract read as a whole, a clear intention that the property shall not pass until the purchase is completed.'

Section 19 provides that the ownership transfers as the parties intend. In *McEntire v. Crossley Brothers Ltd*,[4] the hire-purchase agreement for a gas engine provided that the 'gas-engine shall remain the sole and absolute property of the owners … until all sums of money due under this agreement are paid.' Before paying all the instalments, the lessee became bankrupt and the assets were taken over in settlement. A dispute emerged about whether the assets included the gas engine. Lord Herschell stated the principle as follows:

Upon an agreement to sell, it depends upon the intention of the parties whether the property passes or does not pass. Here, the parties have in terms expressed their intention, and said that the property shall not pass until the full purchase money is paid. I know no reason to prevent that being a perfectly lawful agreement. If that was really the intention of the parties, I know of no rule or principle of law which prevents it from being given effect to.

Applying the principle, as soon as the lessee failed to pay an instalment, the contract was breached. As a result, Crossley Ltd acquired the right either to sue for the remaining money or take possession of the gas engine and claim damages. In this case, the delivery of the machine was given but the ownership never transferred.

Vasantha Vishwanathan v. V.K. Elayalwar

Vasantha was running a transport business and owned nineteen buses.[5] There was an apprehension that the state government of Tamil Nadu was going to impose a ceiling on the number of carriage permits to ten. With this apprehension, Vasantha entered into an agreement with Elayalwar to sell him five buses covered by the route permit. To further the agreement, the two made a joint application to the Regional Transport Authority for the transfer of permits of the five buses to Elayalwar. By the time the Regional Transport Authority came to review the application, the Government of Tamil Nadu passed an ordinance fixing a ceiling limit of ten permits to an individual operator and directing the surrender of excess permits. As Vasantha was required to surrender the excess permits under the ordinance, the Regional Transport Authority refused the transfer to Elayalwar.

Elayalwar went in appeal against the decision to a higher body, the State Transport Appellate Tribunal. Under the ordinance, Vasantha would have had to surrender nine of his permits. He went to the high court challenging the constitutional validity of the ordinance.[6] During the pendency of these processes, Elayalwar sent a letter to Vasantha providing the roadmap for the sale. It was decided that nothing would be done till

---

[4] *McEntire* v. *Crossley Brothers Ltd*, (1895) AC 457.

[5] *Vasantha Vishwanathan* v. *V.K. Elayalwar*, AIR (2001) SC 3367.

[6] The Constitution of India guarantees certain fundamental rights to the citizens. It prohibits the State from making any law which curtails these rights. A citizen can go to the high court or directly to the Supreme Court challenging a law as being in violation of their fundamental rights. If the law is held to be violative by the court, it becomes inoperative.

the permits were transferred in his name. Thereafter, the parties would fix the price of the buses and he would take delivery after making the payment. The letter also said that no amount of sale price had been paid by Elayalwar till then.

Events took a different turn. The ordinance, which had by then been replaced with an act, was struck down as constitutionally invalid. Following this, the State Transport Appellate Tribunal accepted Elayalwar's position and directed the Regional Transport Authority to transfer the permits in his favour. This was done on 21 April 1979. As the law itself had been declared invalid, Vasantha was no longer keen to sell his buses. Elayalwar, however, claimed to have become the owner of the buses as the permits had been transferred in his name. He sought the help of the police and got possession of the buses. Vasantha claimed that ownership had not been transferred, and so the case came before the Supreme Court.

The court noted that the Motor Vehicles Act, 1939, required that when motor vehicles were bought or sold, both the buyer and the seller were required to report and enter into the certificate of registration. The transfer of ownership is not created by the registration; it is the other way round. It only registers the fact of sale that has taken place. The act 'simply prescribes the procedure for entering the factum of transfer in the registration certificate, which is an act posterior to the transfer'. The question of transfer of ownership thus had to be judged according to the Sale of Goods Act, 1930. The Supreme Court noted:

The transfer of vehicles in question would be governed by the provisions of Section 19 of the Sale of Goods Act, according to which property in the vehicle would pass ... at such time as the parties to the contract intend it to be transferred.

Thus, the passing of property in the goods would be dependent upon the intention of the parties as evidenced from the contract. From the contract, it would appear that the parties intended that after the registration formalities were completed, price of the vehicles covered by the permits would be ascertained and thereafter, the same would be paid by the 1st defendant, entitling him to take possession of the vehicles. Thus, the parties intended that property in the vehicles shall pass only after possession of the vehicles was delivered to the 1st defendant after completion of all the aforesaid formalities. In the present case, after the registration formalities were completed, the value of the vehicles covered by the permits was not ascertained, much less paid, rather, on the other hand, possession was forcibly taken by the 1st defendant. Therefore, property in the vehicles did not pass to the 1st defendant as required under Section 19 of the Sale of Goods Act. As the 1st defendant had illegally taken possession of the vehicles which he was entitled to ply, it has been rightly held by the High Court that the plaintiff would be entitled to profits earned by the 1st defendant...

Under Section 19, ownership passes as intended by the parties. The parties can provide for it in express terms or their intention can be inferred. In the above case, the time of passing of the property could be inferred. A contract where the intention of the parties on transfer of ownership can be inferred is called a conditional contract (because the parties have put a condition on the transfer of ownership). A contract where no intention of the parties can be inferred is called an unconditional contract. In an unconditional contract for the sale of specific goods, the principle is that the ownership transfers when the contract is made. We will examine this as the last theme in this chapter. The act raises certain presumptions on the intention of the parties. We will note this first to exhaust a conditional sale contract.

Presumed Intentions: Goods not in a Deliverable State

Section 19(3) is on the presumption of the intention in certain cases: 'Unless a different intention appears, the rules contained in Sections 20 to 24 are rules for ascertaining the intention of the parties as to the time at which the property in the goods is to pass to the buyer.' Section 21 concerns cases where the seller, under the contract, has to do something to put the specific goods in a deliverable state. It reads:

21. Specific goods to be put into a deliverable state: Where there is a contract for the sale of specific goods and the seller is bound to do something to the goods for the purpose of putting them into a deliverable state, the property does not pass until such thing is done and the buyer has notice thereof.

This is how Sections 19 and 21 would work together. Under Section 19(1) and (2), the intention of the parties would be ascertained from the terms of the contract, conduct of the parties, and the circumstances. If the parties intended to pass the ownership even if the goods were not in a deliverable state, the ownership would pass as intended. However, if the above cannot be ascertained, Section 21 would apply. It would be assumed that the parties intended to pass the property only after the goods were put in a deliverable state. Application of Section 21 makes the contract a conditional one, that is, the property is not to pass till the goods are put in a deliverable state. The following is a leading case (and one of the few) on this issue.

Underwood Limited v. Burgh Castle Brick and Cement Syndicate

Underwood Limited entered into a written agreement to sell a condensing engine to Burgh Castle Brick and Cement Syndicate.[7] The engine was affixed to the soil on the premises of Underwood Limited and had to be detached before being dispatched to Burgh Castle by train to Yarmouth, a town in England. The sale and delivery term of the contract was 'free on rail, London'. The meaning of this term, as we will see in Chapter 8, is that the risk, and by implication property, passes when the goods are loaded onto a train by the seller in London. The engine was successfully dismantled but broke while being loaded onto the train. The parties were in dispute as to who would bear the loss. The judges were of the view that as the contract was free on rail London, the intention of the parties was that the risk and ownership would pass only on putting the goods in good condition on the rails. The contention of the seller was that the contract was silent at the time of passing of the property. As we will see, in this case, the ownership transfers at the very time the contract is made. The judges were considering this contention for the sake of the argument. The question was whether Section 18, Rule 2, of the Sale of Goods Act, 1893, which is equivalent to Section 21 of the Sale of Goods Act, 1930, applied. That is, the further requirement that the engine was in a deliverable state must be satisfied.

The seller contended that at the time of making of the contract, the engine was in a deliverable state and the contract was unconditional. Thus, the ownership passed to the buyer at the time of making of the contract. Bankes L.J. rejected the contention. He noted:

The appellants contended that where a specific article is complete in itself, for example a complete

[7] *Underwood Limited* v. *Burgh Castle Brick and Cement Syndicate*, (1922) 1 KB 123.

engine or a complete cart—that is to say, where nothing more has to be done to make it an engine or a cart—it is then in a deliverable state ... I do not accept that test. A 'deliverable state' does not depend upon the mere completeness of the subject matter in all its parts. It depends on the actual state of the goods at the date of the contract and the state in which they are to be delivered by the terms of the contract. Where the vendors have to expend as much trouble and as much money as the appellants had to expend before this engine could be placed on rail, I cannot think that the subject matter can be said to be in a deliverable state.

Scrutton J. noted:

I find it impossible to apply the definition ... of a 'deliverable state' as 'a state in which the buyer is bound to take delivery' of the goods, to this case, where the buyers find an engine so firmly attached that it takes two days before it can be got loose, and in such a state that it cannot be put on rail, where they stipulated to have it, until a further two weeks' work has been done upon it. I decide this case on the ground that the sellers were bound to do something for the purpose of putting this engine in a deliverable state...

Atkin J. noted:

... the vendors were bound to do something to the engine for the purpose of putting it into a deliverable state—namely, to detach it and take it to pieces in order to put it on rail. It is quite plain that the property was not to pass till these things were done and that the appellants took the risk of delivery on to rail.

PRESUMED INTENTIONS: ASCERTAINING PRICE

The second rule for ascertaining the intention of the parties is contained in Section 22. It reads:

22. Specific goods in a deliverable state, when the seller has to do anything thereto in order to ascertain price: Where there is a contract for the sale of specific goods in a deliverable state, but the seller is bound to weigh, measure, test or do some

other act or thing with reference to the goods for the purpose of ascertaining the price, the property does not pass until such act or thing is done and the buyer has notice thereof.

Section 22 has to be read with Section 19. If the intention of the parties under Section 19 is to pass the ownership even if the seller has to weigh or measure to ascertain the price, the property will pass. However, in the absence of this intention, where the goods are specific and in a deliverable state, the ownership will not pass if the goods have to be weighed, measured, or tested by the seller to ascertain the price. The principle is to give protection to the buyer against the seller. The application of the section amounts to the contracting parties putting condition on transfer of ownership. This makes the contract a conditional one. The following case is an illustration of the principle.

Turley v. Bates

Turley ran a colliery.[8] He extracted a quantity of fire clay, which he estimated to be about 1,500 tonnes, and stacked it in a heap on the land of Bates, who had bought it at the rate of 10 pence per tonne. The weighing was to be done at the expense of the buyer. Bates took about 270 tonnes and paid for it, but after that the parties had a dispute. Bates claimed that the property in the clay in heap had not passed to him, and so he was only in breach of contract. As a result, the seller can only claim damages, which would have been nominal. Turley contended that the property had passed to Bates and thus, he should be paid the full amount. Channell B. ruled:

It was argued that the rule ... was, that so long as a price had been agreed upon according to quantity, to be ascertained by weighing, that until the goods

---

[8] *Turley* v. *Bates*, (1863) 2 H & C 200.

had been weighed and the price so ascertained the contract was incomplete … the principle involved in the rule above quoted is, that something remains to be done by the seller. It is, therefore, very doubtful, as before stated, whether the present case comes within the principle of the rule. But, however that may be, it is clear that this rule does not apply if the parties have made it sufficiently clear whether or not they intend that the property shall pass at once, and that their intention must be looked at in every case. … it seems to us clear that the intention of the parties was that the property in the whole heap should pass, notwithstanding the clay was to be weighed at Johnson's machine; and we, therefore, think that the rule to reduce the damages must be discharged.

The rule applies only where the seller has to weigh or measure, not the buyer. In this case, it is the buyer who was to weigh the goods. Thus, there was no intention to presume, and the rule had no application.

Presumed Intentions: Sale or Return Transactions

The third presumption of the intention of the parties is where the seller is in a 'sale or return' transaction. Before looking at the provision, let us see how contracts are formed in 'sale or return' transactions. Suppose Y receives from X a box of chocolates along with the following offer document: 'The box of chocolate, priced at Rs 200, is being delivered to you on a sale-or-return basis. Kindly communicate your acceptance of the offer by signing the counter-foil attached with this note. The ownership will pass only when we have received full payment for the box.'

The offer document has prescribed the modality of acceptance and the time of passing of ownership. Y can accept the offer by following the prescribed modality. Y is free to reject the offer. In this case, no sale contract will be formed and the question of transfer of ownership will not arise. Let us see if the offer

document had not provided for the transfer of ownership. A note attached to the box of chocolate merely read: 'The box of chocolate, priced at Rs 200, is being delivered to you on a sale-or-return basis.' As the person has voluntarily received the goods, he is the bailee. However, he is not the owner as the offer by X is not accepted as yet.

Let us consider the following possible responses by the recipient. Y communicates rejection of the offer to X. The rejection extinguishes the offer. Y must restore the goods to the owner. Y sends an email communicating acceptance of the offer to X. An agreement is made following the communication of acceptance. As the contract is for the sale of specific goods and the parties have not provided for the transfer of ownership, it becomes an unconditional contract. The ownership should transfer on the making of the contract.

Suppose Y makes no communication with X but opens the box and eats a chocolate. What should X understand from Y's action? Y has impliedly accepted the offer and an agreement is formed between the parties. The ownership transfers to Y when he opens the box of chocolate. Section 24, the rule on the assumption of the intention of the parties in the case of 'sale or return', covers these principles. It reads:

Section 24. When goods are delivered to the buyer on approval or 'on sale or return' or other similar terms, the property therein passes to the buyer:

(a) when he signifies his approval or acceptance to the seller or does any other act adopting the transaction;

(b) if he does not signify his approval or acceptance to the seller but retains the goods without giving notice of rejection, then, if a time has been fixed for the return of the goods, on the expiration of such time, and, if no time has been fixed, on the expiration of a reasonable time.

Let us first examine 24(a) by looking at the following leading case dealing with this issue.

Kirkham v. Attenborough and Gill

Kirkham manufactured jewellery. He delivered some jewellery to Winter in early 1895, with a contract note mentioning the price on a sale-or-return basis.[9] Winter pawned some jewellery to Attenborough and some to Gill. In January 1898, Winter died without paying Kirkham for the jewellery, nor intimating that he intended to keep it. Kirkham demanded that Attenborough and Gill return the jewellery, but they refused to do so unless the borrowed amount was paid back to them. Kirkham came before the court against Attenborough and Gill for the recovery of his jewellery. The questions were: had the ownership of jewellery been transferred from Kirkham to Mr Winter? If yes, when? The Court noted:

The contract by which goods are delivered 'on sale or return' means this: the purchaser may return the goods within a reasonable time, and the option of return belongs solely to the purchaser; the other party cannot even ask for the return of the goods, and his only right is to sue for the price if the goods are not returned. That being the meaning of the contract, we have to see how the party who has the option is to exercise that option.

The position of a person to whom goods have been delivered on a contract of 'sale or return' is this: He has an option of becoming the absolute purchaser of the goods, and may become the absolute purchaser in three ways. He may buy them at the price fixed; he may retain them so long as to make it unreasonable to return them; or he may do something inconsistent with a return of the goods

...

[9] *Kirkham* v. *Attenborough*; *Kirkham* v. *Gill*, (1895–9) All ER Rep 450.

I think that, if he retains the goods for an unreasonable time, he does something which is inconsistent with a return of the goods. Again, if he does an act which is inconsistent with a return, as, for instance, if he sells the goods, that is an act 'adopting the transaction,' and the property passes. Again, if he pawns the goods, he adopts the transaction, because he has not then the free control over the goods so as to be able to return them. In all these cases, he comes within the words of the section, as having done an act 'adopting the transaction', and the property in the goods passes. If that is the true construction of the section, it is perfectly clear that the defendants are entitled to retain the goods, because they have been pawned to them. An act has been done which is inconsistent with a return of the goods, and, therefore, the property in the goods passed to Winter, and, therefore, to the defendants.

As we can see, the court did not treat it like a simple offer where the consideration is given as an advance. As the delivery on 'sale or return' is only an offer, the offeror should be free to revoke it at any time before the offer is accepted. The court, however, noted that the seller cannot ask for the goods back. This follows Subsection (b). A long silence by the person to whom the goods are delivered should be taken to be rejection and not acceptance. The subsection, however, treats a long silence as acceptance. The principle, at variance with contract law, has been made for this specific situation. The seller, having delivered the goods is barred from withdrawing the offer, and the buyer has the option of not taking the delivery. Having taken the delivery, however, the buyer is obliged to respond to the offer.

UNCONDITIONAL CONTRACT

Let us look at the following contracts on the intention of the parties to transfer ownership in specific goods to the buyer.

Contract 1: A buyer entered into an agreement to buy a second-hand laptop from a seller. The only agreement the parties had was on the price. The laptop was in a deliverable state.

Contract 2: In an auction, a painting was struck down in favour of X for Rs 25,000. The auction was without any terms. The painting was in a deliverable state.

In both the cases, the parties have not provided, either in express or implied terms, for the passing of ownership. An auction can take any form. Even if we limit it to auction of art work, it does not have to follow a given structure. Thus, in both the cases, there is an agreement to sell specific goods. The goods are in a deliverable state, and therefore Section 21 does not find application. The challenge before the courts was to deal with the cases where the intention of the parties cannot be ascertained on the time of transfer of ownership.

The courts, in the development of common law principles could have taken the following positions. First, as the parties have not provided on an important aspect of the sale, the agreement is not definite, clear, and certain. Thus, no contract has been formed. This position is not tenable as the contracting parties themselves would not accept it. The parties are certain that they have a contract—only the time of transfer of ownership is uncertain. The courts would accept this as they have seen their role as contract makers, not breakers. What then is the right time for the transfer of ownership? It can happen only after the agreement has been formed. Should it be one hour, one day, two days, two weeks, or one month after the agreement has been formed? Any time period set for the transfer of ownership would be without reference to

the intention of the parties, and thus, arbitrary. The only neutral point the courts could find was the time at which the agreement itself was formed. Thus, in contracts of sale of specific or ascertained goods, where the parties have not provided for the transfer of ownership in express or implied terms, the ownership passes when the contract is made. Section 20 states the principle:

Section 20. Specific goods in a deliverable state: Where there is an unconditional contract for the sale of specific goods in a deliverable state, the property in the goods passes to the buyer when the contract is made, and it is immaterial whether the time of payment of the price or the time of delivery of the goods, or both, is postponed.

'Unconditional' means the contract does not contain any express or implied condition which must be met for the passing of property. For example, the contract may provide in express terms that the ownership will not transfer till the price is paid or it is implied in a self-service store that the ownership will transfer only on delivery after the payment is made. The term 'condition' has been used in several different senses, including as the core part of the contract giving the right to terminate the contract. The use of 'unconditional' in the section is not in this sense. It is only about not making the passage of the property dependent upon any event or action of the buyer.

Both Sections 19 and 20 use the terms 'specific goods' and 'ascertained goods'. Thus, in a contract of sale, we first need to check whether the contract is for the sale of specific goods or not. In relation to such specific goods, we would then see whether the intention of the parties regarding the passing of ownership is express or implied. If the parties have not provided for the passing of the ownership, including the presumption raised by Sections 21, 22, and 24, we would conclude that the sale is unconditional. Following this, Section 20 would become applicable to the contract. We also need to assess the significance of Section 20's requirement that the goods need to be in a deliverable state. If the goods are not, Section 21 will apply. It will be presumed that the parties intended to transfer ownership only after the seller had put it in a deliverable state; it will not be an unconditional sale. If the intention of the parties is to transfer ownership even if the goods are not in a deliverable state, the parties must indicate this, and it will be a conditional sale. Thus, the inclusion of the term 'deliverable state' is for added clarity of the application of the section.

Let us examine the principle on passing of property in an unconditional contract when the goods are specific and in a deliverable state when the contract is made. What is peculiar about the principle is the fact of the buyer becoming the owner while the goods are still with the seller. The buyer would have to bear the risk of the loss or damage to the property, even without recourse to making arrangements for its protection. The seller thus becomes a bailee of the goods at the point of time the ownership gets transferred. The principle of bailment is very wide, and applies even if there is no contractual relationship between the parties. The following is a landmark case that illustrates this.

Dennant v. Skinner

George Edward Kenneth Dennant was the owner of the South London Motor Auctions.[10] In one of the auctions, he knocked down a motor car to the highest bidder out of 150

prospective buyers. On inquiry, the highest bidder said that his name was George Albert King. Dennant knocked down four more vehicles to him. After the sales, King said that he would like to pay by cheque. Dennant replied that he did not accept cheques from people he did not know. King assured him that he was the son of the owner of King's Motors, a well-known motor-car dealership in another town. In support of his financial worthiness, he showed the counterfoils in his cheque book, according to which he had been paying large amounts to well-known auctioneers. Dennant then accepted the cheque but made King sign a form which stated: 'I hereby certify my cheque no. will be met on presentation at my bank. Furthermore, I agree that the ownership of the vehicles will not pass to me until such time as the proceeds of my cheque have been credited to South London Motor Auction account at Lloyds Bank.'

Assured with the protection of the undertaking signed by King, Dennant allowed King to remove the vehicle. King sold the car to someone, who in turn sold it to Skinner, another motor-car company. The cheque was dishonoured on presentation and it was found that King had no connection with King's Motors. The police was informed of the matter. King pleaded guilty and was convicted. Dennant sought to recover the car from Skinner, claiming it to be his property. His contention was that the property in the car had never passed to King. Thus, as the valid owner, he had the right to have the car restored to him. Skinner disputed this.

The dispute in the case was whether the property had been transferred to King or not. If the property had indeed been transferred to King, then the subsequent sales would be valid and the car would not be restored to Dennant. If, however, it had not been

[10] *Dennant* v. *Skinner*, (1948) 2 KB 164.

transferred, the property of the car continued to be with Dennant and the car would be restored to him. It was contended that this was a case of mistaken identity, and thus, the contract was not binding. The court did not accept this view. It was clear that the contract was made with the very person bidding, whatever his name was. The contract was for the sale of a specific car. The auctioneer had not announced any terms for the auction. The auction was in the open; and there was a notice put up in the auction hall that contained some of its terms and conditions. However, it was not conspicuous enough for any one to have noted. Further, there was nothing specific in the notice regarding the transfer of ownership. The court referred to Section 18 of the Sale of Goods Act, 1893, the equivalent of Section 20 of the Sale of Goods Act, 1930. It reads, 'Where there is an unconditional contract for the sale of specific goods, in a deliverable state, the property in the goods passes to the buyer when the contract is made, and it is immaterial whether the time of payment or the time of delivery or both be postponed.'

This was a contract of sale by auction. Unless the parties provide otherwise, a contract of sale in an auction is concluded on the fall of the hammer. This follows from the principle of formation of contract through offer and acceptance in contract law. In fact, the Sale of Goods Act reiterates the principle. The court noted:

A contract of sale is concluded in an auction sale on the fall of the hammer, and, indeed, the Sale of Goods Act, 1893, section 58(2), so provides. … Accordingly, on the fall of the hammer, the property of this car passed to King, unless that prima facie rule is excluded from applying because of a different intention appearing or because there was some condition in the contract which prevented the rule from applying.

The argument was placed that the subsequent signing of the document on ownership would mean that ownership had not passed. On this, the court noted:

The document contemplates that the ownership of the vehicle has not passed to the bidder, but, as I have already said, in my judgment, it had passed on the fall of the hammer, and, if subsequently the bidder executed the document acknowledging that the ownership of the vehicle would not pass to him, that could not have any effect on what had already taken place. … In my view, the property had passed on the falling of the hammer.

If the document had instead stated that the ownership will re-vest in Dennant, it would have been a different matter. Further, we will see in Chapter 11 that an unpaid seller has the right to retain possession of goods, even if the ownership is transferred. When Dennant gave up the possession, he lost this right too. The Supreme Court of India relied extensively on *Dennant* v. *Skinner* in the following case.

Consolidated Coffee Ltd v. *Coffee Board, Bangalore*

To maintain the price of coffee, the Coffee Board was given the power to procure coffee from producers and auction it for exports.[11] To be able to bid in these 'export auctions', exporters had to be registered with the Board and procure a permit. The permit holder had to make a security deposit. Several stringent conditions were applied to the permit holders, as the following passage from the judgment shows:

Under Clause 11 no one is allowed to retract his bid when once the same has been entered in the Register of Bids. The highest bid is ordinarily accepted but the Sale Conducting Officer may not

[11] *Consolidated Coffee Ltd* v. *Coffee Board, Bangalore*, AIR (1980) SC 1468.

accept such bid if he has reason to believe that the same is not bona fide or genuine or the same is the outcome of concerted action on the part of the dealers or a section of them for the purpose of controlling or manipulating prices, etc. subject to his recording the reasons for such rejection in the Register of Bids. Clause 19 deals with weighment, delivery and payment of price and contains an overriding provision to the effect that the 'property in the coffee sold shall not pass to the buyer until after he has paid the full price and the coffee sold to him is weighed and set apart for delivery to him'. Clause 26 declares that it is an essential condition of the auction that the coffee sold thereat shall be exported to the destination stipulated in the catalogue of lots or to any other foreign country outside India as may be approved by the Chief Coffee Marketing Officer within three months or within such extended period as shall not exceed one year from the Notice of tender issued to the auction buyer (Registered Exporter) and that under no circumstances, the coffee purchased at such auction shall be diverted to other destinations or sold or be disposed of or otherwise released in India.

Within Section 5 of the Central Sales Tax, penultimate local sales 'in the course of export' were exempted from the local sales tax. The condition was that 'such last sale' was for the purpose of complying with 'the agreement or order for or in relation to such export'. The permit holders argued that the conditions and impositions by the Coffee Board on them were an 'agreement' to export. The Coffee Board required them to bring firm export orders to avail the benefit of Section 5. As a penultimate sale, local sales tax should not be payable on the auctioned coffee.

To work out the tax implications, the nature of the auction sale had to be construed. The Sale of Goods Act, 1930, makes provisions on sales by auction. Subsection (2) of Section 64 provides, 'In the case of a sale by auction ... the sale is complete when the

auctioneer announces its completion by the fall of the hammer or in other customary manner; and, until such announcement is made, any bidder may retract his bid.' It was argued by the permit holders that as it was a sale by auction, the sale was complete on the fall of the hammer. Thus, the auction by the Coffee Board was a sale, entitling them to tax benefit. The Supreme Court interpreted the provision as follows:

Regarding Section 64 (2) of the Sale of Goods Act, it seems to us that that provision does not deal with the question of the passing of the property in the goods sold at auction sale, but instead, it deals with the completion of the contract of sale. It is true that sub-section (2) says that 'the sale is complete' when the auctioneer announces its completion by the fall of the hammer or in other customary manner, but, the next following provision which says: 'and until such announcement is made any bidder may retract his bid' suggests that what is complete at the fall of the hammer or the announcement of closure in other customary manner is that the contract for sale is complete. It is well known that our Sale of Goods Act, 1930 is based upon and is largely a reproduction of the English Sale of Goods Act, 1893 and in principle as well as in most details, the law of sale of goods in both the countries is now the same and, therefore, English authorities on interpretation of different sections, although not technically binding in India, would have great persuasive value.

It will be pertinent to observe that our Section 64 is based upon Section 58 of the English Act ... At foot-note (2), Section 58 (2) of the Sale of Goods Act, 1893 is the provision indicated in support of the aforesaid statement of law and it is further stated: 'In an unconditional sale the property in the goods passes on the fall of the hammer' ... This would show that under Section 58 (2) of the English Sale of Goods Act, 1893, normally, in an auction sale, at the fall of the hammer, a completion of the contract of sale takes place and until such time, the bidder may retract his bid, but if the auction sale happens to be an unconditional sale in respect of specific and ascertained goods, the title to the property passes simultaneously at the fall of the hammer, not by virtue of Section 58 (2) but by reason of the operation of Section 18, Rule 1 of the English Act (which is equivalent to Section 20 of our Act).

The court thus summarized the *Dennant* v. *Skinner* case:

In *Dennant* v. *Skinner* ... the auctioneer knocked down five vehicles including a Standard motor car to King. After the sales, King said that he would like to pay by cheque, but D replied that it was not his practice to accept cheques from people he did not know. King represented that he was the son of the proprietors of King's Motors of Oxford, a well-known firm and produced counterfoils in his cheque books, according to which he had been paying large amounts to well-known auctioneers. D thus accepted the cheque, King signing a form which stated: 'I hereby certify that my cheque No ... will be met on presentation at my bank. Furthermore, I agree that the ownership of the vehicles will not pass to me until such time as the proceeds of my cheques have been credited to South London Motor Auction account at Lloyds Bank.' King was permitted to remove the vehicles and he sold the Standard car to a third party, C, who sold it to the defendant, Section The cheque was dishonoured on presentation and it transpired that King had no connections with King's Motors. D sought from S return of the car or payment of its value. Negativing the claim, the Court held that the contract for sale was unconditional and, therefore, the property in the car passed on the fall of the hammer under the Sale of Goods Act, 1893, Section 18 (1), and D's right under Section 39 (1) (b) of that Act to retain the car until payment was made was relinquished when he gave possession to King.

The Supreme Court, thus, referred to the working of the English law on unconditional auction sale:

It will thus appear clear that because the auction sale was unconditional and it related to specific goods, that it was held that the property in the car had passed to King at the completion of the contract which occurred at the fall of the hammer under Section 58 (2), but the property had passed under Section 18 (1). This case also shows that to an auction sale normally governed by Section 58, the implied rule pertaining to the passing of property contained in Section 18 (1) applied; if so, it stands to reason that the auctioneer could incorporate an express term pertaining to the passing of property, different from the implied rule, in his auction conditions and if he were to do so, it will be operative.

The Supreme Court then moved to the Indian Sale of Goods Act:

Section 64 (2) of our Sale of Goods Act, being in *pari materia* with Section 58 (2) of the English Sale of Goods Act 1893, will have to be interpreted in the same manner and we are, therefore, of the view that it does not deal with the question of passing of the property at auction sale, but merely deals with completion of the contract of sale which takes place at the fall of the hammer or at the announcement of the close of the sale in other customary manner by the auctioneer. It would also be correct to say that if the auction sale of chattels is unconditional and is in respect of specific ascertained goods and nothing remains to be done to the goods for putting them in a condition ready for delivery, the property in the goods pass to the purchaser upon the acceptance of the bid, but that would not be because of Section 64 (2) but because of Section 20 and such would not be the case if the goods sold thereat are non-specific or unascertained goods or the auction sale is conditional.

The question then was whether the auction by the Coffee Board was a conditional sale or an unconditional sale. Contracts are consensual. The parties are free to set their own terms. This basic concept cuts across all provisions in the Sale of Goods Act. The Supreme Court noted the incorporation of the principle in Section 62 of the Act. It reads:

'Where any right, duty or liability would arise under a contract of sale by implication of law, it may be negatived or varied by express agreement or by the course of dealing between the parties or by usage.' Thus, a sale by auction can be conditional or unconditional, as the Supreme Court noted:

… once it is accepted that auction sales to which Section 64 applies could be unconditional or conditional and that the auctioneer can prescribe his own terms and conditions on the basis of which the property is exposed to sale by auction, it must be held that the acceptance of any bid as well as the passing of the property in the goods sold thereat would be governed by those terms and conditions.

Reviewing the numerous terms and condition imposed by the Coffee Board, the Supreme Court ruled that the auction was subject to those numerous conditions. Thus, the auction alone could not be taken to be the penultimate sale to an export. The claim of the permit holders failed.

* * *

In this chapter, we examined the transfer of ownership in sale contracts of specific goods. We first need to examine the sale contract to settle whether the sale is for specific goods. We then need to deduce the intention of the parties from the terms of the contract and the conduct of the parties with regard to when they intended the property to be transferred. At this stage, we also need to ask whether the goods are in a deliverable state or not. If the goods are not in a deliverable state, there would be a presumption that the parties intended to transfer the ownership only after the seller had put it in a deliverable state. Does the seller have to weigh or measure the goods to ascertain the price? If yes, the presumption would be that the ownership was to transfer only if this was done. Another presumption is that if the seller has given the goods to the buyer on a sale-or-return basis, the ownership passes when the buyer communicates his acceptance or adopts the transaction. There would be no such presumptions if the parties indicated otherwise. If nothing can be inferred as the intention of the parties regarding the transfer of ownership, it becomes an unconditional sale. In this case, if the goods are in a deliverable state, the ownership transfers the moment the contract is made. In the next chapter, we will learn about transfer of ownership in a sale contract where the goods are unascertained.

3

Transfer of Ownership
Unascertained Goods

A sale contract whose subject matter is the sale of identified goods is called a sale of specific goods. By contrast, in a sale of unascertained goods, the goods would be described. During the performance of the contract, the parties settle on specific goods meeting that description. To understand the concept of sale of unascertained goods, let us look at the following sale contracts:

Contract 1: A manufacturer was to manufacture a machine of a specific configuration and deliver it to a buyer.

Contract 2: A wholesaler was to supply 100 packs of 1 litre mixed-fruit juice to a retailer on February 15.

Contract 3: A bookseller confirmed he had five copies of a particular book. He was to supply two books to the buyer in the evening.

Contract 4: An oil manufacturer auctioned 1,000 litres of oil from a lot of 5,000 litres lying in a storage tank.

Contract 5: A buyer test drove a car and entered into a contract to buy the car. The delivery was to be done two days later, after the price was paid.

All of the above are sale contracts. In Contract 5, the parties entered into a contract for the sale of a specific car, the one the customer had driven. In Contract 1, the goods did not exist at the time of making of the contract, but will be created by the manufacturer. Goods that are to be created are called future goods. In Contract 2, the description of the product is settled. The wholesaler may have the goods or he may procure and supply them. In Contract 3, the seller has agreed to sell two books from a bulk of five books. However, the parties have not agreed on the two specific books. If the contract were for the sale of all the five books, it would have been a sale of specific goods. In Contract 4 too, 1,000 litres have to be segregated from the bulk. In all these contracts, the goods are not ascertained at the time of making of the contract.

In the case of a sale of specific goods, the buyer cannot give other goods, nor can the seller demand other goods. The sale is of the specific identified goods. As the name suggests, in the sale of unascertained goods, the goods are not ascertained at the time of making of the contract. This is the context in which the term 'sale of unascertained goods' is used. It is left for the parties to subsequently settle on the specific goods. At some point of time, in the course of performance of the contract, the goods become specific. The goods become ascertained at the point of time at which both the buyer and seller are irrevocably committed to the goods towards the performance of the contract. Let us try to understand the concept with the following illustrations.

Illustration: Under a contract, the seller was to deliver a packet of 'Amul milk, 500 ml, Shakti'. The seller came to the premises of the buyer and gave him a packet of milk meeting the description. The buyer took the packet; that is, he took the delivery of the packet. The packet was ascertained at that moment. If the buyer refused to take delivery of the packet by pointing out that the packet was unclean, there would have been no commitment of the parties to the packet; the seller would have given another. Similarly, if the buyer refused to take delivery, the contract would have been breached. If there is no performance of the contract, there is no ascertainment.

Illustration: This case is an agreement for the sale of a packet of 'Amul milk, 500 ml, Shakti'. The seller said to the buyer, 'The packets are lying in the tray. Pick any one of them.' As the buyer did so, that particular packet was committed to the contract. The goods became ascertained by the buyer with the assent of the seller. Now, neither the seller nor the buyer can change the packet. A claim to change would be in breach of the contract.

Illustration: In an agreement for the sale of a book titled *Introduction to Taxation*, the seller was to drop a copy of the book in the mail box of the buyer. When the seller did so, it was he who ascertained the book to the contract with the assent of the buyer. But what if, after dropping the book, the seller realized that of the two books with him, he had to deliver the one whose cover had become dirty in transit. The other book was to be taken for a more valued customer. The mail box was not locked, so he opened it, took out the book, and put another copy. Was the first book committed to the contract or the second one? So long as no one gets to know, there is no dispute between the parties, but if the buyer had somehow found out, the fact would be established. Under the contract, the first book got committed to the contract. The seller would be in breach in replacing the copy.

The ascertainment of the goods in a sale contract will happen through the consent of the parties. The modalities for ascertaining may be provided in the contract itself. Alternately, the parties may work it out later. All the illustrations we saw above were of goods with descriptions. In the case of future goods, the same process would apply. Till the time the goods are no longer in existence, there is no question of the goods being committed to the contract. After the goods come into existence, these are committed by the seller with the consent of the buyer, or by the buyer with the consent of the seller. Similarly, goods in bulk will be ascertained at its separation from the bulk with the consent of the buyer and seller. Let us illustrate this:

Illustration: Under an agreement to sell 1,000 litres of edible oil from a lot in a storage tank belonging to the seller, the buyer, will send his carriage container to receive the goods. The seller pours out 1,000 litres in the container. By separating the goods from the bulk and pouring it into the container, the seller has ascertained the goods. The ascertaining was done by the seller with the consent of the buyer.

Illustration: This is an agreement to sell 5 litres of edible oil from the lot in the warehouse of the seller. The seller shows the lot to the buyer, gives him a 5-litre measuring container, and asks him to take it. The buyer pours out the 5 litres into his container. The buyer has ascertained with the consent of the seller.

Illustration: Under the agreement, the seller was to deliver the first car that rolled out from his factory in the month of September. The goods will automatically be ascertained the moment the car is assembled.

ASCERTAINMENT AND TRANSFER OF OWNERSHIP

Let us now look at the relationship between ascertainment and ownership. In a sale (as a contractual relationship), ownership should transfer when the parties intend for it to transfer. Ownership, by its very nature, can only be in specific goods. Thus, irrespective of the terms of the contract and intention of the parties, ownership cannot transfer till the goods are ascertained. This is one principle that prevails even over the intention of the parties. Section 18 expresses this principle:

18. Goods must be ascertained: Where there is a contract for the sale of unascertained goods, no property in the goods is transferred to the buyer unless and until the goods are ascertained.

Prior to the codification, the principle was explained in *Wait* v. *Baker*: 'property does not pass until there is a bargain with respect to a specific article, and everything is done which, according to the intention of the parties to the bargain, was necessary to transfer the property in it.'[1] The following is a case that took place after the enactment of the Sale of Goods, 1893.

In Re Wait

Wait imported 1,000 tons of wheat from America and sub-sold 500 tons to different buyers.[2] The sub-purchasers had paid the full price. Wait went bankrupt and his property was taken over by the trustees, who took control of the 1,000 tons of wheat. The dispute was whether 500 tons of the wheat belonged to the sub-purchasers. If it did, they would take their goods. If it did not, they could only claim the breach of contract and demand damages. Atkin noted, '"Ascertained" probably means identified in accordance with the agreement after the time a contract of sale is made, and I shall assume that to be the meaning.' As the portion of the sub-buyers was not separated from the bulk, the goods were not ascertained and the property could not have passed to the sub-buyers. Let us examine the notion of transfer of ownership.

Illustration: Under a contract, the ownership in a USB flash drive of 4 GB was to transfer to the buyer on payment of the price. The seller came to the premises of the buyer and gave him a flash drive meeting the description. Under the contract, the buyer was to pay the price within a week of the delivery. In this case, the flash drive is ascertained. However, the ownership in the flash drive has not passed to the buyer.

Illustration: In an agreement for the sale of a packet of Amul milk, 500 ml, Shakti, the ownership was to pass on payment of the price. The seller said to the buyer, 'The packets are lying in the tray. Pick any one of them.' When the buyer did so, the milk packet was ascertained. The packet is also delivered to the buyer, as he now possessed

---

[1] *Wait* v. *Baker*, (1848) 2 Exch 1.

[2] *In Re Wait*, (1927) 1 Ch. 606.

it with the consent of the seller. However, the ownership had not yet been transferred. This will happen only when the buyer approaches the seller and pays him the money.

Illustration: In an agreement for the sale of a book titled *Introduction to Taxation*, the buyer paid the money for it on Monday under the terms of the contract. The seller was to drop a copy of the book in the mail box of the buyer on Tuesday. The ownership in the book was to transfer on Friday. The seller fulfilled his part of the agreement on Tuesday, and so the book is ascertained to the contract. The buyer now has possession of the goods, but the ownership has not transferred to the buyer.

Illustration: Under an agreement, the seller was to pour in 5 litres into a container given by the buyer from a tank containing edible oil and bring it to him. The ownership in the oil was to transfer a week after delivery. The price was already paid. When the seller poured the oil, the goods are ascertained, but not delivered to the buyer. The ownership continues to be with the seller.

Let us now consider the case of a sale contract of unascertained goods where the parties do not express any intention, whether express or implied, on the transfer of ownership. The law has already stated its approach on the unconditional sale contracts in specific goods. The ownership transfers at the very moment the contract is made. As the ownership cannot transfer in unascertained goods, the transfer of ownership must wait till the goods are ascertained. The expression of these principles is in Sections 23 and 25.

23. Sale of unascertained goods and appropriation: (1) Where there is a contract for the sale of unascertained or future goods by description and goods of that description and in a deliverable state are unconditionally appropriated to the contract, either by the seller with the assent of the buyer or by the buyer with the assent of the seller, the property in the goods thereupon passes to the buyer. Such assent may be express or implied, and may be given either before or after the appropriation is made.

(2) Where, in pursuance of the contract, the seller delivers the goods to the buyer or to a carrier or other bailee (whether named by the buyer or not) for the purpose of transmission to the buyer, and does not reserve the right of disposal, he is deemed to have unconditionally appropriated the goods to the contract.

25. Reservation of right of disposal: (1) Where there is a contract for the sale of specific goods or where goods are subsequently appropriated to the contract, the seller may, by the terms of the contract or appropriation, reserve the right of disposal of the goods until certain conditions are fulfilled. In such case, notwithstanding the delivery of the goods to a buyer, or to a carrier or other bailee for the purpose of transmission to the buyer, the property in the goods does not pass to the buyer until the conditions imposed by the seller are fulfilled.

(2) Where goods are shipped or delivered to a railway administration for carriage by railway and by the bill of lading or railway receipts, as the case may be, the goods are deliverable to the order of the seller or his agent, the seller is prima facie deemed to reserve the right of disposal.

(3) Where the seller of goods draws on the buyer for the price and transmits the bill of exchange and bill of lading to the buyer together, to secure acceptance or payment of the bill of exchange, the buyer is bound to return the bill of lading if he does not honour the bill of exchange and if he wrongfully retains the bill of lading the property in the goods does not pass to him.

In the definition above, 'unconditionally' has the same meaning as in 'unconditional contract'. It means that there are no terms on the passing of the property. The expression 'reservation of the right of disposal' in both the sections is superfluous; the very meaning of 'unconditionally' is that there are no reservations on the passing of the ownership. If the seller has 'reserved the right of disposal of the goods', the appropriation is conditional; if the goods are 'unconditionally appropriated', there are no reservations on the passing of property. The act has added the term to make the code comprehensive. Section 25(2) also makes the presumption that if the bill of lading or railway receipt is deliverable to the order of the seller, the seller is maintaining control on the goods. He may withhold it from the buyer. Thus, the assumption is that he has reserved the right of disposal.

Let us see how the terms are networked in Section 25(1). The section applies both to sale of specific as well as unascertained goods. Suppose that X owns a car, and contracts to sell it to Y. Under the terms of the contract, the ownership is to pass only on full payment of the price. X received 50 per cent of the price and gave the car to Y. The relevant part of Section 25(1) would read:

(1) Where there is a contract for the sale of specific goods ... the seller may, by the terms of the contract ... reserve the right of disposal of the goods until certain conditions are fulfilled. In such case, notwithstanding the delivery of the goods to a buyer ... the property in the goods does not pass to the buyer until the conditions imposed by the seller are fulfilled.

X has delivered the car but the ownership has not passed to the buyer. Consider another illustration. A car company entered into an agreement with a customer to sell a particular brand of a car. Under the terms of the contract, the ownership was to pass only on receiving full payment for the car. The car company delivered a car to the customer on the payment of 50 per cent of the sale price. The relevant part of Section 25(1) would read:

(1) Where there is a contract ... where goods are subsequently appropriated to the contract, the seller may, by the terms of the contract or appropriation, reserve the right of disposal of the goods until certain conditions are fulfilled. In such case, notwithstanding the delivery of the goods to a buyer ... the property in the goods does not pass to the buyer until the conditions imposed by the seller are fulfilled.

In this case, the terms of the contract had reserved the right of disposal. Thus, the operating word is 'contract or appropriation'. The car was ascertained on delivery; however, the ownership did not pass to the buyer.

Let us look at another case where a car company entered into an agreement with a customer to sell a particular brand of a car for Rs 6 lakh. The contract was to be completed within one month of signing of the contract. The contract was silent on rest of the details. The seller received 50 per cent of the car's price and delivered the car on the condition that its ownership would transfer only when the seller received the rest of the amount within a week. In this case, the operating part of the section is:

(1) Where there is a contract ... where goods are subsequently appropriated to the contract, the seller may, by the terms of ... appropriation, reserve the right of disposal of the goods until certain conditions are fulfilled. In such case, notwithstanding the delivery of the goods to a buyer ... the property in the goods does not pass to the buyer until the conditions imposed by the seller are fulfilled.

These three cases show the scope of the term 'appropriation'. By ascertaining the goods, both the buyer and seller lose the right to replace it with another. But if this was indeed the intention, why did the drafters not use the term 'ascertainment' instead. This is because the drafters were using the terms and phrases used by the courts in the judgments, which in turn were referring to the prior judgments. The ideas did not crystallize in one mind at one point of time, but came to be expressed over more than a century. In essence, the term 'unconditional appropriation' applies in a contract of sale of unascertained goods where the parties express no intention on the time or condition of passing of property in the contract or at the time of ascertainment of goods. With this in mind, let us see how the courts have given meaning to the term in the section. If the parties express an intention on the passing of the ownership, the courts have no hesitation in giving effect to it. It is only in the cases where the parties have not provided on the passing of ownership that the courts have to give their judgment. Thus, all the cases that came before the court were on 'unconditional appropriation'.

The first case we will examine is *Macklow v. Mangles*, which deals with future goods. To better understand the case, let us look at the following illustration. A person entered into a contract with a carpenter to make a study table for him. The description of the table and the material to be used was settled between the parties, and the table was to be delivered to the buyer on 1 November. The buyer was to pay the full value, Rs 10,000 on 15 October, but the contract was silent on the passing of property. The carpenter started constructing a table. All the workmen knew that the table was for that particular customer. Under the contract, the buyer paid the price on 15 October. After completion of the table on 20 October, the carpenter pasted a sticker on the table with the name of the customer, but it was destroyed in a fire. Had the property passed to the buyer, that he should bear the loss? The answer is obviously no. The table was not appropriated to the contract. The carpenter intended the table for the customer, but the appropriation would happen only if the buyer assented to it. This has not happened, so the property in the table did not pass to the buyer.

Consider another situation where the table had not been destroyed in a fire, but was sold to a customer who visited the carpenter's workshop and took a liking to it. The carpenter then made another one and brought it to deliver to the first customer. The buyer cannot claim the first table as it was not appropriated to the contract. It would have been a different case if the parties in the course of making of the table had committed to the buyer getting that very table.

Mucklow v. Mangles

Royland had undertaken to build a barge for Pocock.[3] Pocock paid him an advance and further sums of money as the work progressed. In the process, Pocock paid the full value of the barge. When the barge was nearly finished, Royland painted Pocock's name on the stern. Two days after the completion of the work, the barge was taken away by the officer of the sheriff under a bankruptcy suit before it could be delivered to Pocock. The dispute was whether the barge had become the property of Pocock. Heath J. said:

A tradesman often finishes goods, which he is making in pursuance of an order given by one person, and sells them to another. If the first customer has other goods made for him within the stipulated time, he has no right to complain.... The painting of the name on the stern in this case makes no difference. If the thing be in existence at the time of the order, the property of it passes by the contract, but not so, where the subject is to be made.

The court was reiterating the future nature of the goods. In another landmark case, *Wait* v.

---

[3] *Mucklow* v. *Mangles*, (1808) 1 Taunton 318.

Baker,[4] the court explained the principle of appropriation:

The word appropriation may be understood in different senses. It may mean a selection on the part of the vendor, where he has the right to choose the article which he has to supply in performance of his contract; and the contract will show when the word is used in that sense. Or the word may mean, that both parties have agreed that a certain article shall be delivered in pursuance of the contract, and yet the property may not pass in either case. For the purpose of illustrating this position, suppose a carriage is ordered to be built at a coachmaker's, he may make any one he pleases, and, if it agree with the order, the party is bound to accept it. Now suppose that, at some period subsequent to the order, a further bargain is entered into between this party and the coachbuilder, by which it is agreed that a particular carriage shall be delivered. It would depend upon circumstances whether the property passes, or whether merely the original contract is altered from one which would have been satisfied by the delivery of any carriage answering the terms of the contract, into another contract to supply the particular carriage … property does not pass until there is a bargain with respect to a specific article, and everything is done which, according to the intention of the parties to the bargain, was necessary to transfer the property in it. … 'Appropriation' may also be used in another sense, … viz. where both parties agree upon the specific article in which the property is to pass, and nothing remains to be done in order to pass it.

As we can see, the judges were using the term appropriation in different senses. While the word was used differently, the concept was understood in the same sense. The following three leading cases, all before making of the English Act, have a common theme. Let us understand the point with a more contemporary case. A contract for the sale of 100 litres of edible oil is silent on the transfer of ownership. Under the contract, the buyer is to give a steel container to transfer the oil, and then take it back. The day after this was done, the price of edible oil increased sharply. The seller poured the oil into another container and sold it to another buyer. Has he breached the contract? Had the oil become the property of the buyer? The first objection that comes to us is how the buyer would ever know that the edible oil was poured in and out. This is an issue of facts. If the seller never disclosed it, the buyer (or his agent) would never get to know, and a dispute would never arise. Taking the fact as given, what conclusion do we reach? On pouring the 100 litres in the container, the goods were ascertained. As the parties had not provided on the passing of the property, filling up the container was 'unconditional appropriation', passing the property to the buyer.

What if the goods get damaged or destroyed? Would the buyer have to bear the risk even without realizing that he has become the owner? The answer would have to be yes. He invited it by getting in a contract of this nature. However, the seller has the possession of the goods as a bailee, and must take good care of the goods, as if it were his own. Should there be a lapse on his part, he would have to compensate the owner.

Aldridge v. *Patrick Johnson*

Aldridge entered into an agreement with Knights to buy 100 quarters of barley from a larger quantity stored with the latter.[5] The rate for the barley was fixed on a per-quarter basis. Aldridge had examined a sample of the barley, and it was further agreed that Aldridge would send his own sacks to Ipswich, where

---

[4] *Wait* v. *Baker*, (1848) 2 Exch 1.

[5] *James Wilsher Aldridge* v. *Patrick Johnson*, (1857) 7 E & B 88.

the barley was stored. Knights filled up 155 sacks for delivery to Aldrige, but in the face of his impending bankruptcy, he had the barley in the sacks emptied onto the heap. Following the bankruptcy, the property of Knights came under the control of trustees. Aldridge claimed the 100 quarters of barley from the trustee to Knights's property following his bankruptcy, while the trustee claimed that the barley had not become Aldrige's property. Lord Campbell C.J. noted:

No rule of the law of vendor and purchaser is more clear than this: that, until the appropriation and separation of a particular quantity, or signification of assent to the particular quantity, the property is not transferred. Therefore, except as to what was put into the 155 sacks, there must be judgment for the defendant (seller). It is equally clear that, as to what was put into those sacks, there must be judgment for the plaintiff (buyer). Looking to all that was done, when the bankrupt put the barley into the sacks eo instanti the property in each sack-full vested in the plaintiff (buyer). I consider that here was a priori an assent by the plaintiff. He had inspected and approved of the barley in bulk. He sent his sacks to be filled out of that bulk. There can be no doubt of his assent to the appropriation of such bulk as should have been put into the sacks. ... There remained nothing to be done by the vendor, who had appropriated a part by the direction of the vendee. As to the question of conversion, the property being in the plaintiff ... It was wrong of the bankrupt to mix what had been put into the sacks with the rest of the barley; ... That being so, the plaintiff's property comes into the hands of the defendant as the bankrupt's assignee.

Erle J. noted:

I also am clearly of opinion that the property in what was put into the sacks passed to the plaintiff. It is clear that, where there is an agreement for the sale and purchase of a particular chattel, the chattel passes at once. If the thing sold is

not ascertained, and something is to be done before it is ascertained, it does not pass till it is ascertained. Sometimes the right of ascertainment rests with the vendee, sometimes solely with the vendor. Here it is vested in the vendor only, the bankrupt. When he had done the outward act which showed which part was to be the vendee's property, his election was made and the property passed. ... Here was an ascertained bulk, of which the plaintiff agreed to buy about half. It was left to the bankrupt to decide what portion should be delivered under that contract. As soon as he does that, his election has been indicated; the decisive act was putting the portion into the sacks.

Langton v. Higgins

For many years a wholesale druggist in London by the name of Langton had made an annual contract with a farmer named Carter, for the purchase of oil distilled from the crop of peppermint that was grown on his farm.[6] Langton used to provide an advance to Carter and send bottles for delivery of the oil to him. He was under an obligation to buy all the oil extracted by the farmer, and pay per pound weight. Further, if more than 250 bottles were supplied, a discount was to be given. Each year, the farmer filled and sealed the bottles and put a label mentioning the weight of the oil. The bottles were delivered to a carrier who took it to the railway station and forwarded it to the buyer in London. The dispute in this case arose when the farmer filled up the bottles, but sold them to another person, Higgins, and disappeared. Langton, as usual, had made a large advance to the farmer, and claimed that the oil was her property and that it should be restored to her. Higgins, for his part, claimed to be a bona fide buyer of the oil. Bramwell delivered the following judgment:

The contract is to sell the whole of the vendor's crop of oil of peppermint grown in a certain year.

---

[6] *Langton* v. *Higgins*, (1859) 4 H & N 402.

I do not think that when the oil was made the property passed ... but it appears to me that when the oil was put into the plaintiff's bottles the property in it vested in her. ... I am of opinion that the property vested in the plaintiff when the oil was put into her bottles. Looking at the principle, there ought to be no doubt. A person agrees to buy a certain article, and sends his bottles to the seller to put the article into. The seller puts the article into the buyer's bottles, then is there any rule to say that the property does not pass? The buyer in effect says, 'I will trust you to deliver into my bottles, and by that means to appropriate to me, the article which I have bought from you.' On the other hand the seller must be taken to say, 'You have sent your bottles and I will put the article in them for you.' In all reason, when a vendee sends his ship, or cart, or cask, or bottle to the vendor, and he puts the article sold into it, that is a delivery to the vendee. If we could suppose the case of a metal vessel filled with a commodity which rendered the vessel useless for subsequent purposes, it would be monstrous if the vendor could say 'I have destroyed your vessel by putting into it the article you purchased, but still the property in the article never passed to you.' Or suppose a vendor was to deliver a ton of coals into the vendee's cellar, could he say 'I have put the coals in your cellar, but I have a right to take them away again?' But, independently of reason, there is an authority on the subject.

Rohde v. Thwaites

The seller agreed to sell twenty hogsheads[7] of sugar to the buyer.[8] The seller delivered four hogsheads to the buyer, and the buyer accepted it. The seller filled up sixteen other hogsheads, and informed the buyer that they were ready to be taken away. The buyer said he would take them as soon as he could, but later refused. The dispute was whether the property in the goods had passed to the buyer

and whether he was to pay the price or was only in breach of contract. Justice Bayley raised the principle as follows:

... the plaintiffs did appropriate, for the benefit of the defendant, sixteen hogsheads of sugar, and they communicated to the defendant that they had so appropriated them, and desired him to take them away; and the latter adopted that act of the plaintiffs, and said he would send for them as soon as he could. I am of opinion, that by reason of that appropriation made by the plaintiffs [seller], and assented to by the defendant [buyer], the property in the sixteen hogsheads of sugar passed to the vendee. That being so, the plaintiffs [seller] are entitled to recover the full value of the twenty hogsheads of sugar, under the count for goods bargained and sold.

The vendor ascertained the goods and the buyer agreed to take the delivery at the earliest. Thus, at the point of time when the buyer assented, the ownership was passed to the buyer. Justice Holroyd noted:

The sugars agreed to be sold being part of a larger parcel, the vendors were to select twenty hogsheads for the vendee. That selection was made by the plaintiffs, and they notified it to the defendant, and the latter then promised to take them away. That is equivalent to an actual acceptance of the sixteen hogsheads by the defendant. That acceptance made the goods his own. ... If the sugars had afterwards been destroyed by fire, the loss must have fallen on the defendant. I am of opinion that the selection of the sixteen hogsheads by the plaintiffs, and the adoption of that act by the defendant, converted that which before was a mere agreement to sell into an actual sale, and that the property in the sugars thereby passed to the defendant; and, consequently, that he was entitled to recover to the value of the whole under the count for goods bargained and sold.

The vendor was entitled to receive the price for the goods. The following are the other cases exploring the principle.

---

[7] A hogshead is a cask that contains a specific volume.

[8] *Rohde* v. *Thwaites*, (1827) 6 B & C 388.

Pignataro v. Gilroy

On 12 February, Gilroy sold 140 bags of rice of '130 Butterfly 10 TYC' description to Pignataro, to be delivered in fourteen days.[9] The sale was by sample. The particular bags that were to satisfy the contract were not then ascertained. Pignataro was told that 125 bags would be delivered at a warehouse called chambers. The remaining fifteen bags were to be collected from Gilroy's place of business, 50 Long Acre. On 27 February, Pignataro sent a cheque for the amount, and asked for a delivery order as contracted. On the following day, 28 February, Gilroy sent a receipt for the cheque and a delivery order for 125 bags from Chambers. With regard to the remaining fifteen bags that were to be collected from Gilroy's place, 50 Long Acre, the letter stated that they 'are ready for delivery, and shall be pleased if you can send for them at once as we are very short of room.'

Pignataro neglected to collect the bags. Gilroy wrote two letters, on 6 March and 12 March respectively, requesting him to collect the bags. It was not until 25 March that Pignataro sent to collect the bags. In this while, the bags had been stolen. Those were the only fifteen bags lying at Gilroy's place. Gilroy took all care and was not negligent. It was the owner of the bags who was to bear the responsibility for the loss. But the question arose: had the ownership transferred from Gilroy to Pignataro? The parties had not provided expressly on the passing of ownership. Nor was there any implied term in relation to the passing of ownership. On the date of the making of the contract, the rice bags were unascertained. The court noted:

The contract being silent as to the time of payment, it is to be taken that this was to be against delivery. ... Under the above contract it would be the duty of the sellers to appropriate the goods to the contract; and if such appropriation were assented to, expressly or impliedly, by the buyer the property would have passed. When they received the cheque for the goods and were asked for a delivery order it was right and proper for them to appropriate and place at the disposal of the buyer the goods for which he thus paid in order to effectuate a delivery or its equivalent concurrently with the receipt of the money. They did send a delivery order for the goods at Chambers' Wharf, and as to the 15 bags, told the plaintiff that they were ready, and asked that they should be taken away. It might well be contended that not only as regards the goods covered by the delivery order, but also as regards the goods at the defendants' own premises which they thus told the plaintiff were ready to be taken away in response to the plaintiff's request for a delivery order, there was an appropriation to which by asking for the delivery order the plaintiff had assented in advance. We do not think it necessary to decide this, because we think there was what amounted to an assent subsequent. If the plaintiff had replied saying that he would remove the goods the case would be precisely the same as Rohde v. Thwaites.

The plaintiff, however, did nothing for a month, and the question is what is the effect of that? If the goods were of the required quality it is difficult to see how the plaintiff could have dissented from the appropriation. He could not object to the place from which he was required to fetch them, because he had inspected rice lying at those premises at the time and for the purposes of this very contract. For the same reason it is not easy to see how he could have objected to their quality unless there happened to be some bags inferior to those which he had inspected. At any rate, he made no objection at all. Now it is obvious that if he makes any objection he ought to do so promptly, because he could not place upon the vendors the risk involved in the continued possession of these goods, nor prolong the encumbrance of the vendors' premises. As he chose merely to say nothing for a whole month in response to an appropriation

---

[9] *Pignataro* v. *Gilroy*, (1919) 1 KB 459.

made in consequence of his own letter, we think that comes to precisely the same thing as if he had written saying he would remove them and did not. The learned judge said that there was no evidence of an appropriation with the assent of the buyer. He could only say this if he was looking for an express assent. As the assent may be implied we think that there was not only evidence of it but that it is the only inference possible upon the facts. For these reasons the appeal must be allowed, and judgment entered for the defendants.

The court considered the request for delivery order by the buyer to be prior assent to ascertainment by the seller. If the delivery order for receiving the bags merely mentioned the number of bags but not specific identifiable bags in the warehouse, there is no ascertainment as yet and the ownership would not pass. Ownership would pass when the warehouse ascertained it. However, if the delivery order was for the specific bags, the delivery order itself had ascertained the goods in the warehouse. In relation to the fifteen bags to be collected from the seller's premises, which were lost, the court decided that first the vendor ascertained and then the buyer impliedly assented to the ascertainment. Silence ordinarily implies rejection. However, in the performance of a contract, parties have rights and obligations to each other. It became the duty of the buyer to respond. As he did not respond even after two reminders, the assent became implied.

Wardar's v. Norwood Ltd

Wardar's, a meat-importing firm, bought two consignments of kidneys from Argentina in the autumn of 1964.[10] The consignments were delivered in London and put into cold storage. They then advertised the product for sale.

[10] *Wardar's (Import & Export) Co. Ltd* v. *W. Norwood & Sons Ltd*, (1968) 2 All ER 602.

On 13 October 1964, there was a telephone conversation between them and Norwood Ltd, during which an agreement was formed to sell 600 of the 1,500 cartons to Norwood Ltd. On the same day, Norwood Ltd made an inspection of the cartons. The goods were in good condition. Following the sale, Norwood Ltd. sub-sold the goods to Drummond in Glasgow. Norwood Ltd. instructed McKay's, an agent for carriage, to pick up the cartons and take them to Drummond. McKay's in turn gave the delivery note for picking up 600 cartons to McBeath, the driver of a lorry that had refrigeration facility. McBeath, however, had brought a consignment from Scotland that did not need refrigeration, and so the lorry was not pre-refrigerated. As a result, the consignment decayed. On whom should the loss fall, the buyer or the seller? This depended on whether the property in the goods had passed from Wardar's to Norwood, and if so, when. At the time the contract was made, the goods were not ascertained; they were ascertained and appropriated to the contract when the driver took delivery of the cartons. The ownership in the goods passed at that moment. The court ruled:

When the driver, Mr McBeath, arrived at the cold store at 8 a.m. on October 14, according to his evidence, the load of frozen kidneys which he was to take to Scotland was there on the pavement waiting for him. There is no doubt that that load of six hundred cartons had been in the cold store the day before and indeed had then been examined by the buyers soon after they made their oral contract of purchase. As far as the evidence goes, there was absolutely nothing the matter with the kidneys on October 13. ... they must have been taken out of the cold store at some time on the morning of October 14 prior to 8 a.m.

...

Under rule 5 of Section 18, the property passes to the buyers in the case of unascertained goods such as these when the goods are unconditionally appropriated to the contract. At 8 a.m. the carrier arrived; and the carrier was the buyers' agent. There were the goods, which had been left on the pavement by the sellers' agent for the purpose of fulfilling the contract. The carrier handed over the delivery note with the clear intention that those goods should be accepted for loading; and the loading commenced.

… there was a clear, unconditional appropriation when the delivery order was handed over in respect of the goods which had been deposited on the pavement for loading. There is certainly no evidence that they were not then of merchantable quality. It would seem from the evidence of Mr McBeath, the driver of the lorry, that at some stage, the porters wished to take a tea-break. The driver was apparently concerned at the goods being left standing on the pavement, but he was told, according to his evidence, that the tea-break would take only five minutes. It appears that it took about an hour; and it was after the tea-break, according to Mr McBeath that he first noticed that some of the cartons were dripping, which would be a strong indication that the goods had by then started to deteriorate. Meantime, however, a good many of the cartons—we do not know how many—had already been loaded into the lorry. Since, however (as I think), the goods were appropriated to the contract when the delivery order was handed over and accepted in respect of the goods standing on the pavement, any deterioration that occurred thereafter was at the risk of the buyers. We know that when the goods arrived at their destination, the vast bulk of them were not of merchantable quality. We also know from the driver of the lorry that he did not turn on the refrigeration, so he says, until the tea-break was taken. At any rate, the refrigeration did not become effective until 3 p.m. It may not be very material, but it does not seem to me to be at all unlikely, if the goods were left in a stuffy lorry, as they were, for some hours, that the deterioration may have occurred during that time. The driver said that this was a hot day. Unless it was a very exceptional day for October 14 in this country, I cannot think that the sun had much strength in it by 8 a.m. In any event, none of

this, I think, matters, because at 8 a.m. these goods were appropriated to the contract and the risk of deterioration then fell on the buyers; and there is no evidence that there was any deterioration before eight o'clock in the morning.

The judgment refers to Rule 5 of Section 18 of the Sale of Goods Act, 1893. The Section reads:

18. Unless a different intention appears, the following are ascertaining rules for ascertaining the intention of the parties as to the intention, time at which the property in the goods is to pass to the buyer.

…

Rule 5.—(1) Where there is a contract for the sale of unascertained or future goods by description, and goods of that description and in a deliverable state are unconditionally appropriated to the contract, either by the seller with the assent of the buyer, or by the buyer with the assent of the seller, the property in the goods thereupon passes to the buyer. Such assent may be express or implied, and may be given either before or after the appropriation is made.

(2) Where, in pursuance of the contract, the seller delivers the goods to the buyer or to a carrier or other bailee or custodier (whether named by the buyer or not) for the purpose of transmission to the buyer, and does not reserve the right of disposal, he is deemed to have unconditionally appropriate the goods to the contract.

Section 23 of the Indian Sale of Goods Act, 1930, reproduces Rule 5. The seller, in anticipation, had ascertained the cartons to be delivered to the buyer. The buyer gave the delivery order in relation to the goods on the pavement. The handing over of the delivery note became the assent to the ascertainment. The property passed to the buyer at this stage.

Carlos Federspiel & Co., S.A. v. Charles Twigg & Co., Ltd

Charles Twigg & Co., Ltd was a UK company, engaged in the business of manufacturing children's bicycles and tricycles.[11] Federspiel & Co., S.A. was a buyer of their products based in Costa Rica. The parties had an established and successful business relationship. The manufacturer sent a quotation which the buyer accepted. Under the terms, the buyer paid the full amount in advance. The goods were sold on FOB terms but some further terms in the contract modified it and made it appear like a CIF contract. FOB and CIF are shipping terms used by traders to indicate who will bear the freight and insurance. In both, ownership does not pass prior to loading of the goods on the ship. The seller manufactured the goods, got them packed according to the requirements of the contract, and made preparations for shipment. However, the company at this stage went in winding-up. The buyer, who had already paid the money, claimed that the property in goods had passed to him. The excerpts from the judgment are as follows:

… this contract was in its true nature an f.o.b. contract, the natural time at which the property would pass would be on shipment. Undoubtedly this contract also contained some c.i.f features, and there is an express reference to what is called 'approximate c.i.f. charges' in the pro forma invoice. If and in so far as it was a c.i.f. contract, the effect of the authorities is that the property would pass not earlier than shipment, perhaps later than shipment. The insurance referred to in a c.i.f. contract is, of course, marine insurance for the sea voyage.

…

Therefore, under the contract, it was to be expected that the ownership of the goods would pass to the buyers on shipment of the goods, or possibly at some later time, when the bill of lading and insurance policy and final definitive invoice would be handed over to the buyers. The goods were not in fact shipped, and indeed they were not even dispatched from the sellers' works to the port of shipment. They were, however, packed, and the packages were marked 'C.F. & Co., San Jose, Costa Rica, Port Limon.' … preparatory steps towards shipment had been taken by the sellers. Goods to the quantity and proper description required had been manufactured. They were packed, and they were marked with these shipping marks. The steps can be regarded, not as intended appropriation, but as being preparation for the shipment. It was contended that in August or September, 1953, there was an appropriation of the goods to the contract by the sellers with the assent of the buyers.

The court reviewed cases on appropriation and concluded

On those authorities, what are the principles emerging? I think one can distinguish these principles. First, Rule 5 of Sect. 18 of the Act is one of the Rules for ascertaining the intention of the parties as to the time at which the property in the goods is to pass to the buyer unless a different intention appears. Therefore the element of common intention has always to be borne in mind. A mere setting apart or selection of the seller of the goods which he expects to use in performance of the contract is not enough. If that is all, he can change his mind and use those goods in performance of some other contract and use some other goods in performance of this contract. To constitute an appropriation of the goods to the contract, the parties must have had, or be reasonably supposed to have had, an intention to attach the contract irrevocably to those goods, so that those goods and no others are the subject of the sale and become the property of the buyer.

---

[11] *Carlos Federspiel & Co., S.A. v. Charles Twigg & Co., Ltd*, (1957) 1 Lloyd's Rep. 240.

Secondly, it is by agreement of the parties that the appropriation, involving a change of ownership, is made, although in some cases the buyer's assent to an appropriation by the seller is conferred in advance by the contract itself or otherwise.

Thirdly, an appropriation by the seller, with the assent of the buyer, may be said always to involve an actual or constructive delivery. If the seller retains possession, he does so as bailee for the buyer. There is a passage in Chalmers' Sale of Goods Act, 12th ed., at p. 75, where it is said:

> In the second place, if the decisions be carefully examined, it will be found that in every case where the property has been held to pass, there has been an actual or constructive delivery of the goods to the buyer.

I think that is right, subject only to this possible qualification, that there may be after such constructive delivery an actual delivery still to be made by the seller under the contract. Of course, that is quite possible, because delivery is the transfer of possession, whereas appropriation transfers ownership. So there may be first an appropriation, constructive delivery, whereby the seller becomes bailee for the buyer, and then a subsequent actual delivery involving actual possession, and when I say that I have in mind in particular the two cases cited, namely, Aldridge v. Johnson , *sup.*, and Langton v. Higgins, *sup.*

Fourthly, one has to remember Sect. 20 of the Sale of Goods Act, whereby the ownership and the risk are normally associated. Therefore as it appears that there is reason for thinking, on the construction of the relevant documents, that the goods were, at all material times, still at the seller's risk, that is *prima facie* an indication that the property had not passed to the buyer.

Fifthly, usually but not necessarily, the appropriating act is the last act to be performed by the seller. For instance, if delivery is to be taken by the buyer at the seller's premises and the seller has completed his part of the contract and has appropriated the goods when he has made the goods ready and has identified them and placed them in position to be taken by the buyer and has so informed the buyer, and if the buyer agrees to come and take them, that is the assent to the appropriation. But if there is a further act, an important and decisive act to be done by the seller, then there is *prima facie* evidence that probably the property does not pass until the final act is done.

Applying those principles to the present case I would say this. Firstly, the intention was that the ownership should pass on shipment (or possibly at some later date) because the emphasis is throughout on shipment as the decisive act to be done by the seller in performance of the contract. Secondly, it is impossible to find in this correspondence an agreement to a change of ownership before the time of shipment…. Thirdly, there is no actual or constructive delivery; no suggestion of the seller becoming a bailee for the buyer. Fourthly, there is no suggestion of the goods being at the buyer's risk at any time before shipment; no suggestion that the buyer should insist on the seller arranging insurance for them. Fifthly, the last two acts to be performed by the seller, namely, sending the goods to Liverpool and having the goods shipped on board, were not performed.

Therefore, my decision that the *prima facie* inference which one would have drawn from the contract is that the property was not to pass at any time before shipment, is in my view not displaced by the subsequent correspondence between the parties. It follows, therefore, that there was no appropriation of these goods and therefore the action fails.

The judgment refers to Rule 5 of Section 18 of the Sale of Goods Act, 1893. We have already seen the section and the corresponding section in the India law, the Sale of Goods Act, 1930. Another section the judgment refers to is Section 20. It reads:

20. Risk prima facie passes with property: Unless otherwise agreed, the goods remain at the seller's risk until the property therein is transferred to the buyer, but when the property therein is transferred to the buyer, the goods are at the buyer's risk whether delivery has been made or not…

Section 26 of the Sale of Goods Act, 1930 reproduces the section. We will look at the principle of risk moving with property in Chapter 4.

Philip Head & Sons Ltd v. Showfronts Ltd

Showfronts Ltd were building contractors who had the contract for reconstruction of showrooms and offices on the first floor of a building.[12] They appointed Philip Head & Sons Ltd as the sub-contractor for tiling work and providing and laying carpets. The sub-contractor submitted an estimate of £1511 16s, including six different items for materials and an additional item, 'Planning and Laying', against which the figure of £147 18s was entered. There was a separate estimate for tiling work. The contractor approved the estimate. The sub-contractor received carpet material from the manufacturer at site, and the carpeting work was completed in the smaller rooms. The showroom, however, was huge; it measured 40 × 20 feet. A single carpet would not have covered it. The manufacturer supplied carpeting for the showroom in lengths at site. The sub-contractor sent the lengths for stitching and got them back at 4.30 p.m. on Friday. The carpet thus stitched was a formidable load. It required six men to move it from the lift into the main showroom, which was the only space where it could be put because of its unmanageable size.

The tiling and carpeting work had been delayed. This, in turn, was delaying certain finishing work such as decorating and touching up. The contractor arranged to allow the sub-contractor complete use of the premises over the weekend so that he might complete the tiling work and make further progress with the carpeting work. The carpet was seen by various men on Saturday, but was missing on Sunday morning. The sub-contractor claimed that the property in the carpet had passed to the contractor, and thus he was entitled to recover the amount in the estimate for the carpet. It was contended that it was not a contract for sale of goods but a work contract. The court reiterated that whether a contract is a work contract or sale of goods has to be judged by assessing the main object of the contract. The court decided that it was a contract of sale of goods: 'the conclusion I have come to is that notwithstanding that the planning in connection with this carpeting and the laying of the carpeting (which, of course, included cutting, stitching and so forth) were of very great importance ... nevertheless this was a contract of sale and one to which the Sale of Goods Act, 1893, applied.'

The next question was if the property passed to the buyer and when. The sale was for future goods, along with their description. The contractor argued that the property in the carpet could not pass until it had been laid in position. He argued that that there could be no assent here by the buyer to the unconditional appropriation of goods to the contract by the seller before the stage of laying the carpet had been concluded. The sub-contractor contended that there was nothing expressed in the contract on the passing of the property. The carpet was ascertained and delivered, and thus, appropriated to the contract. The court ruled:

The problem here is, I think, however, whether it can be said that carpeting in a deliverable state was unconditionally appropriated to the contract. That phrase is defined in sect. 62 (4) of the statute as follows:

Goods are in a 'deliverable state' within the meaning of this Act when they are in such a state that the buyer would under the contract be bound to take delivery of them.

[12] *Philip Head & Sons Ltd* v. *Showfronts Ltd*, (1970) 1 Lloyd's Rep. 140.

There is not much assistance in the authorities as to the meaning of this phrase. It is, however, both interesting and, I think, helpful to read a passage from an opinion of Lord Blackburn in Seath & Co. v. Moore, (1886) 11 App. Cas. 350, in which many of the points subsequently codified in the Sale of Goods Act, 1893, including some of the problems which I have to deal with here, are discussed. It is true that that case was one dealing with problems arising out of a shipbuilding contract, but in this particular passage Lord Blackburn is purporting to state the relevant principles of English law in general terms. He stated in relation to the passing of property:

> It is essential that the article should be specific and ascertained in a manner binding on both parties, for unless that be so it cannot be construed as a contract to pass the property in that article and in general, if there are things remaining to be done by the seller to the article before it is in the state in which it is to be finally delivered to the purchaser, the contract will not be construed to be one to pass the property till those things are done.

> But it is competent to parties to agree for valuable consideration that a specific article shall be sold, and become the property of the purchaser as soon as it has attained a certain stage: though if it is part of the bargain that more work shall be done on the article after it has reached that stage, it affords a strong primâ facie presumption against its being the intention of the parties that the property should then pass. I do not examine the various English authorities cited during the argument. It is, I think, a question of the construction of the contract in each case, at what stage the property shall pass; and a question of fact, in each case whether that stage has been reached.

I find that passage to give valuable guidance here. I have described as best I can the state of the carpeting subsequently stolen at the time that it came back to these premises after having been stitched up; it was plainly a heavy bundle, very difficult to move. Although I have determined that this was a contract to which the Sale of Goods Act, 1893, applied, nevertheless an important feature of it was undoubtedly the laying of the carpeting following on the planning. It seems to me that one has to consider—in each case it is a case of fact—where there is work to be done in relation to the article sold before the contractual obligations of the sellers are completed, what is the relevant importance of that work in relation to the contract when deciding whether the property has passed and in particular whether the article or goods in question is or are at a particular moment of time in a deliverable state under sect. 18, rule 5(1). I think one is entitled to apply everyday common sense to the matter; a householder, for example, purchasing carpeting under a contract providing that it should be delivered and laid in his house would be very surprised to be told that carpeting, which was in bales which he could hardly move deposited by his contractor in his garage, was then in a deliverable state and his property.

I take the view because of the condition of this carpeting at the time it was stolen and the importance of the last stage in the obligations to be performed by the plaintiffs under this contract, that at the moment when this carpeting was stolen it had not been unconditionally appropriated to the contract in a deliverable state, and accordingly, in my judgment, the property had not passed at the moment that the carpeting was stolen. In those circumstances the plaintiffs' case must fail.

An unconditional appropriation of goods happens on delivery. However, delivery can be made to the buyer only if the goods are in a deliverable state. As a result, unconditional appropriation does not happen till the goods are put in a deliverable state by the buyer. The judgment quotes the definition of deliverable state contained in Section 64(4). Section 2(3) of the Indian act borrows the above definition. It reads, '… goods are said to be in a "deliverable state" when they are in such state that the buyer would under the contract be bound to take delivery of them.' The carpet was not in a deliverable state as it was not laid down. Thus, the court ruled that there was no unconditional appropriation of the carpet to the contract. The risk of loss of the carpet remained with the seller.

DELIVERY TO CARRIER

We now turn to the second aspect of sale of unascertained goods contained in Section 23(2). It reads:

(2) Where, in pursuance of the contract, the seller delivers the goods to the buyer or to a carrier or other bailee (whether named by the buyer or not) for the purpose of transmission to the buyer, and does not reserve the right of disposal, he is deemed to have unconditionally appropriated the goods to the contract.

The provision is the same as Section 18, Rule 5(2) of the English Act, the Sale of Goods Act, 1893. The key word in the section is 'delivery'. It is the surest way of ascertainment. Delivery is possible only of specific goods; thus, if the goods have not already been ascertained, their delivery will. Further, if there are no conditions on the transfer of ownership, in the case where the goods are not already ascertained, ownership in the goods will pass to the buyer when delivered. Thus, if the property has not already passed, the goods are unconditionally appropriated when delivered to the buyer. This happens provided the seller 'does not reserve the right of disposal'. Section 25, 'Reservation of Right of Disposal', explains the meaning of the term. The seller may 'reserve the right of disposal of the goods until certain conditions are fulfilled'. In other words, even if the goods are delivered to the buyer, the property would not be transferred to the buyer till the conditions are fulfilled. Let us illustrate this.

Illustration: Under a contract for sale of unascertained goods, the property was to pass only on payment. The payment was to be made five days after delivery to the buyer.

The seller delivered the goods to the seller. The property has not passed to the buyer at the time.

Illustration: Under a contract for sale of unascertained goods that is silent on passing of property, the seller asked the buyer to choose the goods. The buyer selected some goods. The ownership has passed to the buyer even if the goods are not delivered to the buyer at the time.

Illustration: Under a contract for sale of unascertained goods that is silent on passing of property, the price was to be paid two days after delivery. The seller delivered goods meeting the description. The ownership in the goods passed to the buyer at the time of delivery.

Illustration: Under a contract for sale of unascertained goods that is silent on passing of property, the seller asked for the money while delivering the goods to the buyer. As the buyer could not pay immediately, the seller gave him the goods, but insisted that the ownership will not pass till the money was paid. In this case, the buyer has retained the right of disposal. Thus, at the time of delivery, ownership did not pass.

Illustration: Under a contract for sale of unascertained goods that is silent on passing of property, the seller asked for the money while delivering the goods to the buyer. The buyer could not pay immediately, but promised to the next day. The seller gave him the goods. In this case, the seller has made the delivery, but not reserved his right of disposal. Thus, the ownership passed on delivery.

The principle is one aspect of unconditional appropriation. Only specific goods can be delivered. Thus, if goods are not already ascertained, it will definitely be ascertained at the time of delivery. If the parties have not provided on the transfer of ownership and the buyer does not reserve the right of disposal, delivery leads to the passing of property.

Let us take a look at the second aspect, where the buyer and seller are at a distance and a carrier takes the goods to the buyer. In the following illustrations, the contract is silent on the passing of property, the seller has not reserved the right of disposal, and the property has not already passed to the buyer. The actions were done under the contract. What effect would these have on the passing of property?

1. The buyer visits the premises of the seller and takes delivery.

2. The buyer sends an employee to the seller to take delivery.

3. The buyer hires a van and sends him to take delivery.

4. Under the contract, the seller has to hire a van and give the driver the goods to take to the buyer.

In the first three situations, the ownership transfers at the time of delivery. In the third, the carrier is an agent of the buyer. Delivery to the carrier amounts to delivery to the buyer. In the fourth, the carrier is an agent of the seller. Thus, technically, the delivery is not made to the buyer.

When goods are delivered to a carrier, the carrier gives a document confirming the carriage, destination, and person to whom the goods are to be given. The document in the case of shipping is a bill of lading, a railway receipt for carriage by rail, and lorry receipt for carriage by road. If the document is drawn in favour of the buyer, and the documents are given to him, he alone can receive the goods. If the carriage document is drawn in the favour of the seller, even if the goods are being carried to the buyer, the seller or his agent only can get the delivery of

the goods from the carrier. For this reason, Section 23(2) assumes it that delivery to a carrier as equivalent to delivery to the buyer if the seller has not reserved the right of disposal. Further, if the documents are drawn in favour of the seller, delivery will get affected to the buyer only on the consent of the seller. It will amount to the seller reserving the right of disposal. Section 25(2) provides this explicitly for shipping and railway. It reads: 'Where goods are shipped or delivered to a railway administration for carriage by railway and by the bill of lading or railway receipts, as the case may be, the goods are deliverable to the order of the seller or his agent, the seller is prima facie deemed to reserve the right of disposal.'

Healy v. Howlett & Sons

Healy was a fish exporter in county Kerry, Ireland, and Howlett, a fish salesman in London.[13] Healy telegraphed to Howlett that he had 120 boxes of mackerel for sale, quoted the price, and asked him to 'wire order quick'. Howlett telegraphed back, 'Send twenty boxes of hard, bright mackerel'. The same day, Healy consigned by railway from Valentia his order of 190 boxes of mackerel to Holyhead, North Wales. This was for Howlett and other buyers. Healy telegraphed the names of the customers and the number of boxes to be given to each of them to the railway company at Holyhead. This was the standard practice of fish exporters: by not marking the boxes at the point of departure, they would ensure that their customers would not be revealed to rival exporters. The train was to take the consignment to Dublin, where the boxes would be transferred to a boat—also operated by the railway company—that was bound for Holyhead. The train was delayed, and the

---

[13] *Healy* v. *Howlett & Sons*, (1917) 1 KB 337.

consignment missed the boat connection in Dublin. It had to be taken in a later boat to Holyhead. The railway company marked twenty boxes for Howlett and took it to deliver to him in London. The fish was not of merchantable quality by then, and the buyer refused to take the boxes. The goods were sold at a lower price to another buyer. The dispute between the parties was who would bear the loss.

Within the Sale of Goods Act, 1893, if the place for delivery is not stipulated and the goods are delivered to a carrier, delivery to the carrier is taken to be delivery to the buyer. The judge of the City of London Court, the court of the first instance, ruled that the property passed when the boxes were delivered to the railways at Valentia. The time of passing of the property could not be when the boxes were marked by the railways at Holyhead, as the word in the section is 'delivery to the carrier', which clearly was Valentia. Thus, either the property passed to the buyer at Valentia or it passed to him at delivery in London. The court ruled that the property passed from the seller to all the buyers jointly. The case came in appeal before the King's Bench. The court ruled:

When the fish arrived at Dublin they had been delayed—it does not appear where, but they did not catch the boat by which they were intended to be conveyed to Holyhead. In accordance with the practice of the plaintiff—perfectly reasonable no doubt—at Holyhead twenty boxes were marked for the defendants at Billingsgate. It is contended for the plaintiff that that amounts to an appropriation of those twenty boxes out of the 190 boxes to the purchaser's risk, and that it was an appropriation of the goods within the authorities which establish that where there is a contract for the sale of goods which are not specific the property will pass as soon as there has been an appropriation of particular goods to the contract. The result of those authorities is abundantly clear and is that

the goods become the property of the consignee and are at his risk so soon as they are marked off by some distinct act as his, and not the seller's, and are delivered to the carrier as the agent to complete delivery to the purchaser. But in the present instance out of 190 boxes a portion were to belong to the defendants, a London firm, and none had been marked off. I am not aware that in any similar case it has been held that because all the parcels were meant to be divided between three separate purchasers in London there was an appropriation of them all to the risk of the purchasers when it was impossible to say at whose risk any one of the boxes could be. It would follow in the present case that if there was delivery or appropriation, as the learned judge in the Court below put it, up to a certain point, although not completely, at Valentia, some process of lottery or allotment would have to be adopted to decide upon which consignee the loss was to fall if a portion of the goods disappeared and the other portion did not. It is difficult to understand how that could possibly be done. Supposing half the boxes had been lost at sea and the other half were safe, it would be impossible to say whether the boxes which had been lost were the property of the defendants or of one of the other two consignees. In order to bring the present case within the authorities as to appropriation passing the property each box ought to have been marked with the name of its consignee. From that moment the boxes would have remained at the risk of the consignees respectively. That seems to me to be the principle laid down in the Sale of Goods Act, 1893, so far as that statute in terms deals with the matter. Taking the view I do, it is unnecessary to go into the question as to what risks would still have to be borne and by whom. The goods must of course be in a condition good enough to withstand the ordinary risks of transit. It is, however, unnecessary to deal with that point.

…

There are insuperable difficulties in holding that the property has passed in the present case. It is impossible to say which consignee is to bear the loss caused by the deterioration of any particular boxes of the mackerel. The essence of the authorities which decide that appropriation of goods to the contract by delivery to the carrier at the beginning of the transit may be sufficient to pass the property is that it should be known to whom the goods are appropriated, and not that the question as to who is to bear any loss that may happen should be open to any discussion or be determined by accident. That result would follow if the judgment of the learned judge of the City of London Court were upheld. I am of opinion that his decision was wrong and must be reversed.

* * *

To review, in the case of sale of unascertained goods, ownership cannot pass till the goods are ascertained. This will take precedence over the intention of the parties on transfer of ownership. In the course of performance of the contract, goods would get ascertained with the consent of the buyer and the seller. The contract itself may have provided for the process by which ascertainment will happen. Alternately, the contracting parties may do it in the course of performance of the contract. If the contract does not provide on the time of transfer of ownership, the ownership will transfer when the goods are appropriated to the contract. If the seller delivers the goods to a carrier without reserving his right of disposal, it is assumed that the ownership has transferred to the buyer on delivery to the carrier. In the next chapter, we will take up cases from the British and Indian courts reviewing the passing of property in ascertained and unascertained goods to gain a complete understanding of the principles.

4

Transfer of Property
Review of Cases

In the preceding chapters, our goal was to grasp the principles on transfer of ownership of goods in a sale contract. We explored this by taking up illustrations and landmark cases on the theme. Only a court judgment which directly aided in developing our concepts was reviewed. The principles have been used in several cases in the past more than 100 years. Reviewing the significant cases will help us in three ways. One, it will strengthen the concepts learnt. Two, it will make us familiar with the application of the principles in different contexts. Three, as law persons, we should know the case law.

ASCERTAINED AND UNASCERTAINED GOODS

Kursell v. Timber Operators and Contractors

On 10 September 1920, the owner of a tract of forest in Latvia entered into a written contract for the sale of all merchantable timber growing in the specified forest.[1] Merchantable timber was defined to be 'all trunks and

[1] *Kursell* v. *Timber Operators and Contractors, Limited,* (1927) 1 KB 298.

branches of trees but not seedlings and young trees of less than six inches in diameter at a height of four feet from the ground.' The timber was to be cut not more than twelve inches from the ground. The purchasers were given fifteen years in which to cut the timber, and were to have the use of the seller's saw-mills, plant, and huts, as well as the right to occupy every part of the forest.

The Latvian government passed a law on 16 September 1920 that nationalized the forest without any compensation. The dispute between the buyer and seller was whether the contract was performed or not. If the ownership of the contracted goods was already transferred to the buyer, the buyer should pay the price to the seller and bear the loss of the forfeiture by the government. On the other hand, if the forest continued to be the property of the seller, the forfeiture was the seller's loss. He could not perform the contract as he was prevented by the law. This would lead to discharge of the contract due to frustration. Scrutton L.J. noted:

What is the legal result of these facts? In the first place has the property passed? It was said that this was a contract for the sale of specific goods in a deliverable state under s. 18, r. 1, of the Sale of Goods Act. Specific goods are defined as goods identified and agreed upon at the time a contract of sale is made. It appears to me these goods were neither identified nor agreed upon. Not every tree in the forest passed, but only those complying with a certain measurement not then made. How much of each tree passed depended on where it was cut, how far from the ground. Nor does the timber seem to be in a deliverable state until the buyer has severed it. He cannot under the definition be bound to take delivery of an undetermined part of a tree not yet identified. ... For these reasons in my opinion the property had not passed under s. 18, r. 1, and, therefore, the timber was not at the risk of the purchasers.

The first requirement for the passing of property is that the goods have to be specific for the ownership to transfer. In the contract, some of the timber in the forest was to pass to the buyer. This was to happen later, when the buyer ascertained the goods by identifying the timber that met the requirements. The following two cases from the Supreme Court of India are on the same subject.

Badri Prasad v. State of MP

An owner of a patch of forest entered into an agreement with Badri Prasad to harvest the mature teak timber on that patch.[2] The written agreement included the following:

1. ... Out of the area of 1704.46 acres of Mouza Sunderpani Jagir contract of all the teak trees of more than 12 inches girth standing in the 1000 acres of the forest ... given to contractor Badri Prasad Moolchand firm of Timarni for a sum of Rs 17,000 ...

4. For the proper execution of work of the forest the felling of the forest shall have to be done from one side.

...

5. After felling, the stumps of teak trees should be 3 inches high from the ground and slanting so as to drain the water off. ... Till the stumps are passed the wood cannot be removed. Only the pairing can be done. The coupe guard shall make a hammer mark of passing on the stump and end of the paired wood.

The Abolition of Proprietary Rights (Estates, Mahals, Alienated Lands) Act, 1950, came into effect soon after the contract was made. The state had acquired all the proprietary rights existing in the forest. The dispute was whether the ownership in the timber had passed to Badri Prasad. The Supreme Court noted:

It is true that trees which are agreed to be severed before sale or under the contract of sale are 'goods' for the purposes of the Sale of Goods Act. But before they cease to be 'proprietary' right or interest in proprietary rights within the meaning of Sections 3 and 4 (a) of the Act they must be felled under the contract. It will be noticed that under Clause 1 of the contract the plaintiff was entitled to cut teak trees of more than 12 inches girth. It had to be ascertained which trees fell within that description. Till this was ascertained, they were not 'ascertained goods' within Section 19 of the Sale of Goods Act. Clause 5 of the contract contemplated that stumps of trees, after cutting had to be 3 inches high. In other words, the contract was not to sell the whole of the trees. In these circumstances property in the cut timber would only pass to the plaintiff under the contract at the earliest when trees are felled. But before that happened the trees had vested in the State.

Pushpapriyadevi v. State of Maharashtra

A contractor entered into an agreement with the proprietor of an estate on 15 March 1951.[3] The contract was for the felling of trees

---

[2] *Badri Prasad* v. *State of MP*, AIR (1970) SC 706.

[3] *Pushpapriyadevi* v. *State of Maharashtra*, AIR (1978) SC 1076.

from a specified area in the forest, for a sum of Rs 50,000. Under the terms of the contract, Rs 15,000 was to be paid immediately and the balance within six months. The buyer had a right to fell teak trees over 4 inches in girth at the rate of Rs 50 a tree. The contractor had to fell and remove the timber between 15 March 1951 and 14 March 1953. Clause 5 provided: 'The contractor will not remove any forest produce from the site ... until the logs are checked and passed by the Estate Forest Staff by affixing passing hammer mark. The contractor will not remove any forest produce between the sunset and sunrise.' Clause 8 provided that if the contractor fails to pay any instalment within the time fixed, the estate authorities will be entitled to stop and restrain all further extraction or other work in the contract area. Clause 9 provides that the contractor must agree to file accounts of the feeling, logging, and extraction done by him every month.

The Madhya Pradesh Abolition of Proprietary Rights (Estates, Mahals, Alienated Lands) Act, 1950, was brought into force on 31 March 1951. Under the act, all proprietary rights in an estate vesting in a proprietor of such estate were to vest in the state. The dispute in the case was whether the rights in timber were with the estate or had passed to the buyer. The Supreme Court ruled:

... the trees were not felled before 31st March, 1951 and further they were not ascertained as required under the contract, for as pointed out the logs had to be checked and passed by the State Forest staff by affixing the mark before they can be removed by the appellant. ... Holding that the trees were not felled and that the goods were not ascertained, we find that the title in the goods had not passed to the appellant before 31st March, 1951, the date on which the estate vested in the State.

Badriprasad v. State of MP

This case offers an interesting contrast to the ones we've seen here. It relates to an auction by the Forest Department in which a contract was made with a contractor to extract timber from a forest in Harda, in the State of Madhya Pradesh.[4] Awarding a contract for utilization of forest produce was subject to the Forest Act and the rules framed under it. Thus, the terms of the contract would be those that were put up in the auction as well as the provisions in the rules. The auction was conducted by the Divisional Forest Officer on 24 December 1956 for both felled trees and standing trees in the block of the forest. According to the auction, 'The forest produce sold and purchased consists of: "All standing trees bearing hammer mark of marginally shown device at base and breast height. All felled trees marked at the butt end and stumps with the device shown in the margin."' The hammer was struck for the highest bidder at Rs 70,200. After the auction, the DFO and the bidder signed the contract. According to the terms of the auction, the purchase price was to be paid in four instalments; Rs 17,600 was to be paid immediately, and the other instalments were due on 1 March, 15 May, and 15 December 1957.

The forests were extensive. Contracts were awarded only for a block of it. If an unsupervised contractor were left to extract timber that was awarded to him, he might appropriate timber from the adjoining areas as well. Thus, forest contracts had elaborate checks to guard against pilferage. One of them was a certificate showing the area for the operations of the contractor. On 5 February 1957 the Forest Department gave him a certificate showing the boundary of the forest area from

[4] *Badriprasad* v. *State of MP*, AIR (1966) SC 58.

which the produce was to be extracted. The contractor confirmed that the area and timber shown in the certificate was as announced at the auction. Under the contract, the contractor was to start operations within a month of receiving the certificate.

The forest rules provide an elaborate procedure for felling and removal of timber by the contractors. The operations were divided into two categories, cutting and carting. Cutting operations included felling and converting the tree into logs without removing them from the place where it was felled. Carting operations included all transport of the logs and other residues to a depot, saw mill, or other destination.

The rules authorized the Divisional Forest Officer to divide the contract area, called a coupe, into sections going up to 8. A forest contractor would be allowed to carry out cutting operations first only in Sections 1 and 2 of the coupe. As soon as he began cutting operations in Section 3, he was deemed to have surrendered his rights to the standing trees in Section 1, and so on. Through this process, the trees would be felled in all the sections. Carting could be done alongside felling. However, when felling operations in Section 4 started, the right to cart from Section 1 would cease. Where the Forest Department had felled the trees and then given the contract, the rules on carting as stated above applied.

In this case, the coupe was organized in four sections, named A, B, C, and D. The timber felled by the forest department was hammer-marked at two places, at the butt end and at the lower part, somewhere around the stem. The trees were to be felled so as to leave the lower hammer mark in the uncut portion; the portions so cut bore only one hammer mark at one end. A second special

hammer mark was placed on the other end at the check post.

The contractor began his operations in Section A of the coupe in the last week of February 1957. He defaulted on the payment of the second instalment, which was due on 1 March 1957. On 28 March 1957, the following notice was issued to him:

You are being informed through this notice that the removal of goods from the coupe by you is already in excess of the amount deposited by you in the treasury. So please send the challan of the second instalment as soon as possible by the return load carrier, otherwise your removal of goods would be stopped and a report would be made to the higher authority within two days.

On 25 April 1957, the contractor was told by the forest authorities that no further removal of the forest produce would be allowed in view of the default of payment of the second instalment. The licence book and the transit pass were taken back by the government forester. The contractor paid the second instalment on that day, but a fire broke out in the forest on 27 April that destroyed the timber. The claim of the forest department was that the property in timber had passed to the contract, and thus the loss fell on the contractor. The contractor claimed that the property had not passed, and that payment of further instalments was unnecessary. The Supreme Court noted that the sale was of specific goods. This comprised felled timber bearing the hammer mark and trees bearing the hammer mark. To the contention that the property in timber was to pass only on paying of the instalment, the Supreme Court noted:

There is nothing in the contract that possession would not be delivered over the cut timber in sections B, C, and D till the 2nd, 3rd and 4th instalments have been paid. The relevant provisions of R. 18 of the Forest Contract Rules, extracted earlier, do not contain any such restriction. It only provides that the operations necessary to be conducted by the contractor had to start with section A or the first section and that the rights of the contractor to the material purchased would be deemed to be surrendered in certain circumstances. This has nothing to do with the payment of the instalments by the contractor. He can proceed to operate on the entire property purchased, according to his inclination in accordance with the procedure, as regulated by the rules. There is therefore no force in the submission that there could have been no delivery of possession over the produce sold and existing in sections B, C, and D till the various instalments had been paid.

The forest department could stop removal of forest produce sold till the instalment was paid. It was argued that this amounted to the seller reserving the right of disposal under Section 25(1) of the Indian Sale of Goods Act, 1930. The Supreme Court ruled:

There is nothing in the deed of contract or in the Forest Contract Rules which reserved such a right of disposal in the State. Right given to the Government under R. 8 is the right to stop the removal of forest produce when the value of the forest produce already removed exceeded the amount of the instalments paid. This is to regulate the compliance with the conditions of the auction one of which was that ordinary forest produce was to be sold on payment in full at the time of delivery. The contractor had therefore to pay full price he had bid at the date of the sale or any day prior to the delivery of the goods to him in February 1957. The provisions for allowing payment by instalments is a concession for the convenience of the contractor and it is provided in the rules that payment in instalments may however be considered as payment in full at the time of delivery provided there be a clause in the agreement in accordance with the provisions of R. 8 of the Forest Contract Rules.

Reference may here be made to the provisions of S. 83 of the Indian Forest Act, 1927 ... Subsection (1) provides that when any money is payable for or in respect of any forest produce, the amount thereof shall be deemed to be a first charge on such produce, and such produce may be taken possession of by a Forest Officer until such amount has been paid. Rule 8 of the Forest Contract Rules is therefore in pursuance of the statutory provisions of S. 83 of the Forest Act which creates a lien on forest produce for the money payable to Government. Action which the Divisional Forest Officer can take for stopping the removal of the forest produce sold is in pursuance of the statutory authority conferred on him and not in pursuance of any terms of the contract between respondent No. 2 and the Government.

When a contractor is deemed to have paid in full the price there could be no occasion for the Government to reserve a right of disposal of the property even when its delivery had been made to the purchaser. As already stated, it is S. 20 of the Sale of Goods Act which will apply to this case. This section provides that where there is an unconditional contract for the sale of specific goods in a deliverable state, the property in the goods passes to the buyer when the contract is made and it is immaterial whether the time of payment of price or the time of delivery of the goods or both is postponed. The contract was unconditional, the goods sold were specific. They were in a deliverable state and therefore the property in the goods did pass at the time when the contract was made. This section would have applied even if the time of payment of price had been postponed. In the present case, as already stated, the payment allowed by instalments is to be deemed payment in full at the time of the delivery of the goods sold.

This case is in contrast to the preceding ones. In this case, the contract was for the sale of specific goods—the timber logs bearing the hammer mark and the standing trees bearing the hammer mark. We need to be clear that trees attached to the ground are goods if agreed to be severed. Therefore, that the hammer marked trees were still standing was no bar on these being specific goods. The property in these goods could pass while these were still standing.

As the contract for sale was for specific goods, the property in these would have passed as intended by the parties. If no intention was discernible, it would become an unconditional contract. The property in this case would pass at the very time the contract was made. The contract did not provide in express terms on passing of the property. The court constructed the other terms of the contract to see if intent could be discerned on the passing of the property. There were terms on removal of timber from the forests, but these were to prevent pilferage of the neighbouring forest. The court noted that there was no condition that the property would pass only on payment of the instalments. Thus, it was an unconditional sale of specific property and the ownership passed at the very point of time the agreement was made.

Commissioner of Income Tax, Delhi v. M/s P.M. Rathod and Co.

M/s P.M. Rathod and Co. was a firm engaged in the manufacture and sale of perfume and hair oil.[5] The firm was based in Ratlam and sent its agents all over India to canvass orders. One of the ways the ordered goods were sent to the customers was by Value Payable Post (VPP), a service provided by the post office. The goods would be given to the post office for the transmission to the buyer, and the post office would deliver the goods only on payment of the price. If the customer failed to pay the price, the goods would be brought back to the sender. The second arrangement the firm followed was to get railway receipts in its own favour and send the receipts to a bank. The customer could pay the price to the bank and get the railway receipt endorsed in their favour, entitling them to collect the goods. *Commissioner of Income Tax, Delhi v. M/s P.M. Rathod and Co.* was a case on the assessment of Income Tax. Ratlam was then in a state called Madhya Bharat, which was entitled to a concessional rate of income tax. The question was, in relation to the above mode of business, whether the price was received by the firm at Ratlam or at the premises of the customer. This depended on the nature of the relationship between the seller and the post office. Section 25(1) applies to the case. The Supreme Court stated:

Under the VPP system the seller retains control over the goods right up to the time the goods are delivered to the buyer against payment of price and therefore the contract would fall under S. 25 of the sale of Goods Act ... The principle then is that if the seller when sending the articles which he intends to deliver under the contract does so, ... with the direction that the articles are not to be delivered to the purchaser till the payment of price, the appropriation is not absolute but conditional and until the price is paid the property in the goods does not pass to the purchaser.

...

The argument raised ... was that the respondents delivered the goods to the post office at the instance of the buyer and that the post office acted merely as a bailee for the purpose of transmission to the buyer. But even as such bailee it cannot act against the instructions of the bailor and deliver the goods to the buyer without receiving their price and when he does recover he recovers it on behalf of the bailor. Even a bailment for transmission would fall under S. 25 of the Sale of Goods Act and there is only a conditional appropriation and until the condition imposed is fulfilled the goods do not pass. ...

[5] *Commissioner of Income Tax, Delhi v. M/s P.M. Rathod and Co.*, AIR (1959) SC 1394.

Thus the principle governing a despatch of articles by V.P.P. is that the appropriation is conditional and goods only pass when the condition is fulfilled i.e., the price is paid against delivery. The post office is an agent for the seller and receives the price from the buyer at the place of delivery for transmission to the seller.

… as in the case of goods sent by V.P.P. the Railway Receipts in favour of self could not be delivered to the buyer till the money was paid and although the goods had been handed over to a common carrier the appropriation to the contract was only conditional and the performance was completed only when the monies were paid and the Railway Receipts delivered.

Thus, in both the cases, the money was received not in Ratlam but at the location of the buyer.

Seth Pushalal Mansinghka Private Ltd v. *Commr of IT Delhi Rajasthan and MP*

Seth Pushalal Mansinghka Private Ltd was a private limited company whose mines, factory, and head office were at Bhilwara in Rajasthan.[6] It ran a mining business at Bhilwara and was engaged in the cutting, processing, sorting, and packing of mica, which was exported to places in other states: Kodarma and Giridih. According to the income tax law at the time, there was a rebate for income 'arising' or 'accruing' in the state where the company was located. In relation to the sale of the goods to the buyers in the other states, the decisive question was whether the sale was performed in the state of the company or the other state. In other words, the contract of sale had to be analysed to settle where the property in the goods passed to the buyer in the state of the company or the other state.

[6] *Seth Pushalal Mansinghka Private Ltd* v. *Commissioner of IT Delhi Rajasthan and MP*, AIR (1967) SC 1626.

The arrangement for sale was as follows. The representatives of the buyers from Kodarma and Giridih used to visit Bhilwara, inspect the various qualities of mica that the company had, and entered into written contracts for purchase. The contracts were titled 'Bhilwara godowns delivery' and were contigent upon the condition that the consignments would be sent to Kodarma or Giridih by rail and the railway receipts would be sent 'through bank'. There was further stipulation that 25 per cent of the price would be sent by way of an advance. Further, after the consignments left the godowns at Bhilwara, they would be entirely at the buyer's risk. The seller used to consign the goods in their own favour. This was forwarded to Rajasthan Bank by endorsing its name. The Rajasthan Bank used to forward it to its branches in Giridih and Kodarma by endorsing their name. The railway receipt was accompanied by bills of exchange, and given to the buyer only on paying the price to the bank. The Supreme Court took it to be a contract for sale of unascertained goods. The representatives of the buyer only saw the quality of mica and placed order for a certain quantity. The order was not for buying any specific lot. The Supreme Court, referring to Section 23 and 25 noted:

In the case of a contract for sales of unascertained goods the property does not pass to the purchaser unless there is unconditional appropriation, of the goods in a deliverable state to the contract.

…

In the present case, the appellant has reserved the right of disposal over the goods at the time of despatch. The consignment was sent "self" railway receipt was taken in the name of the appellant and the railway receipt along with the bill of exchange was presented by the appellant to the Rajasthan Bank for collection after endorsing the railway receipt in favour of the Rajasthan Bank. The goods were delivered to the buyers only when they paid the price to the bank and obtained the railway receipts endorsed in their favour. The fact that the goods are by the bill of lading made deliverable to the order of the seller or his agent is a prima facie reservation of the right of disposal so as to prevent the property from passing to the purchaser. If the seller deals with or claims to retain the bill of lading, in order to secure the contract price as when he sends forward the bill of lading with a bill of exchange attached, with directions that the bill of ladling is not to be delivered to the purchaser till acceptance or payment of the bill of exchange the appropriation is not absolute but until acceptance of the draft, or payment or tender of the price, is conditional only, and until such acceptance or payment or tender, the property in the goods does not pass to the purchaser— Mirabita v. Imperial Ottoman Bank, (1878) 3 Ex D164 at p. 172. If the seller discounts a draft upon the buyer with a bank, and authorises the bank to hand to the buyer a bill of lading to the order of the seller and endorsed in blank by him upon his acceptance of the draft, the intention to be inferred, according to general mercantile understanding, is that the seller intends to transfer the ownership when the draft is accepted, but intends also to remain the owner until this has been done. So, when the seller draws a hundi or a bill of exchange on the purchaser and delivers the hundi or the bill of exchange with a relative railway receipt to his own banker for the purpose of delivery of the railway receipt to the purchaser on his honouring the hundi the property in the goods cannot be held to pass to the purchaser till he pays the price and takes delivery of the railway receipt from the banker.

It was argued on behalf of the appellant that after the railway receipts had been endorsed in favour of the bank and the appellant got the consideration by discount of the railway receipts the title in the goods had passed from the appellant to the Bank of Rajasthan which became thereafter the agent of the purchaser. We do not think there is any substance in this argument. ... It is apparent from the conditions specified in the discount form of the bank that the responsibility of the appellant did cease till the bank realised payments from the purchaser. The discount form of the bank provided:

'The bank is sending the goods at the risk of the consignor ... In case the bill is dishonoured by the purchaser ... the responsibility will be that of the consignor and the bank will have the right to recover the amount from him ... In case the amount is not recovered from the purchaser, the bank has the right to debit the same amount to the account of the consignor.'

It is clear, therefore, that when the appellant negotiated the hundi with the banker, the latter did so only as a part of its banking business. Even if there was a purchase of the hundi by the banker it cannot mean that there was a sale of the goods to the banker. In the first place, there was no agreement between the banker and the seller for the sale of the goods. Secondly, the banker had only a security over the goods till the price was paid by the buyer. To hold otherwise would mean that the seller committed a breach of contract with the buyer and sold the goods to the banker. That is, however, not the case. The appellant only preferred this contract with the buyer in accordance with the usual commercial practice. Therefore, if any money was paid by the bank to the appellant as price for the hundi it was not the sale price of the goods in any sense and the bank was not acting as the agent of the buyer. On the other hand, the purchase of the hundi by the bank was only a convenient arrangement between the bank and its own customer, the appellant, to avoid freezing of credit of the latter and it was done in the course of its usual banking transactions. It follows, therefore, that the price of the goods sold can be held to be accrued only when the purchaser pays the price or enters into an arrangement with the bank which is the endorsed of the hundi; for, till then, the latter will have a right of recourse against the appellant in case the hundi is dishonoured. In the present case, the appellant became entitled to the purchase money only on the passing of title to the purchasers at Kodama and Giridih...

Commissioner of Income-Tax, Madras v. Mysore Chromite Ltd

Mysore Chromite Ltd, was a company based in the Mysore State, where it owned chromite mines.[7] Chrome ores were extracted from the mines and converted into a merchantable product and then sold to buyers, mostly in America and Europe. The applicability of the income tax then depended upon the fact whether the profits arose outside British India. This, in turn, depended on whether the sale was concluded—that is, the ownership was transferred to the buyer—in British India or abroad.

The arrangement followed by the company was as follows. The buyer used to open a confirmed, irrevocable bankers' credit with a bank in London. The bank would communicate this to the Eastern Bank Ltd, London, who in turn would communicate to its branch in Madras. The bank in Madras would communicate of the credit arrangement to the company. The company would ship the goods on terms FOB Madras; however, the bill of lading would be drawn in its own name. The shipping documents were sent through to London with the bank in Madras with a bill of exchange. The documents would be given to the buyer only on honouring the bill of exchange; that is, on payment. The Supreme Court ruled:

It is suggested that as soon as the assessee company placed the goods on board the steamer named by the buyer at the Madras Port the goods became ascertained and the property in the goods passed immediately to the buyer. This argument, however, overlooks the important word 'unconditionally' used in the section. The requirement of the section is not only that there shall be appropriation of the goods to the contract but that

such appropriation must be made unconditionally. This is further elaborated by section 25 which provides that where there is a contract for the sale of specific goods or where goods are subsequently appropriated to the contract, the seller may, by the terms of the contract or appropriation, reserve the right of disposal of the goods until certain conditions are fulfilled. In such a case, notwithstanding the delivery of the goods to the buyer, or to a carrier or other bailee for the purpose of transmission to the buyer, the property in the goods does not pass to the buyer until the conditions imposed by the seller are fulfilled.

The question in this case, therefore, is: was there an unconditional appropriation of the goods by merely placing them on the ship? It is true that the price and delivery was F.O.B., Madras but the contracts themselves clearly required the buyers to open a confirmed irrevocable Bankers' credit for the requisite percentage of the invoice value to be available against documents. This clearly indicated that the buyers would not be entitled to the documents, that is, the bill of lading and the provisional invoice, until payment of the requisite percentage was made upon the bill of exchange. The bill of lading is the document of title to the goods and by this term the assessee company clearly reserved the right of disposal of the goods until the bill of exchange was paid. Placing of the goods on board the steamer named by the buyer under a F.O.B. contract clearly discharges the contractual liability of the seller as seller and the delivery to the buyer is complete and the goods may thenceforward be also at the risk of the buyer against which he may cover himself by taking out an insurance. 'Prima facie' such delivery of the goods to the buyer and the passing of the risk in respect of the goods from the seller to the buyer are strong indications as to the passing also of the property in the goods to the buyer but they are not decisive and may be negatived, for under section 25 the seller may yet reserve to himself the right of disposal of goods until the fulfilment of certain conditions and thereby prevent the passing of property in the goods from him to the buyer.

[7] *Commissioner of Income-tax, Madras* v. *Mysore Chromite Ltd*, AIR (1955) SC 98.

The facts found in this case are that the assessee company shipped the goods under bill of lading issued in its own name. Under the contract it was not obliged to part with the bill of lading which is the document of title to the goods until the bill of exchange drawn by it on the buyers' Bank where the irrevocable letter of credit was opened was honoured. ... [U]pon the terms of the contracts in question and the course of dealings between the parties the property in the goods could not have passed to the buyer earlier than the date when the bill of exchange was accepted by the buyers' Bank in London and the documents were delivered by the assessee company's agent, the Eastern Bank Ltd, London, to the buyers' Bank. This admittedly, and as found by the Appellate Tribunal, always took place in London. It must, therefore, follow that at the earliest the property in the goods passed in London where the bill of lading was handed over to the buyers' Bank against the acceptance of the relative bill of exchange.

Agricultural Market Committee v. *Shalimar Chemical Works Ltd*

Shalimar Chemical Works Ltd is a Hyderbabad-based company that imports dried coconut kernel from various places in Kerala for manufacturing coconut oil.[8] The Agriculture Market Committee is a body created under the Andhra Pradesh (Agricultural Produce and Livestock) Markets Act, 1966. Section 12 of the Act provides for the levy of fees by the Notified Market Committee. It reads: 'Levy of fees by the Market Committee: (1) The Market Committee shall levy fees on any notified agricultural produce, livestock or products of livestock purchased or sold in the notified market area.' Thus, the Section applied if the 'sale', that is, passing of the ownership happened within the notified market area. The factory of the company was

in the notified market area and dried coconut kernel was a notified produce.

The company followed the following arrangement for procuring coconut kernel. The company placed orders on dealers in Kerala, who would send the goods by lorry. The lorry receipt would be drawn in favour of the company. The dealer sent the documents for collecting the consignment to a bank at Hyderabad. After making the payment to the bank, the company received the documents entitling them to collect the consignment from the transporter. The lorry was unloaded at the premises of the company, and the goods were weighed to verify the quantity sent by the dealers. Shalimar Chemical Works Ltd had running accounts with the dealers in Kerala. The accounts of the dealers were settled within two or three months from the date of despatch. If there was a shortage in the quantity received, which was rare, the company would raise a debit note against the dealer for the shortage. The invoices raised by the dealers mentioned that the despatch of the goods was being made solely at the risk and responsibility of Shalimar Chemical Works Ltd. The invoice also mentioned that the seller took 'no responsibility or liability as to delayed despatches, losses due to theft, pilferage, rain or damage'.

The Committee imposed a market fee on the company. It contended that the goods were unloaded at factory premises of the company and weighed; as the quantity and price could not be ascertained, the ownership could pass only after.[9] Shalimar Chemical Works Ltd claimed that the sale was done in

---

[8] *Agricultural Market Committee* v. *Shalimar Chemical Works Ltd*, AIR (1997) SC 2502.

[9] The rules had provided that if goods were weighed within the market area, it would be presumed that the sale was done within the market area. The Supreme Court struck down the provision as it was beyond the scope given by the act for the executive to make rules.

Kerala, so the location at which the sale had taken place came under dispute. The Supreme Court ruled:

We may, at this stage, consider certain provisions of the Sale of Goods Act, 1930, specially as the Andhra Pradesh (Agricultural Produce and Livestock) Markets Act, 1966 does not contain any definition of sale or purchase. Sections 19 and 20 of the Sale of Goods Act are quoted below

...

We may, before analysing the provisions of Sections 19 and 20, observe that the Indian Sale of Goods Act is based largely upon the English and American Acts. Under these Acts, namely, the English Sale of Goods Act, the American Uniform Sales Act and the Indian Sale of Goods Act, the relevant factor for determining where the sale takes place, is the intention of parties. A contract of sale, like, any other contract, is a consensual act inasmuch as parties are at liberty to settle, amongst themselves, any terms they may choose.

Section 19 attempts to give effect to the elementary principle of the Law of Contract that the parties may fix the time when the property in the goods shall be treated to have passed. It may be the time of delivery, or the time of payment of price or even the time of the making of contract. It all depends upon the intention of the parties. It is, therefore, the duty of the Court to ascertain the intention of the parties and in doing so, they have to be guided by the principles laid down in Section 19(2) which provides that for ascertaining the intention of the parties, regards shall be had to the terms of the contract, the conduct of the parties and the circumstances of the case.

Section 19 indicates that in case of unconditional contract of sale in respect of specified goods in a deliverable state, the property in the goods passes to the buyer at such time as the parties intend it to be transferred. Section 19(3) provides that Sections 20 to 24 contain the rules for ascertaining the intention of the parties as to the time at which the property in the goods shall be treated to have passed to the buyer. Both Sections 19 and 20 apply to the sale of 'specific' or 'ascertained' goods.

Section 20, which contains the first rule for ascertaining the intention of the parties, provides that where there is an unconditional contract for the sale of 'specific goods' in a 'deliverable state', the property in the goods passes to the buyer when the contract is made. This indicates that as soon as a contract is made in respect of specific goods which are in a deliverable state, the title in the goods passes to the purchaser. The passing of the title is not dependant upon the payment of price or the time of delivery of the goods. If the time for payment of price or the time for delivery of goods, or both, is postponed, it would not affect the passing of the title in the goods so purchased.

In order that Section 20 is attracted, two conditions have to be fulfilled: (i) the contract of sale is for specific goods which are in a deliverable state; and (ii) the contract is an unconditional contract. If these two conditions are satisfied, Section 20 becomes applicable immediately and it is at this stage that it has to be seen whether there is anything either in the terms of the contract or in the conduct of the parties or in the circumstances of the case which indicates a contrary intention. This exercise has to be done to give effect to the opening words, namely, 'Unless a different intention appears' occurring in Section 19(3).

...

In the instant case, the goods which were the subject-matter of sale were ascertained goods. They were also in a deliverable state. On the order being placed by the respondent, the seller in the State of Kerala, loaded the goods on the lorry and despatched the same to Hyderabad. It is at this stage that the conduct of the parties becomes extremely relevant. It was one of the terms of the contract between the parties that the seller would not be liable for any future loss of goods and that the goods were being despatched at the risk of the respondent. The respondent had also obtained insurance of the goods and had paid the policy premium. He, therefore, intended the goods to be treated as his own so that if there was any loss of goods in transit, he could validly claim the insurance money. The weighment of the goods at Hyderabad or the collection of documents from the bank or payment of price through the bank at Hyderbad were immaterial, inasmuch as the property in the goods had already passed at Kerala and it was not dependant upon the payment of price or the delivery of goods to the respondent.

We are in disagreement with the application of the law in this case. It is doubtful that the goods were ascertained. It was not a contract for a specific lot or gunny bags of coconut kernel. The company must be placing orders to be supplied with a certain grade and quantity of dried coconut kernel. Thus, it was a case of sale of unascertained goods. The goods were ascertained when the dealer delivered it to the carrier. As the lorry receipt was in the name of the company, only the company could receive at the destination, and the ownership could pass only at this point. As there were no conditions on transfer of property, the point of delivery became 'unconditional appropriation' of the consignment to the contract. Further, the stipulation in the invoice on the risk being with the company further strengthens the view that the intention of the parties was to transfer ownership at the time of delivery.

Separation from Bulk

One way by which goods are ascertained is separation from the bulk. The following case is an example of this.

Collector of Customs v. Pednekar and Co. (Pvt.) Ltd

Pednekar and Co. (Pvt.) Ltd was an importer and dealer in sewing machines that could be imported only against a licence.[10] The company placed two separate orders on Japanese suppliers. One order was for supply of 162 pieces of industrial sewing machine head 'Raruna Brand' and 208 dozen of oscillat-ing rock shafts (an accessory of sewing machines). The second order was for supply of 59 sets of industrial sewing machine. The two Japanese sellers accepted the orders and sent the goods by different ships.

The company had financial difficulties in organizing for a letter of credit. A letter of credit is issued by a bank in favour of the seller on behest of the buyer. The seller hands over the shipping document entitling the buyer to receive a shipment and collects the payment from the bank at his location. The company got another dealer in sewing machines, Cycle Co., to be a guarantor to the bank for the letter of credit. While the goods were en route, the company entered into an agreement with the Cycle Co. to sell it certain quantities of industrial sewing machine and oscillating rock shafts at a future date. The contract of sale was made on 20 February 1959 and read:

Sale Contract
We Messrs. Padnekar and Co. Private Ltd....
hereby agree to sell in forward sale Industrial Sewing Machine Heads ... on the following terms and conditions:
Items and quantity: 221, pos. Industrial Sewing Machine Heads, TA. 1 Model complete with knee Lifter, accessories box Robbin winder made in Japan.
200 dozen Oscillating Rock Shaft 'Cote' brand made in Japan.
Rates and value: ....
Total—Rs. 72,205/-
Payment: ...
Place of delivery: Buyer's Godown at Bombay.
Time of Delivery: June–July 1959.

When the goods arrived at the port, the company had to submit all documents, including the letter of credit and the sale agreement, to the custom officials. The customs department alleged that the importation of the goods had been made by the Cycle

---

[10] *Collector of Customs* v. *Pednekar and Co. (Pvt.) Ltd*, AIR (1976) SC 1408.

Company without any valid import licence in their favour and not Pednekar and Co. (which did have a licence), and that the Cycle Company was the real owner of the goods. Further, Pednekar and Co. had aided and abetted in the unauthorized import of the goods by the Cycle Company. Further, there was another charge that the company had transferred the licence in favour of the latter. The customs department moved to confiscate the goods. The question was whether the ownership had passed to the Cycle Company. The Supreme Court ruled:

It is, in our opinion, not possible to hold that the property in goods passed at the time of agreement dated February 20, 1959. The contract to sell related not to the entire consignment of the goods which were being imported by the respondent but only to part of those goods, even though it may be a major part. Out of 208 dozen rock shafts which were imported, 200 dozen were to be sold by the respondent company to respondent No 2. There was nothing to prevent the respondent company from selecting for itself any eight dozen rock shafts out of the whole consignment. The place of delivery of the goods was buyer's godown in Bombay. The property in the goods could not pass in favour of respondent No. 2 until, after the arrival of the goods in Bombay, two hundred dozen rock shafts to be delivered to the buyer were separated. So far as industrial sewing machines were concerned, the property in them could also not pass to the buyer before the passing of the property in rock shafts as the contract between the respondent company and the buyer was one indivisible contract. The High Court, in our opinion, rightly held that the property in the goods did not pass to the buyer till the time of the delivery of the goods in Bombay. No specific goods in a deliverable state were attached to the contract when it was made.

Now suppose that a seller had a container containing 100 litres of oil. He sold the oil to three buyers in measures of 50, 30, and 20 litres. After giving the first and second customers their shares, is the remainder of the oil in the container already separated from the bulk by the principle of exhaustion? The answer given by the courts is yes. The two cases on this are *Wait & James* v. *Midland Bank*[11] and *Karlshamns Olje Fabriker* v. *Eastport Navigation Corporation (The 'Elafi')*.[12]

As a summary, let us see the application of the principle to a current business practice. In *Re London Wine Co (Shippers) Ltd*,[13] a customer could buy wine from the company but leave it with them for storage. The company issued a 'Certificate of Title' to the buyer that described them as the 'sole and beneficial owner'. The company charged the buyer for storage and insurance. The buyer could take delivery by applying to the company or sell it to another person. On the issuance of a certificate, the wine bottles for the customer were not segregated but continued to be a part of the bulk. A dispute developed between the debtors to the company and the customers over the ownership of the wine. However, there could be no ownership transfer till the goods were ascertained. As the company had not segregated the bottles for the customers, the ownership continued with the company.

Re Goldcorp Exchange Ltd,[14] a case from New Zealand before the Privy Council, dealt with a similar practice. Goldcorp Exchange Ltd used to sell gold coins and gold ingots to the customers. The customers were given certificates for their purchase and ownership. The company charged the customer for storage and insurance. A certificate holder could surrender his certificate and receive

---

[11] *Wait & James* v. *Midland Bank*, (1926) 31 Com Cas 172.

[12] *Karlshamns Olje Fabriker* v. *Eastport Navigation Corporation* (The 'Elafi'), (1982) 1 All ER 208.

[13] *Re London Wine Co (Shippers) Ltd*, (1986) PCC 121.

[14] *Re Goldcorp Exchange Ltd*, (1995) 1 AC 74.

delivery of the gold in seven days or sell to another buyer on the prevailing market price. The practice essentially took away the inconvenience of storing gold for the customers. On a sale, the gold was not appropriated to the buyer. The company promised to maintain adequate stock to be able to deliver whenever called upon by the customers.

When the company was liquidated, the dispute was whether the gold was owned by the company or the customers. The Privy Council ruled that as the gold for the customer was not ascertained, the ownership continued to be with the company. It noted:

It is common ground that the contracts in question were for the sale of unascertained goods. ... For example, 'I sell you 60 of the 100 sheep now on my farm.'

Approaching these situations a priori common sense dictates that the buyer cannot acquire title until it is known to what goods the title relates. Whether the property then passes will depend upon the intention of the parties and in particular on whether there has been a consensual appropriation of particular goods to the contract. ... In fact, however, the case turns not on appropriation but on ascertainment, and on the latter the law has never been in doubt. It makes no difference what the parties intended if what they intend is impossible: as is the case with an immediate transfer of title to goods whose identity is not yet known. As Lord Blackburn wrote in his treatise on *The Effect of the Contract of Sale* (1845), pp. 122–3, a principal inspiration of the Sale of Goods Act 1893:

The first of [the rules] that the parties must be agreed as to the specific goods on which the contract is to attach before there can be a bargain and sale, is one that is founded on the very nature of things. Till the parties are agreed on the specific individual goods, the contract can be no more than a contract to supply goods answering a particular description, and since the vendor would fulfil his part of the contract by furnishing any parcel of goods answering that description, and the purchaser

could not object to them if they did answer the description, it is clear there can be no intention to transfer the property in any particular lot of goods more than another, till it is ascertained which are the very goods sold.

This rule has existed at all times; it is to be found in the earliest English law books. ... It makes no difference, although the goods are so far ascertained that the parties have agreed that they shall be taken from some specified larger stock. In such a case the reason still applies: the parties did not intend to transfer the property in one portion of the stock more than in another, and the law which only gives effect to their intention, does not transfer the property in any individual portion.

Their Lordships have laboured this point, about which there has been no dispute, simply to show that any attempt by the non-allocated claimants to assert that a legal title passed by virtue of the sale would have been defeated, not by some arid legal technicality but by what Lord Blackburn called 'the very nature of things.'

It is interesting to note the court had to go so far back into the past to show that the principles governing the sale of goods are not 'arid legal technicality' but common sense.

Transfer of Ownership and Risk

We have explored the process through which ownership transfers from the buyer to the seller. The transfer of ownership has a profound effect. The first is that risk passes with ownership. Acquiring ownership is the very essence of a sale contract. It vests in the owner the exclusive right in the goods. The obverse side to this is that loss, damage, or deterioration to the goods also falls on the owner. Examples of this are theft, fire, accident, or perishing of the goods. Thus, risk and ownership go together. However, the obligation of risk can be severed and contracted. This is what happens in an insurance contract. Similarly, risk can be transferred through a contract of bailment—the bailee has to compensate the owner for the loss of goods or damage to goods according to the terms of bailment. If there are no terms of bailment, the bailee has a duty to take as good care of the goods as a person would of his own. Failing this, the bailee has to make good the loss to the owner.

Thus, in a sale contract, risk passes to the owner the moment the ownership transfers to him. If the seller has possession, he will become the bailee of the goods. Of course, if the buyer and seller have agreed otherwise, the contractual intent will have effect. Section 26 provides this:

26. Risk prima facie passes with property: Unless otherwise agreed, the goods remain at the seller's risk until the property therein is transferred to the buyer, but when the property therein is transferred to the buyer, the goods are at the buyer's risk whether delivery has been made or not:

Provided that, where delivery has been delayed through the fault of either buyer or seller, the goods are at the risk of the party in fault as regards any loss which might not have occurred but for such fault:

Provided also that nothing in this section shall affect the duties or liabilities of either seller or buyer as a bailee of the goods of the other party.

As we have seen, ownership passes in ascertained and unascertained goods. The following two cases are on the passing of risk.

Demby Hamilton and Company Limited v. Barden

Barden entered into a contract to buy 30 tons of apple juice from Demby Hamilton.[15] Barden had re-sold the goods to third parties. Under the contract between Barden and

Demby, the third parties were to collect the juice at the rate of one truckload per week. The seller crushed the apple for the season and put them into barrels. The buyers were supposed to collect the goods by February 1946, but only two truckloads were collected by then, and there was no collection after. The question was who would bear the risk of the deterioration of the goods. The case involved application of Section 20 of the Sale of Goods Act, 1893, the equivalent of Section 25 in the Indian law, the Sale of Goods Act, 1930. Sellers J. delivered the following judgment:

The first requirement of the proviso in question is that delivery has been delayed through the fault of the buyer. I am satisfied on the facts in the present case that a good delivery, which would have avoided all loss, was delayed through the fault of the buyer, and that of the third parties. The next requirement of the proviso is that, where delivery has been delayed through the fault of the buyer, the goods are at the risk of the party in fault 'as regards any loss which might not have occurred but for such fault.' The goods referred to there must be the contractual goods which have been assembled by the seller for the purpose of fulfilling his contract and making delivery. The goods may have been defined goods, goods manufactured for the purposes of delivery, or goods which had been acquired by the seller from somebody else for the purpose of fulfilling his contract. It does not seem to me that the Act requires to be construed in any narrow sense. The real question is whether the loss which has accrued was brought about by the delay in delivery, and that must have regard to the goods which were there to be delivered. Different circumstances may arise in different cases. It may be that the seller was in a position to sell the goods elsewhere and acquire other goods for the postponed time of delivery, and if he does not do that and there is some loss in the meantime the responsibility for the loss would be held to fall upon him. Again, there may be cases (and I think this is one of them) where the seller has his goods ready for delivery and has to keep them ready for

---

[15] *Demby Hamilton and Company Limited v. Barden (Endeavour Wines Limited) (Third Party)*, 1949 (1) All ER 435.

delivery as and when the buyer proposes to take them. In the present case the position is clear. The casks of apple juice which were not accepted were manufactured at the time of the contract, and the contract required that delivery should be in accordance with sample. It would have been very difficult to have obtained goods which complied with the sample unless the apples had all been crushed at the same time. They would have had to be apples from the same district and the juice from them, when obtained, would have had to be of the same maturity. The condition of apples changes. They may be unripe at one time and too ripe at another. The 30 tons of juice were goods which the sellers rightly and reasonably kept for the fulfilment of their contract. These were the last apples which the sellers had that season for crushing, and, therefore, the goods in question were goods which the sellers had awaiting delivery in fulfilment of their contract with the buyer.

I have to ask myself whether this loss might not have occurred but for the fault of the buyer. I am satisfied that it would not have occurred but for his fault. There is, of course, an obligation on a seller to act reasonably, and, if possible, to avoid any loss. As to that, one or two questions arise for consideration. Was there anything the sellers could reasonably do to dispose of these goods when they still had an outstanding obligation to keep them at the disposal of the buyer and when they had to be ready and willing to deliver them when requested? If delivery had been asked for at a later date and they had let these goods go elsewhere they could not have fulfilled their contract. I do not hesitate to find (although to construe this proviso is not easy) that in a practical and business sense this loss has fallen on the sellers by reason of the fact that the buyer refused to take delivery at the proper time and postponed the date of delivery until the goods had deteriorated, and I come to the conclusion that the liability for that loss falls on the buyer.

Sterns, Limited v. Vickers, Limited

London and Thames Haven Oil Wharves Company, a warehousing company, had stored 200,000 gallons of white spirit in a tank for its owner, Vickers, Limited.[16] The latter entered into a contract to sell 120,000 gallons of the white spirit to Sterns, Limited. Vickers obtained a warrant from the warehouse that it was holding 120,000 on behalf of Sterns, who sold the spirit to Lazarus and endorsed the warrant in his name. Lazarus did not want immediate delivery of the spirit, and paid the warehouse for further storage. Months later, when Lazarus came to take the spirit, it was found to be adulterated. The question arose as to who would bear the risk of the goods. The case shows that ordinarily risk passes with ownership; however, the parties may sever and let risk pass even if the ownership is yet to pass. Scrutton L.J. delivered the following judgment:

In the present case, what happened was that at the date of the contract there was a bulk larger than the quantity sold, and it was of the contract quality according to sample. A delivery warrant was issued by the Thames Haven Company undertaking to deliver that quantity from the bulk which at that time corresponded with the sample. That warrant was accepted by the purchaser and by their sub-purchaser, Lazarus, who proceeded to pay rent for the storage from the date of the warrant. In those circumstances I come clearly to the conclusion that as between the plaintiffs and the defendants the risk was on the plaintiffs the purchasers. The vendors had done all that they undertook to do. The purchasers had the right to go to the storage company and demand delivery, and if they had done so at the time they would have got all that the defendants had undertaken to sell them. What the purchasers here are trying to do is to put the risk after acceptance of the warrant upon persons who had then no control over the goods, for it seems plain that after the acceptance of that warrant the vendors would have had no right to go

[16] *Sterns, Limited* v. *Vickers, Limited*, (1923) 1 KB 78.

to the storage company and request them to refuse delivery to the purchaser. For these reasons, treating the matter as a question rather of the transfer of risk than of the passing of property—for strictly I do not think the property passed, but only a right to an undivided share in the bulk to be selected by a third person—I think the view taken by the judge below was erroneous. He seems to have considered the question of transferring the risk, and thought there was no evidence of it. With that view I cannot agree. I think the only conclusion to be drawn from the evidence is that the risk did pass. The appeal must be allowed.

SALE AND AGREEMENT TO SELL

In the performance of a sale contract, if the ownership is transferred before termination of the contract, the damages will not include re-vesting of the ownership in the seller. Further, to transfer ownership a person has to have ownership in the goods in the first place. Thus, till the ownership transfers to the buyer, it cannot be transferred further. The effect of transfer of ownership is so profound that the Sale of Goods Act, 1930, makes a distinction between sale and agreement to sell. Let us note this distinction and its significance. Section 4 provides:

4. Sale and agreement to sell: (1) A contract of sale of goods is a contract whereby the seller transfers or agrees to transfer the property in goods to the buyer for a price. There may be a contract of sale between one part-owner and another.

(2) A contract of sale may be absolute or conditional.

(3) Where under a contract of sale the property in the goods is transferred from the seller to the buyer, the contract is called a sale, but where the transfer of the property in the goods is to take place at a future time or subject to some condition thereafter to be fulfilled, the contract is called an agreement to sell.

(4) An agreement to sell becomes a sale when the time elapses or the conditions are fulfilled subject to which the property in the goods is to be transferred.

The provision is best understood by studying Subsection 3 first. In an unconditional contract for sale of specific property, the ownership transfers at the very point of time the agreement is made. Similarly, an offer for sale of goods may provide that the ownership will change when the agreement is made. In both cases the transfer of ownership and formation of agreement happen together. In other cases, the ownership has to transfer after making of the contract. These contracts are 'agreements to sell'. Both are contracts of sale.

An agreement to sell ascertained goods would become a sale as discussed in previous chapters. The ownership will pass as intended by the parties. In the case of an agreement to sell unascertained goods, the ownership will pass when the goods get appropriated to the contract. There may be conditions for the passing of property; for example, payment of the price. Section 4(2) refers to these contingencies and conditions on which the transfer of ownership rests. As Section 4(4) provides, an agreement to sell becomes a sale when the conditions are met and the ownership gets transferred.

An agreement to sell need not become a sale. The buyer can be in breach, giving the owner the right to terminate the contract. This will discharge the buyer from the obligation of transferring the ownership. Alternately, the seller can refuse to transfer the ownership, giving the right to the buyer to terminate the contract, freeing the parties of the obligations. In the case unascertained goods, the agreement to sell will become a sale only on 'unconditional appropriation' of the goods to the contract.

The passing of ownership is a significant factor. If the ownership has not passed, the seller can breach the contract and not transfer the property. The property can be taken in execution for his debts. The risk in goods will continue to be with the seller. However, if the property passes, the seller can only claim the price. Even if the contract is not fully performed and something remains to be done— for example, the seller has yet to deliver the goods—the ownership would not re-vest in the seller. The Supreme Court made the distinction in *The Instalment Supply* v. *STO Ahmedabad*.[17] It noted:

The definition is the same as in the English Sale of Goods act, 1893. The points to be noticed are that the essence of sale is the transfer of the property in a thing from one person to another for a price. The term 'contract of sale' includes an agreement to sell. An agreement to sell is known as an executory of sale, while a sale is known as an executed contract of sale. The term 'contract of sale' thus includes both actual sales and agreements for sale. It is important to distinguish clearly between the two classes of contract. An agreement to sell is a contract pure and simple whereas a sale is a contract plus a conveyance. By an agreement to sell a *jus in personam* is created, by a sale a *jus in rem* also is transferred. Where goods have been sold and the buyer makes default, the seller may sue for the contract price on the count of 'goods bargained and sold' but where an agreement to buy is broken, the seller's normal remedy is an action for unliquidated damages. If an agreement to sell be broken by the seller, the buyer has only a personal remedy against the seller. The goods are still the property of the seller, and he can dispose of them as he likes. But if there has been a sale, and the seller breaks his engagement to deliver the goods, the buyer has not only a personal remedy against the seller, but also the usual proprietary remedies in respect of the goods themselves. In many cases, too, he can follow the goods into the hands of third parties. Again, if there be an agreement for sale, and the goods are destroyed, the loss as a rule falls on the seller, while if there has been a sale, the loss as a rule falls upon the buyer though the goods have never come into his possession.

* * *

Law has been evolving just like any other field of knowledge. With the knowledge of contract as the foundation, the law of sale of goods has developed. Other fields have in turn developed where the concept of sale is the foundation. This was in the field of regulation of business and taxation. The laws used the terms 'sale' for the purposes of taxation or regulation of business. This led to the dispute on whether the term 'sale' referred to transfer of ownership or its popular meaning of a contract of sale. Examination of the question also involved other aspects of the Sale of Goods Act, 1930, for example the scope of the term 'goods' and 'delivery'. We will review the theme towards the end of the book.

---

[17] *The Instalment Supply* v. *STO Ahmedabad*, AIR (1974) SC 1105.

5

Transfer of Title

In the previous chapters, we have seen when and how ownership passes from the seller to the buyer. In this chapter, we will see who can transfer ownership to the buyer by examining cases where a third party—often fraudulently—sells the goods of another to a buyer who buys it in good faith. This leaves two innocent parties, the owner and the buyer, claiming ownership right over the goods. This can arise in the following situations: a thief or finder of the goods sells the goods; a person induces another to give goods on credit and sells it; a servant who is in possession of goods sells it; or an agent exceeds the authority given to him and sells the goods.

Clearly, the owner can transfer ownership. So too can an agent of the owner. In a contract of agency, the agent binds the principal in a contractual relationship with others. The agent has to act within the capacity given to him by the principal. Thus, if the agent is authorized, he can transfer ownership to a buyer. Agency can be created through express or implied communication. Further, no consideration is needed to create a contract of agency.

We will now examine the passing of ownership by persons other than the owner or a person authorized by him. There is no case law on the subject from the Indian courts. Thus, our study will be based entirely on British cases.

Ownership and Sale

A person gave his tools to his assistant for temporary safekeeping. The assistant sold the tools to a buyer, who bought it without the knowledge that they did not belong to the seller. The assistant then disappeared with the money. The original owner approached the buyer claiming the tools. Should the tools be restored to the original owner or kept by the bona fide buyer? To dispossess the buyer of the ownership would be establishing the principle that a buyer who purchases in good faith can never be sure of his ownership. If sale is robbed of its sanctity, it would disrupt the foundations of trade and commerce. On the other hand, if we cannot find any remedy for the original owner, we would be implying that property and ownership have no meaning. Any one can appropriate and sell another's property, and this too is fatal to the principles of trade and commerce. Thus, to deal with this contradiction between property and development of commerce, the rights of the property owner have been privileged. Human society has been based on ownership since long before demands of commerce arose. The sanctity of ownership has been too firmly ingrained for the demands of commerce to oust it. As Lord Denning noted:

In the development of our law, two principles have striven for mastery. The first is the protection of property. No one can give a better title than he himself possesses. The second is the protection of commercial transactions. The person who takes in good faith and for value without notice should get a good title. The first principle has held sway for a long time, but it has been modified by the common law itself and by statute so as to meet the needs of our times.[1]

We will later see that the law admits of limited situations in which ownership can be transferred by a person who is not the owner of the goods. The principle that no one can sell a thing he does not own was well stated in the *Rowland* v. *Divall*.[2] Divall bought a motor car in April 1922. He sold it to a motor car dealer, Rowland, in May 1922. Rowland repainted the car and put it for sale in his showroom. Two months later, he found a buyer in Colonel Railsdon. In September, 1922, the police seized the car from Colonel Railsdon on the ground that it had been stolen from the owner and sold to Divall. Rowland refunded the price to Railsdon and came to the court to recover the amount paid to Divall. The court ruled:

… there has been a total failure of consideration, that is to say that the buyer has not got any part of that for which he paid the purchase money. He paid the money in order that he might get the property, and he has not got it. It is true that the seller delivered to him the de facto possession, but the seller had not got the right to possession and consequently, could not give it to the buyer. Therefore the buyer, during the time that he had the car in his actual possession had no right to it, and was at all times, liable to the true owner for its conversion. … there can be no sale at all of goods which the seller has no right to sell.

The principle derives from an old Roman phrase, *Nemo Dat Quod Non habet*, that is, no one can transfer a better title than he himself has. Section 27 of the Indian law, the Sale of Goods Act, 1930, provides:

27. Sale by person not the owner: Subject to the provisions of this Act and of any other law for the time being in force, where goods are sold by a person who is not the owner thereof and who does not sell them under the authority or with the consent of the owner, the buyer acquires no better title to the goods than the seller had, unless the owner of the goods is by his conduct precluded from denying the seller's authority to sell…

The Section states the *nemo dat* principle that only the owner or a person authorized by him can transfer the ownership. The creation of authority is through the contractual process of making the seller an agent of the buyer. The section ends with an exception to the rule in 'unless the owner of the goods is by his conduct precluded from denying the seller's authority to sell'. This may appear like a negative wording of the concept that the authority for the seller could be created by conduct, but this is different. The owner will create authority with the seller through a contractual process of offer and acceptance. The communication between the parties can be express or implied; that is, the owner can constitute the agency not only through words but also conduct. However, this communication is between the owner and the seller.

---

[1] *Bishopsgate Motor Finance Corporation Limited* v. *Transport Brakes Limited*, (1949) 1 All ER 37.
[2] *Rowland* v. *Divall*, (1923) 2 KB 500.

The exception is merely a statement. It does not provide as to what kind of representation or action would be taken to be 'conduct precluded from denying the seller's authority to sell'. The exception before the codification was estoppel. The codification merely indicated that common law principles of estoppel were to be imported in to the section. Thus, in giving meaning to the phrase, the courts have referred to common law on estoppel.

The courts felt that at times strict application of the legal rights could result in harsh and unfair results. The courts would give remedy by suspending the application of the legal right in appropriate cases. The principle on which a legal right could be suspended in some situations came to be called equity. Estoppel is a branch of equity. The principle is: 'Estoppel arises where you are precluded from denying the truth of anything which you have represented as a fact although it is not a fact'.[3] Allowing someone to claim a representation as the truth is a part of the process of the court. Thus, estoppel is a part of evidence law. As it suspends legal rights, it has to be applied with safeguards. There must be representation from the person and the innocent party must rely on the representation.

A 'representation' can take different forms. It can be express in spoken or written communication. It can be implied and inferred from the conduct of the person. When misrepresentation is done by omission to do one's duty, it becomes negligence. Thus, representation from the owner to the buyer can be caused by communicating in express words, by his conduct and negligence in not doing his duty. In any case, the representation must be clear and unambiguous. In relation to sale of goods, its expression would be as follows: The owner represents to the buyer in word, by conduct or negligence that the seller (the third party) is the owner of the goods or has a right to sell the goods. The most widely quoted passage on estoppel is of Blackburn in *Swan* v. *North British Australasian Co.*[4]

It is pointed out by Parke B. (Freeman v. Cooke (1848) 2 Exch. 654) that in the majority of cases in which an estoppel exists, 'the party must have induced the other so to alter his position that the former would be responsible to him in an action for it'; and he had before pointed out that 'negligence,' to have the effect of estopping the party, must be 'neglect of some duty cast upon the person who is guilty of it' and this, I apprehend, is a true and sound principle. A person who does not lock up his goods, which are consequently stolen, may be said to be negligent as regards himself, but inasmuch as he neglects no duty which the law casts upon him, he is not in consequence estopped from denying the title of those who may have, however innocently, purchased those goods from the thief ... What I consider the fallacy of my brother Wilde's judgment is this: he lays down the rule in general terms 'that if one has led others into the belief of a certain state of facts by conduct of culpable neglect calculated to have that result, and they have acted on that belief to their prejudice, he shall not be heard afterwards, as against such persons to show that state of facts did not exist.' This is very nearly right, but in my opinion not quite, as he omits to qualify it by saying that the neglect must be in the transaction itself, and be the proximate cause of the leading the party into that mistake; and also, as I think, that it must be the neglect of some duty that is owing to the person led into that belief, or, what comes to the same thing, to the general public of whom the person is one, and not merely neglect of what would be prudent in respect to the party himself, or even of some duty owing to third persons, with whom

---

[3] *Farquharson Brothers & Co.* v. *C. King & Co. Respondents*, (1902) AC 325.

[4] *Swan* v. *North British Australasian Co.*, (1863) 2 H. & C. 175.

those seeking to set up the estoppel are not privy; and these distinctions make in the present case all the difference.

This quote is on negligence as a form of representation but also covers all aspects of estoppel. The representation should be made to the buyer or the public of which the buyer is a part. Let us illustrate this: The owner makes a representation to the buyer that Y has his authority to sell the goods. Convinced by the representation, the buyer purchases the goods. The owner cannot deny that Y did not have the authority. If the owner had stated on his webpage that Y had the authority to sell, again he could not have denied it as the representation is to anyone who visited it. However, if the owner makes a communication to A that Y has his authority to sell, B cannot estop the owner as the representation was never made to him. A representation on its own is not adequate for the application of estoppel. The party must rely on the estoppel to make the purchase. If the buyer knew the representation to be untrue or went ahead irrespective of the representation, estoppel would not apply.

We now turn to negligence as a form of representation. Negligence is in omitting to do a duty. It is not in 'merely neglect of what would be prudent in respect to the party himself'.[5] That is, being imprudent in relation to one's goods is not neglect. Let us illustrate this: A person carelessly left his camera on a bench in a park. Another person found it and tried in vain to identify the owner. That person then used it for a week, and sold it to a buyer who bought it bonafide. As noted above, only the owner can transfer ownership. Did the ownership transfer to the finder for him to

have transferred the ownership to the buyer? The answer is no. That the owner is negligent in the safekeeping of his property is no excuse for another to appropriate it. Imposing duty of care on the owner for retaining property would create a right and impetus for the others to appropriate the property. Nothing short of absolute protection of ownership would be adequate. Thus, the principle is that no matter how negligent the owner is with his goods, no one else gets a title in them. A thief gets no title in the goods and a finder is only a bailee to them. The ownership continues with the owner.

Estoppel by negligence arises when the owner does not discharge a duty he owes to either the buyer or the public of which the buyer is a part. The specific manifestation of this would be in the owner not discharging a duty that leads the seller to represent that he is the owner of the goods or has the authority to sell the goods. Representation by the seller can take three forms, representation in words, by conduct or negligence. Representation in words is straightforward; it is representation by conduct and negligence which the judgments have elaborated.

Farquharson Brothers & Co. v. C. King & Co.

Farquharson Brothers & Co. were importers and sellers of timber.[6] They warehoused their timber with the dock company Surrey Commercial Docks. The timber merchant would instruct the dock company to release timber through a delivery order. In 1895, the timber company authorized an employee, Mr Capon, to sign for delivery on behalf of the company. This was in addition to the other members of the firm who could sign

[5] Blackburn, J. in *Swan* v. *North British Australasian Co.*, 1 Hurl & C. 181.

[6] *Farquharson Brothers & Co.* v. *C. King & Co.*, (1902) AC 325.

delivery orders. In 1896, Capon began a series of frauds. He obtained an address at a place called Battersea under the name of Brown and professed to King & Co. that he was a commission agent acting on behalf of Messrs Bayley, a well-known company. Capson signed a delivery order on the dock to deliver timber to Brown's order. Brown instructed the dock company to deliver timber to King & Co. In the stock-books of his company, Capon made alterations and false entries of fictitious sales to account for the reduction in the stock. All the parties other than Capson had acted bonafide. The company discovered the fraud and claimed, as the owner, the timber or its value from King & Co., who for its part asserted its right as the owner.

The Court of Appeal ruled in favour of King & Co. on the grounds of estoppel. The case came before the House of Lords, which considered it to be a straightforward case and wrongly decided by the Court of Appeal. The House of Lords was of the view that it was a simple case of theft. Lord Lindsay noted:

What have the plaintiffs done to preclude them from denying, as against the defendants, Capon's right to sell to them? … Absolutely nothing. … I do not myself see upon what ground a person can be precluded from denying as against another an authority which has never been given in fact, and which the other has never supposed to exist.

In the present case, in my view of it, Capon simply stole the plaintiff's goods and sold them to the defendants, and the defendants' title is not improved by the circumstance that the theft was the result of an ingenious fraud on the plaintiffs and on the defendants alike. The defendants were not in any way misled by any act of the plaintiffs on which they placed reliance; and the plaintiffs are not, therefore, precluded from denying Capon's authority to sell.

The court established that for estoppel to arise there must be a representation from the owner to the buyer and the buyer should rely on it. Alternately, the owner can make a representation to the world at large, and the buyer should know of and rely on it. The timber merchant did not make any direct representation to the buyer. The further contention was that authorization to Capson to issue a delivery order was itself a representation by conduct to the world at large. However, the representation should establish that the seller is invested with real or apparent authority to sell. Further, the buyer must rely on that representation. In this case, the buyer had bought the timber from Brown, not Capson. Thus, there was neither a representation nor a reliance on it.

Before taking up the next case, we need to note the effect of a person being in possession of goods. If a thief or a finder of goods sells to a buyer, the ownership, of course, does not transfer to the buyer. However, if the owner voluntarily gives possession of his goods to another, does this on its own amount to a representation to the world at large that the person in possession of goods is either the owner or has the authority of the owner to sell the goods? An owner gives possession of his goods to others for various reasons. The goods of the owner can be in the possession of a servant, warehouse, transporter, or other bailee. That a person is in possession of goods does not establish that he is the owner or has the authority to sell. If it were, nobody would ever part with his goods. *Mercantile Bank of India Limited* v. *Central Bank of India Limited*[7] has firmly stated the principle. There must be something more in addition to the possession to estoppel the owner. This will come up in the next case, where the seller

---

[7] *Mercantile Bank of India Limited* v. *Central Bank of India Limited*, (1938) AC 287.

had the possession of both the car and the registration book of the car.

Central Newbury Car Auctions Ltd v. Unity Finance Ltd

Central Newbury Car Auctions Ltd was the owner of a second-hand Morris car.[8] The car was in their showroom, and its registration book had the name of one C. Ashley, the last owner. Under the law, every car was to be registered with the City Council. The City Council issued a registration book with the name of the owner. The owner was responsible for paying the annual licence fee and meet other responsibilities in relation to the car. On the sale of a car, the new owner was required to get his name entered in the registration book with the City Council, which recorded the change of ownership and stamped it. However, as the motor car dealers bought cars to sell, they were not required to get their names entered in the registration book. This kept the book clean with fewer entries, and explains why Ashley's name still appeared in the registration book. There was a column in the registration book for the owner to sign against his name. Neither Ashley nor the two previous owners had signed against theirs. We will see the relevance of this later.

A distinguished-looking stranger visited the showroom, liked the Morris, and agreed to take it in part exchange for the Hillman Minx car he had come in. The sale was to be under a hire-purchase arrangement. The car company would sell the car to the finance company South Western Securities Ltd, which in turn would give the car to the person on a hire purchase basis. The visitor gave his name as Cullis. He signed a 'proposal form' in which he offered to enter into a hire-purchase

agreement with the finance company. The secretary of the Newbury Auction Co. signed an offer document offering to sell the car to the finance company for a specified amount. Under the offer document, the property was to pass as soon as the finance company accepted the sale offer of the car dealer. The documents were to be sent to the finance company by post.

Having got the forms and papers signed and taken the Hillman car in their possession, the Newbury Auction Co., did not wait for the finance company's reply. They assumed it would come through. They immediately let Cullis have the Morris car and the registration book. He drove off with the car and the log-book, and they never saw him again. The Newbury Auction Co. sent the documents by post that night to the finance company. The very next morning the finance company telephoned to say that they thought Cullis was a fake. The address given by him was fictitious. They refused to accept the sale offer of the car dealer. The Newbury Auction Co. made inquiries about the Hillman Minx car that Cullis had left with them; and they discovered that it on a hire purchase. They paid £100 to the owner to get the ownership and informed the police of the fraud.

Three days later, a man drove the Morris car to Mercury Garage and introduced himself as Ashley. He had signed in the register book against the name. The Mercury Garage was taken in and agreed to buy the car for £ 200. The manager took delivery of the car and the log-book, and he gave the man a crossed cheque for £ 200 in favour of C. Ashley and got a receipt from him for the money. The man came the next day and persuaded the manager to open the crossed cheque. He came in a van with household goods and told him he was moving in the neighbourhood and was yet to open a bank

---

[8] *Central Newbury Car Auctions Ltd* v. *Unity Finance Ltd*, (1957) 1 QB 371.

account. The manager opened it as he noted the signature of Ashley in the register book and in the receipt; he tallied the signature and found that there could be no foul play. Mercury Motors afterwards sold the Morris car to Unity Finance Ltd, who let it on hire purchase terms to Powell.

When the Newbury Auction Co. found out what had happened to the Morris car, they claimed that it still belonged to them. When it was not returned, they brought an action against the Unity Finance Company and Powell for damages for conversion of it. Mercury Motors was brought into the case as a third party. The value of the car had been agreed at £ 240. Morris L.J. framed the question thus:

The question becomes one as to whether by entrusting him with the car and the book they have in effect made a representation which they are precluded from denying that the possessor of the car and book was vested with authority to sell. If Cullis had had the car alone, it is not suggested that authority to sell could be assumed. ... Is the position any different if the registration book is also handed over? This raises the question as to the nature of such a book.

The court noted that the registration book was not a document to record the legal owner of the car. It was for the purposes of taxation. The registration book itself disclaimed that the person who is entered as the owner may or may not be the legal owner. The court noted:

The result, as it seems to me, is that it cannot be assumed that the person in possession of a car and its registration book is the owner of the car. ... The man who went to the garage might have been someone who had been given possession of the car and book without being entitled to part with them. The man might have been merely a thief of the car and book.

...

If the plaintiffs had merely given Cullis the car it is not suggested that there would have been a representation to all the world that the possessor of the car was its legal owner, nor can such a representation be established because possession was also given of a book which does not prove legal ownership and which proclaims a clear warning and intimation that it does not.

For these reasons I do not consider that the plaintiffs were estopped from proving their ownership, and in my judgment they were entitled to succeed against the defendants.

The car dealer never gave the authority to Cullis to sell the car. However, could his handing over both the car and the registration book created an apparent authority in the person to sell the car? Was the fact that the seller had both the car and the book a representation to the world at large that the person in possession had the right to sell? The answer to this question was no. Was the owner negligent in giving the car and the book to the person? There is no duty cast on the owner to the world in relation to protection of his property. Thus, the owner was not negligent in parting with the car and the book.

Eastern Distributors Ltd v. Goldring

Murphy owned a Bedford utility van and wanted to buy a Chrysler car from a motor dealer called Coker on hire purchase.[9] However, he did not have the money to pay the deposit under the agreement. The motor dealer suggested a way: he could sell the van to the finance company, and take the van on hire purchase and pay the amount in instalments. As finance companies did not buy from individual owners and the motor dealer was interested in selling the Chrystler,

[9] *Eastern Distributors Ltd.* v. *Goldring*, (1957) 2 QB 600.

the motor dealer suggested that he would tell the finance company that he was selling both the van and Chrystler to Murphy, and that Murphy had paid the deposit on both the vehicles (none of which was true, of course). To accomplish the plan, Murphy signed the proposal forms for hire purchase agreements on the two vehicles. He also signed a delivery note stating that he had taken the delivery of the Bedford. He later failed to pay the instalments and sold the car. The finance company and the buyer were in dispute on the ownership. Delvin J. ruled:

Coker was armed by Murphy with documents which enabled him to represent to the plaintiffs that he was the owner of the Bedford car and had the right to sell it. The result is that Murphy is, in the words of section 21, precluded from denying Coker's authority to sell, and consequently the plaintiffs acquired the title to the goods which Murphy himself had and Murphy had no title left to pass to the defendant.

As Murphy had represented to the finance company that Coker was the owner of the car, he was barred from claiming that actually Coker was not the owner.

Estoppel by Negligence

We have already noted that for negligence to arise there must be a duty owed which the owner fails to perform. We will further explore negligence with the following case.

Moorgate Mercantile Co. Ltd v. Twitchings

The following paragraph from the judgment of Lord Wilberforce serves as an introduction to the case.[10]

My Lords, this case arises out of a hire purchase agreement of a motor car, a type of transaction

which has provoked much litigation in which hardship to individuals is frequently revealed. This is due to the perennial failure of English law to develop a proper method of charging movable property. The hire purchase agreement is an ingenious invention which has proved itself as a very convenient and economically stimulating method of financing sales of chattels. But by divorcing ownership (vested in a finance company) from possession (held by a dealer or private hirer), by permitting the latter to retain documents of title without any endorsement of the interest of others, and by not requiring registration, in an accessible register, of the agreement, it lends itself, almost ideally, to fraudulent dispositions. In order to reduce these risks the finance companies in about 1938 devised a registration machinery of their own, through a company called Hire Purchase Information Ltd. (HPI) with which the great majority of hire purchase agreements are registered: but the system was neither compulsory nor universal, and there are some transactions which escape it. The present is one.

Moorgate Mercantile Co. Ltd was a finance company that, as the owner, let a motor car on hire purchase to one McLorg. It was their intention, as it was their normal practice, to register the agreement with HPI. By some mistake, the agreement was not registered. McLorg took the car to sell to a motor dealers firm named Twitchings and did not disclose that it was on hire purchase. The motor dealers asked HPI whether there was any hire purchase agreement registered or recorded against the car. When the answer was in the negative, they proceeded with the purchase and resold the car. When Moorgate Mercantile Co. Ltd learnt of this, they sued the motor dealers for damages for conversion. The case came before the House of Lords. Lord Tullybelton noted:

The conduct of Moorgate, by which it is said to be estopped from denying McLorg's authority to sell, is its omission to register with HPI its hire

---

[10] *Moorgate Mercantile Co. Ltd Appellants* v. *Twitchings Respondent*, (1977) AC 890.

purchase agreement with him. That omission is said to have been negligent ... If Twitchings are to succeed under either head they must therefore show (a) that Moorgate owed a duty to them to take reasonable care to register the agreement, (b) that Moorgate negligently failed to perform that duty, and (c) that their negligence was the proximate or real cause of Twitchings's loss.

...

The first question then is whether Moorgate was under such a duty to Twitchings. The mere fact that registering hire purchase agreements was a usual practice in the business of finance houses such as Moorgate will not by itself give rise to a duty on the part of Moorgate towards Twitchings to register its agreements. ... The primary purpose of the HPI scheme is, in my opinion, to provide protection to finance houses. But finance houses which are members of the scheme are under no obligation to anyone else to protect their own property by using the facilities of HPI. The owner of property is entitled to be careless with it if he likes, and even extreme carelessness with his own property will not preclude him from recovering it from a person who has bought it from someone who dishonestly purported to sell it. In my opinion, Moorgate's conduct in not registering the hire purchase agreement with McLorg was, at worst, careless in respect of Moorgate's own property, and it was not in breach of any duty to other parties. ... It is notorious that the person in possession of a motor vehicle is often not the owner of it, and the vehicle log book contains a warning that it is not proof of ownership of the vehicle. The very fact that dealers like Twitchings check with HPI before buying a vehicle from a stranger shows that they are well aware that possession and ownership may be separate. Accordingly, I am of opinion that when Moorgate, having given possession of their vehicle to McLorg under a hire purchase agreement, did not register the agreement with HPI, they were not in breach of any duty owed by them to Twitchings. Twitchings therefore fail to show the first of the three things that they have to establish if their defence is to be upheld.

Estoppel is a rule of evidence. It precludes a person from putting up certain facts before the court. The implication of this would be that the buyer has not become the owner of the goods. The original owner continues to be the owner but he cannot claim the goods due to the application of estoppel. In other words, estoppel does not transfer the title but merely prevents the owner from claiming it. The Court of Appeal in *Eastern Distributors Ltd* v. *Goldring*[11] was of the view that estoppel in relation to sale of goods ' transfer[s] a real title and not merely a metaphorical title'.

MERCANTILE AGENT

The common law maintains that only the owner can pass a title. However, trade and commerce could not be sustained if there was no protection for the buyer to purchase with the confidence that he would be entitled to enjoy his goods. The British Parliament by legislation created some exceptions for the seller who was not an owner to make a valid transfer. This was achieved through the Factors Acts, first enacted in 1823, and the last in 1889, before the enactment of the Sale of Goods, 1893. The term 'factor' is not in commercial use anymore. It refers to commercial agents or mercantile agents whose business is to handle goods or documents of titles of goods to find a buyer. An auctioneer is an example of a mercantile agent. The Factors Act provided that a mercantile agent would pass a valid title if the agent had possession of the goods with the consent of the owner. The Sale of Goods Act, 1893, recognized the provision in the Factors Act, 1889, in Section 21(2), providing 'the provisions of the Factors Acts, or any enactment enables the apparent

[11] *Eastern Distributors Ltd* v. *Goldring*, (1957) 2 QB 600.

owner of goods to dispose of them as if he were the true owner.'

As India did not have a corresponding Factors Act, it borrowed the exceptions from the Factors Act, 1889, and included them in the Sale of Goods Act, 1930:

27. Sale by person not the owner: Subject to the provisions of this Act and of any other law for the time being in force, where goods are sold by a person who is not the owner thereof and who does not sell them under the authority or with the consent of the owner, the buyer acquires no better title to the goods than the seller had, unless the owner of the goods is by his conduct precluded from denying the seller's authority to sell:

Provided that, where a mercantile agent is, with the consent of the owner, in possession of the goods or of a document of title to the goods, any sale made by him, when acting in the ordinary course of business of a mercantile agent, shall be as valid as if he were expressly authorised by the owner of the goods to make the same; provided that the buyer acts in good faith and has not at the time of the contract of sale noticed that the seller has no authority to sell.

Section 2(9) gives the following definition of mercantile agent: '[A] "mercantile agent" means a mercantile agent having in the customary course of business as such agent authority either to sell goods, or to consign goods for the purposes of sale, or to buy goods, or to raise money on the security of goods'. There are no cases from the Indian courts on this. The British cases, as the following review will show, explore different dimensions of the provision.

Lowther v. Harris

Colonel Lowther had a large quantity of valuable furniture and antiques for disposal.[12]

Baron Prior had a shop selling glass and China, and dealt in antiques in a small way. He ran his business under the name 'Period'. Lowther engaged Prior to sell his antique on a commission basis. He took a house close to Prior's shop and stored the furniture and antique. Lowther had appointed a secretary who used to live in the house and take care of the goods. When customers came to Prior's shop, he would bring them to the house to show the furniture. The secretary was on duty during the day. The customers were not told that the property was not his. He would make an invoice in the name of 'Period', collect the price by cheque drawn in his name and account for the sale by paying cash to Lowther. Prior had limited authority. He had no authority to complete a sale or make a delivery without first getting the sanction of Lowther. He used to see him about about four times a week. If the articles were of value less than £ 100, he would seek the secretary's sanction. The collection of Lowther included two tapestries, the Aubusson tapestry, bought for £ 900, and the Leopard tapestry, bought for £ 771.

Lowther discovered that various articles of value had been disposed of by Prior. He was arrested and convicted of larceny. This included the two tapestries. The stories in relation to the two tapestries are different. We will first narrate how the Aubusson tapestry was sold. Prior told Lowther that he had sold the tapestry to a buyer, Corbel Woodhall, for £ 525. Lowther protested that the price was too small, but agreed to the sale on the representation that Woodhall was a valuable customer. He gave the tapestry to Prior, but he did not sell the tapestry to Woodhall at all. He made up the sale to get possession of the tapestry, which he sold to an art dealer, Harris, for £ 250. He had dealt with Prior as a commission agent who

[12] *Lowther* v. *Harris*, King's Bench Division, (1927) 1 KB 393.

called himself 'Period'. He did not know whether he was working for a principal or selling in his own capacity, but he bought it in good faith. Prior stole the second tapestry from the premises later and sold it to Harris, who bought it in good faith. Lowther moved against Harris claiming to be the owner of the tapestries. The question was on the capacity of Prior to transfer ownership to Harris. Was he a mercantile agent in possession of the tapestry with the consent of the owner? If the answer was yes, he would have passed the ownership to Harris. Lowther would have no claim against him. Wright J. ruled:

The first question is whether Prior was a mercantile agent—that is, an agent doing a business in buying or selling, or both, having in the customary course of his business such authority to sell goods. I hold that he was. Various objections have been raised. It was contended that Prior was a mere servant or shopman, and had no independent status such as is essential to constitute a mercantile agent. ... In my opinion Prior, who had his own shops, and who gave receipts and took cheques in his own registered business name and earned commissions, was not a mere servant but an agent, even though his discretionary authority was limited. It is also contended that even if he were an agent he was acting as such for one principal only, the plaintiff, and that the Factors Act, 1889, requires a general occupation as agent. This, I think, is erroneous. The contrary was decided under the old Acts in Heyman v. Flewker, and I think the same is the law under the present Act.

...

The next question is whether Prior was in possession of the Aubusson tapestry, and, if so, with the consent of the plaintiff, and, if he had such possession, whether it was in his capacity as mercantile agent. ... But I do hold that Prior became in possession of the Aubusson tapestry when he was allowed to take it away in the van after the plaintiff had sanctioned a sale to Woodhall. It is true that no such sale had in fact been made or was intended to be made, and that

the possession was obtained by the fraud of Prior. Possession, however, was in fact obtained by Prior, and obtained by him in his capacity as mercantile agent. For the plaintiff it was contended that Prior obtained the tapestry under colour of an actually completed sale, and merely for purpose of delivery and as a sort of carrier between vendor and vendee. I think that is erroneous. Prior's functions as a mercantile agent were not completed even if a bargain had been concluded, but extended to the delivery of the goods, the collecting of the price, and the giving of a receipt and a subsequent accounting to the plaintiff. Delivery of possession to Prior was a necessary step to enable him to complete his office.

...

I accordingly hold that Prior obtained possession of the Aubusson tapestry in his capacity as a mercantile agent and with the consent of the plaintiff, having such possession ... in the ordinary course of business of a mercantile agent, a sale to the defendant, who, it is not contested, acted in good faith and with no notice of Prior's want of authority. I hold that the defendant establishes his defence as regards the Aubusson tapestry under the Factors Act, 1889.

For the second tapestry, as Prior had obtained the possession without the consent of the owner, the ownership was not transferred to the buyer. Lowther was entitled to recover the goods or its value from Harris.

Pearson v. Rose & Young LD
Pearson was a tobacconist who intended to sell his year-old car and buy a new one.[13] One of his customers, Mrs Hunt, told him that her husband was a dealer in new and old cars, and that she would introduce him to her husband. Pearson met Mr Hunt a couple of times and settled on buying a new car. The sale was not on an exchange basis; Pearson had to sell the car independently. He took his car to the

[13] *Pearson* v. *Rose & Young LD*, (1951) 1 KB 275.

business premises of Mr Hunt, the Reliance Motor Haulage Contractors Ld., and left it there, not with the authority to sell it, but only to get offers on it. Hunt intended to sell the car and pocket the proceeds. However, Pearson had retained the registration book of the car, and nobody would buy it without its registration book. To get the registration book, Hunt staged a plan to trick Pearson.

Hunt informed Pearson that there were restrictions on the selling of the car, and that a reference to the registration book was necessary to clear this. Pearson came with the registration book to explain to Hunt that there were no restrictions on selling of the car. To prove this, Hunt took out the registration book to show Pearson. Just then, a message came for Hunt that his wife was outside the office in a distressed condition. Hunt asked Pearson to leave the office so that he could see his wife. Ten minutes later, Hunt emerged and told Pearson that Mrs Hunt had to go to a hospital for an operation, and asked 'if he would be kind enough to go round in a car with Mrs Hunt to the hospital.' Pearson agreed, forgetting that he had left the registration book with Hunt. The case does not give details of what happened when Mrs Hunt reached the hospital. Pearson sold the car to a motor dealer. The car changed hands to finally come to Rose & Young Ld. All the parties had bought the car in good faith. On finding the car with Rose & Young Ld., Pearson demanded it from them, and, on their refusal to deliver it, sued them for conversion.

It was not in doubt that Mr Hunt was a mercantile agent. Pearson had willingly given the car to Hunt. The court, however, was of the view that the registration book constituted goods along with the car. The question the court then had to decide was, when a mercantile agent obtains possession of the goods with fraud or misrepresentation,

does that constitute 'possession with consent' for the mercantile agent to pass property in the goods? The court was of the view that the operating words in the section were possession with consent of the owner. It did not distinguish whether the owner consented due to a fraud or misrepresentation played on him. Lord Denning delivered the following judgment:

In the early days of the common law the governing principle of our law of property was that no person could give a better title than he himself had. But the needs of commerce have led to a progressive modification of this principle so as to protect innocent purchasers. ... The way that Parliament has done it in the case of mercantile agents is this: Parliament has protected the true owner by making it clear that he does not lose his right to goods when they are taken from him without his consent, as for instance when they have been stolen from his house by a burglar who has handed them over to a mercantile agent. The true owner can in that case claim them back from any person into whose hands they came, even from an innocent purchaser who has bought from a mercantile agent. But Parliament has not protected the true owner, if he has himself consented to a mercantile agent having possession of them: because, by leaving them in the agent's possession, he has clothed the agent with apparent authority to sell them; and he should not therefore be allowed to claim them back from an innocent purchaser.

The critical question, therefore, in every case is whether the true owner consented to the mercantile agent having possession of the goods. This is often a very difficult question to decide.

...

Did the plaintiff consent to Hunt's having possession of the registration book as well as the car? ... the answer is clearly 'No'. ... the plaintiff simply let Hunt have the registration book in his hands to inspect for a few moments. The plaintiff gave Hunt the barest physical custody of it whilst he was still there himself. He never consented to Hunt having possession of it. Then Hunt, by a trick, managed to get the plaintiff called away whilst he, Hunt, still held the book. Armed thus with the registration book Hunt was able to sell the car on the very same day to an innocent purchaser, which, without it, he could not have done. But on those facts the plaintiff no more consented to Hunt having possession of the registration book than if Hunt had stolen it from his pocket. The Factors Act, 1889, does not operate, therefore, to give a good title to the dealer who bought from Hunt, nor to the buyers in succession from him.

Thus, so long as the owner has voluntarily given possession of the goods to a mercantile agent, the mercantile agent would be 'in possession of the goods' 'with the consent of the seller' and the exception would come to apply.

Staffs Motor Guarantee, Limited v. British Wagon Company, Limited

Albert Thomas Heap was a dealer in motor cars of a certain make and ran a garage.[14] He applied to British Wagon Company, a finance company, to buy a lorry and let it on hire purchase to a firm called the Thorley Transport Company. The finance company did not accede to the request. Heap came up with another proposal. He asked the finance company to buy the lorry from him and let it to him on hire purchase, giving him the liberty to sub-let it to the Thorley Transport Company. The proposal was accepted, and the parties signed the relevant papers. Later, Heap told Staff Motors that the lorry was his and sold it to them. He continued to pay the instalments to British Wagon Company. When the instalments stopped, British Wagon Company repossessed the lorry. Staff

Motors claimed that under the Factors Act, being a mercantile agent, Heap had passed the title in the lorry to him. The Court of Appeal ruled in favour of British Wagon Company. Mackinnon J. noted:

… it has rightly been pointed out on behalf of the defendants that … the lorry had been sold by Heap to the defendants and had been entrusted by the defendants to Heap not as a mercantile agent dealing in or selling motor vehicles, but to Heap as a hirer of the car and therefore as its bailee. In these circumstances I do not think that it is open to the plaintiffs to say that the defendants entrusted the car to Heap as a mercantile agent.

…

Because one happens to entrust his goods to a man who is in other respects a mercantile agent, but with whom he is dealing not as a mercantile agent but in a different capacity, I do not think that it is open to a third party who buys the goods from that man to say that they were in his possession as a mercantile agent and that therefore he had power to sell them to a purchaser and so give him a good title to them. The claimant must be able to assert not only that the goods were in the man's possession as a mercantile agent, but also that they were entrusted by the owner to him as a mercantile agent.

The exception applies only if the owner gives possession to the other in the capacity of a mercantile agent. In the above case, the company had given possession under a contract of hire and not a mercantile agent.

SALE UNDER A VOIDABLE CONTRACT

B sells goods to C under a voidable contract. C gets the possession of the goods from B. B has the choice of rescinding the contract or leaving it alone. If B leaves it alone, the ownership would transfer to C when B performs the contract. What happens if B rescinds it? It would be assumed that no contract was formed between the parties and thus C got the possession, but not the ownership. The

---

[14] *Staffs Motor Guarantee, Limited v. British Wagon Company, Limited*, (1934) 2 KB 305.

difficult question is if C sells the goods further. The fortunes of the sub-buyer will depend on whether B decides to rescind the contract. The exception in Section 29 addresses this concern. It reads:

29. Sale by person in possession under voidable contract: When the seller of goods has obtained possession thereof under a contract voidable under section 19 or section 19A of the Indian Contract Act, 1872 (9 of 1872), but the contract has not been rescinded at the time of the sale, the buyer acquires a good title to the goods, provided he buys them in good faith and without notice of the seller's defect of title.

There is no case on this from the Indian courts. The following case is from the Court of Appeal.

Car and Universal Finance Co., Ltd v. Caldwell

The facts of this case were not unusual but posed a peculiar problem for the law.[15] Caldwell sold his car to Norris and accepted a cheque as part payment of the price. When he presented the cheque to the bank the next morning, it was dishonoured. From the bank he learnt that the same thing had happened to another person the previous week. Caldwell went to the police to report the fraud. The police showed him a photograph, which he recognized as 'Norris'. The police informed him that a warrant was out for his arrest under the name of Rowley. Caldwell also asked the Automobile Association to trace the car and restore it to him. The fraudster had sold the car in two or three days of its acquisition, and the buyer had sold it forward. Caldwell claimed the car back from the person who had possession of it. He said that informing

the police of his intention to have the car restored to him was an election to rescind the contract. Lord Upjohn summarized the principle on election:

Where one party to a contract has an option unilaterally to rescind or disaffirm it by reason of the fraud or misrepresentation of the other party, he must elect to do so within a reasonable time and cannot do so after he has done anything to affirm the contract with knowledge of the facts giving rise to the option to rescind. In principle and on authority he must in my judgment in the ordinary course communicate his intention to rescind to the other party. This must be so because the other party is entitled to treat the contractual nexus as continuing until he is made aware of the intention of the other to exercise his option to rescind. So the intention must be communicated and an uncommunicated intention, for example by speaking to a third party or making a private note, will be ineffective.

The court noted the 'exceptional contractual circumstances' in cases like this. The fraudster only needs to evade any communication with him to deprive the other party of his right to rescind the contract. The court thus ruled that if the party can 'establish clearly and unequivocally that he terminates the contract and is no longer to be bound by it', the contract should be taken to be rescinded. The communication of Caldwell to the Police and Automobile Associate of his request was confirmed to be an election to rescind the contract.

SELLER IN POSSESSION

An owner sells goods to a buyer but continues to be in possession of the goods. The owner then sells the goods to another buyer and the second buyer takes possession of the goods. This leads to another dispute between two innocent buyers. Should the second buyer be dispossessed of the goods in favour of the

[15] *Car and Universal Finance Co., Ltd* v. *Caldwell,* (1965) 1 QB 525.

first buyer? The British Parliament was of the view that the second buyer should be left alone with the goods. This was done by introducing the provision in the Factors Act in 1877. The Privy Council noted:[16]

The English statutory provision which was the origin of section 28 (1) was introduced in 1877 with the object of mitigating the asperity of the common law towards an innocent party purchasing goods from a person who has all the trappings of ownership but in truth has no proper title to the goods. Nemo dat quod non habet. The purchaser had no defence at common law against the true owner…

This was the case where a buyer under an agreement to sell came to be in possession of the goods, and sold and delivered the goods to another buyer. As the Factors Act was an existing law, the exception to the nemo dat principle, which applied even if the seller was not a factor, was introduced in it. In the codification of the law of sale of goods in the Sale of Goods Act, 1893, the provisions were modified and introduced in the act. The intention was to delete the provisions in the Factors Act after the enactment. However, this was not done. This led to simultaneous application of both acts. Further, the extent to which the provisions in the two acts were different caused a great deal of confusion.

In India, the Sale of Goods Act, 1930, borrowed from the Sale of Goods Act, 1893, on the subject of the seller remaining in possession. However, the provision on the buyer remaining in possession was borrowed from the Factors Act. It did not follow the changes made by the Sale of Goods Act, 1893. Thus, the provisions in the Sale of Goods Act, 1930, are different from the Sale of Goods

Act, 1893. As there is no case law from the Indian courts, we would have to rely on common law cases. However, as the provisions are not similar, we have to be careful in our borrowings. We will first take the case where the buyer is in possession of the goods. Section 30(1) of the Sale of Goods Act, 1930, provides:

30. Seller or buyer in possession after sale: (1) Where a person, having sold goods, continues or is in possession of the goods or of the documents of title to the goods, the delivery or transfer by that person or by a mercantile agent acting for him, of the goods or documents of title under any sale, pledge or other disposition thereof to any person receiving the same in good faith and without notice of the previous sale shall have the same effect as if the person making the delivery or transfer were expressly authorised by the owner of the goods to make the same.

Section 25(1) is the corresponding section in the Sale of Goods Act, 1893:

25. Seller or buyer in possession after sale. (1) Where a person having sold goods continues or is in possession of the goods, or of the documents of title to the goods, the delivery or transfer by that person, or by a mercantile agent acting for him, of the goods or documents of title under any sale, pledge, or other disposition thereof, to any person receiving the same in good faith and without notice of the previous sale, shall have the same effect as if the person making the delivery or transfer were expressly authorised by the owner of the goods to make the same.

Other than the punctuations, the two subsections are identical. The following is a case on the theme.

Worcester Works Finance Ltd. v. Cooden Engineering Co. Ltd

A motor car dealer, Griffiths, bought a Ford Zephyr motor car from Cooden Engineering

[16] *Pacific Motor Auctions Pty Ltd* v. *Motor Credits (Hire Finance) Ltd*, (1965) AC 867.

Co. Ltd for £ 525.[17] He wrote a cheque and took the car along with its log book. He had the car registered in his name in the records of the registration authority. Griffiths was a fraudster; the cheque bounced. He made arrangements with a man named Millerick to sign documents to take the car on hire purchase from a finance company called Worcester Works Finance Ltd. Griffiths submitted the papers to the finance company, which purchased the car and gave it to Millerick on hire purchase. The entire transaction was only on paper. The car continued to be with Griffiths. He received £ 450 for the car. As he did not want his fraud to be discovered, he paid the instalments for a few months in league with Millerick.

Meanwhile, Cooden presented the cheque three times to the bank, and each time it was dishonoured. The company believed that as the cheque had not been cleared, they were entitled to repossess the car. They sent a man to Griffith's premises to do just that. The company kept the car for its use for some time, and then let it out on hire purchase, registering the agreement with the Hire-Purchase Information Bureau. Through the registration, Worcester Finance found out that the car was in Cooden's possession. They claimed the car as theirs and brought action for damages for conversion.

The case fell within Section 25 of the Sale of Goods Act, 1893. Griffiths was the owner who sold the car to the finance company but continued to be in possession of it. Cooden created interest for itself in the car by repossessing it. The dispute was whether the interests of the finance company or of Cooden were to prevail. Lord Denning opined:

The words 'continues in possession' refer to 'the continuity of physical possession regardless of any private transactions between the seller and purchaser which might alter the legal title under which the possession was held': *per* Lord Pearce, at p. 888.[18]

It does not matter what private arrangement may be made by the seller with the purchaser—such as whether the seller remains bailee or trespasser, or whether he is lawfully in possession or not. It is sufficient if he remains continuously in possession of the goods that he has sold to the purchaser. If so, he can pass a good title to a bona fide third person, and the original purchaser will be ousted. But there must be a continuity of physical possession. If there is a substantial break in the continuity, as for instance, if the seller actually delivers over the goods to a purchaser who keeps them for a time, and then the seller afterwards gets them back, then the section might not apply.

Applying these principles it is plain that Griffiths was a person who, having sold goods to the finance company, 'continued in possession' of them until the time when they were retaken by the Cooden company.

The next question is whether the retaking by the Cooden company was 'the delivery or transfer' by Griffiths of the goods to the Cooden company under a 'disposition' thereof. Griffiths did not actually deliver or transfer the car to the Cooden company. But he acquiesced in their retaking it. That was, I think, tantamount to a delivery or transfer by him. But was it under a 'disposition' thereof?

Mr Jacob argued that there was no disposition here: there was, he said, only a retaking by the Cooden company. To my mind the word 'disposition' is a very wide word. ... When the Cooden company retook this car (because the cheque had not been met) there was clearly a transfer back to them of property in the goods. They would not thereafter be able to sue on the cheque. By retaking the goods they impliedly gave up their remedy on the cheque. That retransfer of the property back to the Cooden company was a 'disposition' within the section.

The last question is whether at the time when the Cooden company retook the car they received 'the same in good faith and without notice of the previous sale,' that is, without notice of the sale by Griffiths to the finance company. The word 'notice' here means actual notice, that is to say, knowledge of the sale or deliberately turning a blind eye to it. Our commercial law does not like constructive notice. It will have nothing to do with it. I am quite clear that the Cooden company acted in good faith without notice of the sale to the finance company. They had sold a car and been given a dud cheque for it; and were just retaking it.

So all the requisites of section 25(1) are satisfied. The retaking by the Cooden company has the same effect as if it was expressly authorised by Worcester Finance. It is equivalent to a transfer by Griffiths back to the Cooden company with the express authority of the finance company. So the Cooden company acquired a good title to the car.

This result is consonant with the object of section 25. Worcester Finance did not see the car at all. They did not take possession of it. They simply received documents from the dealer Griffiths and handed out money to him. They relied on his honesty. He was dishonest. He got £ 450 out of them by a trick. In contrast, the Cooden company actually had possession of the car—sold it to Griffiths—and when his cheque was dishonoured, they retook it. Plainly as a matter of commercial good sense the title should remain in the Cooden company and not in Worcester Finance. The Cooden company are protected by section 25. The car is theirs.

Buyer Remaining in Possession

Section 30(2) of the Sale of Goods Act, 1930, makes the following provision on the buyer being in possession of goods and making a further sale. It reads:

30. Seller or buyer in possession after sale: (2) Where a person, having bought or agreed to buy goods, obtains, with the consent of the seller, possession of the goods or the documents of title to

the goods, the delivery or transfer by that person or by a mercantile agent acting for him, of the goods or documents of title under any sale, pledge or other disposition thereof to any person receiving the same in good faith and without notice of any lien or other right of the original seller in respect of the goods shall have effect as if such lien or right did not exist.

The provision is identical to the one on the seller retaining possession and making a sale. The provision in the British law is different. As the provision is similar to the seller remaining in possession, we can draw from that instead. If a person has 'bought' goods from a seller, he has already become the owner and received the right to sell the goods. This part of the provision is surplus. However, there might be a contract of sale where the buyer has been given the delivery of the goods but the ownership has not changed. For example, the term of the contract may stipulate that the ownership will not change till the money is paid. In this case, the buyer will have the possession of the goods but not the ownership. The goods should come to the buyer under a sale contract. A contract of sale must be distinguished from other forms of contract, like hire purchase and bailment. The rights of the sub-buyer prevail over the rights of the original seller.

Both of the above provisions on the buyer or seller retaining possession of the goods uses the phrase 'the goods or the documents of title to the goods'. Thus, possession of the documents of title to goods is equivalent to possessing the goods themselves. Section 2 of the sale of goods Act, 1930, defines 'document of title to goods' as follows:

(4) 'document of title to goods' includes a bill of lading, dock-warrant, warehouse keepers's certificate, wharfingers' certificate, railway receipt, warrant or order for the delivery of goods and any other document used in the ordinary course of

business as proof of the possession or control of goods, or authorising or purporting to authorise, either by endorsement or by delivery, the possessor of the document to transfer or receive goods thereby represented…

The term 'document of title' seems to mean a document that establishes the right of the person over the goods. Thus, the person whose name is mentioned or the bearer of the document can claim to be the owner of the goods. However, this is not the sense in which the act defines it. It mostly refers to documents that do not establish the ownership of the person but merely give him the right to be delivered the goods. In this sense, the term is misleading. The documents mentioned above can be seen to fall in two categories. One, it is an acknowledgement issued by a bailee like a warehouse or a carrier that he has possession of the goods and the person named in the document or any person the named person orders has the right to receive the delivery of the goods. The person who has the right to receive the goods may or may not be the owner of the goods. The bailee, in delivering the goods, has performed his duty. Examples of this kind of a document include a dock warrant, warehouseman's warrant, railway receipt, and lorry receipt. It also includes a bill of lading. However, a bill of lading is quite different. In maritime trade, the seller and buyer used the document in conjunction with other shipping terms like FOB and CIF to transfer the ownership. Thus, the bill of lading, depending on the shipping term, may be the document establishing ownership over the goods.

The second set of documents is issued by the owner of the goods or some other person entitled to possession of the goods to the warehouseman, carrier, or other bailee to deliver the goods to the person named in the document. Such documents are called delivery orders. As mentioned earlier, these documents do not confer ownership rights or are evidence of rights over the goods. However, the delivery of goods is itself a significant event. These documents are important as these confer the right to be delivered the goods.

In the context of the above provisions on the buyer or the seller retaining the possession of these documents, even if these do not confer ownership on their own, become decisive in settling the claims of the two buyers of the same goods. Let us illustrate this: S is the owner of goods that are being transported by a truck. He has the lorry receipt, which is in his favour. S sells the goods being transported to B1 but does not give B1 the lorry receipt. S sells the same goods to B2. B2, unaware that the goods are already sold, buys from S and S delivers the lorry receipt to B2. In settling the ownership issue between two innocent buyers, the fact that B2 has been given the possession of the lorry receipt means that the title in goods passes to him. Of course, S is in breach of contract with B1 and thus he will have to pay damages to him.

The following provision on sale by a joint owner can be readily grasped:

28. Sale by one of joint owners: If one of several joint owners of goods has the sole possession of them by permission of the co-owners, the property in the goods is transferred to any person who buys them of such joint owner in good faith and has not at the time of the contract of sale noticed that the seller has no authority to sell.

* * *

The general principle *nemo dat quod non habet* means that no one can transfer a better title than he himself has. In other words, a person who is not the owner cannot transfer a valid title. Having created the representation that the seller has the authority to sell, the owner may be prevented from establishing that the seller did not have the authority. The second exception is if a person got the possession of the goods with the consent of the owner in the capacity of a mercantile agent; the buyer would then get a valid title. The third exception is where the buyer remains in possession of the goods after having sold it. A sale to another person and giving him the possession would pass a title to the second buyer. The sale by a prospective buyer who has received the possession has a similar effect of passing the title to a sub-buyer.

6

Quality of Goods

If a sale is a specific form of contract, it is as old as contracting itself. The development of contract law itself owes much to trade. As the quality of goods in a sale contract was of crucial importance for the parties concerned, The rights and obligations of the contracting parties on the quality of goods in a sale contract had developed over centuries. In the early stages of the development of trade and commerce, people and traders came from different areas, assembled in the market place, and bought and sold goods. In those open markets, buyers and sellers came face-to-face, examined the goods, satisfied themselves with their quality, and then bought them. After a sale, it was generally difficult to establish who came, bought, and went away. Thus the maxim *caveat emptor* (buyer beware) came into being. In other words, a buyer buys at his own risk. This became the general law.

However, as trade and commerce developed, the *caveat emptor* principle became inadequate, unjust, and a hindrance to trade and commerce. Thus, common law courts developed exceptions to the rule. These exceptions corresponded with different stages of the development of trade and commerce.

The common law courts made a distinction between specific goods and goods sold by description. A person buying the only horse the seller owned was buying that specific horse. He was free to examine the horse before making up his mind. As the sale was of the particular goods, *caveat emptor* continued to apply. To get further assurance, the buyer must ask the seller to make it a part of the contract that the horse was of adequate quality. In contrast, in a sale of goods by description, the buyer does not agree to buy specific goods but a class of goods, for example, long-grain rice. In this case, common law courts developed that the seller was under an obligation to supply the goods of that description. This corresponded with the phase of development where the seller and the buyer were far apart. The seller would put up a description of the goods he possessed. Trade and commerce would have collapsed if the seller were not bound to deliver goods in conformity with the description.

The courts came up with two further exceptions to *caveat emptor*. One was that if the buyer relies on the skill and judgment of the seller to supply him with goods that would be suitable for a particular purpose, the seller would be under an obligation to supply goods fit for that purpose. The second exception was that when the goods' generic name is used when they are sold, they must be fit for their basic purpose. This came to be known as the requirement of merchantability of goods. The common law courts used the term that the seller warrants that the goods are of merchantable quality.

At the time of codification of the law on the sale of goods, the British legislature went further than common law in giving protection to the buyer. Further, the Sale of Goods Act, 1893 used the term 'condition and warranty' from contract law to describe the rights of the buyer. To recall, the condition is a core part of the contract for whose breach the buyer can terminate the contract. A warranty is a subsidiary part for whose breach only damages can be claimed. This was in contrast with common law courts use of the term 'warranty' in its positive sense in describing the undertakings of the seller. The expansion of the substantive law and the change of terminology created its effects in interpretation of the law.

The Sale of Goods Act, 1893, was one of the first acts codifying common law. There was much difference of opinion among the judges in interpreting the provisions. Some maintained that as the act was a statute, one should look at the text of the law alone to interpret it. Others reasoned that as the act codified common law, the prior cases should be referred to give substance and meaning to the provisions. Yet others attempted to work with a combination of the two approaches. While the approach of using common law cases to give substance to the act triumphed, in relation to the quality of goods, as the substance of the law as well as the terms had changed, using the earlier cases was not be of much help on several themes. Thus, we will

not be referring to the cases prior to codification. Instead, we will develop a generalized picture of the evolution of the law and its expression in the act. In the early years after the enactments, the courts struggled with this transition and vacuum, and the position settled with the passage of time. Thus, we will be selective in using the cases towards developing a coherent understanding of the principles.

The provisions in the act are a layering of the principles and ideas developed at different points of time. Let us develop a broad expectation of the rights of the buyer from everyday experiences and from the fact that a sale is a contract.

SALE BY DESCRIPTION

A customer visited an e-shop, selected a shirt and paid for it with his credit card. The shirt was delivered to him a week later. The customer had selected a shirt with the description 'sky blue, pure cotton'. On receiving the shirt, the customer found a label inside the shirt that read, 'cotton 70 per cent, polyester 30 per cent', and demanded that the shirt be taken back by the seller and the money returned. The seller claimed that the buyer was being fussy. According to the seller, such shirts were very popular and better than the pure cotton shirts. Should the buyer be allowed to return the shirt and get his money back? The description of the shirt is what the parties had contracted for. The buyer must get what has been described. Is the description a core part of the contract for whose breach the seller can terminate the contract or only a subsidiary part? As a sale contract is about the goods and its ownership, quality of goods is a core part of the contract. For this reason, the chapter on the quality of goods expresses the rights of the buyer in the terms of condition and warranty.

We know the concept of condition and warranty from contract law. However, the Indian Contract Act, 1872, does not use the terms nor has it defined it. The definitions appear in the chapter on the quality of goods in Section 12 of the Sale of Goods Act, 1930:

12. Condition and warranty: (1) A stipulation in a contract of sale with reference to goods which are the subject thereof may be a condition or a warranty.

(2) A condition is a stipulation essential to the main purpose of the contract, the breach of which gives rise to a right to treat the contract as repudiated.

(3) A warranty is a stipulation collateral to the main purpose of the contract, the breach of which gives rise to a claim for damages but not to a right to reject the goods and treat the contract as repudiated.

(4) Whether a stipulation in a contract of sale is a condition or a warranty depends in each case on the construction of the contract. A stipulation may be a condition, though called a warranty in the contract.

The section merely gives the definition of the terms we are familiar with from our study of contract law. Consider the following scenario: In an art gallery, several paintings were put on display. A customer liked a particular painting depicting a white horse running through water. There was no sign, label, or declaration; only a sticker declaring the price to be Rs 3,000. The customer took the painting to the counter, paid for it and left. Later, he realised that it was not a painting but a good quality re-print of a painting. He tried to return it and claim his money. What the customer offered to buy was the specific goods he had picked up. The store had not described it as an original painting. Therefore, the store was not in breach. This is not a sale by description but a sale of specific goods.

Let us now look at a case where the goods is described as well as specific. A person received an email from a colleague hoping to sell a car. It was described as a 'Maruti Zen, latest model, metal pearl'. The person visited the owner to see the car, took a test drive, and bought the car. A day later, the latter tried to return the car and get his money back as the car was not silver pearl in colour, but white. Should he be allowed to return the car? On the one hand, the seller should be bound to the description. At the same time, in every contract, we must identify what has been offered, accepted, and thus, agreed to between the parties. The offer and acceptance can be express or implied. It must have been apparent to the buyer on an examination of the car that it was white. Thus, even if the car had been earlier described as metal pearl, the description was impliedly modified by the parties to transact a white car.

Let us consider a variation of the case above. The buyer gets a car that is metal pearl in colour. He takes the car to a garage. After inspecting the car, the garage informs him that while the body of the car is of the latest model, engine, and several other components of the car were of an older model. The buyer wants to return the car and get his money back. Should he be allowed to return the car? The buyer had examined the car, but on examination and even a test drive it could not have been apparent to him that the engine inside the car was an older one. Thus, the parties never impliedly agreed on the buying and selling of a car with an older engine. In this case, the description put up by the seller does not get modified as the deviation in the goods is not apparent. We can thus summarize the principles of a sale by description:

1. From the communication between the parties, we must first discern whether there is

any description of the goods and reliance on it by the parties or not. If there isn't one, it is not a sale by description.

2. In a sale by description, the buyer must get the described goods if the buyer has not seen the goods and relies on the description alone.

3. In a sale by description, where the buyer has seen or examined the goods, the description would be modified to the extent of apparent deviations.

5. In a sale by description, where the buyer has seen or examined the goods, the description would not be modified by deviations latent or hidden in the goods.

We can now note Section 15 in the Sale of Goods Act, 1930, on sale by description. It reads:

15. Sale by description: Where there is a contract for the sale of goods by description, there is an implied condition that the goods shall correspond with the description; and, if the sale is by sample as well as by description, it is not sufficient that the bulk of the goods corresponds with the sample if the goods do not also correspond with the description.

The provision in the English act is analogous. Let us examine the section with a review of court judgments.

Varley v. Whipp

Varley offered to sell Whipp a second-hand reaping machine.[1] Varley said that the machine was in another British town, Upton, that it had been bought just the previous year, and had only been used to cut fifty or sixty acres. The reaping machine did not actually belong to Varley at that time; he bought it from the owner and delivered it via rail. After

receiving the machine, the buyer wrote to the seller:

I have had a look at the 'self-binder' you sent me, but it is not what I expected; it is a very old one, and has been mended, and you told me that it had only cut about fifty acres, and was practically new. I think you must never have seen it. It will be no use to me, as I don't care about old things, and especially machinery…

Whipp returned the machine to Varley and moved the court for recovering the money. The court ruled:

The machine which was to be sold had never been seen by the buyer, and it was not the property of the seller at the time. It was described as being at Upton, as being a self-binder, as being nearly new, and as having been used to cut only about fifty or sixty acres. All these statements were made with regard to the machine. … The term 'sale of goods by description' must apply to all cases where the purchaser has not seen the goods, but is relying on the description alone. It applies in a case like the present, where the buyer has never seen the article sold, but has bought by the description. … The most usual application of that section no doubt is to the case of unascertained goods, but I think it must also be applied to cases such as this where there is no identification otherwise than by description.

Thus, where the purchaser has not seen the goods and relies on the description by the seller alone, the buyer must get what has been described. The case becomes different when, along with there being a description, the buyer also sees the goods.

Beale v. Taylor

Taylor described a car through an advertisement as a 'Herald convertible, white, 1961, twin carbs. 190'.[2] He gave a test drive to

[1] *Varley* v. *Whipp*, (1900) 1 QB 513.

[2] *Beale* v. *Taylor*, (1967) 3 All ER 253.

Beale, the buyer. After being bought, the car gave trouble and the buyer took it to a garage. The garage found that the car had been put together from two different cars. Unlike the back portion, the front portion, including the engine, was not a 1961 model as represented by Taylor, but an earlier 948 cc model. The two parts had been welded together about halfway, somewhere under the driver's seat. The issue involved here was what features Beale could have learnt about the car on inspecting it that could have had the effect of modifying the description. He certainly could not have learnt about the latent defects in the car. The court ruled:

… if the buyer has not seen the goods, then in the ordinary way the contract would be one where the buyer relied on the description alone. … the buyer … must get what has been described. If the buyer has seen the good, he must have noted the apparent deviations of the good from the description. Thus, in effect, the buyer has agreed to the deviations. Thus, if the buyer has examined the goods, goods must confirm to the description, other than apparent deviations an examination would have brought out.

The court ruled that the fact of the car being welded from the halves of two cars was latent and could not have been noticed from an ordinary examination. Section 15 does not explicitly provide for exempting apparent deviations on examination. The text, in fact, holds the parties to the description. The common law took only the sale of unascertained goods to be a sale by description. A sale of specific goods was not a sale by description but of the particular goods. *Caveat emptor* applied to these sales. The courts made an exception by recognizing that description was qualified to the extent of apparent deviations on examination. It was in this context of the common law position that the court in

Varley v. *Whipp* had noted: 'The most usual application of that section no doubt is to the case of unascertained goods, but I think it must also be applied to cases such as this where there is no identification otherwise than by description.'[3]

All communications between the parties to a contract of sale do not give rise to a 'sale by description'. The term has a specific meaning. We first need to discern the binding terms of the contract from the communications between the parties. The appropriate expression for the terms that have actually been made part of the contract is 'incorporated terms'. Only if the terms of a contract describe the features or character of the goods does it become a 'sale by description'.

Harlingdon and Leinster Enterprises v. *Christopher Hull Fine Art*

The Christopher Hull Fine Art Limited, owned and controlled by Christopher Hull, was an art dealer.[4] The company carried its business from a gallery in Motcomb Street, London SW1. In the autumn of 1984, Mr Hull received two oil paintings to be disposed of. The paintings were described in an auction catalogue of 1980 as the work of Gabriele Munter (1877–1962), an artist of the German expressionist school. Mr Hull specialized in the works of contemporary British artists. He had no training, experience, or knowledge to conclude from an examination of the paintings whether they were indeed by Munter. He took them to Christie's (another art dealer), who expressed interest in the paintings. He was told that Harlingdon and Leinster Enterprises Limited (Harlingdon),

[3] *Varley* v. *Whipp*, (1900) 1 QB 513.
[4] *Harlingdon and Leinster Enterprises Limited* v. *Christopher Hull Fine Art Limited*, (1990) 1 All ER 737.

who did business as Leinster Fine Art from a gallery in Hereford Road, London W2, had a good reputation as a dealer in German art. In fact, Harlingdon had a special interest in the buying and selling of German expressionist paintings.

The Harlingdon was owned and run by Mr and Mrs Holger Braasch. Hull spoke to Braasch on the telephone, saying that he was in a position to sell two paintings by Gabriele Munter. Braasch expressed an interest in the paintings. Towards the end of November 1984, one of the employees of Harlingdon, Mr Runkel, visited Hull to see the paintings. Hull told Runkel that he did not know much about the paintings, that he had never heard of Gabriele Munter and that he thought little of her work. Runkel and Braasch did not have any special expertise or training for the assessment of German expressionist paintings either. Runkel's examination could not have revealed that the painting in question was not by Munter.

Runkel agreed to buy the painting for £ 6,000 if and when Harlingdon found a customer to purchase it from them. Harlingdon informed Hull on 3 December 1984 that the company had found a customer and would purchase the paintings. The paintings were delivered, along with an invoice that mentioned the paintings as 'GABRIELE MUNTER, 1877–1962 Dorfstrasse in Oberbayern oil on board 39' 48 cm MS No 961 6,000'. The customer purchased the paintings from Harlingdon in February 1985 and sent the paintings for examination to the keepers of the estate of Gabriele Munter in Munich. They communicated to him that the paintings were fake. Following this, in March, Braasch took back the paintings from the purchaser and refunded the price. Braasch then asked Hull to take back the paintings and refund £ 6,000. Hull refused. Was it a sale by descrip-

tion? What was the description put up by the seller? Did the buyer examine the goods?

The painting is described to be by Munter in the catalogue and invoice by the seller. The seller, however, while negotiating with the buyer, tells him that he does not know much about the paintings of Munter and thought little of her work. If the sale was a 'sale by description', the seller would have to supply a genuine Munter painting. If the conversations between the buyer and seller had made the description ineffective, the seller would not be bound to the description. It would just be a painting. The judgment in the case was given by three judges: Nourse, Slade, and Stuart-Smith. The first two maintained that the negotiations between the parties had modified the description, while Stuart-Smith maintained that it was a sale by description. By the majority rule, the opinion of the two judges prevailed.

The case was in appeal. Thus, the judges referred to the judgment of the lower court. Here, plaintiff refers to the buyer and defendant to the seller. Section 13 of the English act provides the equivalent of Section 15 of the Indian act; that is, in a 'sale by description' the goods must correspond with the description. Justice Nourse noted:

The judge found that both at the time when the agreement was made and subsequently when the invoice was made out both Mr Hull and Mr Runkel believed that the painting was by Munter and that, if either had not believed that, the deal would not have been made. He made the following further findings:
'In my judgment Mr Runkel must have known and accepted that Mr Hull was disclaiming any judgment, knowledge or private information which would or could have grounded the latter's earlier statement to Mr Braasch that he had two paintings by Gabriele Munter for sale ... I think the only conclusion which can

be drawn from the unusual facts of this case is that it was Mr Runkel's exercise of his own judgment as to the quality of the pictures, including the factor of the identity of their painter, which induced him to enter into the agreement he made with Mr Hull. However, I am not satisfied that without the attribution given what followed in the circumstances in which it was made, Mr Runkel would not have purchased the painting. If it had never been made Mr Runkel would never have gone to see the paintings. But when he did go and examine the painting he considered whether it was a Munter or not: he did agree to buy it regardless of the attribution, because he relied on his own judgment. ... It was reliance on his own assessment and not on anything said by a man who had gone out of his way to stress his ignorance of the paintings which led Mr Runkel astray.'

Thus did the judge find as a fact that the plaintiffs did not rely on the description of the painting as one by Gabriele Munter They relied only on their own assessment. ... Section 13(1) of the Sale of Goods Act 1979 is in these terms:

> 'Where there is a contract for the sale of goods by description, there is an implied condition that the goods will correspond with the description.'

The sales to which the subsection is expressed to apply are sales 'by description'. Authority apart, those words would suggest that the description must be influential in the sale, not necessarily alone, but so as to become an essential term, i.e. a condition, of the contract. Without such influence a description cannot be said to be one by which the contract for the sale of the goods is made.

I think that the authorities to which we were referred are consistent with this view of s 13(1).

Thus, as the case brings out, in every sale where there is a description, the sale need not be a 'sale by description'. The reverse of this is that a sale of specific goods may be a sale by description. In a sale across a counter in a retail store, the seller shows goods to the buyer. The buyer agrees to buy the specific piece which has been shown to him. Yet, it is understood between the parties that the buyer wants to buy goods of that description and not that specific piece. In *Grant* v. *Australian Knitting Mills Ltd*[5] the Privy Council noted:

> It may also be pointed out that there is a sale by description even though the buyer is buying something displayed before him on the counter; a thing is sold by description, though it is specific, so long as it is sold not merely as the specific thing but as a thing corresponding to a description, e.g., woollen under-garments, a hot water bottle, a secondhand reaping machine, to select a few obvious illustrations.

The position would also apply in a self-service store. While the customers bring in their trolley a specific piece, they offer to buy goods of that description and not that specific piece.

SCOPE OF DESCRIPTION

The formulation of the principle on sale by description, like most of common law, is located in the practices in the past. At a stage when trade and commerce was basic, in primary produce, there were limited features for describing the goods. It was not 'descriptions' of the goods but 'description' of the goods. In the present context, goods are identified by giving multiple descriptions. Some aspects may be central to the contract while others may be subsidiary. For example, the colour of a car may be a subsidiary aspect while the model of the car would be a core part of the contract. This raises the question of the scope of the term 'description'. Let us examine this aspect with the following case.

[5] *Grant* v. *Australian Knitting Mills Ltd*, (1935) All ER Rep 209.

RE MOORE & CO, LTD V. LANDAUER & CO

Moore & Co, Ltd entered into a contract to sell Landauer & Co. 3,100 cases of Australian canned fruits.[6] Each case was to contain thirty cans. When the ship brought the goods to the buyer in the UK, the buyer found that half of the consignment was packed in cases containing thirty cans and the rest was in cases containing twenty-four cans. The buyer had received the contracted number of cans but the packing in the cases was not in accordance with the contract. The buyer rejected the goods. The Court of Appeal was to decide whether the buyer was justified in rejecting under Section 13 of the UK Act which is equivalent of Section 15 of the Sale of Goods Act, 1930. Atkin LJ noted:

… the stipulation that there should be two and a half dozen in a case is part of the description of the goods. There was, therefore, an implied condition that the goods when tendered should correspond with the description, and it appears to me that that condition was broken, and there was a right to reject.

Bankes L.J. noted:

That question of law, in my opinion, admits of a very simple answer. If it is true to say, as I think it is, that this is a sale of goods by description, and the statement in the contract that the goods were packed thirty tins to a case is part of the description, then there is by operation of law an implied condition that the goods should correspond to that description. That is the effect of s 13 of the Sale of Goods Act, 1893. It follows, therefore, that these goods did not correspond with the description.

Goods can be described on multiple parameters. In the above case, the goods had to be cut fruit in cans and packed thirty cans in each case. Once the packing is taken as a description of the goods, it becomes a condition and the buyer can reject the goods for its non-conformity. It cannot be an answer that the description was not material to the goods. The following case is also on this theme.

Arcos, Limited v. E.A. Ronaasen and Son

Arcos Limited was the agent for selling timber for the Russian Government in England.[7] The company entered into an agreement to supply staves to a buyer in the United Kingdom, E.A. Ronaasen and Son. A stave is a long thin curved piece of wood used for making a large container, like a barrel. The dimensions were provided in the contract. The specification admitted margins for length and breadth. However, there was no margin for thickness. The thickness was invariant at half-an-inch.

The buyer had made it known to the seller that he needed the staves for making cement barrels, thus the seller was under an obligation to supply staves that would meet the purpose of making cement barrels. The buyer had been eager to reject the goods, and, when the goods arrived in London, claimed that the goods were not shipped within the stipulated period in the contract. Arbitration did not find this assertion to be correct. The buyer then rejected the goods on the ground that they did not conform to the description in the contract, in that they were not half-an-inch thick.

In arbitration, the dimensions of the goods could be examined only nine months after the goods arrived in London. By this time, the staves had been exposed to rain and moisture. On examination, the arbitrator

---

[6] *Re Moore & Co, Ltd v. Landauer & Co*, (1921) 2 KB 519.

[7] *Arcos, Limited v. E.A. Ronaasen and Son*, (1933) AC 470.

found that none of the staves were less than half-an-inch. About 5 per cent were half-an-inch; a large proportion was over half-an-inch, but not more than nine-sixteenths of an inch. He found that the staves were fit for use in the manufacture of cement barrels and reported: 'their thickness was closer to 1/2 inch than it is now and I am satisfied that the staves when shipped were commercially within and merchantable under the contract specification.' The case came before the House of Lords for decision. Lord Atkin ruled:

On the facts as stated by the umpire as of the time of inspection only about 5 per cent. of the goods corresponded with the description: and the umpire finds it impossible to say what proportion conformed at the time of shipment.

It was contended that in all commercial contracts the question was whether there was a 'substantial' compliance with the contract: there always must be some margin: and it is for the tribunal of fact to determine whether the margin is exceeded or not. I cannot agree. If the written contract specifies conditions of weight, measurement and the like, those conditions must be complied with. ... the conditions of the contract must be strictly performed. If a condition is not performed the buyer has a right to reject.

The real reason for the buyer's rejection was the change in the market conditions. The buyer benefited by rejecting the goods. As the description is a condition, it has to be strictly followed. Deviations would bring uncertainty in commercial contracts where goods may have been sold to sub-buyers. The case also demonstrates that once an aspect of the goods qualifies to be a description, the buyer has a right to it. It can be no defence that the aspect was a secondary aspect or of no material relevance. The courts have not been comfortable with this outcome. In a case on ship charter, *Reardon Smith Line Limited* v. *Hansen-Tangen Hansen-Tangen* v. *Sanko*

Steamship Company,[8] the charter was to hire a ship of a particular description. He argued that the principles of sale by description could be extended to hiring. In that context, Lord Wilberforce commented:

In the first place, I am not prepared to accept that authorities as to 'description' in sale of goods cases are to be extended, or applied, to such a contract as we have here. Some of these cases either in themselves (Re Moore & Co. and Landauer & Co.) or as they have been interpreted (e.g. Behn v. Burness) I find to be excessively technical and due for fresh examination in this House. Even if a strict and technical view must be taken as regards the description of unascertained future goods (e.g. commodities) as to which each detail of the description must be assumed to be vital, it may be, and in my opinion is, right to treat other contracts of sale of goods in a similar manner to other contracts generally, so as to ask whether a particular item in a description constitutes a substantial ingredient of the 'identity' of the thing sold, and only if it does to treat it as a condition ... I would respectfully endorse what was recently said by Roskill L.J. in Cehave NV v. Bremer Handelsgesellschaft mbH [1976] 1 QB 44 at 71: 'In principle it is not easy to see why the law relating to contracts for the sale of goods should be different from the law relating to the performance of other contractual obligations, whether charterparties or other types of contract. Sale of goods law is but one branch of the general law of contract. It is desirable that the same legal principles should apply to the law of contract as a whole and that different legal principles should not apply to different branches of that law.' The general law of contract has developed, along much more rational lines (e.g. Hong Kong Fir Shipping Co. Ltd v. Kawasaki Kisen Kaisha Ltd), in attending to the nature and gravity of a breach or departure rather than in accepting rigid categories which do or do not automatically give a right to

---

[8] *Reardon Smith Line Limited* v. *Hansen-Tangen Hansen-Tangen* v. *Sanko Steamship Company*, (1976) WLR 989.

rescind, and if the choice were between extending cases under the Sale of Goods Act 1893 into other fields, or allowing more modern doctrine to infect those cases, my preference would be clear.

In the above passage Roskill L.J. wondered why the law of sale of goods should be different from contract law. With specialization in society, it is inevitable that different branches of law would appear. It is equally inevitable that the sale of goods, while building on the foundation of contract law, will follow its own trajectory. Lord Wilberforce found the position taken in *Re Moore & Co, Ltd* and *Landauer & Co* excessively technical Legal text emerges in a given context, and as the context changes, a gap develops between the text and the context. The text has to be interpreted to make sense of the changed context. Thus, law always finds itself in such interpretive gaps. On this theme, one can note that the attempts by Denning to make contract law relevant in the changed context failed in *Gibson v. Manchester City Council*.[9] At other times, the legislature changes the law. The re-enactment of the law in the UK has assimilated the above concern on the scope of description. However, as the law in India remains unaltered, the above cases on the scope of description remain relevant.

'BUYER BEWARE' AND EXCEPTIONS

The principle of *caveat emptor* and exceptions to the principle are in Section 16 of the Sale of Goods Act, 1930. Towards exploring the scope of Section 16, let us do some preliminary work with the following illustrations. A buyer placed an order for a mirror of certain dimensions. On taking delivery of the mirror, the buyer realized that the mirror

was scratched. He insists on returning the mirror and getting back his money. The seller says that a few scratches on the mirrors are only to be expected. How would we decide the rival claims? The buyer and seller have contracted for 'a mirror'. The seller is claiming that scratched mirrors fulfil the description of 'a mirror', while the buyer disagrees. We cannot leave it to the buyer and seller to decide among themselves. The seller would try to pass badly scratched mirrors, while the buyer would insist on a mirror without any scratch. The question is not of their relative contentions. It is about giving a meaning to the word 'mirror'. Language and words are used by everyone. To give a meaning to the word, we should step out from this dispute and take an objective view of what buyers, sellers, and consumers generally understand by the word 'mirror' and how badly scratched a mirror might be for one to conclude that it cannot be called one.

One could ask, would buyers buy it under that name? A buyer would buy goods only if the goods are fit for the purpose of his use. Such goods are said to be of merchantable quality. If there are willing buyers for certain goods, merchants would buy from each other and move the goods in the trade channel. Thus, we could alternately ask, would traders buy and sell the goods under that name? Goods would not move in trade if these cannot be used, and goods would be traded only if these are fit for the ordinary purposes for which these are intended.

Now, a mirror that is completely scratched up is certainly not of merchantable quality. It does not deserve to be called a mirror. Other goods that would not be considered to be of merchantable quality could be a pen that does not write, a clock that does not keep time, a computer that does not boot, and a CD player that does not play CDs. But if a mirror is not

---

[9] *Gibson* v. *Manchester City Council*, (1979) 1 All ER 972.

completely scratched, it becomes a matter of degree and the question would be whether, in the given context of society and market, such a mirror would be considered to be of merchantable quality. What could have been an acceptable mirror fifty years back, may not pass as a mirror today. A quality product in one country may be inadequate in another. In a given context, goods of merchantable quality imply a minimum quality of the goods that exists in trade and is used in a society and market.

There is another dimension to merchantability of goods. Some goods can be used for multiple purposes. For example, mirror is used as an everyday household item, as a reflector in solar heating, and in the manufacture of medical and scientific equipment. The buyer may have bought the mirror for use in the manufacturing of medical equipment. From his point of view, it is not adequate that the mirrors are good enough for household use. The mirrors must be of a higher quality than that. However, if the supplied mirrors are fit for any one use (say household use), they deserve the name 'mirror' and are of merchantable quality. The buyer contracted to get a 'mirror' and had been delivered a 'mirror'. If he needed a mirror for a specific use, he should have further stipulated the quality of the mirror required. The criterion of merchantable quality was evolved early. In *Gardiner* v. *Grey*, in 1815, the court ruled: '...the intention of both parties must be taken to be, that it shall be saleable in the market under the denomination mentioned in the contract between them. The purchaser cannot be supposed to buy goods to lay them on a dunghill.'[10]

Another early case demonstrating the concept of merchantability is *Jones* v. *Just*. A buyer bought Manilla hemp. On arrival, the goods were found to be damaged and not saleable under that description. The buyer resold the goods under the description 'Manilla hemp with all faults'. He received about 75 per cent of what merchantable Manilla hemp would have got him. The buyer moved the court to recover the difference as damages. The court ruled: 'It appears to us that, in every contract to supply goods of a specified description which the buyer has no opportunity to inspect, the goods must not only in fact, answer the specific description, but must also be saleable or merchantable under that description.'[11]

Let us take a case where a buyer asks the seller to be given glue that can stick ceramic. The seller gives him a tube of glue that is fit for sticking paper, but not ceramic. The seller was free to tell the buyer that he did not know enough to help. Having made the buyer rely on his judgment, he should be bound to the obligation of supplying glue that would stick ceramic. This is the general sense of the second exception to *caveat emptor*.

We have tried to look at the law of sale of goods as a logical extension of contract law. In addition to this, however, we need to understand that commercial law developed over time to address the changing contexts of trade and commerce. With the development in trade and commerce, the producers and sellers could come to a fixed and definite forum—the marketplace—to buy or sell their goods. Further, through division of labour and specialization, manufacturers and traders became more informed about the goods they traded in. An imbalance developed between the capabilities of the sellers and the buyers.

[10] Cited in *Aswan Engineering Establishment Company* v. *Lupdine Limited*, (1987) 1 All ER 135.

[11] *Jones* v. *Just*, (1861–73) All ER Rep Ext 1975.

By dealing in certain products regularly, the sellers came to possess far greater knowledge in those products than the average buyer. The buyer also recognized this and came to rely on the skill and judgment of the seller. The seller, was, of course, free to tell the buyer that he did not possess sufficient knowledge about a product to be able to help the buyer. However, having represented to the buyer that he could be relied upon, he was required to act accordingly. He must supply goods that would be fit for the purpose asked for by the buyer. Thus came the exception to the maxim of *caveat emptor*: if a buyer described the purpose for which he wanted a thing, and relied on the skill and judgment of a seller who dealt in that particular product, the goods should be fit for that purpose. Section 16 of the Sale of Goods Act, 1930, provides these principles. Let us become familiar with the text of the law.

Section 16. Implied Conditions as to quality or fitness: Subject to the provisions of this Act and of any other law for the time being in force, there is no implied warranty or condition as to the quality or fitness for any particular purpose of goods supplied under a contract of sale, except as follows:

(1) Where the buyer, expressly or by implication, makes known to the seller, the particular purpose for which the goods are required, so as to show that the buyer relies on the seller's skill or judgment, and the goods are of a description which it is in the course of the seller's business to supply (whether he is the manufacturer or producer or not), there is an implied condition that the goods shall be reasonably fit for such purpose:

Provided that, in the case of a contract for the sale of a specified article under its patent or other trade name, there is no implied condition as to its fitness for any particular purpose.

(2) Where goods are bought by description from a seller who deals in goods of that description (whether he is the manufacturer or producer or not), there is an implied condition that the goods shall be of merchantable quality:

Provided that, if the buyer has examined the goods, there shall be no implied condition as regards defects which such examination ought to have revealed.

(3) An implied warranty or condition as to quality or fitness for a particular purpose may be annexed by the usage of trade.

(4) An express warranty or condition does not negative a warranty or condition implied by this Act, unless inconsistent therewith.

We shall summarize, abridge, and rephrase the section for our understanding: The opening lines state the 'buyer beware' principle with the exception that the buyer can claim benefit under Sections 16(1) and 16(2). Section 16(1) provides that if the buyer has relied on the skill and judgment of the seller, the goods should be fit for that purpose. In the cases 'where goods are bought by description', Section 16(2) imposes an 'implied condition' that the goods should be of 'merchantable quality'. The section also requires that the benefit is available only if the seller sells goods of that description. This, however, has never been an important point. It has often been assumed that if a trader has sold goods, he must be selling goods of that description. Section 15 has already provided that the buyer must get what has been described to him. Thus, the goods should not only be what has been described, in addition, it must be merchantable, that is, fit for the basic purpose for which it is used. On the same principles on which Section 15 treated the situation where the buyer has examined the goods, Section 16(2) takes away the benefit of merchantability in relation to apparent defects where the buyer has examined the goods. It assumes that the buyer has impliedly accepted the apparent shortcomings in the goods.

Thus, in a sale of goods, we should ask the following questions: has the buyer relied on the skill and judgment of the seller? Is it a sale by description, with or without examination? Has the buyer got what was described? Is the product merchantable? Only when none of this is available to the buyer would it become a case of 'buyer beware'. We will now explore how the British courts have given meaning to this provision. Section 16 of the Indian law is drawn from Section 14 of the British law, the Sale of Goods Act, 1893.

SECTION 14(1): RELIANCE ON THE SKILL AND JUDGMENT OF THE SELLER

Preist v. Last

Preist asked Last, a chemist, for a hot water bottle.[12] Last showed him one. Preist asked Last if it would stand boiling water. Last said it would not but that it would stand hot water. Preist bought the bottle. Within a week, the bottle burst. It turned out that pure rubber formed a very small proportion of the material in the bottle. The buyer claimed damages for the violation of Section 14(1). The court worked through the key terms in the clause: 'makes known to the seller, the particular purpose for which the goods are required, so as to show that the buyer relies on the seller's skill or judgment'. Justice Collin noted:

There are many goods which, in themselves, have no special efficacy for any particular purpose, but may be fitly used for a multitude of purposes. In a case where goods of that sort are purchased, it would be necessary, in order to bring it within subsection (1) of Section 14, to show what particular purpose the goods were sold for. But when you begin with the fact that the description by which the goods were sold was such as to show that the goods were only capable of being used for one

[12] *Preist and Wife* v. *Last*, (1903) 2 KB 148.

particular purpose, then, as it seems to me, you have a sale for a particular purpose within the meaning of the subsection.

In relation to reliance on the skill and judgment of the seller, Justice Walton noted:

I have no hesitation in finding that when the buyer told the druggist that he required a bottle for use as a hot water bottle, he did it in such a way as to show that he relied on the skill and judgment of the seller. I think that when people go into a shop in which these articles are dealt with, they are entitled to expect that some skill or judgment has been exercised by the shopkeeper in selecting the goods, so that when you buy something which the shopkeeper professes to sell, you may expect to get a thing which is of some use for the purpose for which it is sold and is not mere rubbish.

Jones v. Padgett

Jones, a tailor, ordered some 'indigo blue cloth' from Padgett, who were wool manufacturers. One of the ordinary uses of indigo blue cloth was the making of servants' liveries, though it was also frequently used for other purposes as well, such as for carriage linings, caps, and boots. Jones made servants' liveries from the cloth, but discovered that it was not strong enough for the hard usage to which servants' liveries are subjected. As Jones had not communicated the purpose for which he wanted the goods, he could not claim the benefit of Section 14(1). The court ruled:

There is no doubt that if a manufacturer sells an article which he knows is bought for a particular purpose, he impliedly warrants that it is fit for that particular purpose. That is a principle which was established some sixty years ago in the case of Jones v. Bright and has been acted upon ever since. But the present case is not within that rule, because nothing was mentioned to the seller as to the particular purpose for which this cloth was bought, and there was nothing to fix him with knowledge of that purpose.

It was a case of sale of a fabric by its name. As the fabric was fit for several purposes, it was held to be of merchantable quality. Thus, Jones had no remedy.

Baldry v. Marshall

The proviso to Section 14(1) states that the benefit of the subsection is not available to a buyer where there is a 'sale of a specified article under its patent or other trade name'. *Baldry* v. *Marshall* explores this proviso.

Baldry wrote on 13 April 1923, to Marshalls, who were motor car dealers: 'Can you tell me if the Bugatti eight cylinder is likely to be on the market this year and if so, will you send particulars.'[13] Marshalls, in reply, sent the full particulars and added: 'As no doubt you are already aware, we specialise in the sale of these cars, and are in a position to supply you with all information necessary.' Baldry knew nothing about Bugatti cars except for what he had read in newspapers. He informed Marshalls that he wanted a fast car, comfortable and suitable for the ordinary purposes of a touring car. Marshalls said that the Bugatti car would satisfy those requirements, and he also showed him a specimen. Baldry then gave Marshalls an order on one of their printed order forms on which were printed the following words: 'Please supply me, on the terms and conditions hereinafter specified, with one eight cylinder Bugatti car, fully equipped and finished to standard specification as per car inspected.' The form was signed by Baldry. On the back of the contract, the following disclaimers were printed:

The company reserves the right to withdraw any model or alter specifications or prices without notice. Illustrations and specifications must be taken as a general guide and not as binding details.

[13] *Baldry* v. *Marshall*, (1925) 1 KB 260.

The manufacturer extends guarantee against any breakage of parts due to faulty material.

It also contained the clause: 'Cars are sold on condition that the foregoing guarantee is accepted instead of and expressly excludes any other guarantee or warranty, statutory or otherwise.' The intention was to exclude all conditions as well as warranties. In this context and in view of the above communications and the written contract, the court had to decide whether the case was a sale by trade name or that of reliance on the skill and judgment of the seller. The court ruled:

It is however, clear to my mind upon the evidence that it was not in fact, sold under a trade name within the meaning of the proviso. The mere fact that an article sold is described in the contract by its trade name does not necessarily make the sale a sale under a trade name. Whether it is so or not depends upon the circumstances. I may illustrate my meaning by reference to three different cases. First, where a buyer asks a seller for an article which will fulfil some particular purpose, and in answer to that request, the seller sells him an article by a well-known trade name, there, I think, it is clear that the proviso does not apply. Secondly, where the buyer says to the seller, 'I have been recommended such and such an article'—mentioning it by its trade name—'will it suit my particular purpose?', naming the purpose, and thereupon, the seller sells it without more, there again, I think the proviso has no application. But there is a third case where the buyer says to a seller, 'I have been recommended so and so'—giving its trade name—'as suitable for the particular purpose for which I want it. Please sell it to me.' In that case, I think it is equally clear that the proviso would apply and that the implied condition of the thing's fitness for the purpose named would not arise. In my opinion, the test of an article having been sold under its trade name within the meaning of the proviso is: Did the buyer specify it under its trade name in such a way as to indicate that he is satisfied, rightly or wrongly, that it will answer his purpose, and that he is not relying on the skill or judgment of the seller, however great that skill or judgment may be? Here, there is nothing to show that Baldry, when describing the car in the contract as an 'eight cylinder Bugatti car,' after he had communicated to the Marshalls the purpose for which he wanted it, meant to intimate that he was not relying on their skill and judgment.

Grant v. Australian Knitting Mills Ltd

This Privy Council case is the best summary of the position of the law that emerged after codification. Grant bought two woollen underwear garments from John Marlin and Co., who dealt in such goods.[14] John Marlin had purchased them in the ordinary course, along with other stock, from the Australian Knitting Mills, the manufacturers. Grant put on one suit on the morning of 28 June 1931. By evening, he had started to feel an itch. The next day, redness appeared on the front of each of his ankles over an area of about 2.5 by 1.5 inches. Grant treated himself with calamine lotion, but the irritation was such that he scratched the area till he bled. He changed his underwear and put on the other set that he had purchased from the retailers. Grant's skin trouble continued. On 13 July he consulted a dermatologist, who suspected the undergarments were the cause of dermatitis. Grant returned the garments to the retailers with the intimation that they had given him dermatitis. Grant's condition got worse and worse. For weeks, he remained confined to bed. In November, he became convalescent. The doctor treating Grant feared that he might die.

The manufacturer attempted to attribute the problem to the sensitive nature of Grant's skin and not to a defect in the garment. Detailed evidence was brought out to show

otherwise. The manufacturing process and the treating of the garments with chemicals had left sulphites in the garments. These should have been washed off the cloth but were not. The combination of free sulphites with sweat formed sulphur dioxide, sulphurous acid, and sulphuric acid. Grant moved the courts in Australia seeking remedy for defective goods against the retailer. Australia, like other Commonwealth countries, had borrowed the same provision on implied conditions and warranties in relation to the sale of goods as Britain. Since Britain was the head of the Commonwealth countries, the case came before the highest judicial body, the Privy Council, in Britain. The Privy Council noted:

So far as concerns the retailers, counsel for the respondents conceded that, if it were held that the garments contained improper chemicals and caused the disease, the retailers were liable for breach of implied ... condition, under section 14 of the South Australia Sale of Goods Act, 1895, which is identical with section 14 of the English Sale of Goods Act, 1893.

The Privy Council was of the opinion that the case attracted both the clauses, relying on the skill and judgment of the sellers and the goods not being of merchantable quality. We will note the part of the judgment on reliance on the skill and judgment here. The court noted:

Section 14 begins by a general enunciation of the old rule of caveat emptor, and proceeds to state by way of exception, the two implied conditions by which the old rule has been changed to the rule of caveat vendor: the change has been rendered necessary by the conditions of modern commerce and trade. ... The first exception, if its terms are satisfied, entitles the buyer to the benefit of an implied condition that the goods are reasonably fit for the purpose for which the goods are supplied, but only if that purpose is made known

[14] *Grant* v. *Australian Knitting Mills Ltd*, (1935) All ER Rep 209.

to the seller 'so as to show that the buyer relies on the seller's skill or judgment.' It is clear that the reliance must be brought home to the mind of the seller, expressly or by implication.

In applying the clause, the Privy Council formulated:

The reliance will seldom be express; it will usually arise by implication from the circumstances; thus, to take a case like that in question of a purchase from a retailer, the reliance will be in general, inferred from the fact that a buyer goes to the shop in the confidence that the tradesman has selected his stock with skill and judgment; the retailer need know nothing about the process of manufacture; it is immaterial whether he be manufacturer or not; the main inducement to deal with a good retail shop is the expectation that the tradesman will have bought the right goods of a good make; the goods sold must be, as they were in the present case, goods of a description which it is in the course of the seller's business to supply; there is no need to specify in terms the particular purpose for which the buyer requires the goods; which is none the less the particular purpose within the meaning of the section because it is the only purpose for which anyone would ordinarily want the goods. In this case, the garments were naturally intended and only intended to be worn next the skin. ... the requirements of exception (1) were complied with. The conversation at the shop in which the appellant discussed questions of price and of the different makes did not affect the fact that he was substantially relying on the retailers to supply him with a correct article.

The court was describing that the old rule of *caveat emptor*, overrun by the exceptions, had become *caveat vendor*. This was possible by giving wide expression to the exceptions to the rule in the section. A retailer who sold a product was taken to be dealing in those goods. Thus, other than a private person selling the goods, every sale is taken to be a sale 'in the course of the seller's business'. The reliance of the buyer on the seller need not be express. If the goods are for only one use, it is implied that the buyer relied on the seller in giving goods that would be fit for the purpose.

Cammell Laird & Co, Ltd v. Manganese Bronze and Brass Co, Ltd

Cammell Laird Ltd, a shipbuilding company, had an order to build two ships for a customer.[15] The company approached Manganese Bronze and Brass Co, Ltd, who were specialists in making propellers. The shipbuilding company ordered four, and provided specifications of the dimensions and other particulars, as well as detailed drawings. The drawings indicated the thickness along the midline of the propeller but did not contain further information for thickness and shaping of the blades. The engine type to be used in the ships was communicated to the propeller maker. The propellers supplied matched with the drawings given by the shipbuilder but were not suitable for use in the ships. The case before the court was on the application of Section 14(1). Lord Macmillan noted:

Now there is no question that it is in the course of the respondents' business to supply ships' propellers. But there is room for argument as to whether the appellants made known to the respondents 'the particular purpose' for which the propeller was wanted. On the one hand, it was contended that no particular purpose was expressed or implied which the propeller was to serve, and that if any purpose was implied it was merely the ordinary and general purpose which all ships' propellers serve, namely, as the word itself connotes, the purpose of propulsion. On the other hand, it was contended that the contract disclosed that the propeller was wanted for a particular purpose, the

[15] *Cammell Laird & Co, Ltd* v. *Manganese Bronze and Brass Co, Ltd,* (1934) AC 402.

purpose, namely, of being fitted to and working in association with the ship and engines No 972 which the appellants were building. Having regard to the decision and the reasoning in the case of Manchester Liners, Ltd and another v Rea, Ltd (1) I am of opinion that there was in the present instance sufficient disclosure of a particular purpose within the statutory meaning.

But that is not enough. To get the benefit of s 14(1) the particular purpose must be so made known as to show that the buyer relies on the seller's skill or judgment. The respondents' argument was that the appellants by their detailed specification so tied the respondents' hands as to negative the idea that anything was left or intended to be left to their skill or judgment, except mere matters of material and workmanship, as to which there was no suggestion of failure on their part. That there was an important margin within which the respondents' skill and judgment had scope for exercise is best demonstrated by the fact, already mentioned, that while all the three propellers which they made for this ship were in conformity with the specification, it was only at the third attempt that the respondents succeeded in supplying a propeller that would work.

The defect, whatever it was, which existed in the first two propellers as well as the remedying of that defect achieved in the third propeller, thus lay in the region within which the respondents were free, so far as the specification went, to exercise their skill and judgment. I, therefore, reach the conclusion that there was room here for the exercise of the respondents' skill and judgment, and I hold that the particular purpose for which the propeller was wanted was so made known to the respondents as to show that the appellants relied on their skill and judgment. The appellants are thus entitled, in my opinion, to succeed on both the grounds which I have discussed.

Teheran-Europe Co., Ltd v. S.T. Belton (Tractors), Ltd

This case shows an interesting aspect of reliance on the skill and judgment of the seller. Teheran-Europe Co., Ltd was a company

incorporated in Tehran. It carried on the business of importing and reselling machinery.[16] The company bought machinery in England through an intermediary called Richards Marketing, Ltd, an English company. Richards Marketing Ltd entered into a contract with S.T. Belton (Tractors), Ltd to buy twelve air compressors. The sellers were informed that the compressor were for resale in Teheran. The parties entered into a written contract that described the goods and terms of delivery. The buyers then claimed to terminate the contracts on the grounds that the compressors were not 'reasonably fit for the purpose of resale in Persia as new and unused machines'. The buyers contended that the term was implied under Section 14(1) of the Sale of Goods Act, 1893. Lord Denning delivered the following judgment:

Now, as I read this contract, it was a contract for the sale of goods by description. These were air compressors, described as new and unused—described in the catalogue and in the correspondence. There was clearly an implied term that they should comply with the description as set out in s. 13 (1) of the Sale of Goods Act, 1893.

So far as s. 14 (1) is concerned, it is quite clear that the buyers made known to the sellers that they were required for re-sale in Persia. ... The section of the Act of 1893, however, contains a further requirement before a condition is implied. The particular purpose might be made known to the seller so as to show that the buyer relies on the seller's skill and judgment. The judge held that, once the purpose was made known, there was an inference that the buyer relied on the seller's skill and judgment.

...

We can revert once more to the Act of 1893. The particular purpose must be made known 'so as to show that the buyer relies on the seller's skill

---

[16] *Teheran-Europe Co., Ltd. v. S.T. Belton (Tractors), Ltd.,* (1968) 2 QB 545.

or judgment'. That means that the buyer makes the particular purpose known to the seller in such a way that the seller knows that he is being relied on. That cannot be said here. The defendants here did not know they were being relied on for re-sale in Persia. They knew nothing of conditions in Persia. The plaintiffs knew all about those conditions. The plaintiffs saw the machine here. They read its description. They relied on their own skill and judgment to see that it was suitable for re-sale in Persia and not on the defendants. At all events, they did not make the purpose known to the defendants in such circumstances as to show him that they relied on the defendants' skill and judgment. So I do not think that there was an implied term that they should be fit for the purpose of being re-sold in Persia. So on this point I differ from the judge and I would allow the appeal accordingly.

The buyer can avail of the protection of Subsection 1 only if the seller has made a sale in the course of the seller's business. This requirement is not a significant one. Sale by every manufacturer, retailer, or trader is taken to be in the course of the seller's business. The reliance on the judgment of the seller can be express or implied. If goods have only one use, as the Privy Council in *Grant* v. *Australian Knitting Mills* showed, it is implied that the seller relies on the skill and judgment of the seller to supply goods that serve the purpose. In other cases, two things should happen. The buyer should make it known to the seller the purpose he wants it for and also that he is relying on his skill and judgment. In *Cammell Laird & Co, Ltd v. Manganese Bronze and Brass Co, Ltd*, the seller had made it known for the kind of engine with which the propellers were to be used. As the seller was a specialist in propeller making, it was implied that the buyer was relying on his skill and judgment in supplying propellers that would work with the specified engines. In contrast, in *Teheran-Europe Co., Ltd.* v. *S.T.*

Belton (Tractors), Ltd., it was communicated to the seller that the compressors were for exports to Tehran and sale there. However, this was merely sharing of information. There was no express reliance on the skill and judgment of the seller to supply compressors suitable for use in Tehran. The reliance cannot be inferred as the seller had no knowledge of the conditions in Tehran. It is the buyer who has to establish that he relied on the skill and judgment of the seller.

MERCHANTABLE QUALITY
Section 16(2) provides the following exception to *caveat emptor*: the goods must be of merchantable quality. There are three conditions for its application. First, the goods should be bought from a seller who deals in goods of that description. This is similar to the provision in Section 16(1) requiring the sale to be in the course of the seller's business. It will apply to every sale other than sale by a private person. Two, goods should be bought by description. We noted while discussing sale by description that even if the goods are specific, if the intent is to buy goods of that description, it is a sale by description. The Privy Council noted in *Grant* v. *Australian Knitting Mills* that a sale across the counter is a sale by description. In *Godley* v. *Perry*[17] the court noted: 'That a sale over the counter can be a sale "by description" … that is no less, in my judgment, a "sale by description" than one where an order is placed on the strength of a catalogue.' Similarly, a sale in a self-service store is a sale by description. The third condition is that the goods shall be of merchantable quality. The meaning and scope of merchantability deserves discussion.

The concept of merchantability, as reviewed earlier, had come from prior centuries

[17] *Godley* v. *Perry*, (1960) 1 All ER 36.

where the goods traded in were primary produce with specific use. With the development of manufacturing, trade, and commerce, it is only understandable that if the quality of all the goods were to be described by a single word, 'merchantable quality', the word would find different meanings, and that it would be relevant in different contexts. Other times, the differences may be conceptual. Some early cases emphasized the saleability of the goods, that is, whether the goods could be sold under that description. An expression of this was in *Bristol Tramways* v. *Fiat Motors*.[18] The court noted:

… the implied condition that the goods are of merchantable quality applies to all goods bought from a seller who deals in goods of that description, whether they are sold under a patent or trade rumps or otherwise. … The phrase in section 14(2) is, in my opinion, used as meaning that the article is of such quality and in such condition that a reasonable man acting reasonably would, after a full examination, accept it under the circumstances of the case in performance of his offer to buy that article, and whether he buys for his own use or to sell again so as to make the term 'saleable' apply.

In the subsequent decisions, however, the criterion was not saleability but the fitness for the purpose for which these goods were normally used. It is this meaning that has prevailed. In *Grant* v. *Australian Knitting Mills Ltd*, the Privy Council noted:

… whatever else 'merchantable' may mean, it does mean that the article sold, if only meant for one particular use in the ordinary course, is fit for that use. 'Merchantable' does not mean that the thing is saleable in the market simply because it looks all right; it is not merchantable in that event if it has defects unfitting it for its only proper use…

The reference to 'saleable in the market' was to displace the position taken in *Bristol Tramways* v. *Fiat Motors*. In *Cammell Laird & Co, Ltd* v. *Manganese Bronze and Brass Co, Ltd*,[19] Lord Wright noted, 'What sub-s (2) now means by 'merchantable quality' is that the goods in the form in which they were tendered were of no use for any purpose for which such goods would normally be used and hence were not saleable under that description.'

In *Grant* v. *Australian Knitting Mills Ltd*, the court noted that if a thing is used for only one purpose, the supplied goods should be 'fit for that use'. In contrast, if a thing can be put to multiple uses, the supplied goods would be merchantable if these are fit for any of the uses. In *Jones* v. *Padgett*,[20] fabric was not suited for one use but fit for another. The fabric was held to be of merchantable quality. In *Canada Atlantic Grain Export Company (Inc)* v. *Eilers*,[21] Wright J. noted:

It seems to follow that if goods are sold under a description which they fulfil, and if goods under that description are reasonably capable in ordinary user of several purposes, they are of merchantable quality within Sect. 14(2) of the Act if they are reasonably capable of being used for any one or more of such purposes, even if unfit for use for that one of those purposes which the particular buyer intended.

In *Henry Kendall and Sons* v. *William Lillico and Sons Limited*, reviewed later, the court reiterated the point. The following case took further the concept of merchantability of goods.

---

[18] *Bristol Tramways Carriage Co. Ltd* v. *Fiat Motors Ltd*, (1908–10) All ER Rep 113.

[19] *Cammell Laird & Co, Ltd* v. *Manganese Bronze and Brass Co, Ltd*, (1934) AC 402.

[20] *Jones* v. *Padgett*, (1890) 24 QBD 650.

[21] *Canada Atlantic Grain Export Company (Inc.)* v. *Eilers*, (1929) 35 Ll.L.Rep. 206.

Bartlett v. Sidney Marcus Limited

Bartlett visited Sidney Marcus Limited, a reputed second-hand motor car dealer.[22] The salesman took him for a test drive, and told him that there were some problems in the clutch and oil pressure gauge. Bartlett took them to be minor problems. The seller offered to repair the car and give it to him for £ 575, or the customer could take it for £ 550 and get it repaired himself. A written contract was drawn up, in which it was stated, after noting the price, 'Oil pressure and filter circuit to be checked. Clutch to be bled at client's expense.' The buyer took the car to be repaired after driving it for a month. The car was running fine other than the two problems with the oil gauge and the clutch. At the garage it was found that there were a number of things wrong with the car. Most serious of all was that the clutch thrust had been worn away. This was a far more serious defect than either the seller or the buyer had imagined. The garage took down the engine and repaired other things. Because the clutch thrust was so worn out, the cost of putting it right came to some £ 45. The buyer claimed the sum as damages from the seller. He alleged that there was an express term that the car was in perfect condition except that the clutch needed bleeding. The buyer claimed that the car was not of merchantable quality under Section 14(2). Lord Denning noted:

I take the tests as to merchantability stated by Lord Wright in Cammell Laird & Co. Ltd v. Manganese, Bronze and Brass Co. Ltd, and Grant v. Australian Knitting Mills Ltd. In the Cammell Laird case, Lord Wright said that the goods were unmerchantable if they were 'of no use' for any purpose for which such goods would normally be used. In the Grant case he said that merchantable meant that the article, if only meant for one particular use in the ordinary course, is 'fit for that use'. It seems to me that those two tests do not cover the whole ground. There is a considerable territory where on the one hand you cannot say that the article is 'of no use' at all, and on the other hand you cannot say that it is entirely 'fit for use'. The article may be of some use though not entirely efficient use for the purpose. It may not be in perfect condition but yet it is in usable condition. It is then, I think, merchantable. The propeller in the Cammell Laird case was in usable condition; whereas the underpants in the Grant case were not. I prefer this test to the more complicated test stated by Farwell L.J. in Bristol Tramways etc., Carriage Co Ltd v. Fiat Motors Ltd. It means that, on a sale of a secondhand car, it is merchantable if it is in usable condition, even though not perfect. This is very similar to the position under s 14(1). A secondhand car is 'reasonably fit for the purpose' if it is in a roadworthy condition, fit to be driven along the road in safety, even though not as perfect as a new car.

Applying those tests here, the car was far from perfect. It required a good deal of work to be done on it; but so do many secondhand cars. A buyer should realise that, when he buys a secondhand car, defects may appear sooner or later; and, in the absence of an express warranty, he has no redress. Even when he buys from a dealer the most that he can require is that it should be reasonably fit for the purpose of being driven along the road. This car came up to that requirement. The plaintiff drove the car away himself. It seemed to be running smoothly. He drove it for four weeks before he put it into the garage to have the clutch repaired. Then more work was necessary than he anticipated; but that does not mean that, at the time of the sale, it was not fit for use as a car. I do not think that, on the judge's findings, there was any evidence of a breach of the implied conditions.

On the whole, I would find that this car was reasonably fit for use as a car on the road and, in those circumstances, there was no breach of either s 14(1) or s 14(2) and I would allow the appeal accordingly.

[22] *Bartlett* v. *Sidney Marcus Limited*, 1965 (2) All ER 753.

Merchantability and Examination of Goods

The merchantability clause is not available to the buyer 'if the buyer has examined the goods ... as regards defects which such examination ought to have revealed'. In *Thornett & Fehr* v. *Beers & Son.*,[23] the buyers were given every facility to inspect glue stored in barrels. As they were short of time, they did not fully avail of the opportunity. They looked at the barrels and proceeded with the sale. Later, they claimed the glue was not of merchantable quality. The court referred to the wording of the Section 14(2) and noted that there should be an examination and the examination ought have brought the defect to note. The court noted: 'I think they examined the goods within the meaning of the sub-section. There can be no doubt that such an examination if made in the ordinary way would have revealed the defects complained of. The defects complained of were apparent the moment the casks were opened.'

In a sale over the counter, the customer does get to examine the goods. The Privy Council in *Grant* v. *Australian Knitting Mills Ltd* noted:

... the implied condition only applies to defects not reasonably discoverable to the buyer on such examination as he made or could make. The appellant was satisfied by the appearance of the underpants; he could not detect and had no reason to suspect the hidden presence of the sulphites; the garments were saleable in the sense that the appellant or anyone similarly situated and who did not know of their defect, would readily buy them; but they were not merchantable in the statutory sense because their defect rendered them unfit to be worn next the skin. It maybe that after sufficient washing that defect would have disappeared; but

the statute requires the goods to be merchantable in the state in which they were sold and delivered; in this connection, a defect which could easily be cured is as serious as a defect that would not yield to treatment. The proviso to exception (2) does not apply where, as in this case, no examination that the buyer could or would normally have made would have revealed the defect. In effect, the implied condition of being fit for the particular purpose for which they are required and the implied condition of being merchantable produce, in cases of this type, the same result.

What is a reasonable examination and what such an examination ought to reveal will depend on the facts of the case.

MERCHANTABILITY AND PRICE

Different goods have different prices. Should price be a factor in determining merchantability? Should a buyer paying a high price expect a higher standard of merchantability? We will explore this issue with the following review of judgments.

Henry Kendall and Sons v. William Lillico and Sons Limited

Henry Kendell and Sons, game farmers in Suffolk, bought a compound meal from the Suffolk Agricultural and Poultry Producers Association (SAPPA) to feed their pheasants and partridges.[24] The compound meal contained a proportion of Brazilian groundnut extracts. The SAPPA had bought the groundnuts from third parties, and the third parties from fourth. It was not known to any of them at the time of the sale that the groundnuts were contaminated by afla-toxin. The compound meal, when fed to the peasants and partridges, was fatal. But the groundnuts could be fed safely to cattle and

---

[23] *Thornett & Fehr* v. *Beers & Son*, (1919) 1 KB 486.

[24] *Henry Kendall and Sons (a firm)* v. *William Lillico and Sons Limited*, (1968) 2 All ER 444.

other animals, provided the proportion of groundnuts in the compound feed was kept below a certain level.

SAPPA claimed that the groundnut supplied was not of merchantable quality. The court held that the goods 'were capable in their ordinary use of being ultimately compounded into food for cattle (including a wide variety of animals under that description) or into food for poultry (including a wide variety of birds under that description)'. However, as a compound food for poultry, the goods had proved fatal to very young birds such as day-old ducklings, turkey poults, and pheasant chicks. Judge Havers concluded, 'Though the meal was unfit for use for one purpose, as a compound food for poultry, I cannot find that the meal in the form in which it was tendered was of no use for any purpose for which the meal would normally be used and hence was unsaleable under that description.'

The case went to the House of Lords. Lord Reid noted that there may be several goods of varying quality, price, and use. How does one settle on the question of merchantability in relation to the price? Lord Reid first stated that merchantability refers to the lowest quality commonly sold in the market. He noted:

Merchantable can only mean commercially saleable. If the description is a familiar one, it may be that in practice, only one quality of goods answers that description—then that quality and only that quality is merchantable quality. Or it may be that various qualities of goods are commonly sold under that description—then it is not disputed that the lowest quality commonly so sold is what is meant by merchantable quality; it is commercially saleable under that description.

Similarly, if a particular thing has only one use, as we saw in the case *Grant* v. *Australian Knitting Mills Ltd*, the supplied goods must meet that use. However, if a thing has several uses under a description, the supplied goods would be merchantable if the goods are fit for any of those purposes. Lord Reid noted:

If the description in the contract was so limited that goods sold under it would normally be used for only one purpose, then the goods would be unmerchantable under that description if they were of no use for that purpose. If, however, the description was so general that goods sold under it were normally used for several purposes, then goods would be merchantable under that description if they were fit for any one of these purposes. If the buyer wanted the goods for one of those several purposes for which the goods delivered did not happen to be suitable, though they were suitable for other purposes for which goods bought under that description were normally bought, then he could not complain. He ought either to have taken the necessary steps to bring sub-section (1) into operation or to have insisted that a more specific description must be inserted in the contract.

Since the exceptions were formulated by the courts, trade and commerce has significantly changed. Under the same description, goods of different quality and price sell. Similarly, the buyer need not be the end user. He could be buying for reselling or using for further manufacturing. Lord Reid noted:

I think that it must be inferred from the evidence that buyers who include groundnut extractions in their cattle foods are prepared to pay a full price for goods which may be contaminated; but buyers who only compound poultry foods would obviously not be prepared to buy contaminated goods at any price. Nevertheless, contaminated groundnut extractions are merchantable under the general description of groundnut extractions because, rather surprisingly, some buyers appear to be ready to buy them under that description and to pay the ordinary market price for them. On the face of it, section 14(1) of the Act of 1893 has a narrower scope. It requires that the buyers shall have required the goods for a particular purpose, that that purpose shall have been made known to the seller, and that it shall have been made known to him in such circumstances that he realised or ought to have realised that the buyer was relying on his using his skill or judgment to select goods fit for that purpose.

...

Different qualities normally sell at different prices. If a customer sought from a manufacturer or dealer, cloth for the purpose of making overcoats, the dealer could not know what quality was required. A cut price tailor would not want to pay the price of cloth used in Savile Row, and the tailor in Savile Row would not use the quality which the cut price tailor wants. Unless the seller knew the nature of the buyer's business, his only clue to the quality which the buyer wanted would be the price which the buyer was prepared to pay. If a high price was offered it might no doubt be right to hold that he must supply goods suitable for high quality coats; but it could not be right that if the cloth was sold at a price appropriate for the lower quality, the dealer would have to supply a higher quality simply because the buyer had stated that his purpose was to make overcoats and the lower quality would not always be reasonably fit for making every kind of overcoat.

Perhaps the solution of this problem is to be found in the application of the requirement of the section that the particular purpose must be made known 'so as to show that the buyer relied upon the seller's skill or judgment.' A buyer who is buying for the purpose—known to the seller—of re-selling in the course of his business, may want superior goods for which some of his customers will pay a high price, or he may want goods of lower quality to sell to less demanding customers. If he does not say which he wants, or at least indicate which he wants by the price which he is offering, how can he be relying on the seller to supply something reasonably fit for his purpose?

Thus, Lord Reid looked to the relationship between price, quality, and merchantability, but then suggested that the solution was in the buyer making it known to the seller the purpose for which he wanted the goods. This would give protection to the buyer under Subsection 1. Thus, price was not to be a distinguishing factor on merchantability. However, in a subsequent case, *B.S. Brown & Son Ltd* v. *Craiks Ltd*,[25] Lord Reid thus commented on his judgment.

I see no reason to alter what I said, but judicial observations can never be regarded as complete definitions: they must be read in light of the facts and issues raised in the particular case. I do not think it is possible to frame, except in the vaguest terms, a definition of 'merchantable quality' which can apply to every kind of case. In the Hardwick case ((1969) 2 AC 31) no question as to price arose, because the evidence showed that, even when all the facts were known, the market price was the same for tainted and untainted goods. But suppose that the market price for the better quality is substantially higher than that for the lower quality. Then it could not be right that, if the contract price is appropriate for the better quality, the seller should be entitled to tender the lower quality and say that, because the lower quality is commercially saleable under the contract description, he has fulfilled his contract by delivering goods of the lower quality. But I think that the evidence in this case with regard to prices is much too indefinite to support a case on that basis.

As the case was not decided on the basis of different standards of merchantability depending on the price, the comment remained only a point of view with no binding effect.

Thus, to avail the protection of Subsection 2, the sale should be made by the seller who deals in those goods. This is not a significant point. In the sale by a trader, it is taken that the trader deals in those goods. The sale of future goods and unascertained goods are by description. A sale of specific goods is also by

[25] *B.S. Brown & Son Ltd* v. *Craiks Ltd*, (1970) SC 51.

description if the intent of the parties is to sell goods of that description. In the case of specific goods, there may be an examination by the party. The examination will exempt the seller from the responsibility for defects that may be apparent. Within these exceptions, it is an implied condition that the goods are of merchantable quality. If the goods have only one use, the goods should be fit for that use. If the goods have multiple uses, the supplied goods would be merchantable if these are fit for any of the purposes. We could conclude by noting that there is a significant overlap between Subsections 1 and 2. In the words of Lord Diplock:[26]

... sub-s (1) and sub-s (2) of s 14 of the Sale of Goods Act, 1893, are really two sides of the same coin. If a buyer makes known a particular purpose—those, of course, are the words of sub-s (1)—to the seller so as to show that he relies on the seller's skill and judgment, then the suitability for that particular purpose is a warranty and implied condition of the contract. If he does not make known any particular purpose, then, the assumption being that he requires them for the ordinary purposes for which such goods are intended to be used, the implied condition is one that they are fit for those ordinary purposes, that is to say, that they are merchantable, and I venture to think that there is no other distinction between sub-s (1) and sub-s (2).

SALE BY SAMPLE

In a sale by sample, the buyer examines a sample and approves it. The seller then supplies the bulk amount, which should match the sample. The requirement that the goods must be of merchantable quality became the basic minimum of every sale, unless of course it was waived by the contracting parties. What if goods were ordered on the basis of

a sample, and the bulk matched the sample, but the goods were not of merchantable quality? This is the question that was raised in the following founding case, decided before the codification.

James Drummond v. E.H. Van Ingen & Co.

James Drummond were cloth manufacturers in the UK.[27] Van Ingen contracted to buy fabric from Drummond for sale to traders and tailors in the United States. The fabric bought was described as 'mixed worsted coatings'. Van Ingen had ordered the cloth to a sample, and the goods were to be of the 'quality and weight' of the sample. The goods were of a class that was known in the trade as 'corkscrew twills'. Ingen delivered most of the fabric supplied by Drummond to customers in the United States, but the supplies were returned as not suitable for the purpose. The cohesion in the texture of the fabric between the warp and weft was not adequate. As a result, when made into coats, the fabric tore under the strain of ordinary wear. The problem existed in the sample as well. Drummond argued that the bulk corresponded with the sample, and so they had supplied the contracted goods. Ingen argued that the goods must be of merchantable quality. Lord Herschell summarized the law as it had evolved till then:

My Lords, I think that the general principles of law which have to be applied to the facts of this case are well settled and beyond question. It was laid down in Jones v. Bright that where goods are ordered of a manufacturer for a particular purpose, he impliedly warrants that the goods he supplies are fit for that purpose. This view of the law has been constantly acted upon from the time

---

[26] *Mash and Murrell Limited* v. *Joseph I Emanuel Limited*, 1961 (1) All ER 485.

[27] *James Drummond* v. *E.H. Van Ingen & Co.*, 12 App Cas 284.

of that decision, and was not impeached by the learned counsel for the appellants. It is equally well settled that upon a sale of goods of a specified description, which the purchaser has no opportunity of examining before the sale, the goods must not only answer that specific description, but must be merchantable under that description. This doctrine was laid down in Jones v. Just, where all the previous authorities on the point were reviewed. In the case of Mody v. Gregson, in the Exchequer Chamber, the decision in Jones v. Just was approved of and acted upon, and it was further held that the implied warranty that the goods supplied are merchantable was not absolutely excluded by the fact that the goods were sold by sample, and that the bulk precisely corresponded with it, but was only excluded as regards those matters which the purchaser might, by due diligence in the use of all ordinary and usual means, have ascertained from an examination of the sample. I think that the law enunciated in these cases is sound and not open to doubt.

Lord Macnaghten said:

… it was argued, defect or no defect, the sale was a sale by sample: the goods delivered correspond with the sample, and there is an end to the matter: the seller has fulfilled his bargain. I think the sale was strictly a sale by sample. Certainly the goods corresponded with the sample only too well. But does this exact correspondence, when it is found to involve an unforeseen and unsuspected defect, relieve the seller from his obligation to supply goods fit for the purpose for which they were intended? After all, the office of a sample is to present to the eye the real meaning and intention of the parties with regard to the subject matter of the contract which, owing to the imperfection of language, it may be difficult or impossible to express in words. The sample speaks for itself. But it cannot be treated as saying more than such a sample would tell a merchant of the class to which the buyer belongs, using due care and diligence, and appealing to it in the ordinary way and with the knowledge possessed by merchants of that class at the time. No doubt, the sample might be made to

say a great deal more. Pulled to pieces and examined by unusual tests which curiosity or suspicion might suggest, it would doubtless reveal every secret of its construction. But that is not the way in which business is done in this country. Some confidence there must be between merchant and manufacturer. In matters exclusively within the province of the manufacturer, the merchant relies on the manufacturer's skill, and he does so all the more readily when, as in this case, he has had the benefit of that skill before.

This case became the foundation for the provision on sale by sample in the Sale of Goods Act, 1893. Section 17 is the corresponding one in the Sale of Goods Act, 1930. It reads:

17. Sale by sample: (1) A contract of sale is a contract for sale by sample where there is a term in the contract, express or implied, to that effect.

(2) In the case of a contract for sale by sample there is an implied condition—

(a) that the bulk shall correspond with the sample in quality;

(b) that the buyer shall have a reasonable opportunity of comparing the bulk with the sample;

(c) that the goods shall be free from any defect, rendering them unmerchantable, which would not be apparent on reasonable examination of the sample.

A sale can be by both sample and description. It may describe the goods as well as require a sample for approval. Section 15 has already provided for it. Where a sale is by both sample and description, 'it is not sufficient that the bulk of the goods corresponds with the sample if the goods do not also correspond with the description.' The goods must fully correspond with the description.

OUSTING OF IMPLIED TERMS

Protection to the buyer in the Sale of Goods Act, 1930, is provided as an 'implied condition'. Thus, once the seller has provided goods at variance with the description, goods not of merchantable quality, or not of utility as promised, the buyer has the right to terminate the contract and claim damages. The buyer can, of course, at his discretion, allow the seller to re-perform the contract. The right of the buyer to terminate the contract was adequate in the past, when the goods sold were primary produce. In the context of manufactured goods, however, this principle can lead to unsatisfactory implications. Suppose that a car developed a problem in the electrical circuit two days after its delivery. It would not start. A short circuit had occurred, which can easily be fixed by replacing a wire. Technically, the car is not of merchantable quality. The buyer would be justified in returning the car and claiming damages. The manufacturers have attempted to find answers for themselves. The law only provides the implied terms and conditions. The parties are free to set their own terms on the quality of goods, and express terms would supersede the application of the implied terms. Section 16(4) provides: 'An express warranty or condition does not negative a warranty or condition implied by this Act, unless inconsistent therewith.' In addition, Section 62 of the Sale of Goods Act, 1930, provides:

62. Exclusion of implied terms and conditions: Where any right, duty or liability would arise under a contract of sale by implication of law, it may be negatived or varied by express agreement or by the course of dealing between the parties, or by usage, if the usage is such as to bind both parties to the contract.

In other words, the implied warranty or condition can be cancelled by making an express term detracting from it. For example, the terms of a contract of sale may provide: 'Warranty: The equipment will be warranted for a period of 12 months. The warranty is in lieu of all express or implied condition and warranty.' A term like this prevents the buyer from terminating the contract as the implied condition of merchantability has been substituted by an express warranty. The buyer can only claim damages. The word 'warranty' is also used in business practices to convey a completely opposite meaning; that is, promising, guaranteeing, or undertaking a performance. As Lord Denning noted in *Oscar Chess Ltd* v. *Williams*:[28]

I use the word 'warranty' in its ordinary English meaning, to denote a binding promise. Everyone knows what a man means when he says, 'I guarantee it', or 'I warrant it', or 'I give you my word on it'. He means that he binds himself to it. That is the meaning which it has borne in English law for three hundred years… During the last hundred years, however, the lawyers have come to use the word 'warranty' in another sense. They use it to denote a subsidiary term in a contract as distinct from a vital term which they call a 'condition'. In so doing, they depart from the ordinary meaning, not only of the word 'warranty', but also of the word 'condition'. There is no harm in their doing this, so long as they confine this technical use to its proper sphere, namely, to distinguish between a vital term, the breach of which gives the right to treat the contract as at an end, and a subsidiary term which does not. The trouble comes, however, when one person uses the word 'warranty' in its ordinary meaning and another uses it in its technical meaning.

The varied usage of the term is not only in the legal and non-legal context but also within the legal context itself. At times, the seller intends to use the term 'warranty' in its positive sense of vesting more in the buyer. In each case, the courts, interpret the use of the term from its context. Unless it is clear that the use

[28] *Oscar Chess Ltd* v. *Williams*, (1957) 1 All ER 325.

of the term was made in a legal sense to limit the rights of the seller, the implied condition is not cancelled.

Like other industrial countries, the UK has responded to the changing demands of trade and commerce. The English Sale of Goods Act, 1893, has been amended a few times. The amendments were consolidated through a new act, The Sale of Goods Act, 1979, which has been further amended by the Sale and Supply of Goods Act, 1994; the Sale of Goods (Amendment) Act, 1994; and the Sale of Goods (Amendment) Act, 1995. The Sale and Supply of Goods Act, 1994, and the Unfair Contract Terms Act, 1977, deal with the sale of goods. With the integration of Europe, there are the additional European Union directives that require adoption.[29]

In contrast, the Indian law, the Sale of Goods Act, 1930, has remained unchanged. The reason for the lack of law reforms can be explained by the fact that India's industrialization started only in the 1930s. In post-Independence years, the Indian economy has vastly expanded; however, the Indian economy was tightly controlled and managed by the state. Anyone who wanted to start manufacturing and production had to procure the appropriate licenses. This was intended to protect Indian industries from foreign competition by assuring markets for the manufacturers. There was a perennial shortage of goods in the Indian market. Buyers had no choice but to take what they got. Thus, the economic context did not demand reforms of commercial laws. It was only in the Consumer Protection Act, 1986, that supplementary legislation was brought in.

Further, as it was a seller's market, buyers had to be thankful for just receiving the goods; they could not complain about its quality. As a result, there has been almost no case from the Indian courts on the quality of goods. The opening of the economy since 1990, however, has brought in competition and made the question of law on product quality relevant. We can expect reforms in this area in the coming decades. Below, we review two cases from the Indian high courts.

Raghava Menon v. Kuttappan Nair

A customer bought a watch from a reputed shop, but it proved to be defective.[30] The dispute came before the Kerala High Court, which noted:

In the case before me the plaintiff is a layman and he approaches a fairly reputed firm like the defendant dealing in watches and purchases a watch from them, not for any special purpose, but for the common purpose of knowing the correct time. In such a case, Sec. 16(1) of the Sale of Goods Act must apply, because the buyer makes known to the seller, by implication, the purpose for which he purchases the watch and also relies on the seller's skill or judgment. To put it differently, the purpose being only the common purpose and not any special purpose, the seller knows it, and the purchaser being only a layman, he relies on the seller's skill or judgment. Moveover, the goods, namely the watches, are of a description which it is in the course of the seller's business to supply. Therefore, sub-sec. (1) to Sec. 16 applies, unless the case comes within the proviso to that subsection. There is no evidence in the case to show that the plaintiff wanted a particular watch of a particular trade name or patent and did not rely on the seller's skill or judgment; and therefore the proviso has no application. Moreover, sub-sec. (2) of Sec. 16 may also apply to the facts of this case; for, in this case a layman purchases a wrist-watch,

---

[29] A review of the changes and differences in the current law with the law in India would be beyond the scope of this book, however. The purpose of this book is to understand the prevailing law in India.

[30] *Raghava Menon* v. *Kuttappan Nair*, AIR (1962) Kerala 318.

just by description, from a dealer who deals in goods of that description and the defect detected in the watch is not one which could have been found out by examination, and a watch which does not keep correct time cannot be said to be of merchantable quality (vide Grant v. Australian Knitting Mills: 70 Mad LJ 513: (AIR 1936 PC 34), where the Privy Council says that a thing is not merchantable if it has defects making it unfit for its only proper use but not apparent on ordinary examination). To cap, there is evidence in this case that Kenson Dayter Watches are available only with the defendant-Company and thus they have a special responsibility regarding the fitness of such watches and there is the guarantee certificate as well.

Eternit Everest Limited v. C.G. Abraham

C.G. Abraham constructed a new Cinema hall, 'Geetha Theatre', at Shornur.[31] For the roofing, he purchased asbestos sheets and accessories manufactured by the Eternit Everest Ltd, Coimbatore, through its agent, Haridas Bhagath and Company (P) Ltd, Coimbatore. The purchase was made on 16 November 1985 for a total value of Rs 45,815. The roofing work was completed in December 1985. The sheets leaked during the next monsoons, in June 1985. Abraham sent a representation to the Eternit Everest Ltd. The officials of the company visited the site and advised him to provide more ventilation at the ridge level. Despite this, the leaking during the monsoons continued. The officials of the manufacturer visited the theatre again and concluded that the dripping of water was due to the condensation of moisture inside the structure during the rainy season. The problem could be rectified by providing proper ventilation. The officials of the company advised Abraham to provide a number of radial

exhausts to reduce precipitation. In spite of following these instructions, there was no improvement. The officials of the manufacturer then advised Abraham to provide lime coating. This too failed to stop the leakage, which eventually damaged the ceiling. Money had to be invested in putting waterproofs on the plaster of Paris in the ceiling to prevent further damage. Abraham went to the local court at Shornur.

The court appointed a technical advisor to prepare a report on the supplied goods. The report noted that there were fissures in several sheets and that such fissures occur due to a defective curing of the sheets. Further, because of this, water would definitely leak and drip. The report further said that even without them, water can leak and drip if the sheets have not been cured for the full period. The report was of the definite opinion that the leakage and dripping of water was not due to any structural defect of the theatre, or lack of ventilation, but solely due to the defective quality of the asbestos sheets. The parties came before the Kerala High Court. The court noted:

The rule of 'caveat emptor' applies whenever the buyer voluntarily chooses what he buys. But it does not mean that the buyer should 'take chance' but it means he should 'take care'. The most important exception to the rule of 'caveat emptor' are the implied condition of fitness for a particular purpose and the merchantableness of the product. When a man sells an article, he thereby warrants that it is merchantable i.e. it is fit for some purpose and if he sells it for some particular purpose, he thereby warrants it for that purpose. In order to attract sec. 16 it has to be proved that the buyer expressly or by implication had made known to the seller the particular purpose for which the goods were purchased. Ext. A13 letter sent by the 2nd respondent coupled with the invoice showing the sale of the sheets with accessories for the roofing would indicate that the purpose of purchase of

---

[31] *Eternit Everest Limited* v. *C.G. Abraham*, AIR (2003) Kerala 273.

the semi corrugated asbestos sheets was for roofing and that had been disclosed too. Moreover, the corrugated asbestos sheets are mainly used for roofing of buildings for protecting the building from sun and rain and it is not being used for a variety of purposes. The leakproof of the asbestos sheets is the essential quality of the sheets and only if it is leakproof, it can be said to be a fit for the purpose for which it is purchased. The evidence would further reveal that the plaintiff wanted Everest asbestos sheets and Everest asbestos sheets had the reputation regarding its quality. Thus the plaintiff was trusting the judgment or the skill of the 1st defendant, the manufacturer, or the dealer and thus there was an implied term of warranty that the articles would be reasonably fit for the purpose to which it was applied. The evidence would further reveal that the asbestos sheets supplied by the 2nd defendant had manufacturing defect and thereby it was leaking during rainy season. Ext.C1 report would further reveal that fissures were there on the sheets and that could be due to defective curing also. As the article was purchased for a specific purpose and it was disclosed to the seller, sub-sec. (1) of sec. 16 would be attracted and there was an implied warranty as to the quality of the articles sold that it was fit for the purpose for which it was sold.

Right to Sell

Section 14 makes it an implied condition that the seller has the right to sell the goods. While this aspect is not a quality of the goods but an aspect associated with ownership, it is included in the chapter on quality. The section reads:

14. Implied undertaking as to title, etc: In a contract of sale, unless the circumstances of the contract are such as to show a different intention, there is—

(a) an implied condition on the part of the seller that, in the case of a sale, he has a right to sell the goods and that, in the case of an agreement to sell, he will have a right to sell the goods at the time when the property is to pass;

(b) an implied warranty that the buyer shall have and enjoy quiet possession of the goods;

(c) an implied warranty that the goods shall be free from any charge or encumbrance in favour of any third party not declared or known to the buyer before or at the time when the contract is made.

Section 14 states that in a sale of goods, the buyer can take it that the seller has the right to sell. If it turns out that the seller did not have the right, as ownership is an 'implied condition', the buyer can terminate the contract and claim damages. To focus on the operative part of the above provision, the 'implied condition' is about a 'right to sell'. This is larger than ownership. For example, when an owner gives his goods to an auctioneer to auction, the auctioneer does not become the owner but has a right to sell. The same would be the case in all commercial transactions where the owner authorizes any person as an agent to sell goods for him. An interesting case on the wider import of the right to sell is *Niblett Ltd* v. *Confectioners' Materials Co, Ltd.*[*]

Niblett Ltd v. Confectioners' Materials Co. Ltd

The Confectioners' Materials Co., based in the United States, contracted to sell 3,000 tins of condensed milk to Niblett Ltd, based in England.[32] The goods were delivered in two instalments. The first instalment was of 2,000 tins of the 'Freedom' brand. There was no problem with this lot. The second instalment was of 1,000 tins, bearing the brand name 'Nissly'. The Anglo-Swiss Condensed Milk Co. had a famous registered brand called 'Nestle'. They declared that the 1,000 cases of imported tins infringed their registered

[32] *Niblett Ltd* v. *Confectioners' Materials Co. Ltd*, (1921) 3 KB 387.

trademark. A registered trademark creates a property in the mark for the owner of the trademark. No one can use a deceptively similar name. Niblett Ltd had to admit the objections of the Anglo-Swiss Condensed Milk Co. and gave them an undertaking that they would not sell the tins under the brand name 'Nissly'. Niblett Ltd did the best they could to sell, exchange, or export the goods, but nothing worked out. The only possible way of disposing of the tins was to sell them without marks or labels. Section 14 of the Indian act, the Sale of Goods Act, 1930, is a reproduction of Section 12 of the English act, the Sale of Goods Act, 1893. Atkin L.J. explored the application of Section 12 and concluded that the seller did not have the right to sell the goods:

In a contract for the sale of goods there is an implied condition that the seller has a right to sell the goods 'unless the circumstances of the contract are such as to show a different intention.' I think those words were inserted in s. 12 of the Sale of Goods Act to exclude sales by a sheriff under an execution and other cases where by implication or by express terms there is no warranty of title. In the present case I see no circumstances 'such as to show a different intention,' and therefore I think there was an implied condition that the sellers had a right to sell the goods. The sellers had not the right to sell these goods. They gave an undertaking not to sell them, and having admitted that they were an infringement of the Nestle Company's trade mark they were liable to an injunction restraining the sale. Therefore they had no right to sell these goods at the time when the property was to pass. It may be that the implied condition is not broken if the seller is able to pass to the purchaser a right to sell notwithstanding his own inability; but that is not so here, for the Nestle Company had the same rights against the appellants as they had against the respondents. In my opinion there was a breach of this condition.

...

I think there was also a breach of the implied warranty in sub-s. 2, that the buyer shall have and enjoy quiet possession of the goods. It may be that possession would not be disturbed if the only cause of complaint was that the buyer could not dispose of the goods, and that the warranty is confined to disturbance of possession of the goods delivered under the contract of sale. The warranty so interpreted was broken. The appellants were never allowed to have quiet possession. They had to strip off the labels before they could assume possession of the goods.

Section 14(b and c) of the Sale of Goods Act, 1930, provides for an implied warranty, where the seller has the ownership but there are charges or encumbrances to the goods. Thus, if X sells a car to Y and X was not the owner of the car, Y can repudiate the contract. However, if X had the ownership and there were only some additional charges pending, like warehouse fees, insurance, and unpaid taxes, Y will only have the right to claim damages, not to repudiate the contract. The following case is on the provision that there is an implied warranty that the 'buyer shall have and enjoy quiet possession of the goods'.

Microbeads AC v. Vinhurst Road Markings Ltd

Vinhurst bought a machine for making white lines on roads from a Swiss Company.[33] After the machine was purchased, an English company, Prismo Universal Ltd, was declared to be the patent-rights holder by the Patents Office for the technology used in the machine. The patent holder sought an injunction to prevent the use of the machine. At the time of the sale, neither the buyer nor the seller was aware that the machine might infringe a future patent right. Lord Denning examined

[33] *Microbeads AC and Another* v. *Vinhurst Road Markings Ltd*, (1975) 1 All ER 529.

the application of Section 12 of the British Act:

Before the judge most of the discussion was on s 12(1). It says that there is an 'implied condition on the part of the seller that … he has a right to sell the goods…' That means that he has, at the time of the sale, a right to sell the goods. The words 'a right to sell the goods' mean not only a right to pass the property in the machines to the buyer, but also a right to confer on the buyer the undisturbed possession of the goods.

Now, at the time of the sale in January 1970 the Swiss company were able to confer those rights. They had made the machines out of their own materials and they could undoubtedly pass the property in them to the buyers. Moreover there was no one at that time entitled to disturb their possession. There was then no subsisting patent. The specification had not been published. No one could sue for infringement. The buyers could, at that time, use the machines undisturbed. So I agree with the judge that there was no breach of s 12(1).

Now I turn to s 12(2). It says that there is an 'implied warranty that the buyer shall have and enjoy quiet possession of the goods'. Taking those words in their ordinary meaning, they seem to cover this case. The words 'shall have and enjoy' apply not only to the time of the sale but also to the future; 'shall enjoy' means in the future. If a patentee comes two or three years later and gets an injunction to restrain the use of the goods, there would seem to be a breach of the warranty.

But the main point of counsel for the Swiss company before us—a point which the judge accepted—was that the defects of title must be present at the time of the sale. That is why so much turned on the date of publication, 11th November 1970. After that date the Swiss company, could by taking reasonable steps, have known that their machines were infringing machines and that they could not have a right to use them. So, if they had sold after 11th November 1970, they would be in breach of s 12(2) and of s 12(1) also. But counsel for the Swiss company says that before that date

the Swiss company may have been perfectly innocent. Nothing had been published about this patent. The machines were sold in January and April 1970. There was no defect in title existing at the time of the sale. Accordingly counsel submitted there was no breach of s 12(2).

I cannot accept this submission. It means putting a gloss on s 12(2) by introducing a qualification which is not there. It seems to me that when the buyer has bought goods quite innocently and later on he is disturbed in his possession because the goods are found to be infringing a patent, then he can recover damages for breach of warranty against the seller. It may be the seller is innocent himself, but when one or other must suffer, the loss should fall on the seller; because, after all, he sold the goods and if it turns out that they infringe a patent, he should bear the loss in the present case Prismo sue for infringement now and stop the buyer using the machines. That is a clear disturbance of possession. The buyer is not able to enjoy the quiet possession which the seller impliedly warranted that he shall have. There is a breach of s 12(2) of the 1893 Act.

* * *

In this chapter, we have explored the rights and obligations of the contracting parties in relation to the sale of goods. The law implies rights for the protection of the buyer. The rights are implied in the language of condition (for whose breach the buyer can terminate the contract) and warranty (for whose breach the buyer cannot terminate the contract but only claim damages). The contracting parties are free to cancel the implied terms by including express terms. It is an implied condition in every sale by description that the goods correspond with that description and are of merchantable quality. Further, if the buyer relies on the skill and judgment of the seller to be provided goods for a purpose, it is an implied condition that the goods are fit for that purpose.

7

Performance of Contract

There are several aspects to the successful performance of a sale contract. They include quality of goods, transportation, delivery, ownership, and payment of price. All of the aspects relate to one another; one cannot be fully understood without understanding the other. To unravel this, we will try to understand how parties go about performing an agreement once the parties have got into it. However, before examining the performance of a contract, we will look at the situations in which the parties are discharged from the contract and are freed from the obligation of performance.

VOID, VOIDABILITY, AND FRUSTRATION

As a sale is a contract, contract law on void and voidable contract will apply to it. A void contract is a nullity in the eyes of the law, and is treated as if it was never made. A voidable contract gives the right to the innocent party to rescind the contract. Frustration also discharges a contract. Suppose that B contracts to sell his second-hand car to C. Can B deliver to C a car of similar description in its place? The answer would be no. The parties have entered into a contract for sale of a specific car, and the delivery must be of the specific car. Let us consider a variation. B entered into a contract to sell his second-hand car on Wednesday to C. The ownership in the car was to transfer on Friday and the delivery was to be made on Friday. The car was destroyed in a fire on Thursday. Can C demand a car of similar description from B towards performance of the contract? The answer would be no, as the contract was for the specific car.

It is impossible for B to transfer the ownership when the goods do not exist. One of the early cases on frustration was *Taylor* v. *Caldwell*,[1] where the hall to be rented out had been gutted in a fire. The position of the court was that as the subject matter of the contract itself was destroyed, it was beyond the parties to perform the contract. The precedence for this was the sale contract for a horse where the horse died after making of the contract. Thus, destruction of the specific goods leads to frustration and discharge of the parties. Consider a case where B entered into a contract to sell his second-hand car on Wednesday to C. The car was destroyed in a fire on Monday. Can C demand a car of similar description

---

[1] *Taylor* v. *Caldwell*, (1863) 3 B & S 826.

from B towards performance of the contract? As the parties entered into a contract to do something that was impossible, the contract was void since inception. The Sale of Goods Act, 1930, expresses both the principles. Section 7 and 8 read:

7. Goods perishing before making of contract: Where there is a contract for the sale of specific goods, the contract is void if the goods without the knowledge of the seller have, at the time when the contract was made, perished or become so damaged as no longer to answer to their description in the contract.

8. Goods perishing before sale but after agreement to sell: Where there is an agreement to sell specific goods, and subsequently the goods without any fault on the part of the seller or buyer perish or become so damaged as no longer to answer to their description in the agreement before the risk passes to the buyer, the agreement is thereby avoided.

Couturier v. *Robert Hastie*,[2] a House of Lords, pre-codification case, provided the basis for the provision. In the case, the master of a ship, fearing decay of a cargo of corn, sold it at an intermediate port; unaware of this, the buyer had subsequently sold the corn to a sub-buyer. The following case shows the scope of the provision.

Barrow, Lane & Ballard, Ltd v. Phillip Phillips & Co., Ltd

Phillips contracted to sell Ballards a parcel consisting of 700 bags of Chinese ground nuts held in a warehouse.[3] The contract was made on 11 October. Unknown to both parties, 109 bags were stolen before the contract was made. After delivery of 150 bags, the remaining bags were also stolen. The claim of

---

[2] *Couturier* v. *Robert Hastie*, (1856) 5 HL Cas 673.
[3] *Barrow, Lane & Ballard, Ltd* v. *Phillip Phillips & Co., Ltd*, (1929) KB 574.

the seller was that as the goods were specific, the ownership in the goods had been transferred to the buyer. The warehouse company was in liquidation. If the above claim were right, the risk of loss of the goods would have fallen on the buyer. Justice Wright delivered the following judgment:

When the contract ... was made there was not in existence any parcel such as is described in the contract. There was a parcel of 591 bags, but there was not a parcel of 700 bags. If the whole 700 bags had been stolen without the knowledge of either party on Oct. 11, or if it had been destroyed by fire, or if it did not for any such reason exist as a parcel at all on Oct. 11, there could be no doubt at all that Sect. 6 of the Sale of Goods Act, 1893, would have applied. Sect. 6 says:—

> Where there is a contract for the sale of specific goods, and the goods without the knowledge of the seller have perished at the time when the contract is made, the contract is void.

There is no contract, in other words, because the intention of both parties is completely frustrated; they are contracting about something which has no existence in fact, and the law then says that, the contract having reference to specific goods, and those specific goods not existing, there is nothing on which the contract can operate; and the rule has been established for many years that the seller is not treated as warranting the existence of those specific goods, but the case is one of a failure of intention and of mistake.

This case further raises a problem which, so far as I know ... has never come before the Court before. The problem is this. Where you have a contract for the sale of specific goods such as the parcel in this case, and some of the parcel—not all of the parcel—has ceased to exist at all times relevant to the contract, because it has been stolen and taken away and cannot be followed or discovered anywhere, what then is the position? Does the case come within Sect. 6 of the Sale of Goods Act, so that the case would be the same as if the whole parcel had ceased to exist? In my judgment that is so. The contract is for a parcel of 700 bags. A contract for a parcel of 700 bags is something different from a contract for a parcel of 591 bags, and in my judgment the position is no different from what would have been the case if the whole 700 bags had ceased to exist. The result is that the parties are contracting about something which, without the knowledge or fault of either party, at the date of the contract does not exist, and to compel the buyer under those circumstances to take 591 bags would be to compel him to take something which he had not contracted to take, and would in my judgment be unjust.

There is a difference in the wording of the British and the Indian law. The British law only mentions 'perished', while the Indian law mentions 'perished or become so damaged as no longer to answer to their description in the contract'. The significance is this: 'Perish' might refer to the loss or destruction of the goods. At times, the goods may not be lost or destroyed but deteriorated, thus no longer meeting the contract description or being of commercial value. The Indian law addresses this by broadening the scope of the sections to include loss in a commercial sense. Sections 6 and 7 of the Sale of Goods Act, 1930, which we have reviewed above, deal with frustration arising from the subject matter of the contract. Other grounds for frustration would apply under the general contract law, the Indian Contract Act, 1872.

Delivery and Payment

A buyer may buy goods and leave them with the seller only under a contractual arrangement, for example, a lease. This, however, is an exception. In most cases, the buyer would get the possession of the goods. Thus, delivering the goods to the buyer is an integral part of a sale contract. Ownership is a concept that vests the owner with the right of physical control over the goods. Delivery is the acquisition of physical control over the goods.

Ownership has no meaning if the buyer does not get to possess the goods and enjoy its benefits. Thus, for a sale contract to be complete, not only should the ownership transfer to the buyer, but the seller must also deliver the goods to the buyer. Section 2(2) of the Sale of Goods Act, 1930, defines delivery to mean 'voluntary transfer of possession from one person to another'. The term 'possession' has not been defined. It is to be given the general meaning as assigned by the courts. Section 33 of the Sale of Goods Act, 1930, elaborates different ways by which delivery can be made in a sale contract: 'Delivery of goods sold may be made by doing anything which the parties agree shall be treated as delivery or which has the effect of putting the goods in the possession of the buyer or of any person authorised to hold them on his behalf.'

A seller delivers the goods to the buyer by performing an act that has the 'effect of putting the goods in the possession of the buyer'. This is broader than the seller physically putting the goods in the hands of the buyer. Delivery can be made through different means, such as physically delivery, symbolic delivery, and constructive delivery. In a physical delivery, the seller hands over goods to the buyer. The seller and buyer can do this themselves or through others on their behalf. This can take different forms. The seller can hand over the goods to a carrier who is acting on the instructions of the buyer. The carrier is effectively an agent of the buyer. In a symbolic delivery, the goods are not physically delivered but something that represents or symbolizes the goods are delivered to the buyer. Examples of this are giving the key to a warehouse or the ignition key of a vehicle. Commercial application of this mode is in delivering the documents of title of the goods. Section 2(4) defines the document of title as follows:

(4) 'document of title to goods' includes a bill of lading, dock-warrant, warehouse keepers's certificate, wharfingers' certificate, railway receipt, warrant or order for the delivery of goods and any other document used in the ordinary course of business as proof of the possession or control of goods, or authorising or purporting to authorise, either by endorsement or by delivery, the possessor of the document to transfer or receive goods thereby represented…

These documents create the right to receive the goods. A bill of lading is the most prominent instrument of the kind. There can be different ways by which the holder of the document can acquire the right to receive the goods. The bill of lading may have mentioned the person by name and the person is given the document. The bill of lading may have been drawn in favour of the bearer. Any person who has the document will be entitled to receive it. Another means is by endorsement. X may be named in the bill of lading. X may endorse the document in favour of Y and give the instrument to Y. Giving such documents may be equivalent to giving the possession of the goods. Thus, handing over the documents of title may amount to delivery. We will take up this aspect in another chapter dealing with CIF and FOB contracts.

Constructive delivery is done through attornment. S is the owner of the goods that are in the physical custody of another person, T. Following the sale, S instructs T to hold the goods for the buyer, B. T acknowledges the change to both B and S. This is called attornment. T comes to hold the goods as a bailee for B. The delivery is not complete unless the third party acknowledges that he holds on behalf of the buyer. Section 36(3) provides this rule: 'Where the goods at the time of sale are in the possession of a third person, there is no delivery by seller to buyer unless and until such third person

acknowledges to the buyer that he holds the goods on his behalf.'

Scrutton L.J. in *Laurie and Morewood* v. *Dudin and Sons*[4] noted on attornment:

Therefore one is left with the question whether the mere handing in without more amounts to an attornment by the warehouseman … Is it enough to constitute an attornment by the warehouseman to the person presenting the delivery order that, the order being sent by a messenger, it should be received by a clerk and nothing said? I think, myself, that a very little will suffice to create an attornment. If the warehouseman writes on the order in the presence of the messenger the word 'accepted,' so that he sees it; if he makes delivery of part of the goods … if he makes a claim for charges on the person presenting the delivery order; or if he tells him that he has entered his right to the goods in his books. In each of those cases I think it ought to be found that the warehouseman had attorned. But I do not see how it is possible to get an attornment or recognition of the title of the person named in the order out of the mere fact that an order is brought by a messenger and given to a clerk, where nothing is done which is communicated to the other party.

It need not be emphasized that the delivery of the goods to the agent of the buyer is delivery to the buyer himself. Further, prima facie, a carrier is taken to be an agent of the buyer. Thus, unless the contract shows otherwise, delivery to the carrier is delivery to the buyer himself. Section 39(1) provides:

39. Delivery to carrier or wharfinger: (1) Where, in pursuance of a contract of sale, the seller is authorised or required to send the goods to the buyer, delivery of the goods to a carrier, whether named by the buyer or not, for the purpose of transmission to the buyer, or delivery of the goods to a wharfinger for safe custody, is prima facie deemed to be a delivery of the goods to the buyer.

[4] *Laurie and Morewood* v. *Dudin and Sons*, (1926) 1 KB 223.

On the other hand, if the carrier is a servant or an agent of the seller, delivery to the carrier cannot be delivery to the buyer. Thus, to give possession of the goods, the seller must deliver the goods to the buyer in the sense discussed above. As contracts are voluntarily formed, the parties are free to settle on their own mode of delivery or when it should be taken that the goods are delivered. For example, a buyer who buys a bench to install it in a public park may have a term in the contract that the goods would be delivered by installing them in the public park. In this case, the possession has not been given to the buyer, yet the goods are delivered. A contract can provide that the seller would sell the goods, but keep it as the hirer of the goods. The time of delivery could be a fixed date. In this case, at no point of time does the seller voluntarily transfer possession of the goods. Yet the goods are taken to be delivered as the parties have agreed to it. We can now explore the rights and obligations of the buyer and seller.

Section 31 provides: 'It is the duty of the seller to deliver the goods and of the buyer to accept and pay for them, in accordance with the terms of the contract of sale.' The section is self-explanatory. When should the seller deliver the goods to the buyer? The seller should deliver as provided in the contract. When should the buyer pay for it? The buyer would pay as provided in the contract. However, what if the contract does not provide on this? Section 32 provides the answer. It reads:

32. Payment and delivery are concurrent conditions: Unless otherwise agreed, delivery of the goods and payment of the price are concurrent conditions, that is to say, the seller shall be ready and willing to give possession of the goods to the buyer in exchange for the price, and the buyer shall be ready and willing to pay the price in exchange for possession of the goods.

The section is ambiguous as to who should move first. The seller could claim that he was willing and ready to deliver but the buyer did not come forward with the money. And the buyer could claim that he was ready with the money but the seller did not come forward. Section 35 clarifies this: 'Apart from any express contract, the seller of goods is not bound to deliver them until the buyer applies for delivery.' If the contract does not provide on the time of delivery, the buyer should inform the seller that he is ready to receive the delivery and the goods be delivered to him. And if the contract does not provide for the time of payment, the buyer should be ready and willing to pay cash at the time of delivery. In this case, the buyer would give the goods with one hand and take the money with the other, so to speak. Both the buyer and the seller should be 'ready and willing' to do their parts.

In *De Medina* v. *Norman*,[5] 'readiness and willingness' was taken to imply 'not only the disposition but the capacity to perform the contract.' In *Levey and Company* v. *Goldberg*,[6] the seller extended the date for delivery on the request of the buyer. The buyer subsequently refused to take delivery and contended that the seller was not willing and ready to deliver on the original schedule of delivery. The court ruled:

... the plaintiffs [seller] had till the end of August to deliver and that they voluntarily abstained from delivering in August at the request of the defendant [buyer]. The defendant [buyer] therefore cannot rely upon the omission to tender delivery within that period. ... The plaintiffs were not bound actually to tender delivery; it was sufficient if they were ready and willing to deliver. ... The question of

---

[5] *De Medina* v. *Norman*, (1842) 9 M & W 820.

[6] *Levey and Company* v. *Goldberg*, (1922) 1 KB 688.

readiness and willingness is substantially a question of fact. If the defendant had desired delivery in August I entertain no doubt that the plaintiffs could have secured delivery from their manufacturers without the slightest difficulty. I find that the plaintiffs were always ready and willing to carry out their bargain...

Section 32 of the Sale of Goods Act, 1930, requires the seller to be 'ready and willing' to give possession to the buyer. In *Pulgaon Cotton Mills* v. *Gulabai*,[7] before the due date for delivery, the buyer applied for insolvency. In this context, the court noted on the obligation of the seller to deliver:

It is also clear that the plaintiff was not 'ready and willing' to perform the contract. He put in a petition for insolvency even before the due date arrived and thus he lacked not only the disposition but also the capacity to fulfil the contract. The effect of his application was to publish his inability to work out the contract and his want of readiness and willingness. The insolvency of the party may not by itself be sufficient to amount to a total refusal to perform the contract but under the circumstances of this case it was equivalent to a notice by the insolvent that he did not intend to perform his obligation.

Sujanmal v. Radhey Shyam

Through a written contract, entered into on 23 December 1963, the seller was to supply 200 tins of a particular brand of Vanaspati at the rate of Rs 44 per tin.[8] The tins were to be supplied FOR Choti Sadri. The contract did not provide the time of delivery or payment of money. By a letter dated 2 January 1964, the seller demanded payment of the price in advance, to be paid within two or three days, so that the delivery could be made in time.

The buyer did not reply to the letter, but took the demand of the price before supplying the goods to be a breach of the contract. The buyer served a notice on the seller on 18 February 1964 claiming Rs 500 by way of nominal damages and Rs 870 as loss of profits at the rate of Rs 4.35 per tin. The seller responded that it was the buyer who was in breach of the contract and it is the buyer who should pay damages to the seller. The court noted that as the contract had not provided for the time of delivery, under Section 36(2) delivery has to be done by the seller within a reasonable time. The court noted that the contract was also silent on the time of payment of the price. The court noted that, according to the law, unless the parties have provided otherwise in the contract, delivery of goods and payment of money are concurrent conditions. The court ruled:

... a contract of sale always involves reciprocal promises, the seller promising to deliver the goods sold and the buyer to accept and pay for them. In the absence of a contract to the contrary they are to be performed simultaneously and each party should be ready and willing to perform his promise before he can call upon the other to perform his. The seller owes to the buyer as onerous a duty to deliver the goods, as the buyer owes to the seller the duty to accept and pay for them. In Firm Birdhi Chand v. Ramdeo, 1970 Raj LW 148 = 1969 (19) ILR(Raj) 481 it was held,

'In a contract for sale of goods unless otherwise agreed, delivery of goods and payment of price are concurrent conditions and where the plaintiff in a suit on breach of contract happens to be a seller, he must allege and prove that he was ready and willing to deliver the goods.'

Similarly where the plaintiff in a suit for breach of contract happens to be a buyer he must prove that he applied for delivery and he was ready and willing to pay the price of the goods. This proposition of law is clearly borne out from the provisions of the Sale of Goods Act...

---

[7] *Pulgaon Cotton Mills* v. *Gulabai*, AIR (1953) Nagpur 345.

[8] *Sujanmal* v. *Radhey Shyam*, AIR (1976) Rajasthan 98.

The court decided that the seller was not justified in asking for the price in advance and added:

... in the absence of an express contract the plaintiffs [buyer] were not bound to pay the price in advance, though he was prepared to take delivery and pay the price of the goods as soon as the delivery was effected. By not having said so the plaintiffs [buyer] did not show their readiness and willingness to pay the price in accordance with the provisions of Section 32 of the Act.

The court noted:

When there is no contract to the contrary, the law says that the payment and delivery are the concurrent conditions. The general rule is very well laid down in Section 32. It is to the effect that the obligation of the seller to deliver and that of the buyer to pay are implied concurrent conditions in the nature of mutual conditions precedent, and that neither of them can enforce the contract against the other without showing performance, or offer to perform, or averring readiness and willingness to perform his own promise. In the plaint as well, the plaintiffs did not disclose that in spite of having received letter ... they applied for delivery of the goods and they made it clear to the defendants that they were ready and willing to pay the price as soon as the delivery was to be made to them. In this view of the matter I am unable to see how the plaintiffs can justifiably hold the defendants responsible for breach of contract. On this ground alone the plaintiffs claim deserves to be dismissed.

The court considered what a reasonable time for delivery might be:

However, the contract ... having not mentioned the date of delivery, the court can always find a reasonable time for performance of the contract under Section 36 (2) of the Act. As to what is the reasonable time in a given case, is a question of fact, which can be determined on the facts and circumstances of each case. The law implies a reasonable time within which the contract is to be performed when the contract itself is silent as to the time of performance. Once a reasonable time is implied within the meaning of Section 36. subclause (2), the contract becomes a contract to be performed at a fixed time as much as if the parties themselves have fixed a specific time. In the one case it is the act of parties which determines the time when the contract is to be performed; in the other case it is by implication of law that the time is determined. As to what is a reasonable time, this depends upon the particular circumstances, the nature of the commodity, the question of transport, the time during which the contract was entered into and so on. According to the contract the delivery was to be effected at Chhoti Sadri. The seller was to supply the goods from Neemuch. It has come in the judgment of the lower appellate Court that the distance between Chhoti Sadri and Neemuch is only 12 miles and this has not been disputed. According to the statement of Radhey Shyam, he had on the date of the contract more than 200 tins of Rasada Vanaspati, Chhoti Sadri is not a railway station, but there is a railway out agency, and the goods could also be transported by road. In the circumstances of the present case, I, therefore, find that one month's time is reasonable within which the contract was to be performed by the parties. The contract having been made on 27-12-63, it could be performed by 27-1-64.

TIME AND PLACE OF DELIVERY

Under the general contract law, unless provided otherwise by the parties, time is not of essence to contract. Section 11 reiterates this:

11. **Stipulations as to time:** Unless a different intention appears from the terms of the contract, stipulations as to time of payment are not deemed to be of the essence of a contract of sale. Whether any other stipulation as to time is of the essence of the contract or not depends on the terms of the contract.

It is presumed that the time of payment is not of essence to the contract. The terms of the contract must show otherwise to remove the presumption. This can be done by removing the assumption in express terms. In relation to other aspects of the contract, for example, transfer of ownership and delivery, it has to be construed whether or not time is of essence. However, courts have long maintained that transfer of ownership and delivery are of essence in commercial contracts. Not delivering the goods at the specified time mentioned in the contract in a commercial contract is a breach of condition. The buyer can terminate the contract even if the delay has caused no harm or loss to him. Of course, this can be nullified if the contract specifies that the time of delivery is not of essence. The duty cannot be only for one party. If time is of essence when the seller has to make the delivery, it is equally important for the buyer to receive it. Further, there may be several other additional acts in making a delivery; for example, giving notice and loading on the carrier. The courts have taken these too to be necessary in a commercial contract.

In *Bowes* v. *Shand*,[9] the contract provided for the goods to be 'shipped at *Madras*, or coast, for this port, during the months of March and/or April.' The goods were shipped earlier than the stipulation, in February. The buyer terminated the contract and refused to take the goods. The House of Lords held the stipulation to be of essence. Lord Cairns noted, 'It is a mercantile contract, and merchants are not in the habit of placing upon their contracts stipulations to which they do not attach some value and importance, and that alone might be a sufficient answer.' If the contract does not provide a specific date or time period for delivering the goods, the goods have to be delivered in a reasonable period. Section 36(2) provides, '36(2) Where under the contract of sale the seller is bound to send the goods to the buyer, but no time for sending them is fixed, the seller is bound to send them within a reasonable time.'

The seller's failure to deliver the goods on time is a breach of condition. The buyer has the option to terminate the contract. However, if the buyer takes the delivery, he has impliedly elected to not exercise his right to terminate the contract. Thus, having taken the delivery he cannot terminate the contract. On the failure of the seller to deliver the goods, the buyer can extend the time for delivery instead of terminating the contract. This can happen in the following ways. Suppose the seller fails to deliver the goods on time but the buyer does not terminate the contract. Instead, the buyer continues to communicate with the seller towards delivering the goods. The seller may give advance notice that he would not be able to deliver the goods on time. This is an anticipatory breach. The buyer has the option of terminating the contract but elects to continue with it. If the latter, the buyer may give a new date or leave it open. If a new date is fixed, this obviously replaces the old. If no date is fixed, it should be taken to mean supplying within a reasonable period. The buyer can, of course, specify the date after which he would not accept delivery while waiving the supply on time.

Hartley v. Hymans

In a sale contract for delivery of a specified amount of cotton yarn per week for several weeks, the buyer could terminate the contract if the seller failed to deliver the goods within the stipulated time.[10] As it happened, the seller was in breach week after week in making deliveries. The buyer complained and demanded timely deliveries. Did the parties

---

[9] *Bowes* v. *Shand*, (1877) 2 App Cas 455.

[10] *Hartley* v. *Hymans*, (1920) 3 KB 475.

continue to have contractual obligations to each other. McCardie J. noted:

In ordinary commercial contracts for the sale of goods the rule clearly is that time is prima facie of the essence with respect to delivery. ... Now, if time for delivery be of the essence of the contract, as in the present case, it follows that a vendor who has failed to deliver within the stipulated period cannot prima facie call upon the buyer to accept delivery after that period has expired. He has himself failed to fulfil the bargain and the buyer can plead the seller's default and assert that he was not ready and willing to carry out his contract. That this is so seems clear. It is, I take it, the essential juristic result when time is of the essence of the contract...

The court noted, however, that the buyer could waive the requirement 'either by writing or by word of mouth or by conduct'. The waiver would continue the contract under Section 11; alternately, or in addition, having waived the requirement, the buyer is barred from claiming that there was no subsisting contract. The court noted:

Now in considering the present case it is well to bear in mind s. 11, sub-s. 1 (a), of the Sale of Goods Act, 1893, which provides: 'Where a contract of sale is subject to any condition to be fulfilled by the seller, the buyer may waive the condition, or may elect to treat the breach of such condition as a breach of warranty, and not as a ground for treating the contract as repudiated.' This provision seems to apply as much to conditions as to time as to other conditions.

... I hold that (in so far as estoppel differs from waiver) the defendant is estopped from saying that the period for delivery expired on November 15, 1918, or from asserting that the contract ceased to be valid on that date. Inasmuch as the defendant led the plaintiff to believe by letter, as well as conduct, that the contract was still subsisting, and inasmuch as the plaintiff acted on that belief at serious expense to himself, it would be unjust to allow the

defendant to assert that the delivery period ended on November 15.

The net effect of the waiver is that a new agreement is created between the parties over the supply of the goods. The court noted: 'I hold that upon the letters passing between the parties I can, and ought to, imply a new agreement that the contract period should be extended beyond November 15, 1918—i.e., until the defendant had given a notice to the plaintiff requiring delivery within a reasonable period. I here imply such agreement.'

In the following case, Denning L.J. took a different route to explain the waiver by the buyer and its implications.

Charles Rickards L.D. v. Oppenheim

Charles Rickards Ltd, a motor car trader, entered in a contract to fabricate the body of a car and deliver to the buyer, Oppenheim, 'within six or, at the most, seven months.'[11] When the time elapsed without delivery, the buyer waived the stipulation of time. For three months after the time had expired he pressed them, then, tired of waiting any longer, gave four weeks' notice and said, 'at all events, if you do not supply it at the end of four weeks I must cancel the contract'. As the seller failed to deliver after this period, the buyer did just that. The seller challenged the cancellation of the contract by the buyer. Lord Denning noted:

If the defendant [buyer], as he did, led the plaintiffs [seller] to believe that he would not insist on the stipulation as to time, and that, if they carried out the work, he would accept it, and they did it, he could not afterwards set up the stipulation as to the time against them. Whether it be called waiver

---

[11] *Charles Rickards LD. v. Oppenhaim*, (1950) 1 KB 616.

or forbearance on his part, or an agreed variation or substituted performance, does not matter. It is a kind of estoppel. By his conduct he evinced an intention to affect their legal relations. He made, in effect, a promise not to insist on his strict legal rights. That promise was intended to be acted on, and was in fact acted on.

...

So, if the matter had stopped there, the plaintiffs [seller] could have said, notwithstanding that more than seven months had elapsed, that the defendant [buyer] was bound to accept; but the matter did not stop there, because delivery was not given in compliance with the requests of the defendant. Time and time again the defendant pressed for delivery, time and time again he was assured he would have early delivery; but he never got satisfaction; and eventually at the end of June he gave notice saying that, unless the car were delivered by July 25, 1948, he would not accept it.

...

The question thus arises whether he was entitled to give such a notice, making time of the essence ... the defendant [buyer] was entitled to give a notice bringing the matter to a head. It would be most unreasonable if the defendant, having been lenient and waived the initial expressed time, should, by so doing, have prevented himself from ever thereafter insisting on reasonably quick delivery. In my judgment he was entitled to give a reasonable notice making time of the essence of the matter. Adequate protection to the suppliers is given by the requirement that the notice should be reasonable.

Dinkerrai Lalit Kumar v. Sukhdayal Rambilas

This case involved a written sale contract where the parties had not provided the time of delivery.[12] The buyer applied to the seller for delivery but the seller failed to deliver the goods. The question was the date of breach for working out the damages. The court ruled:

Now under this contract, as I have pointed out, no time is fixed for delivery of the goods sold; and under Section 36, Sub-clause (2), of the Indian Sale of Goods Act, where under the contract of sale the seller is bound to send the goods to the buyer, but no time for sending them is fixed, the seller is bound to send them within a reasonable time. Therefore the law implies a reasonable time within which the contract is to be performed when the contract itself is silent as to the time of performance. In our opinion once a reasonable time is implied within the meaning of Section 36, Sub-clause (2)3 the contract becomes a contract to be performed at, a fixed time as much as if the parties themselves have fixed a specific time. In the one case it is the act of parties which determines the time when the contract is to be performed; in the other case it is by implication of law that the time is determined.

...

I see no reason in principle to distinguish between a contract where the time for delivery is fixed and a contract where the time for delivery is, not fixed. If the time for the performance of a contract or the time for delivery is fixed, it cannot be extended by the unilateral act of a party.

Equally so time cannot be extended in the case of a contract where the law implies a reasonable time for the performance of the contract. In the first case, when the fixed time has expired there would be a breach; in the latter case, when the reasonable time implied by the law has expired, equally so there would be a breach unless either in the one or in the other case there is an agreement between the parties to extend the time for the performance of the contract.

Food Corporation of India v. M/s Arosan Enterprises Ltd

The Government of India needed sugar urgently to meet the scarcity in the festival season.[13] Its procurement arm, the Food Corporation of India, made a contract with

---

[12] *Dinkerrai Lalit Kumar* v. *Sukhdayal Rambilas*, (1946) 48 BOMLR 821.

[13] *Food Corporation of India* v. *M/s Arosan Enterprises Ltd*, AIR (1996) Delhi 126.

a foreign seller to supply a huge quantity of sugar within a short period of time. The seller failed to supply the sugar within the stipulated period and the buyer cancelled the contract. Later, at the request of the seller, it withdrew the cancellation of the contract. The buyer kept communicating with the seller to deliver at the earliest, and the seller kept promising to supply the goods. Eventually, the buyer cancelled the contract. At the arbitration, the arbitrator held that there was obligation on the buyer to fix a fresh date of delivery after withdrawal of cancellation. Further, after withdrawal of the cancellation, the buyer had waived his right to again cancel the contract on the ground that shipment had not been made up to stipulated date and thus, the subsequent cancellation was on a non-existent ground and therefore illegal. The case came before the Delhi High Court. The court noted:

The delivery period stipulated in the contract was 31st Oct. 1989. The supply was not made within the delivery period. If the buyer still asks for goods after 31st Oct. 1989 and specifies no fixed delivery date, it would mean that the goods would have to be delivered in a reasonable time (Refer Section 36 of Sale of Goods Act). In such a case it would be assumed that the contract is silent as to the time of performance. The law implies a reasonable time within which the contract is to be performed when the contract itself is silent as to the time of performance. Once a reasonable time is implied within the meaning of Section 36(2), the contract becomes a contract to be performed at a fixed time as much as if the parties themselves have fixed a specified time. In such a case if the delivery is not made within a reasonable time there would be breach unless such a time is extended. What is reasonable time depends upon facts and circumstances of each case. In the present case, however, the supply was never effected and the goods never entered the Indian Waters.

The seller should deliver the goods at a place agreed between the parties. Where should the goods be delivered if the parties do not provide for this in express or implied terms? Section 36 provides the answer on this and other aspects of delivery:

36. Rules as to delivery: (1) Whether it is for the buyer to take possession of the goods or for the seller to send them to the buyer is a question depending in each case on the contract, express or implied, between the parties. Apart from any such contract, goods sold are to be delivered at the place at which they are at the time of the sale, and goods agreed to be sold are to be delivered at the place at which they are at the time of the agreement to sell, or, if not then in existence, at the place at which they are manufactured or produced.

Whether the buyer will take possession of the goods from the seller or the seller will have the goods sent to the buyer is to be decided by the terms of the contract between the parties. Taking possession of the goods is delivery. Thus, the section provides for where the goods should be delivered if the contract is silent on the place of delivery. The section covers three situations: The first is a sale of specific goods where the ownership transfers at the time of making the contract. This can happen because either the contract is silent on transfer of ownership or provides that the ownership will transfer at the time of making the contract. In this case, the delivery is done where the goods were at the time of making of the contract. In the second case, the parties enter into an agreement for the sale of specific goods where the ownership is to transfer at a later time. In this case too the delivery will be done where the goods were at the time of making of the agreement to sell. The third case deals with future goods. These are delivered at the place where they are manufactured or produced. As the delivery is where the goods are or manufactured or produced, it is for the buyer to take delivery of the goods.

DELIVERY OF WRONG QUANTITY

The buyer may reject or accept the delivery of a smaller or larger quantity than contracted for. Section 37 of the Sale of Goods Act, 1930, deals with the options for the buyer. It reads:

37. Delivery of wrong quantity: (1) Where the seller delivers to the buyer a quantity of goods less than he contracted to sell, the buyer may reject them, but if the buyer accepts the goods so delivered he shall pay for them at the contract rate.

(2) Where the seller delivers to the buyer a quantity of goods larger than he contracted to sell, the buyer may accept the goods included in the contract and reject the rest, or he may reject the whole. If the buyer accepts the whole of the goods so delivered, he shall pay for them at the contract rate.

(3) Where the seller delivers to the buyer the goods he contracted to sell mixed with goods of a different description not included in the contract, the buyer may accept the goods which are in accordance with the contract and reject the rest, or may reject the whole.

(4) The provisions of this section are subject to any usage of trade, special agreement or course of dealing between the parties.

The section is self-explanatory. The 'contract rate' would refer to the unit price of the goods. This can be provided in the contract or the parties would have to work it out from the terms of the contract. Section 38 is related to this. Unless provided in the contract, the buyer is not bound to accept goods in instalments. Section 38 reads:

38. Instalment deliveries: (1) Unless otherwise agreed, the buyer of goods is not bound to accept delivery thereof by instalments.

(2) Where there is a contract for the sale of goods to be delivered by stated instalments which

are to be separately paid for, and the seller makes no delivery or defective delivery in respect of one or more instalments, or the buyer neglects or refuses to take delivery of or pay for one or more instalments, it is a question in each case depending on the terms of the contract and the circumstances of the case, whether the breach of contract is a repudiation of the whole contract, or whether it is a severable breach giving rise to a claim for compensation, but not to a right to treat the whole contract as repudiated.

The following is a founding case on the topic.

Behrend & Company, Limited v. Produce Brokers Company, Limited

By two contracts, Behrend & Co., Ltd sold 176 tons of two different varieties of cotton seeds to Produce Brokers Co., Ltd.[14] The contracts contained identical terms. The goods were to be shipped on steamer from Alexandria and delivered in London to the buyer's craft alongside the steamer. Payment was to be made in London in exchange for the shipping documents. The buyer made the payment, received the shipping documents, and sent his craft to collect the goods. The steamer *Port Inglis* delivered only a part of the two parcels. It discovered that the rest of the seeds were lying under cargo to be delivered at another port, Hull. The *Port Inglis* stopped delivery and left for Hull, promising to return and deliver the rest of the seeds. She returned in about a fortnight's time and the seeds were tendered to the buyers. Meanwhile, the buyer had informed the seller that they regarded the departure of the *Port Inglis* with the remainder of the seeds on board as a failure to deliver and a breach of contract. They kept so much of the seeds as had been delivered to them and demanded repayment of so much

[14] *Behrend & Company, Limited* v. *Produce Brokers Company, Limited*, (1920) 3 KB 530.

of the contract price as the undelivered seeds represented. The dispute was referred to an arbitrator who ruled in favour of the buyer. The case came before the court. Bailhache J. ruled:

The umpire has decided in the buyers' favour and I am asked to say whether he was right. Everything depends upon whether the departure of the *Port Inglis* for Hull with the greater part of both parcels of seed on board was a failure to deliver, notwithstanding the promise to return and complete delivery. Both contracts between the parties are in the same terms and neither has any express provision on the subject. In my opinion, the buyer under such a contract, and where each parcel of goods is indivisible, as here, has the right to have delivery on the arrival of the steamship, not necessarily immediately or continuously; he must take his turn or the goods may be so stowed that other goods have to be discharged before the whole of the buyers' parcel can be got out. To such delays and others which may occur in the course of unloading the buyer must submit, but in the absence of any stipulation to the contrary the buyer, being ready with his craft, is entitled to delivery of the whole of an indivisible parcel of goods sold to him for delivery from a vessel which has begun delivery to him before she leaves the port to deliver goods elsewhere. If this is so the rest of the case is covered by s. 30 of the Sale of Goods Act, and the buyer can either reject the whole of the goods, including those actually delivered, in which case he can recover the whole of his money; or he may keep the goods actually delivered and reject the rest, in which case he must pay for the goods kept at the contract price, and he can recover the price paid for the undelivered portion. I think that the award is right.

Shipton, Anderson & Co. v. Weil Brothers & Co.

This case is about the seller supplying a larger quantity than the contracted amount. Under a contract for the sale of a cargo of wheat, the seller was to deliver 10 per cent more or less than 4,500 tons.[15] The seller tendered the buyer 55 lbs more than 4950 tons, the maximum number of tons that the seller was to deliver under the contract. The buyer rejected the tender on the ground that the quantity of cargo tendered was 55 lbs in excess of the contract quantity. The price payable for the 55 lbs would have been about 4s, the whole contract price being more than £ 40,000 for 4950 tons, but the seller never claimed payment of the 4s. The seller contested the rejection of the delivery. The court stated:

Now the excess quantity is trifling, so trifling that it is quite impossible to suppose that any business man would regard it as in any way affecting the substance of the contract or as making the contract any the more or any the less an advantageous contract to enter into. It is an excess of 55 lbs. in a total cargo of 4950 tons; approximately it is an excess of 1 lb. in every 100 tons tendered. If one considers the excess in money, it seems more trifling still; it is an excess of 4s. on a contract price of over 40,000l; or putting it again in still plainer figures an excess of 1s. in 10,000l. Counsel for the defendants, however, say that that is an excess which by law entitles the buyer to reject, and they rely upon s. 30, sub-s. 2, of the Sale of Goods Act of 1893. ... They contend, as they must to be consistent, that any excess that can be measured in weight or in currency would have this effect, that, if it is only sixpence or indeed anything that can be measured, there is a discrepancy between the contract and the tender which is fatal.

...

I have found a case which I think is more in point. It is true that the actual point was not decided, because it was not necessary to decide it; but there was a dictum of Bigham J. in that case which exactly, in my opinion, applies to this case. The case to which I refer is Harland v. Burstall ((1901)

---

[15] *Shipton, Anderson & Co.* v. *Weil Brothers & Co.*, (1912) 1 K.B. 574.

6 Com. Cas. 113). A smaller quantity was there delivered than the contract quantity, thirty loads out of 500, of course a very different proportion to this, and Bigham J. held that there was a deficiency which entitled the buyers to reject. The learned judge says this: 'Of course, in carrying out a commercial contract such as this, some slight elasticity is unavoidable; no one supposes that the delivery is to be within a cubic foot of the named quantity, but it must be substantially of the quantity named; and in my judgment 470 loads is not substantially 500.' I think that the question is whether there has been a substantial departure from the contract. As I pointed out during the argument, the right to reject is founded upon the hypothesis that the seller was not ready and willing to perform, or had not performed, his part of the contract. The tender of a wrong quantity evidences an unreadiness and unwillingness, but that, in my opinion, must mean an excess or deficiency in quantity which is capable of influencing the mind of the buyer. In my opinion, this excess is not. I agree that directly the excess becomes a matter of possible discussion between reasonable parties, the seller is bound to justify what he has done under the contract; but the doctrine of de minimis cannot, I think, be excluded merely because the statute refers to the tender of a smaller or larger quantity than the contract quantity as entitling a buyer to reject.

I wish to add this. The reason why an excess in tender entitles a buyer to reject is that the seller seeks to impose a burden on the buyer which he is not entitled to impose. That burden is the payment of money not agreed to be paid. It is prima facie no burden on the buyer to have 55 lbs. more than 4,950 tons offered to him, and there is nothing to suggest that these sellers would have ever insisted, or thought of insisting, upon payment of the 4s. over the 40,000l. The sellers' original appropriation appeared to be within the proper quantity. The excess of 55 lbs. appears when the quantity shipped is converted from kilos into tons. If the sellers had expressly or impliedly insisted upon payment of the 4s. upon their view of the contract, the case would have been different; but nothing of that kind can be supposed to have taken place here.

Wilensko Slaski Towarzystwo Drewno v. Fenwick & Co. (West Hartlepool), Ltd

In this case, the goods were mixed as well as in short supply. Under a sale contract, the seller was to deliver timber of a specific measurement.[16] About 1 per cent of the timber shipped did not conform to the contract description, and so the buyer refused to take delivery. The court agreed:

It is said … that the proportion of goods appearing in the invoice and specifications which did not conform to the contract description—amounting to something under one per cent. of the cargo—was so small that the doctrine of de minimis non curat lex should be invoked. But I cannot accede to that argument. It seems to me that the shipping documents showed on the face of them goods of the contract description mixed with goods of a different description, and that relatively small though the number of the goods of the different description were, it is sufficient to entitle the buyers to refuse to take up the documents.

Suresh Kumar v. K. Assan Koya and Sons

In a sale contract between two rice traders based in Kerala, one in Cochin and the other at Mattancherry, the seller was selling 'Nepal Rice'.[17] The goods were loaded onto a train at a station called Jogbani and sent to Cochin. The terms of sale were 'bilticut' ready RR 'Jogbani' to Calicut. 'Bilticut' was a local name for a FOR contract, which refers to a contract where the seller delivers the goods to the buyer at the designated railway station for transmission to the buyer. As loading on the train is the delivery to the buyer, the seller has to do this within the time fixed by

[16] *Wilensko Slaski Towarzystwo Drewno* v. *Fenwick & Co. (West Hartlepool), Ltd*, (1938) 3 All ER 429.

[17] *Suresh Kumar* v. *K. Assan Koya and Sons*, AIR (1990) Kerala 20.

the contract. If no time is fixed, this has to be done within a reasonable period. The seller has to pay for all expenses till the goods are loaded on the train. Following Section 39(2), the seller makes a reasonable contract for the protection of the goods. Risk and ownership prima facie pass to the buyer at the time of delivery. The buyer refused to take delivery of the sixth wagon on several grounds, of which all but two were baseless. The agreed quantity was 160 bags of rice having a total weight of 16,000 kg. The buyer was getting a supply of 522 kg. Further, some of the bags were lightly damaged. The court ruled:

… under the bilticut contract the seller's responsibility is to deliver the goods in a reasonably safe manner to the Railway for carriage to the place of destination and the risk of deterioration of goods in quantity and quality necessarily incidental to the course of transit is that of the buyer. This is also the general law unless otherwise agreed is clear from the provisions contained in S. 40 of the Indian Sale of Goods Act which is to the following effect.

> Where the seller of goods agrees to deliver them at his own risk at a place other than that where they are when sold, the buyer shall, nevertheless, unless otherwise agreed, to take any risk of deterioration in the goods necessarily incident to the course of transit.

In the light of the facts and circumstances of the case we are of the view that a shortage of 522 Kgs. of rice out of an agreed quantity of 16, 000 Kgs. of rice and the slight wetness in respect of about 40 bags of rice can reasonably be characterised only as deterioration in the quantity and quality necessarily incidental to the course of transit from Jogbani to Calicut and the loss if any on account of such deterioration is liable to be borne by the defendant and the defendant was not justified in refusing to take delivery on those grounds. We accordingly confirm the finding of learned Judge that the defendant was not justified in refusing to accept the 6th wagon of rice supplied by the plaintiff.

The buyer contended that the seller had delivered a shorter quantity than contracted to the railway. Following Section 37(1), the seller was entitled to reject the goods. The court noted:

Even though it is true that S. 37(1) of the Act provides for rejection of the goods when the seller delivers to the buyer a quantity of goods less than what was contracted for, we find that the said rule is subject to a general rule of law namely 'de minimis non curat lex'. It has been held so by Ahmadi, J. in a decision reported in Dudhia Forest Co-op. Socy. v. Mohamed and Co., 1980 GujLR 272, where it was observed thus:

> It is the duty of the seller to deliver to the buyer the quantity of goods stipulated in the contract. However a slight deficiency in the quantity will not entitle the buyer to reject the goods or claim damages on the principle de minimis non curat lex, because some flexibility in such contracts of sale of goods in bulk is unavoidable and trivial shortfall in quantity must be overlooked. If the difference is, however, substantial, the buyer would be justified in resorting to S. 37(1) of the Sale of Goods Act.

We also find that the scope, purpose and effect of the 'De minimis rule' as applied to the law of sale of goods have been succinctly explained in Benjamin's Sale of Goods thus:

> A deficiency or excess in quantity which is 'microscopic' and which is not capable of influencing the mind of the buyer will not entitle him to reject the goods, for de minimis non curat lex. Some slight elasticity in carrying out a commercial contract for the supply of goods in bulk is unavoidable, and the Courts will not allow the buyer to take advantage of a merely trivial difference in quantity if the delivery is substantially of the quantity named. (Benjamin's Sale of Goods—Second Edition (1981), para-623, page 298)

In view of the legal position explained above we are of the view that a shortage of 522 Kgs out of a quantity of 16,000 Kgs. contracted to be supplied, is only a slight deficiency which comes within the 'de minimis rule' and we hold that the defendant was not justified in rejecting the goods even under S.37(1) of the Sale of Goods Act.

Duties of the Buyer

Section 44 is on the duty of the buyer to take delivery from the seller. It reads:

44. Liability of buyer for neglecting or refusing delivery of goods: When the seller is ready and willing to deliver the goods and requests the buyer to take delivery, and the buyer does not within a reasonable time after such request take delivery of the goods, he is liable to the seller for any loss occasioned by his neglect or refusal to take delivery, and also for a reasonable charge for the care and custody of the goods:

Provided that nothing in this section shall affect the rights of the seller where the neglect or refusal of the buyer to take delivery amounts to a repudiation of the contract.

The buyer has a duty to take delivery of the goods from the seller within a reasonable time. The refusal by the buyer will make him liable to pay damages for the loss caused to the seller, including charges for care and custody of the goods. In addition, if the refusal by the buyer is a breach of a condition of the contract, the seller will have the right to terminate the contract. However, as noted earlier, if the seller makes a defective tender, such as featuring the wrong quantity, the buyer has the option of rejecting it. Section 42 provides the meaning of the term acceptance:

42. Acceptance: The buyer is deemed to have accepted the goods when he intimates to the seller that he has accepted them, or when the goods have been delivered to him and he does any act in relation to them which is inconsistent with the ownership of the seller, or when, after the lapse of a reasonable time, he retains the goods without intimating to the seller that he has rejected them.

The buyer can accept the goods through three means. The first is by communicating the acceptance of the goods to the seller. The second is by performing an act that is inconsistent with the ownership of the seller, such as consuming or using the goods. The third is lapse of a reasonable time. Section 41 gives the buyer a reasonable opportunity to examine the goods.

41. Buyer's right of examining the goods: (1) Where goods are delivered to the buyer which he has not previously examined, he is not deemed to have accepted them unless and until he has had a reasonable opportunity of examining them for the purpose of ascertaining whether they are in conformity with the contract.

(2) Unless otherwise agreed, when the seller tenders delivery of goods to the buyer, he is bound, on request, to afford the buyer a reasonable opportunity of examining the goods for the purpose of ascertaining whether they are in conformity with the contract.

As noted earlier, under Section 31, the buyer has to accept the goods and pay in accordance with the contract. However, under Section 32, 'unless otherwise agreed', delivery and payment are concurrent conditions. If the contract does not set other terms for payment, the buyer is not required to make payment unless the seller is willing to give possession of the goods for the price.

Mohanlal Manilal v. Firm Dhirubhai Bavajibhai

Under a sale contract, the seller delivered a wagonload of a particular quality of coal to the buyer.[18] The buyer had made arrangements to sell the coal to sub-buyers. The delivery was delayed considerably, and the buyer did not examine the quality of coal when it finally arrived. He delivered it to some of the sub-buyers and took the rest to

[18] *Mohanlal Manilal v. Firm Dhirubhai Bavajibhai,* AIR (1962) Gujarat 56.

his warehouse. The sub-buyers complained that the coal was of an inferior quality. The buyer terminated the contract as the goods supplied were not of the quality settled in the contract. The seller contended that the buyer had accepted the goods under Section 42. As the seller had further sold the goods, under the section it was an act that was 'inconsistent with the ownership of the seller'. The buyer accepted this, but contended that Section 41 allows a 'reasonable opportunity' to the buyer to examine the delivered goods. As the buyer had promptly rejected the goods, the rejection was valid. The high court noted:

This contention ... raises an important question as to the relation between Sections 41 and 42 of the Indian Sale of Goods Act.

This view is, in my opinion, incorrect and the contention ... must be rejected. And I think the reason is obvious. One of the acts upon the doing of which the buyer is deemed to have accepted the goods is that he intimates to the seller that he has accepted them. It is clear that such an intimation may be made by the buyer before he has had a reasonable opportunity of examination and if such an intimation is made, it is obvious that without more Section 42 would operate, and the buyer would be deemed to have accepted the goods. In the same way when the buyer does an act in relation to the goods which is inconsistent with the ownership of the seller, Section 42 must be treated as coming into operation notwithstanding that the reasonable opportunity of examining the goods has not expired. Suppose the buyer after taking delivery of the goods and before he has had a reasonable opportunity of examining them consumes them or 'turns them or part of them, at once into his mill and uses them in the manufacture', can it be said in such a case that the buyer is not deemed to have accepted the goods because he used or consumed them before he had a reasonable opportunity of examining them for the purposes of ascertaining whether they were in conformity with the contract? The act of the buyer

in using or consuming the goods would certainly be deemed to constitute acceptance of the goods by the buyer. Section 42 is, in my opinion, independent of Section 41 and must be given effect to whenever any one of the acts specified in that Section is done by the buyer irrespective of the question whether such act is done during the currency or after the expiration of the reasonable time for examination of the goods. Even if during the currency of the reasonable time within which the examination of the goods is to be made the buyer does any one of the acts specified in Section 42, he must be deemed to have accepted the goods. The language of Section 42 is plain and simple. There is no ellipsis and no redundance nor is there anything vague or ambiguous about the language. That being so, I must read Section 42 in its natural and ordinary sense. Section 42 expresses a meaning which is single and sensible and I see no reason why the precise words used by the lawmaker in that Section should not be given their full meaning and effect. Section 42 declares in clear and unambiguous language that when any one of the acts specified therein is done by the buyer, the buyer shall be deemed to have accepted the goods and does not introduce or admit any qualification or exception. Under these circumstances I do not see why the plain meaning and effect of Section 42 should be cut down by introducing a qualification by reference to Section 41. Section 41 confers on the buyer a right of examination of the goods for the purpose of ascertaining whether they are in conformity with the contract. On principle this right is conferred on the buyer for 'no acceptance can properly be said to take place before the purchaser has had an opportunity of rejection' and 'a right of inspection to ascertain whether such condition has been complied with is in the contemplation of both parties to such a contract; and no complete and final acceptance so as irrevocably to vest the property in the buyer can take place before he has exercised or waived that right.'

Now the last words of the preceding sentence provide the answer to the apparent conflict between Sections 41 and 42. The right of examination of the goods for the purpose of ascertaining whether they are in conformity with the contract is a right which is conferred or; the buyer for the purpose of enabling him to decide whether to accept the goods or to reject them. But it is open to him to waive that right and he may choose to accept the goods without exercising that right. It will thus be seen that no conflict is created between Sections 41 and 42 by reading Section 42 as independent of Section 41 and not limiting the provisions of Section 42 by Section 41. Where the buyer does any of the acts specified in Section 42 before the reasonable opportunity of examining the goods has expired the buyer waives the right of examination of the goods conferred by Section 41 and is deemed to have accepted the goods. This is in my opinion the only construction which can be placed on Sections 41 and 42. I am fortified in this opinion by a decision of the Court of Appeal in England in Hardy and Co. v. Hillems and Fowler (1923) 2 KB 490, where the Court of Appeal has taken the same view regarding the construction or Sections 34 and 35 of the English Sale of Goods Act which are in the same terms as Sections 41 and 42 of the Indian Sale of Goods Act with which I am concerned in the present case. In this view of the matter it is clear that the defendant must fail. The act of the defendant in selling and delivering a part of the goods to the sub-purchasers was an act in relation to the goods which was inconsistent with the ownership of the plaintiffs and the defendant was, therefore, deemed to have accepted the goods by selling and delivering a part of the goods to the sub-purchasers. It was immaterial whether the act of selling and delivering a part of the goods to the sub-purchasers was done by the defendant before the reasonable opportunity of examining the goods had expired or was done by the defendant after the expiration of the reasonable time for examination of the goods.

Mahadev Ganga Prasad v. Gouri Shankar

The seller was a manufacturer of sarees, and the buyer, a trader. The parties had entered into a contract for the sale of five bales of sarees.[19] The contract was under the standard terms set by the manufacturer. The clauses on delivery included the following:

Clause 2. Details of purchase will be debited to the customer on the day of the booking of the goods in the Railway. The purchaser shall send money direct to the seller as soon as the RR [railway receipt] will reach him. The seller is at liberty either to send the RR through the Bank or to realise money in advance or to proceed as he thinks proper.

Clause 4. If the purchaser does not release the RR for any reason or fails to take delivery of the goods from the Railway, the seller will be at liberty to release and store the goods in his warehouse at the risk of the purchaser … the seller is further empowered to sell or auction the goods after 7 days notice to the purchaser.

The seller sent the goods by rail and sent the railway receipt through a bank. The buyer claimed that it was a sale by sample and the seller should give a guarantee that the supplied goods would tally with the sample. The buyer declared that if the guarantee did not come through, he would not receive the goods. The seller replied that the sale was not on the basis of a sample but by description of the goods being of merchantable quality. The buyer replied that he had cancelled the contract. The seller claimed that the buyer was in breach of his contractual obligations and claimed damages. The court ruled:

The duties of the seller and the buyer are laid down in chap. IV, Sale of Goods Act. The buyer is bound to accept and pay for the goods in accordance with the terms of the contract for sale.

Section 36, Sale of Goods Act lays down the rules as to delivery. One such rule is that if the goods are not in existence at the time of the contract, the delivery shall be made at the place at

[19] *Mahadev Ganga Prasad* v. *Gouri Shankar*, AIR (37) (1950) Orissa 42.

which they are manufactured or produced. This is also incorporated in paras. 2 and 3 of the printed agreement. Paragraph 2 says that the details of the purchase will be debited to the customers on the day of the booking of the goods in the railway. ... The seller is at liberty either to send the RR through the Bank or to realise money in advance or to proceed as he thinks proper. Paragraph 3 says that as soon as the goods arrive at the station, the risk shifts on to the purchaser. There was, therefore, delivery of the goods to the purchaser under the terms of the contract and the only right of the purchaser thereafter was the right to examine the goods as provided for under S. 41 of the Act. That section makes a distinction between the delivery of the goods to the buyer and his acceptance of the same after examination. There is, however, no provision for the buyer to refuse to receive the goods. He may receive the articles and yet not accept them. The plaintiff's case that he was justified in not receiving the goods at all, does not find support either from the express terms of the contract, as stipulated between the parties, or from any of the provisions of the Sale of Goods Act.

Thus, as the seller has delivered the goods under the contract, the buyer has to receive the goods from the carrier. The buyer retains his right of examination and rejection. However, this can be done only after receiving the goods from the carrier.

G.N. Behere v. N.B. Rice Mills

The seller was a manufacturer of machinery at Dahanu Road in District Thana.[20] The buyer ran an oil mill in Bongaingaon, Assam, and ordered a paddy separator box. The contract was free on rail. The seller drew the railway receipt in the name of the seller and despatched the machine in a good condition. Unfortunately, it was damaged in transit. The

[20] *G.N. Behere* v. *N.B. Rice Mills*, AIR (1966) Assam and Nagaland 95.

seller had sent the railway receipt to a bank for buyer's collection. But when the buyer learnt of the damage to the machine, he refused to take the railway receipt from the bank and collect the goods. The buyer approached the court for a refund of Rs 800, the advance he had paid to the buyer. His contention was that as the goods were not in conformity with the contract, he was free to terminate the contract. The court ruled:

Section 40 of the Sale of Goods Act provides:
> 'Where the seller of goods agrees to deliver them at his own risk at place other than that where they are when sold, the buyer shall, nevertheless, unless otherwise agreed, take any risk of deterioration in the goods necessarily incident to the course of transit.'

This section also shows that although the seller undertakes to take the goods at his own risk to a place other than that where they are when sold, if any deterioration takes place in the course of the transit, the buyer would be liable for it. Whether there was any deterioration for which the buyer would have been liable or not within the meaning of Section 40 could only have been determined after delivery had been taken and it cannot be said that under no circumstances the buyer was bound to refuse delivery of the goods as soon as be found that the goods were in a damaged condition.

The court below has relied upon Section 41, which lays down as follows:

> 'Section 41. (1) Where goods are delivered to the buyer which he has not previously examined, he is not deemed to have accepted them unless and until he had a reasonable opportunity of examining them for the purpose of ascertaining whether they are in conformity with the contract.
>
> (2) Unless otherwise agreed, when the seller tenders delivery of goods is the buyer, he is bound on request to afford the buyer a reasonable opportunity of examining the goods for the purpose of ascertaining whether they are in conformity with the contract.'

This section only gives the buyer a right of examination. It does not give a right to the buyer to repudiate the contract. The right of inspection under this section can only arise either when the delivery has already been taken or when it is tendered for delivery. In the present case the respondent did not take delivery and thus Section 41(1) will not be attracted and if the argument of the respondent is accepted that it was tendered for delivery at the railway station when it reached Bongaigaon, the only right which could be exercised by the plaintiff under Section 41(2) was to ask for the inspection of the goods but he could not repudiate the contract and further that when the goods reached the destination under the railway receipt, it cannot be said that they were tendered for delivery at Bongaigaon station.

Dharampal and Company, Agra v. Firm Kila Gatla Ram Chandra Rao and Company, Vizianagaram

Under the contract, the seller was to deliver 250 bags of peas of a particular quality on the terms FOR Vizianagaram.[21] The seller arranged for a railway wagon and dispatched the peas. He then sent the railway receipt through a bank to the buyer for collecting the peas by paying the required price. The buyer did not collect the railway receipt and receive the goods. He alleged that the peas despatched were not of adequate quality, and attempted to repudiate the contract by not collecting the railway receipt. The seller had to collect the railway receipt from the bank, pay for the demurrage to the railway, and sell the peas in the market at a lower rate. The seller claimed that by failing to collect the railway receipt from the bank and collect the goods, the buyer had breached the contract. The seller further claimed that the

goods were in accordance with the contract. The seller moved the court to claim damages. The high court ruled:

Section 41 of the Sale of Goods Act provides that a reasonable opportunity of examining the goods for the purpose of ascertaining whether they are in conformity with the contract has to be afforded to the buyer. This opportunity is necessary where the buyer had no previous occasion to examine the goods. From the facts of this case it is evident that the buyer had no opportunity of examining the goods earlier. The contract was made on the telegram and the plaintiff despatched the goods without the buyer examining them at the dispatching station. He could examine the goods at Vizianagram where the goods were carried by the Railways. … He did not take the R.R. Consequently, there was no question of his examining the goods or coming to the conclusion that the goods were of an inferior quality or below the quality stipulated. It is only after he had received the goods that he could have examined them. He could not have repudiated the contract, but ask for damages for the breach of warranty. He did not do so, without examining the goods he took the stand that the goods were of an inferior quality than what was contracted for. … When the buyer had contracted the purchase of certain items of farm goods indicating a particular quality that quality could only be ascertained after visual and other inspection. It was his bounden duty to have received the goods, made the inspection and then if it was found to be of a quality inferior to that contracted for he could have sued for damages.

Section 41 of the Sale of Goods Act only gives a buyer a right of examining the goods and not a right to repudiate the contract. The right of inspection could only arise either when the consignee had taken the delivery from the carrier or when it was tendered for delivery to the buyer. Where the buyer was the consignee the question of affording an opportunity could arise only after the consignee received the consignment. Where the seller was the consignee, it was his duty to take delivery of the goods and give an opportunity to the buyer to inspect and examine the goods. It means that

---

[21] *Dharampal and Company, Agra* v. *Firm Kila Gatla Ram Chandra Rao and Company*, AIR (1980) Allahabad 316.

when the seller tenders the goods to the buyer he is bound to afford an opportunity for the inspection of the goods. In the present case the goods were loaded FOR Vizianagaram at the instance of the buyer. The Railway became the carrier and the agent for the buyer. The buyer, therefore, could not compel the seller to offer the goods for an examination at Vizianagaram. That was not part of the contract. That could have been understood if the defendant had contracted with the plaintiff that the goods will be acceptable to him only after inspection at Vizianagaram but such is not the case here. The goods were to be despatched FOR along with the relevant papers which meant that the goods were entrusted to the carrier for being collected by the defendant at the destination. The buyer was obliged to receive the goods and make an examination and if he found that it was substandard or contrary to specification, he could sue for the refund of the price or sell the goods and sue for the damages.

Jain Mills and Electrical Stores, M/s v. State of Orissa

Jain Mills and Electrical Stores were awarded a contract to supply electrical goods to a department of the Government of Orissa for a lift irrigation project.[22] The contract stipulated 1 per cent of the total amount of contract for each day's delay in delivery. The government could terminate the contract for a delay exceeding ten days. There was indeed a delay in the delivery. The government took the delivery and retained the goods, but despite repeated reminders did not pay the seller. The seller came before the court claiming damages. The court noted:

The contract of sale in the present case is governed by the provisions of the Indian Sale of Goods Act, 1930 (hereinafter referred to as 'the Act'). S. 42 of the Act provides:

---

[22] *Jain Mills and Electrical Stores, M/s v. State of Orissa*, AIR (1991) Orissa 117.

'The buyer is deemed to have accepted the goods when he intimates to the seller that he has accepted them, or when the goods have been delivered to him and he does any act in relation to them which is inconsistent with the ownership of the seller, or when, after the lapse of a reasonable time, he retains the goods without intimating to the seller that he has rejected them.'

Section 63 of the Act provides that 'The question "what is a reasonable time" is a question of fact'. In the present case, there was delay of some days in the delivery of the goods. So the parties aggrieved, if at all, are the defendants. As earlier stated, the plaintiffs are not definite as to what exactly was the period of delay, whether it was delay of more than ten days or less than ten days. If the delay was less than ten days, then the defendants could not have rejected the goods, but they were entitled to claim damages as stipulated in the contract. If only the delay had been for a period of more than ten days, the defendants had a right to reject the contract under Cl. (3). But in the present case, after the goods were received by the defendants, they have retained the goods without intimating to the seller within a reasonable time that they have rejected them. So it can be safely inferred, that in view of the provisions of Ss. 42 and 63 of the Act, the defendants must be deemed to have accepted the goods long prior to August, 1973.

INSTALMENT CONTRACT

In some contracts, the delivery of goods may be in instalments. In such contracts, is the contract a single one for the supply of goods in instalments or should each instalment could be taken as a separate contract? For example, a seller supplying different size of plates of the same crockery set to a buyer on three different days is not a divisible contract. The intent of the parties is to sell the set as a whole. However, a contract by a raw material supplier to a manufacturer to supply 500 kg of wheat on every Monday of the week for the year may be a divisible contract.

Whether a contract is divisible or not will have to be decided by the general principles of contract law. The Sale of Goods Act, 1930, provides guide on only some aspects of this. Section 38 provides on instalment contract: 'Section 38(1) provides that unless the parties have agreed for delivery in instalments, the buyer is not bound to accept delivery in instalments nor can the buyer require delivery in instalments.'

Behrend & Company, Limited v. *Produce Brokers Company, Limited*[23] is a judgment that relates to this. We reviewed this case on the subject of the seller supplying a lesser quantity than contracted. The ship delivered part of the goods to the buyer, went to another port to deliver a consignment and came back to deliver the rest. This became delivery in instalment, which was contrary to the contract. The seller was free to reject all the goods or accept the first lot but reject the second lot. The court noted:

the buyer can either reject the whole of the goods, including those actually delivered, in which case he can recover the whole of his money; or he may keep the goods actually delivered and reject the rest, in which case he must pay for the goods kept at the contract price, and he can recover the price paid for the undelivered portion. I think that the award is right.

Section 38(2) provides for a breach of a contract where the goods are to be supplied in instalments and the price is to be paid for each instalment:

38(2) Where there is a contract for the sale of goods to be delivered by stated instalments which are to be separately paid for, and the seller makes no delivery or defective delivery in respect of one or more instalments, or the buyer neglects or

refuses to take delivery of or pay for one or more instalments, it is a question in each case depending on the terms of the contract and the circumstances of the case, whether the breach of contract is a repudiation of the whole contract, or whether it is a severable breach giving rise to a claim for compensation, but not to a right to treat the whole contract as repudiated.

The subsection refers to the case where the seller defaults in making a delivery or the buyer defaults in paying for a delivery. Whether the breach is to be taken as of the entire contract, giving the option in the other party to terminate the contract, or only a breach of the particular instalment is a question to be decided on the terms of the contract and circumstances of the case.

Maple Flock Company, Limited v. *Universal Furniture Products (Wembley), Limited*

Universal Furniture Products, Limited, contracted to deliver to Maple Flock Company, Limited, 100 tons of rag flock in three loads of one-and-a half tons each per week as required.[24] The weekly deliveries were to be paid for separately at a fixed per-ton rate. By law, the government regulated chlorine in flock, so as a term of the contract, the seller gave a written guarantee that all flock supplied conformed to the government standard. The buyer accepted eighteen instalments. By then, the results of the chemical analysis of the sixteenth instalment indicated the chlorine content to be eight times the minimum level set by the government. The buyer intimated termination of the contract. Negotiations took place between the parties and the buyer took two more instalments. But the buyer

---

[23] *Behrend & Company, Limited* v. *Produce Brokers Company, Limited*, (1920) 3 KB 530.

[24] *Maple Flock Company, Limited* v. *Universal Furniture Products (Wembley), Limited*, (1934) 1 KB 148.

held to his intimation and terminated the contract. The seller claimed breach of contract and the buyer damages. Lord Hewart C.J. observed:

The decision of this case depends on the true construction and application of s. 31, sub-s. 2, of the Sale of Goods Act, 1893, which is in the following terms:

'Where there is a contract for the sale of goods to be delivered by stated instalments, which are to be separately paid for, and the seller makes defective deliveries in respect of one or more instalments, or the buyer neglects or refuses to take delivery of or pay for one or more instalments, it is a question in each case depending on the terms of the contract and the circumstances of the case, whether the breach of contract is a repudiation of the whole contract or whether it is a severable breach giving rise to a claim for compensation but not to a right to treat the whole contract as repudiated.'

That sub-section was based on decisions before the Act, and has been the subject of decisions since the Act. A contract for the sale of goods by instalments is a single contract, not a complex of as many contracts as there are instalments under it. The law might have been determined in the sense that any breach of condition in respect of any one or more instalments would entitle the party aggrieved to claim that the contract has been repudiated as a whole; or on the other hand the law as established might have been that any breach, however serious, in respect of one or more instalments should not have consequences extending beyond the particular instalment or instalments or affecting the contract as a whole. The sub-section, however, which deals equally with breaches either by the buyer or the seller, requires the Court to decide on the merits of the particular case what effect, if any, the breach or breaches should have on the contract as a whole.

The language of the Act is substantially based on the language used by Lord Selborne L.C. in Mersey Steel and Iron Co. v. Naylor, Benzon & Co., where he said:

'I am content to take the rule ... as I understand it, that you must look at the actual circumstances of the case in order to see whether the one party to the contract is relieved from its future performance by the conduct of the other; you must examine what that conduct is, so as to see whether it amounts to a renunciation, to an absolute refusal to perform the contract, such as would amount to a rescission if he had the power to rescind, and whether the other party may accept it as a reason for not performing his part.'

The court referred to several cases and continued:

With the help of these authorities we deduce that the main tests to be considered in applying the sub-section to the present case are, first, the ratio quantitatively which the breach bears to the contract as a whole, and secondly the degree of probability or improbability that such a breach will be repeated. On the first point, the delivery complained of amounts to no more than 1½ tons out of a contract for 100 tons. On the second point, our conclusion is that the chance of the breach being repeated is practically negligible. We assume that the sample found defective fairly represents the bulk; but bearing in mind the judge's finding that the breach was extraordinary and that the appellant's business was carefully conducted, bearing in mind also that the appellants were warned, and bearing in mind that the delivery complained of was an isolated instance out of 20 satisfactory deliveries actually made both before and after the instalment objected to, we hold that it cannot reasonably be inferred that similar breaches would occur in regard to subsequent deliveries. Indeed, we do not understand that the learned Judge came to any different conclusion. He seems, however, to have decided against the appellants on a third and separate ground, that is, that a delivery not satisfying the Government requirements would or might lead to the respondents being prosecuted under the Act. Though we think he exaggerates the likelihood of the respondents in such a case being held responsible, we do not wish to underrate the gravity to the respondents of their being even prosecuted. But we cannot follow the Judge's reasoning that the bare possibility, however remote, of this happening would justify the respondents in rescinding in this case. There may indeed be such cases, as also cases where the consequences of a single breach of contract may be so serious as to involve a frustration of the contract and justify rescission, or furthermore, the contract might contain an express condition that a breach would justify rescission, in which case effect would be given to such a condition by the Court. But none of these circumstances can be predicated of this case. We think the deciding factor here is the extreme improbability of the breach being repeated, and on that ground, and on the isolated and limited character of the breach complained of, there was, in our judgment, no sufficient justification to entitle the respondents to refuse further deliveries as they did.

Withers v. Reynolds

Reynolds agreed to supply Withers with straw, to be delivered at the latter's premises, at the rate of three loads in a fortnight.[25] Withers was to pay Reynolds on a per-load basis for each load of straw so delivered. After the straw had been supplied for some time, Withers refused to pay for the last load delivered, and insisted on always keeping one payment in arrears. Parke J. ruled:

The substance of the agreement was, that the straw should be paid for on delivery. The defendant clearly did not contemplate giving credit. When, therefore, the plaintiff said that he would not pay on delivery, (as he did, in substance, when he insisted on keeping one load on hand,) the defendant was not obliged to go on supplying him.

Patteson J. ruled:

If the plaintiff had merely failed to pay for any particular load, that, of itself, might not have been an excuse to the defendant for delivering no more straw: but the plaintiff here expressly refuses to pay for the loads as delivered; the defendant, therefore, is not liable for ceasing to perform his part of the contract.

Warinco A.G. v. Samor S.P.A.

The facts of the case are not important. Justice Donaldson judgment, however, is worth quoting:[26]

It is a popular myth, which lawyers do little to dispel, that the law is a highly technical matter with mysterious rules leading to results which are contrary to commonsense. Nothing could be further from the truth, both in general and in the particular instance of the law relating to the repudiation of contracts.

If a buyer under a contract calling for delivery by instalments commits a breach of that contract before all the deliveries have been made and that breach is so serious as to go to the root of the contract—in other words, to destroy the basis of the contract—commonsense suggests that the seller should not be expected to go to the trouble and expense of tendering later instalments if he does not want to. The law so provides.

Again, if it becomes clear that the buyer will be unable to accept or to pay for later instalments, commonsense suggests that the seller should, if he wishes, be discharged from any obligation further to perform his part of the contract. The law so provides.

Finally, if a buyer acts or speaks in a manner which declares in clear terms that he will not in future perform his part of the contract, the seller should, in common sense and fairness, have the option of being discharged from further obligation under the contract and that is the law.

But common sense also suggests that there can be borderline cases in which it is not quite so clear what should happen. The law is at a disadvantage here in that it must draw a line. The line which it

---

[25] *Withers* v. *Reynolds*, (1831) 2 B & Ad 882.

[26] *Warinco A.G.* v. *Samor S.P.A.*, (1977) 2 Lloyd's Rep. 582.

draws is indicated by the question: 'Has the buyer evinced an intention to abandon or to refuse to perform the contract?' In answering this question, the law has regard to such factors as the degree to which the delivery of one instalment is linked with another, the proportion of the contract which has been affected by the allegedly repudiatory breach and the probability that the breach will be repeated. However, these are merely part of the raw material for answering the question. They cannot be conclusive in themselves.

Devi Lal v. Govind Lal

Under a sale contract, the seller was to supply a particular amount of ghee at a fixed rate per unit by a specified date.[27] The seller supplied only a part of the specified quantity, so the buyer did not pay the full contract price. The specified date went by and the seller did not supply the remaining quantity. The buyer claimed damages for breach of contract while the seller claimed that as the buyer did not tender the full amount and apply for delivery of the remainder, it was the buyer who was in breach of the contract. The Rajasthan High Court ruled:

There was no agreement between the parties to supply the ghee by instalments. There was also no agreement to pay the price of part of the ghee as and when it was applied. The case is, therefore, governed by the principles of law enunciated by Park, J, in Oxendale v. Wetherell, (1829) 109 ER 143. In that case, there was a contract of sale of 250 bushels of wheat within a specified time by the vendor to the vendee. The vendor delivered 130 bushels of wheat but did not deliver the residue. It was observed by Park, J.

'Where there is an entire contract to deliver a large quantity of goods, consisting of distinct parcels, within a specified time, and the seller delivers part, he cannot, before the expiration of that time, bring an action to recover

[27] Devi Lal v. Govind Lal, AIR (1961) Raj 28.

the price of that part delivered, because the purchaser may, if the vendor fail to complete his contract, return the part delivered. But if he retains the part delivered after the seller has failed in performing his contract, the latter may recover the value of the goods which he has so delivered.'

…

The same is the position under the Indian Sale of Goods Act. Section 31 of that Act casts duty on the seller to deliver the goods and on the buyer to accept and pay for them in accordance with the terms of the contract of sale. Under Sec. 38(1) of that Act, the buyer of goods is not bound to accept delivery of goods by instalments unless otherwise agreed. Even where there is an agreement for delivery by instalments and no agreement to pay the price of these instalments, the contract does not cease to be an entire contract for the delivery of the whole quantity. The position in law is as stated by Benjamin on Sale (8th Edition) at Page 719.

'Where there is an agreement (which may be inferred) for delivery by instalments, the contract is not split up into separate contracts for each instalment; the contract is still an entire contract for the whole quantity, though it is divisible in performance. The seller is, therefore, liable if he fails to make up the complete quantity, and cannot recover any part of the price unless there be a provision that instalments are to be separately paid for.'

American law is in no way different. Reference in this connection may be made to Williston on Sales, Vol. II (Revised Edition), Page 466a—

'Where by the terms of a contract the performance is to be paid for at a certain rate so that the contract price for a portion of the performance can readily be calculated, it is still true that in the absence of an agreement express or implied to that effect, no part of the price is payable until the whole performance has been received. It is essential not only that the price for a part can be calculated, but that expressly or impliedly there shall be a promise to pay for a part.'

I am, therefore, of the opinion that the defendant appellant Devi Lal could not insist on the payment of the price of the part of ghee supplied by him before supplying the entire quality of ghee as had been agreed upon. It follows, therefore, that he could not refuse to supply the remaining part of the quantity of the ghee. If he refused to do so he committed the breach of the contract for which the plaintiff could hold him liable. In this case, the defendant appellant had refused to supply the entire quantity of ghee even before the final date of delivery ... No question arises in this case, therefore, of the, application of Sec. 35 under which the duty has been cast upon the buyer to apply for delivery.

It would have been an idle formality on the part of the buyer to apply for delivery in the circumstances of this case as the seller had refused to perform, his part of the contract without any justification even before the final date of delivery had arrived. In the case of anticipatory breach of contract on the part of the seller, Sec. 35 has no application when the buyer treats the contract as rescinded by virtue of Sec. 60 of the Sale of Goods Act. The evidence on record shows that the plaintiff respondent treated the contract as rescinded even before the last date of delivery had arrived.

There are several grounds on which the buyer can reject the goods: the quality of the goods might not conform to the contract, or there could be an excess or short supply, or supply in instalments contrary to the contract. Section 43 provides:

43. Buyer not bound to return rejected goods: Unless otherwise agreed, where goods are delivered to the buyer and he refuses to accept them, having the right so to do, he is not bound to return them to the seller, but it is sufficient if he intimates to the seller that he refuses to accept them.

The buyer does not have to return the goods to the seller. He only has to inform him of the rejection. However, the principles of bailment have a wide application. The buyer would invariably be a bailee of the goods till the seller takes possession of it.

* * *

There are several aspects to the performance of a contract. A sale contract can be frustrated on the grounds of the perishing of the specific goods, which discharges the parties from their obligations. The parties are free to provide on delivery, payment, and other aspects of the performance of the contract. If not provided, however, delivery and payment are concurrent conditions. The buyer can reject the goods if the quantity supplied is short or in excess of the contracted amount. The buyer has the right to examine the goods and reject them. However, unless provided otherwise in the contract, the examination can be done only after receiving the goods. The seller cannot deliver the goods in instalments if the contract does not provide for it.

8

Carriage and Delivery
CIF and FOB Contracts

The principles on delivery of goods by the buyer to the seller are simple. However, once a carrier is involved, the possible legal relations among the three parties multiply. The carrier is only an intermediary whose role is to move the goods from the seller to the buyer. He does not hold the goods for himself, but only on behalf of one of the parties. Who he holds the goods for becomes an important question while deciding the delivery and transfer of ownership to the buyer. The practices of maritime trade developed to deal with these concerns. Different shipping arrangements that apportion risk and costs between the buyer and seller, such as free on board (FOB) and cost, insurance, and freight (CIF) became common. These international commercial terms have been examined by common law courts to adjudicate on their meaning. The general development of the law on delivery in a sale contract and of international commercial terms have overlapped.

The contracting parties are free to provide, even when a carrier is involved, when delivery would be deemed to have taken place and the ownership transferred from the buyer to the seller. The law has to provide the answer when the contract is silent on it. If the carrier is an agent for the buyer, the delivery of the goods would happen when the seller delivers the goods to the carrier. If the carrier is an agent of the seller, the delivery to the buyer would happen when the carrier delivers the goods to the buyer.

Whether the carrier is an agent of the buyer or seller depends on a particular aspect of how the carrier operates. When a carrier is employed, it will receive goods from one person and give it to another. On receiving the goods, the carrier gives a receipt mentioning the details of the consignment, the destination, and the person to whom the goods are to be delivered. The party employing the carrier is free to decide whom he wants the goods to be delivered to. The carrier will deliver the goods at the destination only on production of the receipt to the named person. The seller could have the receipt drawn in favour of the buyer and give it to him to collect the goods at the destination. The seller could have the document drawn in his own favour or in that of his agent at the destination. In this case, although the goods are headed to the buyer, he does not have the right to receive the goods. The seller will receive the goods from the carrier and can do what he likes with them. However, if the receipt is drawn in favour of the buyer, once the carrier receives the goods from the seller, he is duty-bound to deliver it to the buyer alone.[1] In this case, the carrier receives the goods for the buyer. Delivery of the goods to the carrier is delivery to the buyer.

Shipping was the earliest form of carriage. The receipt given by the master of the ship was called a bill of lading. Other forms of carriage developed their own receipts; the one given by railways is called a railway receipt; by road transport, lorry receipt; and by airway transport, airway bill. Section 39 states the principle we have seen above:

39. Delivery to carrier or wharfinger: (1) Where, in pursuance of a contract of sale, the seller is authorised or required to send the goods to the buyer, delivery of the goods to a carrier, whether named by the buyer or not, for the purpose of transmission to the buyer, or delivery of the goods to a wharfinger for safe custody, is prima facie deemed to be a delivery of the goods to the buyer.

(2) Unless otherwise authorised by the buyer, the seller shall make such contract with the carrier or wharfinger on behalf of the buyer as may be reasonable having regard to the nature of the goods and the other circumstances of the case. If the seller omits so to do, and the goods are lost or damaged in course of transit or whilst in the custody of the wharfinger, the buyer may decline to treat the delivery to the carrier or wharfinger as a delivery to himself, or may hold the seller responsible in damages.

(3) Unless otherwise agreed, where goods are sent by the seller to the buyer by a route involving sea transit, in circumstances in which it is usual to insure, the seller shall give such notice to the buyer as may enable him to insure them during their sea transit, and if the seller fails so to do, the goods shall be deemed to be at his risk during such sea transit.

Section 39(1) uses the expression 'for the purpose of transmission to the buyer'. Only if the receipt is drawn in favour of the buyer will the goods be transmitted to the buyer. If the seller draws the receipt in his own favour, while the goods may be transported to the location of the buyer, the seller will receive the goods from the carrier. The carrier, in this case, will not deliver the goods to the buyer. Thus, if the parties do not provide otherwise, giving the goods to the carrier to take it to the buyer is taken as delivery to the buyer.

The property in specific goods passes as intended by the parties and if the contract is unconditional, at the very point of time the contract is made. Thus, delivery of the specific goods is not related to the transfer of ownership. In the case of unascertained goods, ownership transfers as intended by the parties. However, if the contract is silent on the transfer of ownership, the ownership transfers when goods are appropriated to the contract. The appropriation of the goods happens when the goods are delivered to the buyer.

Section 23(2) states, 'Where, in pursuance of the contract, the seller delivers the goods to the buyer or to a carrier or other bailee (whether named by the buyer or not) for the purpose of transmission to the buyer, and does not reserve the right of disposal, he is deemed to have unconditionally appropriated the goods to the contract.' The wording of the section is similar to Section 39(1). The two complement each other. In a sale of unascertained goods, goods are certainly ascertained on delivery. Further, if the contract

---

[1] The lien of an unpaid seller is an exception to this. We will study this in Chapter 11.

has no terms on passing of property (reserving the right of disposal), the ownership will pass at the time of delivery. Thus, Section 39(1) stipulates delivery of the goods to the carrier for transmission to the buyer to be delivery to the buyer as the prima facie rule, and Section 23(2) takes it as the moment when the ownership is transferred. Of course, both are presumptions only if the contract does not provide otherwise.

INTERNATIONAL COMMERCIAL TERMS

Maritime trade had to deal with the numerous issues in relation to delivery, costs, and risk. When the buyer and seller are at two different locations and goods have to be transported by a carrier, the sale price on its own has no meaning. The cost has to include the cost of carriage and insurance. Who bears the risk of loss or damage to the goods in transit, the buyer or the seller? As maritime trade developed practices allocating cost and risk between the buyer and seller, those practices were given rather peculiar names. Disputes developed between the parties over the terms, and courts gave judgments on their scope and meaning. Among the two most significant terms are cost insurance freight (CIF) contracts and free on board (FOB) contracts.

As trade expanded, such terms became widely used in international and domestic trade. Unsurprisingly, people in different jurisdictions would understand and interpret these terms differently. This led to disputes and uncertainty in international trade. To respond to this, the International Chamber of Commerce (ICC), a non-governmental body based in Paris, took the initiative to standardize such terms. It picked up the terms in usage in international trade in relation to sale of goods, affixing responsibilities and liabilities between the buyer and seller. It called such terms 'International Commercial Terms', abbreviated as 'Incoterms'. They were defined for the first time in 1936. It has updated its definitions several times. The last edition of Incoterms came out in 2011. It has become effective from 1 January 2011. The ICC is not a law-making body, and thus the terms do not apply to contracts automatically. The contracting parties have to specifically mention in the contract that the terms are Incoterms and they have the same meaning as is given in the ICC's report.

As shipping was followed by other modes of transportation—the railways and airways—some terms were developed specifically for maritime trade while other terms are used generally, for any mode of transportation. The Incoterms 2010 follows this as the basis for classification of the terms in two categories (see Table 8.1).

TABLE 8.1   Classification of commercial terms by the ICC

All modes of transport	CIP	– Carriage and Insurance Paid to
	CPT	– Carriage Paid to
	DAP	– Delivered at Place
	DAT	– Delivered at Terminal
	DDP	– Delivered Duty Paid
	EXW	– Ex Works
	FCA	– Free Carrier
Sea and inland waterways	CFR	– Cost and Freight
	CIF	– Cost, Insurance and Freight
	FAS	– Free alongside Ship
	FOB	– Free on Board

The terms bear F, C, and D as their first letters, which is another way of categorizing them.[2] As the seller and buyer are distant from each other, there can be two extreme arrangements. The parties can agree as a part of their sale contract that the buyer will take

---

[2] In fact, Incoterms 2000 had categorized the Incoterms into four groups, Groups E, F, C, and D.

delivery of the goods at the seller's premises. From there, the buyer will take the goods to his destination at his own cost and risk. This is called an 'ex' term contract, for example, an ex-warehouse contract. The other extreme arrangement could be one where the parties agree that the seller will bring the goods, at his own cost and risk, all the way to the premises of the buyer and make the delivery to him. This is called a 'D' term contract. It covers different terms under which the seller brings the goods to the country of the buyer at the seller's own risk and cost. In between are the 'F' term and 'C' term contracts. The 'F' term contracts begin with the word 'free', which signifies that the seller will bring the goods at his own cost and deliver them to a carrier, as instructed by the buyer. In the C group, the seller takes up the further costs of carriage of the goods as well. We shall now give a brief description of all the terms in the Incoterms 2010:

EXW: 'Ex works' contract. The seller makes the goods available to the buyer at the seller's premises. The buyer bears all the costs and the risk in taking the goods from the seller's premises to his own. 'Works' stands for the premises of the seller. The other terms used for 'works' are 'factory', 'plant', and 'warehouse'.

FCA: 'Free carriage'. The buyer organizes for the carriage of the goods and informs the seller about the carrier and the place where the goods would be handed over to the carrier. The risk passes when the goods are handed over. The term is followed by the name of the place.

CPT: 'Carriage paid to'. The seller pays the freight for the carriage of the goods to the specified destination. The risk in goods passes to the buyer on delivery of the goods to the first carrier. The term is followed by the

destination at which the carrier has to deliver the goods.

CIP: 'Carriage and insurance paid to'. The seller pays for carriage and insurance to the specified destination point. The risk passes when the goods are handed over to the first carrier. The term is followed by the destination point at which the carrier has to deliver the goods.

DAT: 'Delivery at terminal'. The seller bears the cost and risk of carriage of the goods to a specified terminal in the country of the buyer. At the point when the seller delivers the goods to the buyer at the terminal, the risk passes to the buyer. The seller organizes the export clearance. However, the buyer is responsible for the import clearance and for paying the import duty. The terminal can be a quay; warehouse; container yard; or road, rail, or air terminal. The term is followed by the name of the terminal, port, or place of destination.

DAP: 'Delivery at place'. The seller pays for carriage to the named destination in the country of the buyer. However, the import duty is paid by the buyer. The risk passes to the buyer at the named destination when the goods are made ready for unloading by the buyer. The term is followed by the place of destination.

DDP: 'Delivery duty paid'. The seller pays for carriage to the named destination in the country of the buyer. In addition, the seller organizes import clearance and pays the custom duties. The term is followed by the place of destination.

The following four terms are used exclusively in maritime trade or waterways.

FAS: 'Free alongside ship'. The seller pays for the transportation of the goods to the port of shipment in his country. The buyer pays the loading costs, freight, insurance, unloading costs, and transportation from the port of destination to his premises. The passing of risk occurs when the goods are delivered to the quay at the port of shipment. The term is followed by the place from where the goods are to be shipped.

FOB: 'Free on board'. The seller pays for the transportation of the goods to the port of shipment and for their loading on the ship. The buyer pays the freight, insurance, unloading costs and transportation from the port of destination to his destination. The passing of risk occurs when the goods pass the ship's rail at the port of shipment. The term is followed by the name of the place where the goods are put on the ship.

CFR: 'Cost and freight'. The seller pays the costs and freight to bring the goods to the port of destination. However, risk is transferred to the buyer once the goods are loaded on the ship. The seller is not to bear the cost of maritime insurance. The term is followed by the port of destination.

CIF: 'Cost, freight and insurance'. The seller pays for the transportation of the goods to the port of shipment, loading, and freight, as well as for marine insurance. The risk of loss or damage is transferred from the seller to the buyer when the goods pass over the ship's rail at the port of shipment. The term is followed by the port of destination. The term is the same as CFR except that the seller also pays for marine insurance.

Can the Incoterms be used for domestic trade? The Incoterms have been developed specifically for international trade, but the use of the terms is voluntary. There is no bar on a domestic sale contract using the Incoterms. Further, several variants of the Incoterms have been developed for domestic trade. Some examples of these are variants of

FOB—'free on rail' and 'free on truck'. Such terms used in domestic trade are interpreted according to the meaning given to these terms by common law. We can now explore what meaning the courts have assigned to the two key terms—CIF and FOB.

FOB Contracts

The classic type of FOB contract was where the buyer nominated the ship that would transport the goods. The seller entered into a carriage contract with the ship. The bill of lading was issued in the name of the buyer. Once the goods crossed the railings of the ship, the risk in goods passed to the buyer. The seller was to bear the cost of putting the goods on board, and the cost of carriage and insurance was to be borne by the buyer. However, buyers and sellers have come to modify the classical understanding of FOB in several ways.

The fob contract has become a flexible instrument. In what counsel called the classic type as described, for example, in Wimble, Sons & Co v Rosenberg & Sons, the buyer's duty is to nominate the ship and the seller's to put the goods on board for account of the buyer and procure a bill of lading in terms usual in the trade. In such a case the seller is directly a party to the contract of carriage, at least until he takes out the bill of lading in the buyer's name. Probably the classic type is based on the assumption that the ship nominated will be willing to load any goods brought down to the berth or at least of which she is notified. Under present conditions, when space often has to be booked well in advance, the contract of carriage comes into existence at an earlier point of time. Sometimes the seller is asked to make the necessary arrangements, and the contract may then provide for his taking the bill of lading in his own name and obtaining payment against the transfer, as in a cif contract. Sometimes the buyer engages his own forwarding agent at the port of loading to book space and to procure the bill of lading;

if freight has to be paid in advance this method may be the most convenient. In such a case the seller discharges his duty by putting the goods on board, getting the mates receipt and handing it to the forwarding agent to enable him to obtain the bill of lading.[3]

In *Ian Stach Ltd* v. *Baker Bosley Ltd*[4] it was noted, 'It cannot be said that because a contract is an f.o.b. contract certain consequences must invariably follow. There are different types of f.o.b. contracts...' A FOB contract certainly determines how the goods will be delivered, the expenses to be borne by the seller, and the passing of the risk to the buyer, but it does not determine the passing of the property. Further, there can be several arrangements. The seller can enter into a contract with the carrier as a principal or agent of the buyer. Alternately, the buyer can enter into a contract with the carrier and the seller with an agent of the buyer collecting the shipping documents.

In the classic FOB contract, where the seller makes the contract with the carrier, Section 39(2) applies. In a FOB contract, the seller's duty is to deliver the goods to the carrier. Once this is done, the seller has delivered it to the buyer and the risk passes to him. The loading of the goods may be unconditional appropriation to the contract. As the risk passes with ownership, it leads to the conclusion that ownership passes on shipment. However, this is only a prima facie position; the details of the contract may change this. The seller may get the bill of lading in his name and endorse it in favour of the buyer only on receiving payment. In this case, the seller has reserved the right of disposal, and

thus the property does not pass till the buyer receives the document. At the same time, merely taking the bill of lading in the seller's name may not necessarily be indicative of the intent to hold the transfer of property. The seller could be doing this as the agent of the buyer and may surrender the bill of lading immediately. In this case, prima facie, the property would have passed in shipment.

Shree Bajarang Jute Mills, Ltd, M/s Guntur v. State of AP

Shree Bajarang Jute Mills, Ltd, was a manufacturer of jute bags in Guntur.[5] It had an arrangement with a company called ACC, a manufacturer of cement with factories in different states, to supply packing bags for the different factories. The seller was to despatch the goods for a specific factory outside the state of Andhra Pradesh on a 'free on rail Guntur' basis. The seller obtained the railway receipt in the name of ACC. Against payment, it delivered the receipt to Krishna Cement Works, an agent for ACC in charge of receiving railway receipts and making payments. The receipt was received in Andhra Pradesh, where the agent was based. To avoid multiple taxation, the Constitution of India had made a provision that sales tax is to be levied in the state where there is actual delivery of the goods. The tax authorities levied the tax on the transaction, reasoning that as the railway receipts were delivered within Andhra Pradesh and the price was also realized there, the goods must be deemed to have been delivered to the buyer in the state. The department found support in Section 39, which provides that delivery to the carrier is prima facie delivery to the buyer. The Supreme Court ruled:

---

[3] *Pyrene & Co.* v. *Scindia Navigation*, (1954) 2 QB 402.

[4] *Ian Stach Ltd* v. *Baker Bosley Ltd*, (1958) 2 QB 130.

[5] *Shree Bajarang Jute Mills, Ltd, M/s Guntur* v. *State of AP*, AIR (1966) SC 376.

... the expression 'actually delivered' in the context in which it occurs, can only mean physical delivery of the goods, or such action as puts the goods in the possession of the purchaser: it does not contemplate mere symbolical or notional delivery e.g., by entrusting the goods to a common carrier, or even delivery of documents of title like railway receipts.

...

S. 39 of the Indian Sale of Goods Act, 1930 ... provides ... delivery of the goods to a carrier for the purpose of transmission to the buyer, is prima facie deemed to be delivery of the goods to the buyer. But that provision will not make mere delivery of the railway receipts representing title to the goods actual delivery of goods for the purpose of Art. 286. The rule contained in S. 39(1) of the Indian Sale of Goods Act raises a prima facie inference that the goods have been delivered if the conditions prescribed thereby are satisfied: it has no application in dealing with a constitutional provision which while imposing a restriction upon the legislative power of the States entrusts exclusive power to levy sales tax to the State in which the goods have been actually delivered for the purpose of consumption.

B.K. Wadeyar, Sales-Tax Officer, IV Division Licence Circle, Bombay v. M/s Daulatram Rameshwarlal

Under the sales tax law prevailing in 1955, in exporting goods, sales in which the goods remained the seller's property till they had been brought on board the ship were exempt from sales tax.[6] The contract in question required the seller–exporter to sell the goods on FOB terms. The sales tax department claimed that the ownership in the goods passed to the buyer before the goods had been loaded on to the ship, and therefore the seller had to pay sales tax on the transaction. The Supreme

---

[6] *B.K. Wadeyar, Sales-tax Officer, IV Division Licence Circle, Bombay v. M/s Daulatram Rameshwarlal*, AIR (1961) SC 311.

Court expounded the transfer of ownership in a FOB contract. It ruled:

The normal rule in FOB contracts is that the property is intended to pass and does pass on the shipment of the goods. In certain circumstances, e.g., if the seller takes the bill of lading to his own order and parts with it to a third person the property in the goods, it has been held, does not pass to the buyer even on shipment. We are not concerned here with the question whether the passing of property in the goods was postponed even after shipment. The correctness of the proposition that in the absence of special agreement the property in the goods does not pass in the case of a FOB contract until the goods are actually put on board is not disputed before us.

As has however been rightly stressed by the learned Solicitor-General it is always open to the parties to come to a different agreement as to when the property in the goods shall pass. The question whether there was such a different agreement has to be decided on a consideration of all the surrounding circumstances. ... The first circumstance on which he relies is that the bill of lading was taken in the name of the buyer. Along with this fact we have to consider however the fact that the bill of lading was retained by the sellers, the contract being that payment will be made on the presentation of the bill of lading. It is not disputed that the term in the contract for 'payment at Bombay against presentation of documents' means this. It was the sellers who received the bills of lading and it was on the presentation of these bills of lading along with the invoices, that the buyer paid the price. When the bills of lading, though made out as if the goods were shipped by the buyer, were actually obtained and retained by the sellers, that fact itself would ordinarily indicate an intention of the parties that the property in the goods would not pass till after payment.

...

We have therefore come to the conclusion that there is no circumstance which would justify a conclusion that the parties came to a special agreement that though the sales were on FOB contracts property in the goods would pass to the buyer at some point of time before shipment.

Within the terms of the contract, as the documents were to be given only on payment, the property would pass only at that point.

Marwar Tent Factory, M/s v. Union of India

Marwar Tent Factory won a tender to supply tents to the defence establishment at Kanpur.[7] As a part of the contract, the tents were to be inspected at the Marwar Tent Factory's premises at Jodhpur. After the tents were approved by the inspector, they were to be despatched to the Commandant, COD, Kanpur. They were to be put on rails at Jodhpur under the terms of FOR Jodhpur. The delivery note was to be sent to the COD Kanpur by registered post. On receipt of the delivery note, the COD was to pay 95 per cent of the price to the Marwar Tent Company, and the remaining 5 per cent would be paid after receipt of the goods in a good condition. A consignment of 1,500 tents was despatched, but as a result of pilferage in transit, only 1,276 tents were received. The payment to Marwar Tent Company was, therefore, reduced for the loss of 224 tents.

Marwar Tent Company argued that under the terms of the FOR contract, the ownership in the tents was transferred once they were loaded on the train. Therefore, the risk was transferred to the COD when the goods were loaded on the train, and it is they who must bear the loss. The COD argued that the ownership could be transferred only on delivery. In a FOR contract, the seller bears the costs up to the loading of the goods on rails, but the buyer pays all expenses incurred afterwards.

The court examined the meaning of FOR contracts:

In order to decide the question as to whether the rights in the goods passed from the seller ... as soon as the goods were loaded in railway wagons at Jodhpur and the railway receipt was sent to the consignee, it is pertinent to refer to the meaning of the words, f.o.r Jodhpur. In Halsbury's Laws of England, 4th Edition (Volume 41) at page 800, para 940 it has been mentioned that:

'Under a free on rail contract (f.o.r) the seller undertakes to deliver the goods in to railway wagons or at the station (depending on the practice of the railway) at his own expense, and (commonly) to make such contract with the railway on behalf of the buyer as is reasonable in the circumstance prime facie the time of delivery f.o.r. fixes the point at which property and risk pass to the buyer and the price becomes payable.'

In Benjamin's Sale of Goods (2nd edn.), at para 1799 it is stated as under

'Stipulations as to time of delivery'
'Provisions as to the time of deliver in an f.o.b. contract are taken to refer to the time of shipment and not to the time of arrival of the goods; and this may be so even though the provision in question contemplates the arrival of the goods by a certain time. Thus in Frebold and Stuznickel (Trading as Panda O.H.D.) v. Circle Products Ltd. ([1970] 1 Lloyd's Rep 499) German sellers sold toys to English buyers f.o.b. Continental port on the terms that the goods were to be delivered in time to catch the Christmas trade. The goods were shipped from Rotterdam and reached London on November 13; but because of an oversight for which the sellers were not responsible the buyers were not notified of the arrival of the goods until the following January 17. It was held that the sellers were not in breach as they had delivered the goods in accordance with the requirements of the contract by shipping them in such a way as would normally have resulted in their arrival in time for the Christmas trade.'

---

[7] *Marwar Tent Factory* v. *Union of India*, AIR (1990) SC 1753.

The question as to the meaning of f.o.r. contract fell for consideration in the case of Girija Proshad Pal v. National Coal Co. Ltd. 1949 AIR(Cal) 472) P.B. Mukharji, J. as his Lordship then was observed in para 11 as follows: 'The words f.o.r. are well known words in commercial contracts. In my judgment they mean when used to qualify the place of delivery, that the seller's liability is to place the goods free on the rail as the place of delivery. Once that is done the risk belongs to the buyer.' It is also convenient to refer to the provision of Section 23(2) of the Indian Sale of Goods Act, 1930. This sub-section provides that

(2) Where, in pursuance of the contract, the seller delivers the goods to the buyer or to a carrier or other bailee (whether named by the buyer or not) for the purpose of transmission to the buyer, and does not reserve the right of disposal, he is deemed to have unconditionally appropriated the goods to the contract.

In the instant case, in view of the terms and conditions of the contract embodied in clause 11 of the Schedule of acceptance of tender regarding the place of delivery 'F.O.R. Jodhpur', the property in the goods passed immediately on to the seller after delivering the goods and loading the same in the railway wagons at Jodhpur for transmission to the buyer, the consignee, without reserving any right of disposal. The seller is deemed to have unconditionally appropriated the goods to the contract only under Section 26 of the said Act, the goods remained at seller's risk until the property therein is transferred to the buyer. As stated earlier that the property in goods has been transferred to the buyer by the seller by delivery of the goods and loading the same at Jodhpur in railway wagons. In this connection reference may be made to S. 39(1) of the said Act. Considering the aforesaid provisions of the Sale of Goods Act, 1930 as well as, the terms and conditions of delivery i.e. 'F.O.R. Jodhpur' the irresistible conclusion that follows is that the property in the goods together with the risk passed from the seller to the buyer i.e. from, consignor to the consignee as soon as the goods were loaded in the railway wagons at Jodhpur as per the terms of delivery i.e. F.O.R. Jodhpur. Therefore, the finding of the trial Court

that the risk throughout remained with the appellant until the goods were actually delivered to the Commandant, C.O.D., Kanpur is wholly wrong and illegal. The further finding of the trial Court that the risk was governed with the condition No. 4(l) of the Schedule of Acceptance of Tender and the property in the goods i.e. the tents did not pass until the same were actually delivered to the Commandant, C.O.D., Kanpur and the Commandant, C.O.D., Kanpur was not liable for loss of the tents during the period of transit by the railways is also illegal and bad.

Cost Insurance Freight (CIF) Contracts

In a CIF contract, the seller brought the goods to the port of shipment and had them loaded (both at his cost), and paid for carriage by ship to a pre-appointed destination. The seller also bore the cost of insurance. The seller moved the documents through a faster mode of transportation, and handed them over to the buyer against payment of the price. The documents entitled the buyer to collect the goods from the seller at the pre-appointed destination. The bill of lading could be drawn in favour of the buyer or endorsed in his favour at the time of handing over of the documents. The following is a description of a CIF contract in *Ross T. Smyth & Co Ltd* v. *T.D. Bailey Son & Co*:[8]

The contract in question here is of a type familiar in commerce, and is described as a cif contract. The initials indicate that the price is to include cost, insurance and freight. It is a type of contract which is more widely and more frequently in use than any other contract used for purposes of sea-borne commerce. An enormous number of transactions, in value amounting to untold sums, are carried out every year under cif contracts. The essential characteristics of this contract have often been described. The seller has to ship or acquire

[8] *Ross T. Smyth & Co. Ltd* v. *T.D. Bailey Son & Co.,* (1940) 3 All ER 60.

after that shipment the contract goods, as to which, if unascertained, he is generally required to give a notice of appropriation. On or after shipment, he has to obtain proper bills of lading and proper policies of insurance. He fulfils his contract by transferring the bills of lading and the policies to the buyer. As a general rule, he does so only against payment of the price, less the freight, which the buyer has to pay. In the invoice which accompanies the tender of the documents on the 'prompt'—that is, the date fixed for payment—the freight is deducted, for this reason. In this course of business, the general property in the goods remains in the seller until he transfers the bills of lading. These rules, which are simple enough to state in general terms, are of the utmost importance in commercial transactions.

The following cases will illustrate the nature, rights, and obligations of the parties in a CIF contract.

Manbre Saccharine Co., Ltd v. Corn Products Co., Ltd

The parties had entered into a contract for the sale of American pearl starch and corn syrup.[9] The sale was on CIF terms. The vessel was sunk by a German submarine. The seller and buyer knew that the vessel was sunk. The seller tendered the document but the buyer refused to accept the documents and pay the money. McCardie J. delivered the following judgment:

The first question arising can be briefly stated is follows: Can a vendor, under an ordinary cif contract, effectively tender appropriate documents to the buyer in respect of goods shipped in a vessel which at the time of tender the vendor knows to have been totally lost?

... the essential feature of a cif contract as compared with an ordinary contract for the sale of goods rests in the fact that performance of the

bargain is to be fulfilled by delivery of documents and not by the actual physical delivery of goods by the vendor. All that the buyer can call for is delivery of the customary documents. This represents the measure of the buyer's right and the extent of the vendor's duty. The buyer cannot refuse the documents and ask for the actual goods, nor can the vendor withhold the documents and tender the goods.

In Arnhold Karberg & Co v Blythe, Green, Jourdain & Co (7) SCRUTTON, J, described a cif contract as being a sale of documents relating to goods and not a sale of goods. But when the Court of Appeal considered that case ([1916] 1 KB at pp 510, 514) BANKES and WARRINGTON, LJJ, commented on the language of SCRUTTON, J, and indicated their view that a cif contract is a contract for the sale of goods to be performed by delivery of documents. But I respectfully venture to think that the difference is one of phrase only. For in reality, as I have said, the obligation of the vendor is to deliver documents rather than goods—to transfer symbols rather than the physical property represented thereby. If the vendor fulfils his contract by shipping the appropriate goods in the appropriate manner under a proper contract of carriage, and if he also obtains the proper documents for tender to the purchaser, I am unable to see how the rights or duties of either party are affected by the loss of ship or goods, or by knowledge of such loss by the vendor prior to actual tender of the documents. If the ship be lost prior to tender, but without the knowledge of the seller, it was, I assume, always clear that he could make an effective proffer of the documents to the buyers. In my opinion, it is also clear that he can make an effective tender even though he possessed at the time of tender actual knowledge of the loss of the ship or goods. For the purchaser in case of loss will get the document he bargained for, and if the policy be that required by the contract and if the loss be covered thereby, he will secure the insurance moneys. The contingency of loss is within and not outside the contemplation of the parties to a cif contract. ... I therefore hold that the plaintiffs were not entitled to reject the tender of documents in the present case, upon the ground

[9] *Manbre Saccharine Co., Ltd* v. *Corn Products Co., Ltd*, (1918–9) All ER Rep 980.

that the Algonquin had, to the knowledge of the defendants, sank prior to the tender of documents. This view will simplify the performance of cif contracts and prevent delay either through doubts as to the loss of ship or goods or through difficult questions with regard to the knowledge or suspicion of a vendor as to the actual occurrence of loss.

Kwei Tek Chao and Others (Trading as Zung Fu Co.) v. British Traders and Shippers LD

London exporters (British Traders and Shippers Ltd) contracted under a CIF contract to sell a quantity of Rongalite C to a group of merchants in Hong Kong.[10] The shipment was to be done not later than 31 October 1951 on CIF terms. The seller was to receive payment against a letter of credit on production of 'shipped' bills of lading at the buyer's bank. The goods were not shipped until 3 November 1951. However, the seller's forwarding agents at the port of loading forged the date of shipping. The seller had no knowledge of the forgery, and presented the documents to the bank on 10 November 1951. As the documents appeared to be in order, the bank gave the money to the seller.

The seller had made a sub-sale of the goods. Due to the delay in shipment of the goods, the buyer lost his contract for resale in Hong Kong. The goods finally arrived on 17 December. He knew that the shipment had not taken place before 31 October. Despite this, he took the goods from the ship to a godown, and gave the godown warrants to the bank as his security. The buyers subsequently discovered that the bills of lading had been forged. He was unable to sell the goods owing to a serious fall in the market price in Hong

Kong. He moved the court, claiming that it was the foundation of the contract that the bill of lading would be genuine. As it was forged, it was a nullity and the consideration had wholly failed. Alternately, the buyer claimed damages for breach of contract and loss of profit. The judge, Devlin, did not accept that the forgery made the bill of lading a nullity. He noted, 'If the bills of lading are a nullity, no doubt the property does not pass by their tender, but if a man, with knowledge of a bill of lading and the fact that it is a nullity, takes delivery of the goods, acts upon it and keeps them, it is not then open to him to avoid the transaction.'

As the buyer continued with the contract, he had no right to terminate the contract but only the right to damages. The amount of damages has to be worked out from the time the breach took place and the nature of breach. In this context, the judge noted:

There is not, in my judgment, one right to reject; there are two rights to reject. A right to reject is, after all, only a particular form of a right to rescind the contract. Wherever there is a breach of condition there is a right to rescind the contract, and if there are successive breaches of different conditions committed one after the other, each time there is a breach there is a right to rescind in respect of that breach. A right to reject is merely a particular form of the right to rescind, which involves the rejection of a tender of goods or of documents; and a rightful rejection of either is a rescission which brings the contract to an end.

Here, therefore, there is a right to reject documents, and a right to reject goods, and the two things are quite distinct. A c.i.f. contract puts a number of obligations upon the seller, some of which are in relation to the goods and some of which are in relation to the documents. So far as the goods are concerned, he must put on board at the port of shipment goods in conformity with the contract description, but he must also send forward documents, and those documents must

---

[10] Kwei Tek Chao and Others (Trading as Zung Fu Co.) v. British Traders and Shippers LD, (1954) 2 QB 459.

comply with the contract. If he commits a breach the breaches may in one sense overlap, in that they flow from the same act. If there is a late shipment, as there was in this case, the date of the shipment being part of the description of the goods, the seller has not put on board goods which conform to the contract description, and therefore he has broken that obligation. He has also made it impossible to send forward a bill of lading which at once conforms with the contract and states accurately the date of shipment. Thus the same act can cause two breaches of two independent obligations.

However that may be, they are distinct obligations, and the right to reject the documents arises when the documents are tendered, and the right to reject the goods arises when they are landed and when after examination they are found not to be in conformity with the contract. There are many cases, of course, where the documents are accepted but the goods are subsequently rejected. It may be that if the actual date of shipment is not in conformity with the contract, and the error appears from the documents, the buyer, by accepting the documents, not only loses his right to reject the documents, but also his right to reject the goods, but that would be because he had waived in advance reliance on the date of shipment.

The court further noted:

… as a matter of principle … the second breach cannot affect his right to damages on the first breach. They are distinct not merely in law, but also as a matter of business. Having a right to reject the documents separately from a right to reject the goods, it is obvious that as a matter of business very different considerations will govern the buyer's mind as he applies himself to one or other of those questions.

…

If I might call the breach of the term to deliver correct documents breach A, and the failure to ship goods on the contract date as breach B, it seems to me that the right to damages for breach A vests when the breach is committed, that the measure is then determined as being the proper measure required to put the buyer in as good a

position as he would have been in if the breach had not been committed; and that when a separate breach, breach B, is committed the buyer has a separate and independent right to elect upon that breach as to the way in which he is going to deal with it, whether he treats it as a condition or as a warranty, and that he cannot be fettered in the exercise of that right as he would be if by his election he altered the measure of damage for breach A. That measure of damage must remain the same however the buyer elects to deal with breach B.

A point brought before the court was the buyer by pledging the goods had accepted the goods on landing and thus lost his right to terminate the contract. The court noted:

Clearly, it would create a great deal of embarrassment and inconvenience in the ordinary forms of credit in these transactions if the normal act of pledging goods to the bank, which is done in ninety-nine cases out of a hundred, resulted in the buyer losing his right to reject. Yet, on the face of it, it seems that by pledging the goods he is doing an act, inconsistent with the ownership of the seller, which amounts to an acceptance under section 35.

Section 35 provides:

The buyer is deemed to have accepted the goods when he intimates to the seller that he has accepted them, or when the goods have been delivered to him, and he does any act in relation to them which is inconsistent with the ownership of the seller, or when after the lapse of a reasonable time, he retains the goods without intimating to the seller that he has rejected them.

Interpreting the provision, the court noted:

In Hardy & Co. (London) Ld. v. Hillerns and Fowler the question which arose for decision was whether the buyers had accepted the goods under section 35. The goods had arrived, and the case showed that the time during which he had the right to examine them was still running. During that time the buyer delivered some of the goods to a sub-buyer. That was an act which was inconsistent with the ownership of the seller. The case for the buyer was that section 35 was machinery which came into action only after the machinery in section 34 had been completed. The Court of Appeal held otherwise. The court held that, notwithstanding that his time for examination was still open, the buyer could, if he chose to commit an act under section 35 such as intimating that he accepted the goods, accept them.

Mr Roskill has argued that when the goods are delivered to the buyer and he does any act in relation to them which is inconsistent with the ownership of the seller the word 'delivered' there means physical delivery of the goods from the ship. If that is so, no dealing with the documents would be within the meaning of the clause, because it would all have been done before the goods had been delivered. I cannot take that view of it. 'Delivery' as defined by the Act means a voluntary transfer of possession, and I think that it means, therefore, transfer of possession under the contract of sale. In a c.i.f. contract the goods are delivered, so far as they are physically delivered, when they are put on board a ship at the port of shipment. The documents are delivered when they are tendered. A buyer who takes delivery from the ship at the port of destination is not taking delivery of the goods under the contract of sale, but merely taking delivery out of his own warehouse, as it were, by the presentation of the document of title to the goods, the master of the ship having been his bailee ever since he became entitled to the bill of lading.

I think that the true answer may be found rather differently. Atkin L.J., in the course of his judgment in Hardy & Co. (London) Ld. v. Hillerns and Fowler, dealt with the situation which is always a little puzzling under the c.i.f. contract: if the property passes when the documents are handed over, by what legal machinery does the buyer retain a right, as he undoubtedly does, to examine the goods when they arrive, and to reject them if they are not in conformity with the contract? Atkin L.J. put forward two views for consideration. One was that the property in

the goods, notwithstanding the tendering of the documents, did not pass until the goods had been examined or until an opportunity for examination had been given. The other was that it passed at the time of the tendering of the documents, but only conditionally and could be revested if the buyer properly rejected the goods. Mr. Roskill argues (and I think rightly) that for the first possible view indicated by Atkin L.J. no other authority can be found, and it would clearly create considerable complications. If there is no property in the goods, how can the buyer pledge them? It would provide a simple answer to the point had it arisen in this case, since there could not be a pledge. I think that the true view is that what the buyer obtains, when the title under the documents is given to him, is the property in the goods, subject to the condition that they revest if upon examination he finds them to be not in accordance with the contract. That means that he gets only conditional property in the goods, the condition being a condition subsequent. All his dealings with the documents are dealings only with that conditional property in the goods. It follows, therefore, that there can be no dealing which is inconsistent with the seller's ownership unless he deals with something more than the conditional property. If the property passes altogether, not being subject to any condition, there is no ownership left in the seller with which any inconsistent act under section 35 could be committed. If the property passes conditionally the only ownership left in the seller is the reversionary interest in the property in the event of the condition subsequent operating to restore it to him. It is that reversionary interest with which the buyer must not, save with the penalty of accepting the goods, commit an inconsistent act. So long as he is merely dealing with the documents he is not purporting to do anything more than pledge the conditional property which he has. Similarly, if he sells the documents of title he sells the conditional property. But if, as was done in Hardy & Co. (London) Ld. v. Hillerns and Fowler, when the goods have been landed, he physically deals with the goods and delivers them to his sub-buyer, he is doing an act which is inconsistent with the seller's reversionary interest. The seller's reversionary interest entitles him, immediately upon the operation of the condition subsequent, that is, as soon as opportunity for examination has been given, to have the goods physically returned to him in the place where the examination has taken place without their being dispatched to third parties. The dispatch to a third party is an act, therefore, which interferes with the reversionary interest. A pledge or a transfer of documents such as that which takes place on the ordinary string contract does not.

The case thus resolved the issue of how the buyer can reject the goods in a CIF contract after becoming the owner of the goods. In a CIF contract, the ownership passes to the buyer with the condition that the property will re-vest in the buyer if the goods are rejected on examination after landing.

Marketing Socy v. K.M.G. and Sons

In this case, the buyer had purchased potatoes from the seller in Burma through agents in India. The terms of sale were CIF Madras.[11] The parties knew that the potatoes were to be used as seeds. In addition to the description of the potatoes, the seller had to present a Phyto Sanitary Certificate, issued by the Government of Burma, to establish that potatoes were disease-free. On receiving the goods at Madras, the buyer found that the potatoes were rotting and rejected them. The court examined the right of rejection under a CIF contract:

A C.I.F. contract is one which is commonly resorted to by persons dealing in international trade. In the case of such contracts the cost of the goods, insurance charges and the freight in respect of the goods in question upto the place of destination have to be borne by the buyer. The payment of the price to the seller is generally arranged to be

[11] *Marketing Socy* v. *K.M.G. and Sons*, AIR (1974) Mysore 20.

effected in those cases through the mechanism of a Letter of Credit issued by a banker at the instance of the buyer who undertakes to reimburse the issuing banker to the extent of such payment. The issuing Bank arranges payment of the price to the seller on his producing either before it or before another banker on whom the Letter of Credit is drawn, as the case may be, the invoice, the bill of lading and the insurance policy in respect of the goods which are the subject-matter of sale. While doing so, the bankers concerned do not act as the agents of either the seller or the buyer in connection with the sale. The delivery of invoice, bill of lading and the insurance policy to the bank and receipt of money by the seller pursuant to a Letter of Credit opened for the said purpose cannot be considered as delivery of goods to the buyer.

The question whether a purchaser under a C.I.F. contract is entitled to reject the goods as not being in accordance with the terms of the contract notwithstanding that the property in the goods has passed to him by delivery of the bills of lading when he had no opportunity to inspect the goods before, was considered by the High Court of Madras in Muthukrishha Reddiar v. Madhavji Devichand and Co. Ltd., (AIR 1953 Mad 817), wherein Venkatarama Aiyar, J. in the course of the judgment observed as follows:

'On the question whether the plaintiffs are entitled to reject the goods there has not been much of an argument before us. There is authority for the position that in a C.I.F. contract the purchaser is entitled to reject the goods as not being in accordance with terms of the contract notwithstanding that the property in the goods has passed to him by delivery of the bills of lading if he had no opportunity to inspect the goods before. It is only when he does any act which is inconsistent with the ownership of the seller that he loses his right of rejection under Section 42, Sale of Goods Act...'

It is settled law that even in the case of C.I.F. contracts, the goods which are the subject-matter of sale should be of merchantable quality at the time they are delivered to the buyer at the place of destination and during a reasonable time thereafter. A summary of several decisions of English Courts bearing on the question is set out at page 650 in Benjamin on Sale, 8th Edn, as follows:

'The rule deductible from the authorities is, it is submitted, as follows: The goods despatched, if they are perishable, will not be merchantable unless they can so stand the journey in the ordinary course of transit to the buyer as to be merchantable (saving necessary deterioration) on arrival, and until the buyer has a reasonable opportunity of dealing therewith in the ordinary way of business. Of deterioration arising from exceptional or accidental causes the owner must take the risk; that is to say, the seller if he contracted to deliver the goods at their destination, or has otherwise retained the right of disposal until the arrival of the goods, or the buyer if the goods were merely to be sent off. The rule is, of course, subject to any contrary intention as to the incidence of the risk.'

In paragraph 297 of Volume 34 of Halsbury's Laws of England (Third Edn.) which deals with C.I.F. contracts, we find the following passage:

'The buyer by acceptance of the documents does not thereby lose his right to reject the goods on actual delivery, if the goods are not in accordance with the contract. The place of delivery is prima facie the proper place for inspection, but the circumstances of the case may show some other place or later time to be appropriate. In particular, where goods to the knowledge of the seller are purchased by the buyer for delivery to a further destination, and the nature of the goods and the way in which they are packed makes it unreasonable to inspect immediately on delivery, the right to reject will be extended to the later date.'

From the foregoing, it is clear that even in case of C.I.F. contracts, unless there is a contract to the contrary, a buyer has the right of inspection of the goods before accepting them and to reject them if they do not answer the agreed specifications or when he accepts, to sue the seller for recovery of excess price paid in respect of the quantity which is not of merchantable quality under Section 59 of the Sale of Goods Act (hereinafter referred to

as the Act). The burden of establishing the claim however is on the plaintiff.

The mere fact that defendant 1 has produced the Phyto Sanitary Certificate and the Fumigation Certificate in respect of the goods issued by the Burmese authorities does not deprive the plaintiff of its right of inspection of the goods at the time of delivery and to reject the goods if they are not in order or to accept the goods and to claim the relief under Section 59 of the Act.

Mahabir Commercial Co. Ltd v. *CIT, West Bengal*

Mahabir Commercial Co. Ltd dealt in the sale and purchase of jute in India and what was then East Pakistan.[12] The company sold goods to a buyer on CIF terms. The seller forwarded the shipping documents through the banking channels for the buyer to receive and pay through letter of credit. Within the taxation law prevailing in 1951, the tax would have been applicable if the property in goods passed to the buyer in India but not if it passed in East Pakistan. It is not possible to reproduce the terms of the contract and arrangement for encashment of letter of credit, but the review of the law on CIF contracts by the Supreme Court is interesting.

Before we examine the terms of the contract and the dealings between the parties to ascertain where exactly the unconditional appropriation of the goods under the contract was effected, it is, we think appropriate to set out the principles which are applicable for the determination of that question. It would also be useful to an understanding of the terms of the contract and the intention of the parties, if we were to ascertain what exactly is the significance of an irrevocable letter of credit. In this case we are dealing with the sale of unascertained goods in a delivered state in respect of which where the property in

---

[12] *Mahabir Commercial Co. Ltd* v. *CIT, West Bengal,* AIR (1973) SC 430.

the goods passes is the question to be determined. Sections 23 and 39 of the Sale of Goods Act which are in identical terms with rule 5 of S. 18 and S. 32 of the English Sale of Goods Act lay down the principles for ascertaining where the property in the goods passes.

...

It is apparent that for the purposes of sub-s. (1) of S. 23 there should be an unconditional appropriation with the assent of the parties as indicated before the property in the goods passes to the buyer. This sub-section is quite independent of sub-s. (2) and does not contemplate an unconditional appropriation in pursuance of the contract. Sub-s. (2) on the other hand requires the delivery to a carrier in pursuance of a contract which operates or is deemed to operate as an unconditional appropriation. Where in pursuance of the contract the seller delivers the goods to the buyer or to a carrier or other bailee whether named by the buyer or not for the purposes of transmission to the buyer and does not reserve the right of disposal he is deemed to have unconditionally appropriated the goods to the contract. The buyer's assent to the passing of the property in the said circumstances is implied and that when the seller despatches the goods and delivers them to the common carrier for purposes of transit to the buyer, the common carrier not only receives the goods as agent of the buyer but also assent to the appropriation made by the seller. Where however the intention is clearly indicated and the carrier assents it is immaterial by what document the consignment is effected. In cases where the seller bears the freight for the transmission of the goods free of cost to the buyer, the property in the goods passes to the buyer as soon as they are sent to the carrier though there may be a provision that they are to be paid for by the buyer on behalf of the seller after the arrival of the goods. But where however the seller exercises a right of disposal or where he agrees to deliver the goods at their destination the carrier is the seller's agent and the delivery is not a final appropriation. The intention of the parties is therefore one of the important elements in determining the situs where the property passes to the buyer in pursuance of

the contract. The decided cases are of little help and are only illustrative of the principles which are applicable for determining when the goods are unconditionally appropriated to the contract.

In the case of transactions of sale of goods between the buyer and seller living in two different countries the contract may envisage the seller sending the goods through a carrier and the payment being made either at that place or at the place where the buyer resides. In such a transaction the banks have come to play an important part and the bankers' commercial credit system facilitates merchants domiciled in different countries and assures payment to the seller on the one hand and delivery of the goods contracted for to the buyer on the other. This is done by means of what are known as letters of credit which under the terms of the contract the seller may insist on the buyer to provide for in a bank doing business in the place of the seller's domicile. This may be effected by the buyer requesting the bank to facilitate a letter of credit in the country of the seller where the bank or its constituent assumes liability for payment of the price for some consideration which may either be by loan or an over-draft arrangement or perhaps on the security by the pledge of documents of title to the goods or by some other arrangement arrived at between them.

...

It will be seen from the contract between the parties and the irrevocable confirmed letter of credit that the transaction is one known as c.i.f. contract, that is carriage, insurance and freight, which in the commercial parlance indicates that the contract for the sale of goods is at a price to cover cost, insurance and freight and ex-ship. In f.o.b. contract (free on board) in the absence of a contract to the contrary, the buyer must nominate the ship and notify the seller when it is likely to arrive which is a condition precedent to the seller's duty to bring the goods to the port. On the ship's arrival the seller must deliver the goods on board at his own expense. Thereafter the goods are at the buyer's risk and he is responsible for the freight and any subsequent charges. In a c.i.f. contract the seller has first to ship at the port of shipment goods of the description contained in the contract.

He must then procure the shipping documents (contract of affreightment) as contemplated by the contract upon the terms current covering the whole transit of the goods. He must arrange for an insurance for an amount equal to their reasonable value of shipment upon the terms current in the trade which will be available and it should be for the benefit of the buyer. He must also make out an invoice which is a written account of the particulars of goods delivered to the buyer with value of the goods or their price and charges etc. annexed. This invoice is made out debiting the buyer with the agreed price and giving him credit for the amount of freight which he will pay the ship owner on actual delivery. And lastly the shipper should tender the shipping documents to enable the buyer to deal with the goods in the usual way of business. He is also required to tender such other documents as are specified in the contract and if the contract is silent it is sufficient if the seller tenders the bill of lading, policy of insurance and invoice. All these documents must be valid on tender. Under the c.i.f. contract prima facie the property in the goods passes once the documents are tendered by the seller to the buyer or his agent as required under the contract. But where the seller retains control over the goods by either obtaining a bill of lading in his name or to his order, the property in the goods does not pass to the buyer until he endorses the bill to the buyer and delivers the documents to him.

The appropriation of the goods to the contract by itself would not be such as to pass the property in the goods if it appears or can be inferred that there was no actual intention to pass the property. But if however the seller's dealing with the bill of lading is only to secure the contract price not with the intention of withdrawing the goods from the contract, and he does nothing inconsistent with an intention to pass the property, the property may pass either forthwith subject to the seller's lien or conditional on performance by the buyer of his part of the contract. Kennedy, L.J. in Biddell Brothers v. E. Clemens Horst Company, (1911) 1 KB 934 at p. 952 dissenting with the majority stated the principles for ascertaining in a c.i.f. contract when the property in the goods passes which

was later confirmed in an appeal against that judgment in E. Clemens Horst Co. v. Biddell Brothers, 1912 AC 18, the Lord Chancellor describing it as 'the remarkable judgment illuminating as it does, the whole field of controversy.' In that case the seller was to ship a cargo of hops was to contract for freight, had to effect insurance and was to receive 90s. per 112 lbs. of hops. The buyer had to pay cash. The contract did not when the price was to be paid. The buyer said that he is to pay cash against physical delivery and acceptance of the goods when they come to England. Under Section 28 of the Sale of Goods Act the payment was to be against delivery. But when is the delivery of the goods which are on board the ship said to take place? The Earl Loreburn L. C. said:

'The answer is that delivery of the bill of lading when the goods are at sea can be treated as delivery of the goods themselves, this law being so old that I think it is quite unnecessary to refer to authority for it.

Now in this contract there is no time fixed at which the seller is entitled to tender the bill of lading. He therefore may do so at any reasonable time; and it is wrong to say that he must defer the tender of the bill of lading until the ship has arrived and it is still more wrong to say that he must defer the tender of the bill of lading until after the goods have been landed, inspected and accepted.'

By a reference to Section 32 of the Sale of Goods Act (corresponding to Section 38 of the Indian Sale of Goods Act) Kennedy, L.J. at p. 956 of the judgment to which we have referred observed:

'Two further legal results arise out of the shipment. The goods are at the risk of the purchaser, against which he has protected himself by the stipulation in his c.i.f. contract that the vendor shall, at his own cost, provide him with a proper policy of marine insurance intended to protect the buyer's interest, and available for his use, if the goods should be lost in transit; and the property in the goods has passed to the purchaser, either conditionally or unconditionally. It passes conditionally where the bill of lading for the goods, for the purpose of better securing payment of the price, is made out in favour of the vendor or his agent or representative: see the judgments of Bramwell L.J. and Cotton L.J. in Mirabita v. Imperial Ottoman Bank (1878-3 Ex. D. 164). It passes unconditionally where the bill of lading is made out in favour of the purchaser or his agent or representative, as consignee. But the vendor, in the absence of special agreement, is not yet in a position to demand payment from the purchaser; his delivery of the goods to the carrier is, according to the express terms of S. 32 only 'prima facie deemed to be a delivery of the goods to the buyer'; and under S. 28 of the Sale of Goods Act, as under the common law (an exposition of which will be found in the judgments of the members of the Exchequer Chamber in the old case of Startup v. Macdonald, ([1843] 6 Man. and G. 593), a tender of delivery entitling the vendor to payment of the price must, in the absence of contractual stipulation to the contrary, be a tender of possession. How is such a tender to be made of goods afloat under a c.i.f. contract? By tender of the bill of lading, accompanied in case the goods have been lost in transit by the policy of insurance. The bill of lading in law and in fact represents the goods. Possession of the bill of lading places the goods at the disposal of the purchaser.'

Again dealing with the argument of the plaintiffs that a right under the c.i.f. to withhold payment until delivery of the goods and after having had an opportunity of examining them, the learned Judge says that this cannot possibly be effected except in one of the two ways. At page 959 he stated:

'Landing and delivery can rightfully be given by the shipowner only to the holder of the bill of lading. Therefore, if the plaintiff's contention is right one of two things must happen. Either the seller must surrender to the purchaser the bill of lading, where-under the delivery can be obtained, without receiving payment, which, as the bill of lading carries with it an absolute power of disposition, is, in the absence of a special agreement in the contract of sale, so unreasonable as to be absurd or, alternatively, the vendor must himself retain the bill of lading, himself land and take delivery of the goods, and himself store the goods on quay (if the rules of the port permit), or warehouse the goods, for such time as may elapse before the purchaser has an opportunity of examining them. But this involves a manifest violation of the expression terms of the contract '90 s. per 112 lbs. cost freight and insurance'. The parties have in terms agreed that for the buyer's benefit the price shall include freight and insurance, and for this benefit nothing beyond freight and insurance. But if the plaintiff's contention were to prevail, the vendor must be saddled with the further payment of those charges at the port of discharge which ex necessitate rei would be added to the freight and insurance premium which alone he has by the terms of the contract undertaken to defray.'

Even though the property in the goods may pass to the buyer when the documents are handed over, the buyer may yet retain the right to examine and repudiate the goods but this right generally which a buyer has in c.i.f. contract does not by itself indicate that the property in the goods has not passed to him. This supposed incongruity was sought to be explained per curiam in Kwei Tek Chao v. British Traders and Shippers Ltd. (1954) 2 KB 459 that if property passed when the documents are transferred that property is subject to the condition that the goods should re-vest in the seller if on an examination by the buyer he finds them not to be in accordance with the contract. It is not necessary to consider this aspect because in any case the ascertainment of the obligations under the contract will determine to what extent the transfer of property is subject to a condition or if the property passes conditionally whether the ownership left in the seller is the reversionary interest in the property in the event of the conditions subsequent operating to restore it to him. In any case where the performance of some condition is imposed upon the buyer but is not made a condition of the transfer of the property, the property once passed is not revested in the seller by the buyer's subsequent default. But where however the purchase is financed by an irrevocable credit the transaction would not be affected by rejection of the goods after acceptance of the documents if the latter were such as were called for by the credit or where under that credit the payment of the invoice value is payable on presentation of the documents.

It will be seen from the course of the transactions between the parties that all the conditions of a c.i.f. contract are fulfilled subject to the variations which the parties under the contract agreed, and to which a reference has been earlier made. The bill of exchange which he had to draw in accordance with the invoice was for the price of the goods less the premium and freight which the buyer was paying in India on account of the seller. On the presentation of the shipping documents as noted already, the bank in Pakistan under the irrevocable letter of credit was to make payment of the invoice value in terms of the contract to the sellers in equivalent Pakistan currency at the exchange rate ruling on the date of presentation of the documents at the bank. Once the seller has performed his part and presented the documents for being sent to the seller for acceptance and received payment in Pakistan he has no longer any control over the goods and the property in the goods passes to the buyer. The bill of lading when it is handed over to the buyer by the bank [sic] on the buyer accepting the bill of exchange and paying the amount specified in the invoice, confers on him the right to take delivery of the goods at the place of disembarkation.

...

There is nothing in the agreement which envisaged the property in the goods being in the seller even after the value of the invoice had been paid by the bank under the letter of credit in Pakistan. It may be further noticed that the bills of lading and/or railway receipts have to be made out to order and endorsed in blank. In all transactions of sale of goods the time and place of appropriation are important elements for determining when the property in the goods passes. It is well settled that an appropriation takes place where the goods are situated at the time of appropriation not where the contract of sale is made. There may be an authority given by one party to the other to appropriate and that appropriation is presumed to be finally made whereby the terms of the contract the party so authorised has determined his election by doing such act or thing which cannot be done until the goods are appropriated. Generally, subject to the limitations already discussed a seller appropriates the goods by the delivery of the bill of lading the document giving control of the goods in exchange for payment of the price by which he shows that he does not intend to retain the right of disposal of the property in the goods.

* * *

Thus, in a CIF contract, the seller arranges for the carriage of goods by ship and insurance. He delivers the goods to the carrier and tenders the documents to the buyer. The buyer must then pay the price and accept the documents. He has to receive the documents even if the goods are lost or destroyed. A CIF contract is not a contract for the sale of the document but of the goods. If the goods are lost, the documents give the right to the buyer to receive insurance compensation. In a business sense, the documents become the equivalent of goods. However, if the documents are not in conformity with the contract, the buyer may refuse to receive the documents. If the breach is a condition of the contract, the buyer would have the right to terminate it. By taking the documents, the buyer takes over the entire commercial venture from the seller. In relation to the carrier, the buyer replaces the seller. Thus, ownership passes when the documents are received, and symbolically, delivery is made at this time.

9

Remedies for the Seller

What are the ways in which things can go wrong for the seller? The buyer may not pay the price as agreed upon in the contract. If the contract does not provide for delivery and payment, delivery and payment would be concurrent conditions. The buyer may do neither, or he may take delivery but not pay. Alternatively, the buyer may wrongfully reject the goods. In this chapter, we will examine the remedies available to a seller against breach by the buyer. Let us consider the following cases on the basis of the principles of contract law and the sale of goods that we have learnt so far.

ACTION FOR PRICE

X entered into an agreement to sell specific goods to the buyer on the first day of the month. The agreement was silent on transfer of ownership. The seller delivered the goods to the buyer on the 5th of the month. Under the contract, the price was to be paid on the 20th. Now that the seller has delivered the goods, can he instead demand the price on the 10th? If the seller fails to pay the money on the 20th, can the seller approach the court to regain the ownership over the goods?

In this case, as the contract of sale was unconditional, the ownership passed to the buyer at the time of making of the contract, and the rights and obligations of the parties are as provided in it. The parties can settle on any schedule for payment of the price. The seller can demand payment only as provided in the contract. Thus, the seller cannot demand payment till 20th, even if the goods have already been delivered. The passing of ownership has a significant effect. Ownership is exclusive control over the goods. Only the owner can dispossess himself of his goods. Thus, the seller cannot reclaim the ownership, but only the money due to him.

Consider an agreement for the sale of twenty laptops of a particular brand and specification. The ownership was to pass on delivery, and the price was to be paid within two weeks of it. What if the buyer refuses to take delivery of the goods? Or if the buyer takes delivery of the goods but refuses to pay the money? If the buyer refuses to take delivery, the ownership does not transfer. The buyer is only in breach of contract. The ownership of the goods remains with the seller, who may only claim damages. If the buyer takes delivery but refuses to pay within two weeks, the seller can only approach a court for the payment. He cannot reclaim ownership over the goods.

Suppose that a sale contract for specific goods made on Monday was silent on the transfer of ownership. The seller was to give delivery of the goods to the buyer on Wednesday and the buyer was to pay the price on Friday. Despite the seller's adequate precautions, the goods were destroyed. The seller now refuses to pay money to the buyer. As the sale is for specific goods and the contract is silent on transfer of ownership, the ownership was transferred to the buyer when the contract was made. The risk of loss must fall on the owner. Thus, the buyer should pay the price to the seller.

Now consider a sale contract where the buyer was to make an advance payment on the 10th of the month and the seller was to deliver the goods and transfer the ownership on the 20th. The buyer failed to pay the price. What are the remedies available to the seller? The buyer is in breach of a term of the contract. Every breach gives the innocent party the right to seek remedy. If the payment of the price on the stipulated date is a condition to the contract, he will also have the option of terminating it. Section 55 of the Sale of Goods Act, 1930, provides:

55. Suit for price: (1) Where under a contract of sale the property in the goods has passed to the buyer and the buyer wrongfully neglects or refuses to pay for the goods according to the terms of the contract, the seller may sue him for the price of the goods.

(2) Where under a contract of sale the price is payable on a day certain irrespective of delivery and the buyer wrongfully neglects or refuses to pay such price, the seller may sue him for the price although the property in the goods has not passed

and the goods have not been appropriated to the contract.

Let us consider the following scenarios with reference to Section 55.

Scenario 1: Under a contract for sale of specific goods, the ownership transferred to the buyer on the 10th of the month. The buyer was to pay the price three months later. The seller demanded the price from the buyer on the 11th as he had transferred the ownership. Can the seller file a suit for the price? The answer is no. The ownership is transferred but the refusal of the seller to pay is consistent with the contract, and therefore not 'wrongful'. The buyer must breach the terms of payment for his refusal or neglect to be considered wrongful.

Scenario 2: Under a contract for a sale of unascertained goods, the buyer was to pay on the 10th of the month and the goods were to be appropriated to the contract on the 20th. The buyer failed to pay the money. In this case, Subsection 2 applies. The seller has neither delivered nor transferred the goods, but as a term of the contract on payment of the price has been breached, the seller can file a suit. Subsection 2 is worded in a similar fashion to Subsection 1 in using the phrase 'wrongfully neglects or refuses to pay such price'. Curiously, it does not add 'according to the terms of the contract', which is also present in Subsection 1. The omission is not relevant as the action of the parties can be wrongful only for a breach of the contract.

Scenario 3: Under a contract, the ownership in goods was to pass at the time of delivery. The buyer was to pay for the goods soon after delivery. The buyer refused to take delivery or pay the price. Can the seller sue for the latter? In this case, neither of the Subsections apply. The buyer is in breach of the contract in not accepting the goods. The seller can claim damages for breach but not sue for price. Section 56 provides this principle: 'Where the buyer wrongfully neglects or refuses to accept and pay for the goods, the seller may sue him for damages for non-acceptance.'

Colley v. Overseas Exporters

Colley, a leather merchant at Sheffield, sold a quantity of leather belting to Overseas Exporters, FOB Liverpool.[1] The goods were unascertained at the date of the sale. There was no special agreement making the price payable on a stipulated day irrespective of delivery. The buyer instructed the seller to consign the goods to the Alexandra Dock Station at Liverpool for shipment on board the steamship *Kenuta*. The seller duly dispatched the goods to the station, but unfortunately the *Kenuta* had been withdrawn from service by her owners. Four other vessels that were in turn substituted by the buyer for the *Kenuta* were all prevented from taking the belting on board for one reason or another. As a result, the goods had been lying at the dock station for more than two months awaiting shipment. The seller moved the court to claim the price for the goods. McCardie J. ruled:

The defendants [buyer] committed no deliberate breach of contract; they suffered a series of misfortunes. They failed however to name an effective ship. The plaintiff [seller] on his part did all he could to carry out his obligations. Under these circumstances the plaintiff seeks to recover the price of the goods in question. ... An action for the price of goods is, of course, essentially an action for a liquidated sum. It involves special and technical elements. By special bargain the price of goods may be payable before delivery or before the property has passed from vendor to buyer.

[1] *Colley* v. *Overseas Exporters*, (1921) 3 KB 302.

In ordinary cases and unless otherwise agreed delivery of the goods and payment of the price are concurrent conditions: see s. 28 of the Sale of Goods Act, 1893. Now the full meaning of the word 'price' is not actually defined by the Sale of Goods Act, except perhaps in s. 1, which says: 'A contract of sale of goods is a contract whereby the seller transfers or agrees to transfer the property in goods to the buyer for a money consideration, called the price.' The circumstances however under which a claim to the price may be made (as distinguished from a claim of damages for breach of contract) are indicated in s. 49 of that Act. Sect. 49 provides, sub-s. 1:

'Where, under a contract of sale, the property in the goods has passed to the buyer, and the buyer wrongfully neglects or refuses to pay for the goods according to the terms of the contract, the seller may maintain an action against him for the price of the goods.'

Sub-s 2:

'Where, under a contract of sale, the price is payable on a day certain irrespective of delivery, and the buyer wrongfully neglects or refuses to pay such price, the seller may maintain an action for the price, although the property in the goods has not passed, and the goods have not been appropriated to the contract.'

Here sub-s. 2 of s. 49 does not apply ... The parties before me here made no special agreement as to the payment of the price. Nor can it be said that sub-s. 1 of s. 49 applies here, for the property in the goods has not in fact and law passed to the buyer. Several rules for the passing of property in sale of goods contracts are indicated in ss. 16, 17, 18, and also in s. 32. The Act does not deal specifically with f.o.b. or c.i.f. contracts. Judicially settled rules exist however with respect to them. I need only deal with f.o.b. contracts. The presumed intention (see s. 18 of the Act) of the parties has been settled. It seems clear that in the absence of special agreement the property and risk in goods does not in the case of an f.o.b. contract pass from the seller to the buyer till the goods are actually put on board.

...

In my opinion … no action will lie for the price of goods until the property has passed, save only in the special cases provided for by s. 49, sub-s. 2. This seems plain both on the code and on common law principle. I have searched in vain for authority to the contrary. A clear distinction exists between cases where the default of the buyer has occurred after the property has passed and cases where that default has been before the property has passed.

It follows therefore for the reasons given that the plaintiff is not entitled to recover the price of the goods in question. If he desires to claim damages he must amend his writ. On the record at present before me he cannot ask for judgment.

Section 55 of the Sale of Goods Act, 1930, is the equivalent of Section 49 of the Sale of Goods Act, 1893. In *Workman, Clark & Co., Limited* v. *Lloyd Brazileño*,[2] the contract was for the construction and sale of a vessel. The buyer was to pay the price in five instalments for the different stages of the ship's construction. When the first instalment was due, the buyer failed to pay it. The court ruled that each instalment can be sued for at the moment it was due.

Consider the case of a sale of specific goods where the contract is silent on the transfer of ownership as well as the time of payment. The ownership passes to the buyer the very moment the contract is made. The seller becomes a bailee of the goods. Despite adequate care, the goods are destroyed. Can the seller claim the price of the goods from the buyer? Applying Section 49(1), the answer would tend to be 'no'. The contract does not provide for a time for payment. Thus, the seller is not in breach of a term for it. Delivery and payment would be concurrent requirements. The goods no longer exist; they cannot be delivered, and so the buyer has no obligation to pay for them.

In fact, the buyer may be in no breach of contract for the seller to claim any damages. This is an anomaly that seems to have been overlooked in codification. The common law principles recognized the right of the seller to sue for price (*Castle v. Playford*),[3] and this has been applied by the British courts even after the codification (*Manbre v. Cord Products Co. Ltd*).[4]

W.B. Decorating Co., M/s v. *M/s Damodar Das Daga* is a case on Section 55 from the Calcutta High Court.[5] The Civil Procedure Code makes provisions for a suit to recover a debt or a liquidated demand in money arising 'on an enactment'. The question was whether a suit for price under Section 55 was one arising from an enactment. The court ruled:

It is apparent upon a reading of the section … that the claim for the price of the goods really arises from the terms of the contract of sale. It would be unreasonable to hold that because the Act enables the seller to sue the buyer for the price, the claim must be held to arise on the enactment. That it is not so is apparent on the language of the section itself. A cause of action does not arise under or on an enactment unless it arises out of and depends on the enactment, so that the plaintiff must show both in stating and in proving his case that his right to recover stands on the enactment. In our view the claim of the nature as made in this suit cannot be said to arise on an enactment. It arises from the contract of sale and the breach thereof.

DAMAGES FOR NON-ACCEPTANCE

If a buyer fails to perform any obligation under a sale contract, this qualifies as a breach of the contract. The breach may be of a

---

[2] *Workman, Clark & Co., Limited* v. *Lloyd Brazileño*, (1908) 1 KB 968.

[3] *Castle* v. *Playford*, (1872) LR 7 Exch 98.

[4] *Manbre* v. *Cord Products Co. Ltd*, (1919) 1 KB 198.

[5] *W.B. Decorating Co., M/s* v. *M/s Damodar Das Daga*, AIR (1982) Calcutta 386.

condition of the contract, that is, of a term that is central to the contract. The seller would then—and only then—have the right to terminate the contract. Whether the breach is of a condition or warranty will depend on the terms of the contract. In both the cases, the seller should have a remedy for the breach of the contract by the buyer. Going by contract law, the seller should be able to claim damages and compensation for the loss suffered. The principle would be to put the parties in the same situation as if the contract were performed. For instance, in case of the buyer being in breach of not paying the price, as per the principle elaborated above, the price should be paid to the seller. This is the reason for giving a separate treatment for the money due to the buyer.

For other kinds of breach, damages need to be worked out according to the general principles of contract law. If the buyer does not accept the goods but has already paid the money to the seller, the latter will incur the losses in keeping the goods till the buyer accepts it. If the buyer is to pay on delivery or after delivery, the buyer is refusing delivery and paying the money. In this case, the seller will get damages for non-acceptance by the buyer. Section 56 provides: 'Where the buyer wrongfully neglects or refuses to accept and pay for the goods, the seller may sue him for damages for non-acceptance.'

The contract law provides principles for award of damages. We shall summarize the principles of contract law on awarding damages and review its application to the sale of goods. The different aspects involved in the award of damages include remoteness of damage, measure of damage, liquidated damages, and specific performance. In most cases, a monetary equivalent is provided to compensate the innocent party for the breach of the contract.

As we have already seen, contract law was developed to deal with the disputes and practices of traders. For the traders, what mattered was not the goods in themselves but their monetary value and profit from trade. As has been noted in *Ruxley Electronics and Construction Ltd* v. *Forsyth*:[6]

Damages for breach of contract must reflect, as accurately as the circumstances allow, the loss which the claimant has sustained because he did not get what he bargained for. There is no question of punishing the contract breaker. Given this basic principle, the court, in assessing the measure of the claimant's loss, has ultimately to determine a question of fact ... Since the law relating to damages for breach of contract has developed almost exclusively in a commercial context, these criteria normally proceed on the assumption that each contracting party's interest in the bargain was purely commercial and that the loss resulting from a breach of contract is measurable in purely economic terms.

As a result, the courts do not insist on specific performance of contract as a remedy for the parties. Specific performance is granted under the Specific Relief Act, 1963, which allows It only if monetary compensation would be inadequate to do justice to the party. Further, compensation is not a penalty. It is only aimed at putting the parties in the position they would have been in if the contract had been performed and not breached. This raises two questions, remoteness of damage and measure of damage. A breach leads to several consequences. How far do we go for awarding compensation to the innocent party? This is remoteness of damage. Having limited the extent of the damage, how do we measure the money equivalent for award of compensation? This is measure of damage.

[6] *Ruxley Electronics and Construction Ltd* v. *Forsyth*, (1996) AC 344.

REMOTENESS OF DAMAGE

Hadley v. Baxendale

The principle for remoteness of damages comes from the *Hadley* v. *Baxendale*,[7] a case on the sale of goods. Hadley operated a flourmill at Gloucester that was powered by a steam engine. A crankshaft of the engine broke and the mill had to be shut down. The engineers who had made the steam engine were based at Greenwich. The shaft had to be sent to them to serve as a model for making a new one. It was sent with the carriers Pickford & Co., represented by Baxendale. The carriers promised to deliver the shaft at Greenwich the next day and collected two pounds for the job. However, the delivery was delayed by one week, because the carriers sent it by canal rather than by rail. As a result, the new shaft was delivered late, and the mill had to stay closed, resulting in a loss of profit. Hadley claimed £ 300 as loss of profit for five days.

To decide on what damages were to be awarded, the court sought to find out what the parties knew of the situation. The judge noted that the only communication that had taken place between the parties at the time of the contract was that 'the article to be carried was the broken shaft of a mill and that the plaintiffs (Hadley) were the millers of that mill.' The actual situation was not explicitly known to the parties since Hadley had not told Baxendale about the circumstances under which the shaft was being sent and the carrier had not explicitly agreed to the terms of being responsible for the closure of the mill on account of any delays. There had been no special arrangement of this kind.

In the absence of any explicit communication, the court reasoned that the carriers had no way of knowing that Hadley would lose profits if the shipment was delayed. For all they knew, the mill had a spare shaft that they would put into service. Also, the mill could have been shut down for reasons other than the broken shaft. One can, of course, imagine any sequence of events. As the court put it: 'But it is obvious that, in the great multitude of cases of millers sending off broken shafts to third persons by a carrier under ordinary circumstances, such consequences would not, in all probability, have occurred...' The court, thus, inferred: 'It follows, therefore, that the loss of profits here cannot reasonably be considered such a consequence of the breach of contract as could have been fairly and reasonably contemplated by both the parties when they made this contract.'

Another way of expressing the same principle of inferring from their actions what the parties had known and intended at the time of the formation of the contract is: 'Where two parties have made a contract which one of them has broken, the damages which the other party ought to receive in respect of such breach of contract should be such as may fairly and reasonably be considered either arising naturally, i.e., according to the usual course of things, from such breach of contract itself.' The court thus stated that to determine the contemplation of the parties, we should first look for any explicit or special arrangements. If there is none, we should look at the practices that happen 'naturally' in a 'majority of the cases'. The principle formulated in this case has been applied to all cases on compensation since.

The Indian Contract Act adopted the principle formulated in the *Hadley v. Baxendale* case. Section 73 of the Indian Contract Act provides:

73. Compensation for loss or damage caused by breach of contract: When a contract has been

---

[7] *Hadley* v. *Baxendale*, (1854) 9 Exch 341.

broken, the party who suffers by such breach is entitled to receive, from the party who has broken the contract, compensation for any loss or damage caused to him thereby, which naturally arose in the usual course of things from such breach, or which the parties knew, when they made the contract, to be likely to result from the breach of it.

Such compensation is not to be given for any remote and indirect loss or damage sustained by reason of the breach.

Compensation for failure to discharge obligation resembling those created by contract—When an obligation resembling those created by contract has been incurred and has not been discharged, any person injured by the failure to discharge it is entitled to receive the same compensation from the party in default, as if such person had contracted to discharge it and had broken his contract.

Explanation—In estimating the loss or damage arising from a breach of contract, the means which existed of remedying the inconvenience caused by the non-performance of the contract must be taken into account.

The principles of *Hadley* v. *Baxendale* are in the first two paragraphs. They limit the consequences of breach in two ways. First, if the parties have—in express terms or impliedly—provided for the consequences, these should be followed. We infer from the conduct of the specific parties as well as their negotiations and dealings. The law implies terms from the manner in which such contracts usually happen in practices. Thus, the second option is to take the contract and its breach to be as it usually happens in practice. Referring to common law principles and Section 73, the Supreme Court noted:[8]

Although the Contract Act makes separate provisions for the consequences in each case, the rule laid down as to measure of damages is the same, namely, the party in breach must make compensation in respect of the direct consequences flowing from the breach and not in respect of loss or damage indirectly or remotely caused, which is also the rule in English common law. The rule is based on the broad principle ... that the party who has suffered the loss should be placed in the same position, as far as compensation in money can do it, as if the party in breach had performed his contract or fulfilled his duty.

The Supreme Court has recognized that Section 73 codifies the judgment in *Hadley* v. *Baxendale*. In *Pannalal Jankidas* v. *Mohanlal* it noted:

The rule stated by Alderson B. has consistently been accepted as correct; the only difficulty has been in applying it. The distinction drawn is between damages arising naturally (which means in the normal course of things) and cases where there were special and extraordinary circumstances beyond the reasonable provision of the parties. The distinction between these types is usually described in English Law as that between general and special damages; the latter are such that if they are not communicated it would not be fair or reasonable to hold the defendant responsible for losses which he could not be taken to contemplate as likely to result from his breach of contract.

Realizing the difficulties in working out the remoteness of damage, business parties have come up with terms in the contracts to avoid getting into it. Most commercial contracts have a clause stating, 'Neither party shall be liable to the other party for indirect or consequential losses.' Thus, damages are limited to the losses that are direct. The question then is, what is a direct loss? A businessperson enters into a contract to earn a profit. Thus, in a contract where a party is a businessperson, parties usually understand that there would be a loss of profit for them if the contract is breached. Thus, loss of profit for a businessperson is taken to be a direct loss.

[8] *Pannalal Jankidas* v. *Mohanlal*, AIR 1951 SC 144.

MEASURE OF DAMAGES

As we've seen above, the principle for awarding damages is to give the innocent party a sum of money that will put him in the position in which he would have been but for the breach. In a sale contract, as the goods are referred to a selling price, this becomes the reference for judging the losses. In a sale contract, a businessperson enters into a contract to earn a profit. The profit or loss, however, reflects in the market prices. The loss can be quantified with reference to the market prices. Section 73 of the Indian Contract Act, 1872, has several illustrations on the award of damages in sale contracts:

Illustration (a): 'A contracts to sell and deliver 50 maunds of saltpetre to B, at a certain price to be paid on delivery. A breaks his promise.' If a higher price is paid when the buyer purchases the goods from another source, the loss is the difference between the two prices. 'B is entitled to receive from A, by way of compensation, the sum, if any, by which the contract price falls short of the price for which B might have obtained 50 maunds of saltpetre of like quality at the time when the saltpetre ought to have been delivered.'

Illustration (o): 'A contracts to deliver 50 maunds of saltpetre to B on the first of January, at a certain price. B afterwards, before the first of January, contracts to sell the saltpetre to C at a price higher than the market price of the first of January.' As a result, A had no saltpetre to deliver to B on 1 January. How should the damages payable by A to B be calculated? The contracts of A with B and with C are different. A is in breach of the contract with B when he fails to deliver it on 1 January. B would have to buy from another source on that day. The damages payable by A will be the difference in the market price on 1 January and the contract price. 'In estimating the compensation payable by A to B, the market price of the first of January, and not the profit which would have arisen to B from the sale to C, is to be taken into account.'

Illustration (d): 'A contracts to buy B's ship for 60,000 rupees, but breaks his promise.' In this case, the buyer is in breach. The seller would have to find another buyer. If the sale price is lower, the difference from the contract price would be his loss. 'A must pay to B, by way of compensation, the excess, if any, of the contract price over the price which B can obtain for the ship at the time of the breach of promise.'

Illustration (h): 'A contracts to supply B with a certain quantity of iron at a fixed price, being a higher price than that for which A could procure and deliver the iron. B wrongfully refuses to receive the iron.' In this illustration, the seller is buying as well as reselling. The profit of the seller is the difference between the sale and the purchase price. 'B must pay to A, by way of compensation, the difference between the contract price of the iron and the sum for which A could have obtained and delivered it.'

Re Vic Mill Ltd

A supplier got an order to make a machine of a particular specification, but the order was later cancelled by the purchaser.[9] The supplier got another order for somewhat similar machinery, and to mitigate his losses, made necessary alterations in the machinery and sold to the second purchaser. The first purchaser claimed that the measure of damages was merely the cost of the conversion of the machinery for the second purchaser and his slight loss on the resale. The supplier claimed

[9] *Re Vic Mill Ltd*, (1913) 1 Ch 473.

that the measure of his damages was the loss of his profit. Hamilton L.J. ruled:

That was a reasonable mode of mitigating the damages, but it by no means follows that the damages are confined to the cost, a trivial one, of adapting the machines to the needs of the second customer, and the loss on re-sale to him, which was only £23, making £28 in all. The fallacy of that is in supposing that the second customer was a substituted customer, that had all gone well, the makers would not have had both customers, both orders, and both profits. In fact, what they did, acting reasonably, and I think very likely more than reasonably in the interests of the Vic Mill was to content themselves with earning the profit on the second contract at the cost of adapting the machines, which has been taken at £ 5; but they are still losers of the profit which they would have made on the Vic Mill contract, because they could, if they had been minded, have performed both the contracts, and have made the profit on both the contracts but for the breach by the Vic Mill Company of their contract.

Thus, loss of profit was the basis for the award of damages.

W.L. Thompson Limited v. R. Robinson (Gunmakers) Limited

R. Robinson Ltd signed an order form to buy a Standard Vanguard from motor car dealers and agents W.L. Thompson Ltd.[10] Robinson Ltd breached the contract by refusing to take delivery. To mitigate damages, the motor dealer immediately rescinded the contract with the manufacturer, George Thompson Ltd, for the supply of the car. The manufacturer had already supplied the car to the dealer, but took it back and sold it to another purchaser without charging the dealer for

any damages. This was to maintain amicable business relations.

Thompson Ltd claimed that if the buyer had performed the contract, he would have earned a profit of £ 61. This was calculated on the basis of standard margins given by the manufacturers to the dealers. The prices at which the dealers could sell the car was fixed by the manufacturer. The dealer's profit on the transaction was also fixed—£ 61 in the case of a Standard Vanguard. The dealer's argument was that as he has lost the sale, he should be awarded £ 61 in damages. The argument from Robison Ltd was that there was no loss to the dealer as he could have sold the car to another customer, or, as it had happened in this case, get the supplier to release the dealer from liability. In either case, there is no loss to the dealer. And thus, the loss or damages should be nominal. Upjohn J. noted:

… it would seem to me on the facts to be quite plain that the plaintiff's loss in this case is the loss of their bargain. They have sold one Vanguard less than they otherwise would. The plaintiffs, as the defendants must have known, are in business as dealers in motor cars and make their profit in buying and selling motor cars, and what they have lost is their profit on the sale of this Vanguard. … True the motor car in question was not sold to another purchaser, but the plaintiffs did what was reasonable, they got out of their bargain with George Thompson Ltd but they sold one less Vanguard, and lost their profit on that transaction.

However, while the above would be true following the general principles, the Sale of Goods Act, 1893, has provided on damages where a seller refuses to accept the goods. Section 50 provides:

(1) Where the buyer wrongfully neglects or refuses to accept and pay for the goods, the seller may maintain an action against him for damages for non-acceptance.

[10] *W.L. Thompson Limited* v. *R. Robinson (Gunmakers) Limited*, (1955) 1 All ER 154.

(2) The measure of damages is the estimated loss directly and naturally resulting, in the ordinary course of events, from the buyer's breach of contract.

(3) Where there is an available market for the goods in question the measure of damages is prima facie to be ascertained by the difference between the contract price and the market or current price at the time or times when the goods ought to have been accepted, or, if no time was fixed for acceptance, then at the time of the refusal to accept.

The case explored the working of the provision. The judge interpreted 'available market' thus:

… an available market merely means that the situation in the particular trade in the particular area was such that the particular goods could freely be sold, and that there was a demand sufficient to absorb readily all the goods that were thrust on it, so that if a purchaser defaulted the goods in question could readily be disposed of. … in March, 1954, there was not a demand in the East Riding which could readily absorb all the Vanguard motor cars available for sale. If a purchaser defaulted, that sale was lost and there was no means of readily disposing of the Vanguard contracted to be sold, so that there was not, even on the extended definition, an available market.

The judge further noted:

But there is this further consideration: even if I accepted the defendants broad argument that one must now look at the market as being the whole conspectus of trade, organisation and marketing, I have to remember that s 50(3) provides only a prima facie rule, and, if on investigation of the facts, one finds that it is unjust to apply that rule, in the light of the general principles mentioned above it is not to be applied. In this case, as I said in the earlier part of my judgment, it seems to me plain almost beyond argument that, in fact, the loss to the plaintiffs is 61. Accordingly, however

one interprets s 50(3), it seems to me on the facts that I have to consider one reaches the same result.

Why should the demand and supply make any difference to a bargain being lost and the loss of profit not being awarded? The argument was explained in clearer terms in a later case, *Charter* v. *Sullivan*, also involving a car dealer and a buyer:[11]

The plaintiff, however, is a motor car dealer whose trade for the present purpose can be described as consisting in the purchase of recurrent supplies of cars of the relevant description from the manufacturers, and selling the cars so obtained, or as many of them as he can, at the fixed retail price. He thus receives, on each sale that he is able to effect, the predetermined profit allowed by the fixed retail price, and it is obviously in his interest to sell as many cars as he can obtain from the manufacturers. The number of sales that he can effect, and consequently the amount of profit which he makes, will be governed, according to the state of trade, either by the number of cars that he is able to obtain from the manufacturers, or by the number of purchasers whom he is able to find. In the former case demand exceeds supply, so that the default of one purchaser involves him in no loss, for he sells the same number of cars as he would have sold if that purchaser had not defaulted. In the latter case supply exceeds demand, so that the default of one purchaser may be said to have lost him one sale.

Ordinarily, the difference between the buying and selling price indicates the loss of profit in a sale contract. In exceptional cases, where the demand far exceeds the supply, the breach may not lead to any loss to the vendor. In this case, the court may allow only nominal damages.

We should note the provisions quoted above in the court judgment. Section 50(1)

---

[11] *Charter* v. *Sullivan*, (1957) 1 All ER 809.

is reproduced as Section 56 in the Sale of Goods, 1930; however, the subsequent two subsections, 2 and 3, are not reproduced. The reason for this is that contract law is not codified in the UK. Thus, the UK law of sale of goods codified contract law as it applies to the sale of goods on award of damages. In India, this was covered by the Indian Contract Act, 1872, and so the Sale of Goods Act, 1930, did not consider it necessary. Section 50(2) is the principle from *Hadley* v. *Baxendale*, and Section 50(3) is the principle from contract law for working out damages with reference to the market price.

Murlidhar Chiranjilal v. Harishchandra Dwarkadas

Chiranjilal and Dwarkadas were Kanpur-based traders who entered into a contract for the sale of canvas at a specified rate per yard.[12] The delivery was to be made through a railway receipt for Calcutta; that is, the goods were to be put on the train and a receipt obtained, entitling the holder to collect the goods in Calcutta. The cost of transport from Kanpur to Calcutta and the labour charges were to be borne by Dwarkadas. It was agreed that the railway receipt would be for 5 August 1947. However, Chiranjilal failed to deliver the railway receipt and informed Dwarkadas on 8 August 1947 that booking from Kanpur to Calcutta was closed. Thus, he had not been able to deliver the goods. Dwarkadas moved the court, proving that the rate of canvas on or about the date of the breach was significantly higher in Calcutta, and claiming the difference as damages.

Chiranjilal contended that the relevant price for calculating damages should be the price prevalent in the Kanpur market.

According to him, Dwarkadas should have bought similar canvas from the Kanpur market and sent it to Calcutta, and if he had suffered damages due to a higher price, he would have been eligible to that amount instead. Dwarkadas argued that it was not necessary for him to worry about the prices in the Kanpur market. According to him, the contract clearly stated that the goods were to be transported to and sold in Calcutta, and therefore, it was the price in Calcutta that should be taken into account while arriving at the measure of damages, for the parties knew when they made the contract that the goods were to be sold there. The Supreme Court laid down the principle as follows:

If therefore the contract was to be performed at Kanpur it was the respondent's duty to buy the goods in Kanpur and rail them to Calcutta on the date of the breach and if it suffered any damage thereby because of the rise in price on the date of the breach as compared to the contract price, it would be entitled to be re-imbursed for the loss. Even if the respondent did not actually buy them in the market at Kanpur on the date of breach it would be entitled to damages on proof of the rate for similar canvas prevalent in Kanpur on the date of breach, if that rate was above the contracted rate resulting in loss to it.

Union of India v. M/s Commercial Metal Corpn

The Union of India entered into a contract with the Commercial Metal Corporation to purchase 200 metric tonnes of leaded bronze ingots.[13] The Corporation supplied 163.020 metric tonnes and wrote a letter to the Union of India dated 7 November 1973 to the effect that because of an exorbitant increase in the price of basic raw material, it was not possible

---

[12] *Murlidhar Chiranjilal* v. *Messrs Harishchandra Dwarkadas*, AIR (1962) SC 366.

[13] *Union of India* v. *M/s Commercial Metal Corpn*, AIR (1982) Delhi 267.

for them to supply the remaining goods at the contract price of Rs 12.37 per kg. They asked the government to increase the price to Rs 19.45 per kg. The Union of India did not agree to the price increase but extended the time for delivery, and finally cancelled the contract on 15 February 1975. The Union of India claimed damages for a short supply of 36.980 metric tonnes at the rate of Rs 7.08 per kg, the increase indicated by the Corporation. The main claim of the Corporation against the demand was that the Union of India had made no purchase; thus, it had not suffered any loss. The Delhi High Court disagreed. It noted:

I cannot accept the broad contention that unless the purchaser repurchases the equivalent goods in the market after the date of the breach he cannot claim damages against the seller. In case of non-delivery by the seller the measure of damages is the difference between the market price and the contract price. The market price on the date following the breach is the yardstick by which the buyer's claim for damages is evaluated and quantified. The market value is taken because it is presumed to be the true value of the goods to the purchaser. If he does not get his goods he should receive by way of damages enough to enable him to buy identical goods in the open market.

...

The rule that measures the buyer's damages by the difference between the contract price and the market price at the time and place of delivery is so well entrenched in the law that no one has questioned it since its formulation in 1854 by Alderson. B. in the Court of Exchequer in Hadley v. Baxendale ... This 'breach-date rule' does not require him actually to go into the market and buy the substitute goods before he can succeed in his action for damages. ... No one has said that the buyer in a case of non-delivery by the seller must go into the market and buy like goods in order to claim damages. This has never been the law. The decisive element is the date of breach and the market price prevailing on that date. But not the fact that the buyer actually went into the market and got similar goods and suffered loss thereby. The law does not penalise the buyer's inaction. Even if the buyer does not go into the market he is entitled to damages all the same if he can show that the market had risen on the date of the breach.

...

The object of an award of damages for breach of contract is to place the plaintiff, so far as money can do it, in the same situation, with respect to damages, as if the contract had been performed. He is thus enabled to recover damages in respect of the loss of gains of which he has been deprived by the breach. He is entitled to sue for the loss of his bargain, that is to say, for the loss of the particular benefit which he expected to receive by the contract which has been broken. This is the benefit which the buyer expects from the promised performance. With the amount of money, that is, the difference between the contract price and the market price the buyer should therefore be in the same financial position as he would have been if the seller had performed his contractual obligation to deliver the goods. In other words, the plaintiff is entitled to compensation for the loss of his bargain, so that his expectations arising out of or created by the contract are protected. This protection of expectations is the distinguishing mark of an action for damages for breach of contract.

MITIGATION OF DAMAGES

While the innocent party has a right to receive damages, he must also mitigate his losses and not unnecessarily increase the liabilities of the party in breach. This is the principle of mitigation of damages. Cockburn C.J. in *Frost* v. *Knight*[14] expressed the principle as follows: 'In assessing the damages for breach of performance ... take into account whatever the plaintiff has done, or has had the means of doing, and, as a prudent man, ought in reason to have done, whereby his loss has been, or would have been, diminished.' The following

[14] *Frost* v. *Knight*, ((1872) LR 7 Ex. 111.

passage from the judgment by Viscount Haldane L.C. in *British Westinghouse Electric & Manufacturing Co. Ltd* v. *Underground Electric Rys Co. of London Ltd*[15] is often quoted as a synopsis of the principle of mitigation:

… there are certain broad principles which are quite well settled. The first is that, as far as possible, he who has proved a breach of a bargain to supply what he contracted to get is to be placed, as far as money can do it, in as good a situation as if the contract had been performed. The fundamental basis is thus compensation for pecuniary loss naturally flowing from the breach; but this first principle is qualified by a second, which imposes on a plaintiff the duty of taking all reasonable steps to mitigate the loss consequent on the breach, and debars him from claiming any part of the damage which is due to his neglect to take such steps.

The following statement of the principle from the judgment of James L.J. in *Dunkirk Colliery Co.* v. *Lever*[16] is also a leading summary of the principle: 'The person who has broken the contract is not to be exposed to additional cost by reason of the plaintiffs not doing what they ought to have done as reasonable men, and the plaintiffs not being under any obligation to do anything otherwise than in the ordinary course of business'.

In the case of sale of goods, the principle of mitigation is related to the principle of award on the basis of the market price; here too it is assumed that there is an available market and that the seller would sell the goods for the best price available in the market if a breach occurs. If he fails to do this, the party in breach cannot be responsible for the whole of the loss. Let us review a few cases to understand the principles better.

Payzu, Limited v. *Saunders*

Saunders was a dealer in silk who agreed to sell to Payzu Ltd over a period of ten months.[17] The payment for the supplies was to be made on a monthly basis. Payzu Ltd failed to make payment for the very first delivery. Saunders grew suspicious of Payzu's intent. Considering the failure to pay to be a breach of the contract, she refused to supply any more instalments. By a letter dated 16 January she offered to deliver goods at the contract price if Payzu paid immediate cash. Payzu refused and tried to get the supplies from the market, but in the meanwhile, the price of silk had risen. In middle of February, Payzu claimed the difference between the reigning price and the price contracted with Saunders as damages. In fact, Payzu Ltd. did not purchase the silk as it was not adequately available in the market.

Saunders claimed that Payzu had breached the contract and that she had a right to terminate it. The court did not agree with the contention. A contract can be terminated only for the breach of an essential term. On this aspect, the court noted:

It is essential to remember in the present case that by s. 10 of the Sale of Goods Act, 1893, it is provided that unless a different intention appears from the terms of the contract, stipulations as to time of payment are not deemed to be of the essence of a contract of sale, and by s. 31 where there is a sale of goods to be delivered by stated instalments which are to be separately paid for, and the buyer refuses to pay for one or more instalments, 'it is a question in each case depending on the terms of the contract and the circumstances of the case, whether the breach of contract is a repudiation of the whole contract or whether it is a severable breach giving rise to a claim for compensation but not to a right to treat the whole

---

[15] *British Westinghouse Electric & Manufacturing Co. Limited* v. *Underground Electric Rys Co. of London Limited*, (1912) AC 673.

[16] *Dunkirk Colliery Co.* v. *Lever*, (1878) 9 ChD 20.

[17] *Payzu, Limited* v. *Saunders*, (1919) 2 KB 581.

contract as repudiated.' It is to be observed that in the present case the contract did not provide for delivery in any particular number of instalments. The deliveries were to be extended over the period from January to September, and it was contemplated that there would be an unspecified number of deliveries and a corresponding number of payments. ... I entertain no doubt whatever that the plaintiffs' failure to make punctual payment for the November delivery did not amount to a repudiation of the contract, nor did it go to the root of the contract...

In fact, the court noted that it was Saunders who had repudiated the contract:

... on the other hand, in my opinion, the defendant's letter of January 16 did in fact and in law amount to an unjustifiable refusal by her to carry out her contractual obligations, for she announced in clear terms that she would thenceforth deliver no further goods to the plaintiffs under the contract unless the plaintiffs paid cash to cover each invoice.

The case instead became that Saunders was in breach of the contract, and Payzu should be compensated for the losses arising from it. The question then was, what should have Payzu done to mitigate its loss? Should it not have taken up the offer of Saunders to pay cash for the supplies? Relying on the settled principles of mitigation quoted earlier in the chapter, the court noted:

The question, therefore, is what a prudent person ought reasonably to do in order to mitigate his loss arising from a breach of contract. ... the plaintiffs in deciding whether to accept the defendant's offer were fully entitled to consider the terms in which the offer was made, its bona fides or otherwise, its relation to their own business methods and financial position, and all the circumstances of the case; and it must be remembered that an acceptance of the offer would not preclude an action for damages for the actual loss sustained. Many illustrations might be given of the extraordinary results which would follow if the plaintiffs were entitled to reject the defendant's offer and incur a substantial measure of loss which would have been avoided by their acceptance of the offer. The plaintiffs were in fact in a position to pay cash for the goods, but instead of accepting the defendant's offer, which was made perfectly bona fide, the plaintiffs permitted themselves to sustain a large measure of loss which as prudent and reasonable people they ought to have avoided.

The case was taken in appeal to the Court of Appeal. Bankes L.J. approved the decision and noted:

It is plain that the question what is reasonable for a person to do in mitigation of his damages cannot be a question of law but must be one of fact in the circumstances of each particular case. There may be cases where as matter of fact it would be unreasonable to expect a plaintiff to consider any offer made in view of the treatment he has received from the defendant. If he had been rendering personal services and had been dismissed after being accused in presence of others of being a thief, and if after that his employer had offered to take him back into his service, most persons would think he was justified in refusing the offer, and that it would be unreasonable to ask him in this way to mitigate the damages in an action of wrongful dismissal. But that is not to state a principle of law, but a conclusion of fact to be arrived at on a consideration of all the circumstances of the case. ... I think the learned judge came to a proper conclusion on the facts, and that the appeal must be dismissed.

Scrutton L.J. noted in the judgment:

I am of the same opinion. Whether it be more correct to say that a plaintiff must minimize his damages, or to say that he can recover no more than he would have suffered if he had acted reasonably, because any further damages do not reasonably follow from the defendant's breach, the result is the same. ... In certain cases of personal service it may be unreasonable to expect a plaintiff to consider an offer from the other party who has grossly injured him; but in commercial contracts it is generally reasonable to accept an offer from the party in default. However, it is always a question of fact. About the law there is no difficulty.

The appeal was dismissed.

Strutt v. Whitnell

Strutt was a property developer and friend of Norman Whitnell and Christine Marjorie Whitnell.[18] The Whitnells purchased a house from him for £ 4,650 and let it to a tenant. Within a year structural defects became apparent in the house. Strutt was the property developer, but not the builder. As the Whitnells did not have privity of contract, they could not sue the builder. Being a friend of the couple, Strutt arranged that he would buy back the house so that he could make the claim on the builder. Accordingly, Strutt bought the house back on 3 March 1971.

The contract of resale of the house provided that Whitnells would give vacant possession; however, tenancy laws gave the tenant the right to not vacate the premises. The Whitnells had thought that the tenant would be willing to leave; as it turned out, they were wrong. As a result, the Whitnells were in breach of the contract to Strutt. In a meeting of the parties, Strutt said that he might have to sue them for damages for breach of the term on vacant possession. The Whitnells offered to buy back the house, but by this point their friendship with Strutt had turned sour. He refused the offer and sued the Whitnells for damages amounting to the difference in the value of the house with and without vacant possession.

On the basis of the value of surveyors, the damages were assessed to be £ 1,900 by the

judge. The contention of the Whitnells was that Strutt could have reduced his damages to nothing simply by accepting their offer to buy back the house. According to them, there was no good reason for refusing that offer as he did not want the house for personal use. It was only a part of his business to buy and sell houses. Mackenna J. noted:

I shall state and consider three different cases.

Case 1: A buyer agrees to buy property having a certain quality and the seller delivers the property without that quality. There is a difference between the market value of the property with the quality and without it. The buyer is clearly entitled to recover the difference between the two values.

Case 2: Suppose, in addition to the facts stated in case 1, that after the sale and after the defect in quality has been discovered, the seller offers to buy back the property at the contract price and the buyer refuses to resell. In that case does the buyer lose his right to recover the difference between the two values? Is he limited to the recovery of nominal damages? I would answer that he is entitled to retain the property and to recover the difference between the values. The seller cannot compel him to forego his right to substantial damages as the price of retaining what has become his own property.

Case 3: Suppose, in addition to the facts stated in case 2, that the seller proves that the buyer had no good reason for refusing to accept his offer to buy back the property. Does that make any difference? I would answer, No. I would say that the buyer is entitled to retain his property without any investigation of his reasons for wishing to do so and that his right to recover the difference between the two values is not contingent on his having acted reasonably in the matter of the seller's offer to repurchase.

Payzu Ltd v Saunders ([1919] 2 KB 581) is distinguishable. In that case the defendant in breach of contract had failed to deliver goods to the plaintiff at the contract price and on the contract conditions, but had offered him goods of the same kind at the same price but on less favourable

---

[18] *Strutt* v. *Whitnell and Another*, (1975) 2 All ER 510.

conditions. If the plaintiff had accepted them he would have suffered only a small loss because of the less favourable conditions, which he could still have recovered by way of damages. But he refused the offer. In those circumstances it was held that he could not recover the difference between the market price and the contract price. He would not have suffered this loss if he had accepted the defendant's offer which it was reasonable for him to do. There was no question in that case of the plaintiff being required to return goods which had already become his property or forfeit his right to substantial damages. That is the difference between Payzu Ltd v Saunders and cases 2 and 3.

...

It looks as if the plaintiff has behaved badly towards the defendants, who were his friends, and has merited the description of Shylock which the registrar has given him, and perhaps that additional epithet which would be appropriate to an untruthful witness. If that is so, it is a pity that he must recover substantial damages but this is no ground for deciding his case otherwise than in accordance with the principles of the law of damages which are, I think, well settled in the plaintiff's favour.

Bismi Abdullah and Sons, M/s v. Regional Manager, FCI, Trivandrum

The Food Corporation of India (FCI) accepted the tender of Bismi Abdullah and Sons for the purchase of a quantity of rice, but the latter failed to pay the contract amount and lift the stock.[19] The FCI sold the stock four-and-a half months after the breach. By then, the market for rice had crashed. The FCI claimed the difference between the contract price and the price realized by the sale as damages. The Kerala High Court noted:

One of the fundamental principles of law of damages is that the person entitled to claim damages must do all that is within his power to mitigate damage. In case where there is no right to the difference in price on resale available to the seller as per the contract he can claim only the difference between the contract price and the market price on the date of the breach. Where the seller has got such a right the resale must nevertheless be conducted within a reasonable time from the date of breach. The damages must have relation to the market price on the date of breach whether or not the contract empowers the vendor to resell and claim the difference. In other words, the resale can only be taken as a step to enable the party to establish the market price on the date of the breach. Viewed in this manner the resale must be within a reasonable time from the date of breach so that there may not be much variance in market price between the date of resale and the date of the breach. ... more than 4½ months after the date of breach ... [can] by no stretch of imagination, be said to be a reasonable period.

M. Lachia Setty and Sons Ltd v. Coffee Board, Bangalore

The Coffee Board was a statutory body incorporated under the Coffee Act, 1942.[20] It collected all coffee grown and auctioned to the traders, and had a near monopoly in internal and external trade. In 1952, the price of coffee soared very high, and it took several steps to lower them. M. Lachia Setty and Sons Ltd was a trader in coffee. The company was awarded a lot in an auction, it they did not collect it. The Coffee Board re-sold the coffee and collected the difference from the trader. The contention of the trader was that if the Coffee Board had acted quickly, it could have mitigated the loss. The main priority of the Coffee Board, however, was not the mitigation of the loss of individual traders but bringing the prices down. The Supreme Court relied on

---

[19] *Bismi Abdullah and Sons, M/s v. Regional Manager, F.C.I., Trivandrum,* AIR (1987) Kerala 56.

[20] *M. Lachia Setty and Sons Ltd v. Coffee Board, Bangalore,* AIR (1981) SC 162.

the following passages in *Halsbury's Laws of England*, fourth edition, Volume 12, on mitigation of damages:

The plaintiff must take all reasonable steps to mitigate the loss which he has sustained consequent upon the defendant's wrong, and, if he fails to do so, he cannot claim damages for any such loss which he ought reasonably to have avoided.

...

The plaintiff is only required to act reasonably, and whether he has done so is a question of fact in the circumstances of each particular case, and not a question of law. He must act not only in his own interests but also in the interests of the defendant and keep down the damages, so far as it is reasonable and proper, by acting reasonably in the matter ... In cases of breach of contract the plaintiff is under no obligation to do anything other than in the ordinary course of business, and where he has been placed in a position of embarrassment the measures which he may be driven to adopt in order to extricate himself ought not to be weighed in nice scales at the instance of the defendant whose breach of contract has occasioned the difficulty...

The plaintiff is under no obligation to destroy his own property, or to injure himself or his commercial reputation, to reduce the damages payable by the defendant. Furthermore, the plaintiff need not take steps which would injure innocent persons.

The Supreme Court concluded:

From the above statement of law it will appear clear that the non-defaulting party is not expected to take steps which would injure innocent persons. If so, then steps taken by him in performance or discharge of his statutory duty also cannot be weighed against him. In substance the question in each case would be one of the reasonableness of action taken by the non-defaulting party.

Here the material on record clearly shows that internal coffee prices in the year 1952, particularly from March to October 1952, had soared very high on account of malpractices indulged in by coffee dealers and even the government of India felt itself very much concerned about it and suggestions had been made by Government officials as well as by the members of the Coffee Board to take steps to bring down the coffee prices at reasonable level in the interest of both the trade as well as the consumer and, in fact, several measures, including the step of accepting lower bids in preference to the higher bids, with a view to regulate coffee prices were taken by the Coffee Board pursuant to the Government's directive in that behalf. Clearly, these measures were being taken by the Board in discharge of their main function and duty to maintain the coffee prices at proper level in the interest of all concerned, particularly the consumer and were not directed against the defaulting dealers at the concerned pool auction.

* * *

A seller who has not been paid the price in accordance with the contract can file a suit for it. This is irrespective of whether the ownership has passed to the buyer or not. If the contract is silent on the time of paying of the price, it will be concurrent with delivery. If the buyer refuses to take the goods and pay for it, the seller can claim damages for the seller being in breach in not accepting the goods.

10

Remedies for the Buyer

What are the ways in which things can go wrong for the buyer? The seller can delay the delivery of the goods or fail to deliver them entirely. The delivered goods may fail to correspond with the contract in various ways. The quality of the goods may be different. The buyer may deliver the wrong quantity of the goods, in which case the seller has the option of accepting or rejecting the goods. If the seller accepts the goods, however, he must pay for the additional goods received.

The question we began with will be assessed with the application of all the terms implied by the Sale of Goods Act, 1930. The remedies for a buyer parallel the remedies for a seller, and we shall examine them in this chapter.

REJECTION OF GOODS

The rejection of goods raises a curious question. The contracting parties may have settled that the ownership to the buyer will pass before delivery. This happens in an unconditional sale for specific goods. In a CIF contract, the ownership passes when the buyer gets the documents. How would this be reconciled with the right of the buyer to reject the delivered goods? How can the buyer re-

ject the goods when he is already the owner? The following case deals with this question.

Kwei Tek Chao v. *British Traders and Shippers Limited*

London exporters contracted under a CIF contract to sell a quantity of a chemical known as Rongalite C to merchants in Hong Kong.[1] Under the contract, property passed to the buyer when the price was paid in exchange for the shipping documents. This happened on 12 November. The goods arrived in Hong Kong on 17 December. Meanwhile, the buyer discovered that the goods were shipped after the agreed shipping date and the shipping documents were concealed to hide this fact. The buyer had pledged the documents with a bank. The question was on the right of the buyer to reject the goods even after the property in the goods had passed to the buyer. The right of the buyer to reject the goods was with reference to Section 35, which provides:

The buyer is deemed to have accepted the goods when he intimates to the seller that he has accepted

---

[1] *Kwei Tek Chao* v. *British Traders and Shippers Limited*, (1954) 2 QB 459.

them, or when the goods have been delivered to him, and he does any act in relation to them which is inconsistent with the ownership of the seller, or when after the lapse of a reasonable time, he retains the goods without intimating to the seller that he has rejected them.

Devlin J. delivered the following judgment:

In Hardy & Co. (London) Ld. v. Hillerns and Fowler the question which arose for decision was whether the buyers had accepted the goods under section 35. The goods had arrived, and the case showed that the time during which he had the right to examine them was still running. During that time the buyer delivered some of the goods to a sub-buyer. That was an act which was inconsistent with the ownership of the seller. The case for the buyer was that section 35 was machinery which came into action only after the machinery in section 34 had been completed. The Court of Appeal held otherwise. The court held that, notwithstanding that his time for examination was still open, the buyer could, if he chose to commit an act under section 35 such as intimating that he accepted the goods, accept them.

Mr. Roskill has argued that when the goods are delivered to the buyer and he does any act in relation to them which is inconsistent with the ownership of the seller the word 'delivered' there means physical delivery of the goods from the ship. If that is so, no dealing with the documents would be within the meaning of the clause, because it would all have been done before the goods had been delivered. I cannot take that view of it. 'Delivery' as defined by the Act means a voluntary transfer of possession, and I think that it means, therefore, transfer of possession under the contract of sale. In a c.i.f. contract the goods are delivered, so far as they are physically delivered, when they are put on board a ship at the port of shipment. The documents are delivered when they are tendered. A buyer who takes delivery from the ship at the port of destination is not taking delivery of the goods under the contract of sale, but merely taking delivery out of his own warehouse, as it were, by the presentation of the document of title to the

goods, the master of the ship having been his bailee ever since he became entitled to the bill of lading.

I think that the true answer may be found rather differently. Atkin L.J., in the course of his judgment in Hardy & Co. (London) Ld. v. Hillerns and Fowler, dealt with the situation which is always a little puzzling under the c.i.f. contract: if the property passes when the documents are handed over, by what legal machinery does the buyer retain a right, as he undoubtedly does, to examine the goods when they arrive, and to reject them if they are not in conformity with the contract? Atkin L.J. put forward two views for consideration. One was that the property in the goods, notwithstanding the tendering of the documents, did not pass until the goods had been examined or until an opportunity for examination had been given. The other was that it passed at the time of the tendering of the documents, but only conditionally and could be revested if the buyer properly rejected the goods. Mr. Roskill argues (and I think rightly) that for the first possible view indicated by Atkin L.J. no other authority can be found, and it would clearly create considerable complications. If there is no property in the goods, how can the buyer pledge them? It would provide a simple answer to the point had it arisen in this case, since there could not be a pledge. I think that the true view is that what the buyer obtains, when the title under the documents is given to him, is the property in the goods, subject to the condition that they revest if upon examination he finds them to be not in accordance with the contract. That means that he gets only conditional property in the goods, the condition being a condition subsequent. All his dealings with the documents are dealings only with that conditional property in the goods. It follows, therefore, that there can be no dealing which is inconsistent with the seller's ownership unless he deals with something more than the conditional property. If the property passes altogether, not being subject to any condition, there is no ownership left in the seller with which any inconsistent act under section 35 could be committed. If the property passes conditionally the only ownership left in the seller is the

to those contracts in which no mention of time is made and which therefore are to be performed within the indefinite period known as a reasonable time under the circumstances.

In regard to other cases of which this is one the prima facie measure of damages is said to be the difference between the contract price and the market price at the time the goods ought to have been delivered—in this case the period between January 10 and February 10, 1917. In a constantly fluctuating market and if the prices during that period had ruled higher than the contract prices there might have been some difficulty in determining the proper price to be taken, but in this case that point does not arise, as at all times between those dates the market prices were below the contract prices.

Sect. 51 does not in terms deal with an anticipatory breach, and in the case of a breach by effluxion of time it is clear that it makes no difference to the measure of damages whether a buyer goes into the market or is content to take the difference in price without troubling to buy against the defaulting seller. The question to be decided is whether the same rule applies in the case of an anticipatory breach.

An anticipatory breach occurs when the seller refuses to deliver before the contractual time for delivery has arrived and the buyer accepts his refusal as a breach of contract.

In that case the following rules are well established, subject of course to any express provisions to the contrary in any particular contract.

Immediately upon the anticipatory breach the buyer may bring his action whether he buys against the seller or not.

It is the duty of the buyer to go into the market and buy against the defaulting seller if a reasonable opportunity offers. This is expressed by the phrase 'It is the buyer's duty to mitigate damages.' In that event the damages are assessed with reference to the market price on the date of the repurchase. If the buyer does not perform his duty in this respect the seller is none the less entitled to have damages assessed as at the date when a fresh contract might and ought to have been made.

As a corollary to this rule the buyer may if he pleases go into the market and buy against the seller as he is bound to do so to mitigate damages, so he is entitled to do so to cover himself against his commitments or to secure the goods. In that case again the damages are assessed with reference to the market price at the date of the repurchase.

It is also settled law that when default is made by the seller by refusal to deliver within the contract time the buyer is under no duty to accept the repudiation and buy against him but may claim the difference between the contract price and the market price at the date when under the contract the goods should have been delivered.

Further, in the case of an anticipatory breach the contract is at an end and the defaulting seller cannot take advantage of any subsequent circumstances which would have afforded him a justification for non-performance of his contract had his repudiation not been accepted.

In logical strictness it would appear to follow that equally the defaulting seller cannot take advantage of a fall in the market before the due date for delivery to escape liability for damages.

It looks therefore at first sight as though the date at which the difference between the contract price and the market price ought to be taken for the assessment of damages when the buyer does not buy against the seller should follow by analogy the rule adopted where the buyer goes into the market and buys, or where the breach is failure to deliver at the due date and should be at or about the date when the buyer intimates his acceptance of the repudiation though he does not actually go into the market against the seller. If so, in this case, the date would be about December 14, when the buyer claimed arbitration and so the arbitrators have found.

As against this line of reasoning it must be remembered that the object of damages is to place a person whose contract is broken in as nearly as possible the same position as if it had been performed. This result is secured by measuring damages either at the date of the repurchase, in the case of repurchase on an anticipatory breach, or at the date when the goods ought to have been delivered when there is no anticipatory breach whether there is a repurchase or not. In these cases the buyer gets a new contract as nearly as may be like the broken contract and the defaulting seller pays the extra expense incurred by the buyer in restoring his position.

Where however there is an anticipatory breach but no buying against the defaulting seller, and the price falls below the contract price between the date of the anticipatory breach and the date when the goods ought to have been delivered, the adoption of the date of the anticipatory breach as the date at which the market price ought to be taken would put the buyer in a better position than if his contract had been duly performed. He would if that date were adopted be given a profit and retain his money wherewith to buy the goods if so minded on the fall of the market. It would be in effect, to use a homely phrase, to allow him to eat his cake and have it. Perhaps it is better to avoid figures of speech however picturesque and to say, to make a profit from the anticipatory breach while the contract if duly performed would have shown a loss—a position which is I think irreconcilable with the principles upon which damages are awarded as between buyer and seller.

In my opinion the true rule is that where there is an anticipatory breach by a seller to deliver goods for which there is a market at a fixed date the buyer without buying against the seller may bring his action at once, but that if he does so his damages must be assessed with reference to the market price of the goods at the time when they ought to have been delivered under the contract. If the action comes to trial before the contractual date for delivery has arrived the Court must arrive at that price as best it can.

To this rule there is one exception for the benefit of the defaulting seller—namely, that if he can show that the buyer acted unreasonably in not buying against him the date to be taken is the date at which the buyer ought to have gone into the market to mitigate damages.

...

The result in this case is that the damages are nominal.

The following two cases bring out an important principle: where the 'market price' rule applies, the buyer can buy the equivalent goods in the market. In fact, he has a duty to do this to mitigate losses. Access to the goods would allow him to make a profit from any resale he may have made prior to the breach by the seller. Following this, the loss of profit is not awarded even if the seller knew that the buyer was buying for resale. The buyer only gets the difference in the contract price and the market price. The following two cases bring this out.

Williams v. Reynolds

On 1 April 1865, two Liverpool cotton brokers entered into a contract for the sale of a specific quantity and description of China cotton.[3] The goods were to be delivered in August. It was a common practice at Liverpool for purchasers of cotton to resell before the time for delivery. The buyer entered into an agreement on 25 May to sell the same description and quantity of cotton to Mayall & Anderson, also to be delivered in August. Unfortunately, the first seller could not fulfil the contract on the last day of August, and the buyer lost the profit on resale to M&A. The dispute was about the damages to be paid by the seller to the buyer. Blackburn J. noted:

The question is, whether the plaintiff is entitled to recover a further sum, this being a contract, not for the delivery of specific cotton, but of cotton of a particular description bought on speculation. It was admitted that in the ordinary course of business at Liverpool such contracts are, to a certain extent, the subject of sale, which is not quite an accurate description, for the buyer does not sell or transfer the contract, like a bill of lading, but he makes a contract with some other persons to sell

[3] *Williams v. Reynolds*, (1865) 6 B & S 495.

the same quantity of goods of a like description to those he has bought, relying on his contract to enable him to supply the persons who have purchased from him. The additional facts here are that, on the 25th May, nearly two months after the original contract and three months before its completion, the plaintiff made a contract to supply Mayall & Anderson, at Liverpool, with the same quantity and quality of cotton at 19¾ d., to be delivered in August. If the defendants had fulfilled their contract the plaintiff would have handed over the cotton to his purchasers, and would have gained a considerable profit by the transaction. It was argued that because this purchase was made on the Liverpool Cotton Exchange, where all persons know that cotton is bought on speculation to sell again, the defendants would be aware that the plaintiff would enter into a fresh contract, relying on the performance by them of their contract, and that the nonfulfilment of it would occasion the breach of the second contract, and so the loss of profit by the resale would be a natural consequence of the defendants' breach of contract. Mr Williams admitted that there is no case in point. The remarks made from the bench on some of those cited in the argument shew that they are not in point, and I cannot see that loss of profit from a contract subsequently made by the purchaser (which is not properly a sub-contract) follows as a natural consequence from the original seller's breach of contract. Though the purchaser might naturally rely on the seller's contract to enable him to fulfil his own, it is not necessary that he should do so; and if the seller was a slippery customer it would be imprudent to do it: in that case the purchaser would, as a prudent man, go into the market and supply himself from thence. Here the plaintiff had reason to rely on the defendants, but that does not entitle him to throw upon them the loss of the profit he would have made.

Williams Brothers v. ET Agius, Limited

E.T. Agius, Limited, contracted to sell a quantity of coal to Williams Brothers, who in turn contracted to sell the same description and quantity of coal to Ghiron.[4] As Agius failed to deliver the goods, the Williams could not realize their profit from the sub-sale. The question was whether damages should include the loss of profit of the Williams. Lord Moulton delivered the following judgment:

My Lords, the question for the decision of your Lordships in this appeal is set out very plainly in the award, in the form of a special case, which forms the basis of this litigation. It is whether the appellants are right in their contention that the measure of damages put forward by them in respect of the admitted breach by the respondents of the contract to deliver a cargo of coals in November, 1910, is correct. That contention is that the proper measure of damages is the difference between the contract price of 16s. 3d. per ton and the market price on the date of the breach of contract, which the arbitrator finds to be 23s. 6d. per ton.

Inasmuch as this is a plain case of a failure to deliver a specified quantity of an article obtainable in the market, the measure of damages is well established. The case comes under the rule laid down in the case of Rodocanachi v. Milburn, and regularly and repeatedly followed ever since, and ultimately embodied in the Sale of Goods Act, 1893, s. 51, sub-s. 3. The contention of the appellants is in accordance with that rule, and the question put to the Court in the special case must accordingly be answered in their favour.

This consideration is, in my opinion, sufficient to decide this appeal, but, in deference to the opinions expressed by the majority of the Court of Appeal, I propose to examine the matters which it is suggested make the measure of damages in the present case other than that given by the recognized rule to which I have already referred.

From the facts of the case as found in the award, and the documents therein referred to, we learn that the appellants made a contract to sell a cargo of coal to the Italian firm of P. Ghiron, and that they intended to fulfil that contract by the cargo

---

[4] *Williams Brothers* v. *E.T. Agius, Limited*, (1914) AC 510.

to be delivered by the respondents in November. The price to be paid by the said P. Ghiron was 19s. per ton, and the respondents contend that it is the difference between 19s. per ton and the contract price of 16s. 3d. per ton which is the true measure of damages.

If these were the only facts of the case the contention of the respondents would be precisely that view of the damages in the case of an article purchasable in the market which was negatived by the decision in Rodocanachi v. Milburn. That case rests on the sound ground that it is immaterial what the buyer is intending to do with the purchased goods. He is entitled to recover the expense of putting himself into the position of having those goods, and this he can do by going into the market and purchasing them at the market price. To do so he must pay a sum which is larger than that which he would have had to pay under the contract by the difference between the two prices. This difference is, therefore, the true measure of his loss from the breach, for it is that which it will cost him to put himself in the same position as if the contract had been fulfilled.

DAMAGES FOR LATE DELIVERY
The Sale of Goods Act, 1930, does not have specific provisions where the buyer accepts late delivery. This has to be worked out in accordance with the principles of contract law. The buyer could buy the goods at the scheduled time from the market and sell them on receiving the goods from the seller. Thus, the difference in price on the day the delivery was to be made and the day it actually was made becomes the damages that the buyer must be paid. *Koufos* v. *C Czarnikow Ltd. The Heron II* is an illustration of this.[5]

SPECIFIC PERFORMANCE
Section 58 provides for the remedy of specific performance for the buyer. It reads:

[5] *Koufos* v. *C Czarnikow Ltd The Heron II*, (1969) 1 AC 350 HL.

58. **Specific performance:** Subject to the provisions of Chapter II of the Specific Relief Act, 1877 (1 of 1877), in any suit for breach of contract to deliver specific or ascertained goods, the Court may, if it thinks fit, on the application of the plaintiff, by its decree direct that the contract shall be performed specifically, without giving the defendant the option of retaining the goods on payment of damages. The decree may be unconditional, or upon such terms and conditions as to damages, payment of the price or otherwise, as the Court may deem just, and the application of the plaintiff may be made at any time before the decree.

The benefit of specific performance is available only in relation to a contract of sale for specific or ascertained goods. Note that in some cases the contract may be for the sale of unascertained goods or future goods that become specific in the course of performance of the contract. For example, the seller may have separated the goods from a bulk for delivering to the buyer. Thus, the buyer acquires an interest in the goods to be delivered that have been separated. The court, subject to the provisions of the Specific Relief Act, 1877, has a discretion in granting the relief of specific performance. The court does not exercise it if the contract is concerned with ordinary goods that the buyer intends to resell.

REMEDY FOR BREACH OF WARRANTY
In several cases, the buyer may not have the right to terminate the contract but only the right to claim damages. This can happen in the following situations. The seller may be only in breach of a warranty to the contract. The seller may have breached a condition of the contract giving the right to the buyer to terminate the contract, but the buyer may have elected to continue with it regardless. In these cases, the buyer can only claim damages. Section 59 lists this general principles.

59. Remedy for breach of warranty: (1) Where there is a breach of warranty by the seller, or where the buyer elects or is compelled to treat any breach of a condition on the part of the seller as a breach of warranty, the buyer is not by reason only of such breach of warranty entitled to reject the goods; but he may—

(a) set up against the seller the breach of warranty in diminution or extinction of the price; or

(b) sue the seller for damages for breach of warranty.

(2) The fact that a buyer has set up a breach of warranty in diminution or extinction of the price does not prevent him from suing for the same breach of warranty if he has suffered further damage.

Let us first review a few points that we have learnt so far. Section 12 defines the concepts of condition and warranty. Implied conditions include the goods meeting the description, goods being of merchantable quality, and goods being fit for the described use where there is reliance on the skill and judgment of the seller. Time is of essence in commercial contracts. Further, as contracts are consensual, the parties are free to provide anything as a condition. The parties are also free to provide any of the above terms as only a warranty. Thus, a sale contract will have express and implied conditions, and all other terms will be warranties. On the breach of a condition, the buyer may elect not to terminate the contract but continue with it. The buyer has converted a condition into a warranty. In all the cases of the breach of warranty or where a condition has been converted into a warranty, where the buyer has not paid the price, he can 'set up' against the seller to deduct the damages suffered by the breach from the price. The buyer is also free to sue for damages for the breach of warranty. The basis for working out the damages is again derived from contract law; the amount

of the value of the goods delivered compared with the value the goods would have had if these met the warranty.

Muthukrishna v. Madhavji Devichand and Co.

In a sale on CIF terms, the buyer paid and received the documents.[6] On receiving the goods, he complained to the seller of the inferior quality of the goods. The person the seller sent to check confirmed this. It was agreed between the parties that the seller would refund and receive the goods. However, the buyer subsequently sent a legal notice to the seller, who disclaimed any liability. The parties continued to be in communication. The buyer, with a notice to the seller, auctioned the goods and claimed damages from the seller. The court ruled that the buyer's sale of the goods was an act inconsistent with the ownership of the seller, and that this amounted to the buyer accepting the goods. Thus, the buyer no longer had the right to reject the goods. However, the buyer could still claim damages for the goods being of inferior quality. The court noted:

... when the goods were auctioned, thereafter their right is only to damages for breach of warranty. ... When once that conclusion is reached and it is found that the warranty has been broken, then the rights of the parties are thereafter determined by S. 59, Sale of Goods Act. Under that section the only point for determination is what damages should be awarded for breach of warranty. ... The principles applicable to the case are thus well settled and applying them to the present case, we have to ascertain what the value of good chillies was on 9-10-1945 which is the date of delivery; what the value of the damaged chillies was; and award the difference as damages to the plaintiffs.

6 *Muthukrishna* v. *Madhavji Devichand and Co.,* AIR (1953) Madras 817.

Mohanlal Manilal v. *Firm Dhirubhai Bavajibhai*[7] is the same case that was reviewed in Chapter 7. The buyer was delivered inferior quality coal and he sub-sold it without examining the delivered goods. As a result, the buyer lost the right to terminate the contract but could claim damages. The court noted:

No doubt the description of the goods was a condition of the contract and since the plaintiffs committed a breach of the condition by delivering goods which were not of the contract description, the defendant was entitled to treat the breach of the condition as a breach of warranty on the part of the plaintiffs and to claim damages from the plaintiffs for the loss suffered by the defendant as a result of the breach committed by the plaintiffs.

Bengal Corporation v. Commrs for the Port of Calcutta

Commissioners for the Port of Calcutta entered into a contract to be supplied wire ropes by the seller.[8] Various specifications of the ropes were given, including that they must be of non-rotating types. The seller, who specialized in such ropes, was explicitly informed that the ropes would be required for use in cranes. Thus, it was an implied condition that the ropes would be in accordance with the description and intended use. The rope delivered seemed fine on external examination, but when it was put to use, proved otherwise—it was not the non-rotating type. The buyer brought this to the notice of the seller. As there was no stock of wire ropes available in the market and ships carrying food grains had to be continuously unloaded, the buyer was compelled to use the rope. The

buyer had estimated the difference in price between the contract price and the supplied goods and withheld it, but the seller claimed the withheld sum. The court noted on the application of Section 59:

Section 59 of the Act which clearly postulates that even when a buyer has accepted the goods, he is entitled to set up against the seller a breach of warranty in diminution or extinction of the price or to sue the seller for damages for breach of warranty. The only handicap of such a buyer who has accepted the goods is that he is precluded from treating the breach of a condition as a ground for repudiating the contract. He is compelled to treat the breach of a condition as a breach of warranty and seek his remedies as provided for in Section 59 of the Act.

. . .

The legal position on this question is well established. In a suit by the seller where the buyer sets up a breach of warranty and claims damages in diminution or extinction of the price claimed by the seller by exercising his right under Section 59 of the Act, actual damages have to be proved. The measure of damages again is really not different from the measure adopted in the law of contract. In assessing the damages which the buyer would be entitled to under Section 59 of the Act, two things have to be found out. The first conclusion that the Court has to arrive at is what is the value or price of the goods which were contracted to be bought and sold. The Court has further to find out as to what is the value or price of the goods in respect of which a breach of warranty is being set up. Having done so, the Court has to deduct the second figure from the first and the difference would be the measure of damages which the buyer is entitled to in diminution or extinction of the price claimed by the seller.

National Traders v. Hindustan Soap Works

Hindustan Soap Works entered into a contract with Alfred Mackenzie and Co., Ltd,

---

[7] *Mohanlal Manilal* v. *Firm Dhirubhai Bavajibhai*, AIR (1962) Gujarat 56.

[8] *Bengal Corporation* v. *Commrs for the Port of Calcutta*, AIR (1971) Calcutta 357.

Madras, to supply them '5 tons of caustic soda solid No. 97/98 U.S.A. origin'.[9] The goods were stocked in Alfred Mackenzie's godown, so the sale was of specific goods as well as by description. The buyer had not examined the goods before entering into the contract, but did before paying the price. After receiving the goods, the buyer claimed that the goods were not of merchantable quality and repudiated the contract. The court noted:

... under S. 15 if there is a contract for the sale of goods by description there is an implied condition that the goods shall correspond with the description. Under S. 16(2) there is a further implied condition where there had been no previous inspection by the buyer, that the goods are of merchantable quality. The effect of these two definitions is to give a right or an occasion to the buyer to reject the goods in case what was tendered did not answer the description or was not of merchantable quality.

The passing of property in the goods is not the test as to the applicability of this right. If the goods do not conform to the description there is no performance of the contract at all. If the goods are not of the merchantable quality the thing for which the buyer bargained for was not given. In either case the default of the seller goes to the root of the transaction and therefore the occasion would arise to the buyer to reject the goods and sue for the price if he had paid the price. It was also open to the buyer to accept the goods and sue on the basis of a warranty. S. 59 of the Indian Sale of Goods Act states thus:

...

The remedy of a buyer where he has accepted the goods is only to sue for damages. As to when a buyer is deemed to have accepted the goods is provided for by S. 42 which runs thus:

'The buyer is deemed to have accepted the goods when he intimates to the seller that he has accepted them, or when the goods have been delivered to him and he does any act in relation to them which is inconsistent with the ownership of the seller, or when, after the lapse of a reasonable time, he retains the goods without intimating to the seller that he has rejected them.'

It therefore remains to consider whether the appellant is entitled to reject the goods and sue for the prices as he has done, or whether he has precluded himself from so doing by accepting the goods. We have already held that although the appellant did not have inspection of the goods before the contract was entered into they did have such inspection before the price was paid.

The fact that the appellant paid the price to the respondent after such inspection and the unexplained delay thereafter in complaining about the defect in the goods would clearly show that they had accepted the goods. The appellant having accepted the goods regardless of the breach of the conditions as to the description and quality precluded themselves from rejecting the goods and suing for a refund of the price. They can however treat the breach as one of warranty and sue for damages.

City and ID Corpn of Maharashtra Ltd v. Nagpur Steel and Alloys Pvt. Ltd

City and Industrial Development Corporation of Maharashtra (CIDCO) awarded a tender to Nagpur Steel and Alloys Pvt. Ltd to supply 650 metric tonnes of mild steel round bars and cold twisted bars of various specified sizes.[10] The seller was to get the goods tested by a government institution and send the test reports. The goods were sent in sixty consignments. Each consignment was followed by a test report. The seller utilized the goods, but withheld the payment for the last two instalments on the ground that the some of the goods supplied were over-sized. The dispute was on the right of the seller to refuse

[9] *National Traders* v. *Hindustan Soap Works*, AIR (1959) Madras 112.

[10] *City and ID Corpn of Maharashtra Ltd* v. *Nagpur Steel and Alloys Pvt. Ltd*, AIR (1992) Bombay 55.

payment for the last two instalments. The court noted:

Section 13 of the Act deals with the subject 'when condition to be treated as warranty'. Sub-Section (1) lays down that the buyer may either (a) waive the condition or (b) elect to treat the breach of the condition as a breach of warranty.

It seems to us clear that in the instant case the condition about size was for the benefit of the buyer, it could be waived voluntarily and has been waived by the buyer. The buyer was fully aware of the so called over size of the goods and yet did not reject the goods though specifically provided for in the contract, consumed the goods without giving any opportunity to the buyer to replace the same and even paid the price for 58 consignments. All this amounted to waiver.

Section 59 of the Act provides for remedy for breach of warranty. It lays down that where there is a breach of warranty by the seller, or where the buyer elects to treat any breach of condition as a breach of warranty, he is not entitled to reject the goods, but he may set up against the seller the breach of warranty in diminution or extinction of the price. Now, this Section comes into play only when the buyer does not waive the condition. That apart, the buyer has failed to prove that it has, in fact, elected to treat the breach of condition as a breach of warranty as contemplated under Section 59. It is not the case of the buyer that it had given notice of its intention of such election or to claim compensation for a breach of warranty or to set up the breach in diminution or extinction of price In any case, no evidence to that effect is adduced by the buyer. [The cousel for seller] has stated that no such intention was ever expressed and had it been done, he would have easily replaced the over-sized goods. Remedies under Section 59 are not absolute and cannot be resorted to at any point or strategic point suitable to the buyer. He is duty bound to give notice of his intention. Its proper time, form and manner will, of course, depend upon the facts and circumstances of each case. To hold otherwise, would amount to placing the seller in an awkward and indefinite position—not warranted either by law or by equity.

Useful reference may be made to the following observations made in the context of Section 59 of the Act in the case of Bohre Brij Kishore v. Firm Shripatram Chironji Lal, ILR (1959) 9 Raj 260 at page 270:

'It was incumbent upon the plaintiff to give a notice to the defendant in order to enable him to explain whether or not the quality supplied by him was according to the sample. He should also have been given an opportunity to take the goods back and repay the money which he had received from the plaintiff, if he wanted to do so. This opportunity was also denied to him. It may be further pointed out that the plaintiff has also failed to prove what was the actual loss in the transaction.'

INTEREST ON UNPAID PRICE

Section 61 provides on payment on interest on the price. It reads:

61. Interest by way of damages and special damages: (1) Nothing in this Act shall affect the right of the seller or the buyer to recover interest or special damages in any case where by law interest or special damages may be recoverable, or to recover the money paid where the consideration for the payment of it has failed.

(2) In the absence of a contract to the contrary, the Court may award interest at such rate as it thinks fit on the amount of the price—

(a) to the seller in a suit by him for the amount of the price—from the date of the tender of the goods or from the date on which the price was payable;

(b) to the buyer in a suit by him for the refund of the price in a case of a breach of the contract on the part of the seller—from the date on which the payment was made.

The section states the general principle that the buyer's money has to be returned if the consideration moving from the seller has failed. In addition, it provides for interest and special damages. One application of Section 61(1) is as follows: Under a contract, the seller sent goods on a FOR basis and sent the railway receipt through a bank for the buyer to collect against payment. The buyer did not, thereby breach the contract. The seller had the goods collected from the railways and sold. In addition to the difference in the price, the seller claimed freight charges, demurrage, commission, and brokerage paid at the time of resale. The court ruled:[11]

The next question which has to be determined is whether the plaintiff is entitled to the railway freight incurred by him as special damage under S. 61 of the Act. ... There is no doubt that the contract was F.O.R. and the defendant was bound to pay these charges at the time of taking delivery. The damages are such which the parties knew when they made the contract to be likely to result from breach of it, and are special damages within the meaning of S. 61 of the Act.

...

In regard to demurrage charges paid ... they cannot be allowed inasmuch as the plaintiff was bound to clear the goods when the defendant refused to take delivery. Similarly, in regard to the commission and brokerage paid by the plaintiff at the time of resale, I hold that the plaintiff cannot claim those charges as I have found that he was not entitled to exercise the right of resale under S. 54(2) of the Act.

Section 61(2) is the familiar principle of unjust enrichment and restitution. If an amount of money belongs to someone, so does the yield on it. Unless the contract provides that no interest will be paid, the courts have the freedom to award interest. In *Rajpati Prasad* v. *Kaushalya Kuer*[12] the court explained the provision:

In view of the provisions of Section 61(2) aforesaid, it is manifest that even in the absence of a contract to pay interest, so long as no contract to the contrary was pleaded and proved, the Court has a discretion to award to the plaintiff interest at such rate as it thinks fit on the amount of the price of the goods sold by him from the date of which the price was payable. The defendant did not allege that there was a contract to the contrary within the meaning of the expression as used in Sec. 61(2). He was denying the existence of any contract whatsoever between him and the plaintiff. Therefore, even if the plaintiff had failed to prove the existence of a contract entitling him to recover interest on the amount due to him from the defendant on account of the price of goods supplied, the Court had the power to grant him interest on the amount of the price at such rate as it thought fit.

In *S. Balasubramanian Chettiar* v. *Arvind Enterprises, Tirunelveli*[13] the court explored the wide scope of the provision:

But, according to the Sale of Goods Act, the only condition for denying the interest for the seller is that there should be a contract contrary to the above perception. In this matter, since there is no express or implied contract for the amount not carrying any interest, it goes without saying that the seller is entitled to the award of interest on the price of the goods sold ...

In *Marwar Tent Factory* v. *Union of India*,[14] a case we have studied in Chapter 8, the seller sent goods on a FOR basis. As there was pilferage of goods in transit, the buyer deducted the loss from the price. The seller claimed the amount deducted and the interest on it. The Supreme Court ruled that

---

[11] *M. Balakrishna Rao* v. *MDO and Sons*, AIR (1959) Andhra Pradesh 30.

[12] *Rajpati Prasad* v. *Kaushalya Kuer*, AIR (1981) Patna 187.

[13] *S. Balasubramanian Chettiar* v. *Arvind Enterprises, Tirunelveli*, AIR (2001) Madras 86.

[14] *Marwar Tent Factory* v. *Union of India*, AIR (1990) SC 1753.

in a FOR contract, the ownership and risk passed to the buyer on the loading of the goods on the rails. Thus, the retained amount should be paid. On payment of interest on the amount, the Supreme Court noted:

It is appropriate to refer in this connection to the relevant provisions of S. 61(2) of the Sale of Goods Act, 1930...

In the instant case, undoubtedly, it has been found by the Courts below that the short delivery of 224 tents occurred during the transit of the said goods by the railways. It is also an admitted fact that ... the Commandant, C.O.D., Kanpur deducted the price of the said 224 tents from the other bills of the contractor i.e. the appellant and did not pay the same. The appellant has claimed interest in respect of the price of the said goods being not paid to the appellant within a reasonable time from the date of delivery of the goods i.e. for the period from 1-1-1969 to 1-12-1971.

...

In the case of B.B. Bose v. National Coal Trading Company, AIR 1966 Pat 346, the plaintiff filed a suit for recovery of price of goods sold to the defendant. ... It was urged on behalf of the defendant that there was no stipulation for payment of interest in case the price remained unpaid in the contract and as such the plaintiff could not claim any interest on the unpaid amount. This was negatived by the High Court, Patna and it was held (at p. 351):

'... That is, no doubt true, out the demand clearly was for the outstanding balance price of coal which the plaintiff had supplied to the defendant. The supplies had been effected up to the 26 June, 1954, and in the normal course, the price ought to have been paid by the defendant within a reasonable time of the deliveries, but the payment had been delayed for nearly three years and plaintiff was obliged to institute the present suit for recovery of the price. In such circumstances, it was within the discretion of the Court to award interest to the plaintiff at a reasonable rate on the amount of the price

under Sec. 61(2) of the Sale of Goods Act. The price was undoubtedly payable when the notice of demand (Ex. 2) was served by the plaintiff upon the defendant and there can be no doubt that the rate of 6 per cent per annum which the Court awarded was a reasonable rate.'

Similar question cropped up for decision in the case of M/s M.K.M. Moosa Bhai Amin, Kota v. Rajasthan Textile Mills, Bhawanimandi. In this case the plaintiff filed the suit for price of the goods delivered as well as for interest on the unpaid price. The claim regarding interest was disallowed by the District Judge on the ground that there was no stipulation for payment of interest in case the price of the goods supplied remained unpaid. It was contended on behalf of the plaintiff that even in the absence of the contract, the plaintiff was entitled to reasonable interest under Sec. 61(2) of the Sale of Goods Act, 1930. The supply had been effected up to September 18, 1962 and in normal case the price of the goods ought to have been paid by the defendant within a reasonable time of the deliveries but the payment had been delayed for nearly a year which compelled the plaintiff to bring the suit for recovery of the price. It has been held that in such circumstances, the lower Courts should have exercised discretion in favour of the plaintiff and awarded interest on the amount of the price of the goods under S. 61(2) of the Sale of Goods Act. The High Court of Rajasthan allowed interest @ 6% per annum which was considered to be a reasonable rate of interest.

On a conspectus of all the decisions referred to before as well as the provisions of Sec. 61(2) of the Sale of Goods Act, we are constrained to hold that the plaintiff is entitled to get a decree of interest on the unpaid price from 1-1-1969 to 1-12-1971 @ 6% per annum which is considered to be a reasonable rate of interest, as claimed by the plaintiff appellant.

* * *

The remedies of a buyer against a seller include the right to reject the goods if they are not in conformity with the contract. If the seller does not deliver the goods in accordance with the contract, the buyer can claim damages from the seller. The buyer can also claim damages for late delivery and breach of warranty. Specific performance can be claimed only for specific or ascertained goods. The courts have the freedom to award specific performance of the contract, but this is done in rare cases.

11

Rights of the Unpaid Seller

In Chapter 9, we noted that the seller could file a suit for price and damages. The principle was a reiteration of the principles of contract law in relation to the sale of goods. The common law courts developed an additional remedy for an 'unpaid seller'. This 'unpaid seller' acquires certain rights in the goods in his possession even if the ownership has transferred to the buyer. Let us try to understand the rationale for the right with the following example.

According to the terms of a sale contract, the ownership in the goods transferred to the buyer on Monday. The goods were in the seller's possession. The buyer was to pay the price on Tuesday and take delivery on Wednesday. The buyer failed to pay the price on Tuesday but was nevertheless ready to take the delivery of the goods on Wednesday. Let us consider the options available to the seller. As the ownership has been transferred to the buyer, the goods have to be given to him. The seller can only claim damages. Even if the seller could terminate the contract, the goods would be given to the owner and he would be paid the price. Instead of going to the court, the seller may have had a more effective remedy by refusing to deliver the goods till he was paid. This is called a lien. Further, if the seller remained unpaid, he could resell the goods and recover the price. He could not re-appropriate the ownership as his claim is over the price and not over the goods.

Unpaid Seller

Sections 47 to 54 provide on this remedy for the unpaid seller. Section 47 states:

46. Unpaid seller's rights: (1) Subject to the provisions of this Act and of any law for the time being in force, notwithstanding that the property in the goods may have passed to the buyer, the unpaid seller of goods, as such, has by implication of law—

(a) a lien on the goods for the price while he is in possession of them;

(b) in case of the insolvency of the buyer a right of stopping the goods in transit after he has parted with the possession of them:

(c) a right of re-sale as limited by this Act.

(2) Where the property in goods has not passed to the buyer, the unpaid seller has, in addition to his other remedies a right of withholding delivery similar to and co-extensive with his rights of lien and stoppage in transit where the property has passed to the buyer.

The section allows an unpaid seller a lien over the goods by retaining possession and even reselling to recover the price. The additional right conferred by Section 46(1)(b) is that if the buyer is insolvent, the unpaid seller can even regain possession while the goods are in transit to the buyer. Let us now look at an illustration of the provision in Section 46(2). Under a contract, the buyer was to pay the price on Monday, the seller was to deliver the goods on Tuesday, and the ownership was to pass on Wednesday. The buyer failed to pay the price on Monday but demanded that the goods be delivered on Tuesday. The seller may have the right to terminate the contract, if payment on time were a condition of the contract. In addition, he could retain possession of the goods till he was paid. Similarly, if the buyer turned insolvent, he could regain possession while the goods were in transit. There was no question of reselling the goods as the ownership was still with the seller. Section 45 defines an 'unpaid seller' as follows:

45. Unpaid seller defined: (1) The seller of goods is deemed to be an 'unpaid seller' within the meaning of this Act—
> (a) when the whole of the price has not been paid or tendered;
> (b) when a bill of exchange or other negotiable instrument has been received as conditional payment, and the condition on which it was received has not been fulfilled by reason of the dishonour of the instrument or otherwise.

(2) In this Chapter, the term 'seller' includes any person who is in the position of a seller, as, for instance, an agent of the seller to whom the bill of lading has been indorsed, or a consignor or agent who has himself paid, or is directly responsible for, the price.

We shall now look at a few illustrations and see if they qualify as unpaid sellers.

Under a sale contract, the seller was to deliver the goods on the 10th of the month and receive the price on the 30th. Is the seller an 'unpaid seller' on the 21st of the month?

The provision does not refer to the terms of the contract for the decision. A seller who has not as yet received full payment is unpaid. Obviously, the law could not be giving the benefits of retaining possession and resale to a seller who has given credit to the buyer. The subsequent sections will bring this out and give the rights to the unpaid seller only when the buyer is in default of a contractual term.

Under a sale contract, the seller was to deliver the goods on the 10th and receive 95 per cent of the sale value. The remaining 5 per cent was to come to him on the 30th of the month. Is he an 'unpaid seller' on the 20th of the month? As the seller has not been fully paid on the 20th, he is indeed an unpaid seller.

Under a sale contract, the seller was to deliver the goods on the 10th of the month and receive the price on the 20th of the month. The seller visited the office of the buyer on the 10th with the money. The buyer asked him to come on the 30th and give the money as he was very busy at the time. On the 25th, is he an 'unpaid seller'? The answer is no, as the buyer had tendered the money.

Under a sale contract, the seller was to deliver the goods on the 10th of the month and receive the price on the 20th. The buyer gave him a cheque on the 20th. The seller put it in his bank account the next day. The buyer received an intimation from the bank on the 25th that the cheque was dishonoured. On the 28th, is the seller an 'unpaid seller'? The answer is yes, as the seller is interested in receiving the price, not a cheque. Receiving a cheque as the price will always be subject to the condition that the price is realized.

LIEN OVER GOODS

Sections 47 and 48 provide on the lien of the seller. They read:

47. Sellers lien: (1) Subject to the provisions of this Act, the unpaid seller of goods who is in possession of them is entitled to retain possession of them until payment or tender of the price in the following cases, namely:

(a) where the goods have been sold without any stipulation as to credit;

(b) where the goods have been sold on credit, but the term of credit has expired;

(c) where the buyer becomes insolvent.

(2) The seller may exercise his right of lien notwithstanding that he is in possession of the goods as agent or bailee for the buyer.

48. Part delivery: Where an unpaid seller has made part delivery of the goods, he may exercise his right of lien on the remainder, unless such part delivery has been made under such circumstances as to show an agreement to waive the lien.

Let us see whether the seller can retain possession of the goods in the following situations:

Under a sale contract, the seller was to deliver the goods on the 10th of the month and receive the price on the 30th of the month. On the 10th, is the seller an 'unpaid seller'? Can he exercise the right to retain possession of the goods? The seller is an 'unpaid seller' as he is yet to receive the price. However, the seller has provided credit to the buyer till the 30th of the month. As the time period of credit has not expired, he cannot retain possession of the goods.

Under a sale contract, the ownership was transferred to the buyer on Monday. The seller had given time to the buyer till Wednesday to pay the price. The buyer was free to take delivery of the goods any time. The buyer failed to pay the money on Wednesday but came to take delivery of the goods on Thursday. Can the seller retain possession of the goods? The seller had given credit to the buyer till Wednesday. If the buyer came to take delivery on Tuesday, the seller could not have retained possession. However, on Thursday, the credit period is over and the seller can retain possession of the goods.

A sale contract for specific goods was silent on the time for paying the money. The ownership had already transferred in the buyer. The buyer came to take delivery of the goods. Can the seller retain possession of the goods till he is paid? In this case, there is no stipulation on the time of payment of the price. Thus, the price becomes payable concurrently with delivery. The seller can retain possession till he is paid.

Under a contract, a seller was to give delivery of the goods on Monday and the buyer was to pay the price on Tuesday. The seller fulfilled his part of the agreement but the buyer did not. On Wednesday, the seller hired the same goods for two days from the buyer. On Friday, the seller was still unpaid, in default of the contract. Can the seller claim lien over the hired goods and not return it to the buyer till he is paid? No; the object of the provision is to provide a self-remedy for the buyer. Much the same way the seller cannot retain goods that come his way to recover the price, he cannot retain the goods he sold and delivered to the buyer. For this reason, Section 47 uses the expression 'the unpaid seller of goods who is in possession of them is entitled to retain possession.'

A seller is considered unpaid even if only a small part of the price is due. The unpaid seller has rights over the goods irrespective of the magnitude of his claim. Further, Section 47 reminds us that the seller need not be the owner of the goods; he can be an agent or a bailee. The right of lien extends to the seller regardless of whether he is the owner. Section 49 details the circumstances in which the seller can lose the right of lien. Let us first look at some situations where the unpaid seller could possibly lose the lien over the goods.

An unpaid seller had lien over the goods as the buyer had defaulted in paying to the seller. However, he did make the payment later. Can the seller still claim a lien over the goods? The answer should be no, as the right of the lien is given for the limited purpose of receiving the money.

An unpaid seller had a lien over the goods as the buyer had defaulted in paying. He informed the buyer that he had waived his lien over the goods. However, the seller then declined to deliver the goods claiming a lien. Is the unpaid seller justified in doing so? Having voluntarily waived the right, the seller should not be allowed to extend a lien over the goods.

An unpaid seller hired a carrier to carry the goods to the location of the buyer. The carriage document was made in favour of the seller. Does the lien of the seller continue while the goods are in transit? Yes, as the seller has the right to receive the goods at the other end, the carrier is holding the goods on behalf of the seller. Thus, the seller has not transferred possession of the goods to the buyer. We know this as the seller reserving the right of disposal. Section 49 provides:

49. Termination of lien: (1) The unpaid seller of goods loses his lien thereon—

(a) when he delivers the goods to a carrier or other bailee for the purpose of transmission to the buyer without reserving the right of disposal of the goods;

(b) when the buyer or his agent lawfully obtains possession of the goods;

(c) by waiver thereof.

(2) The unpaid seller of goods, having a lien thereon, does not lose his lien by reason only that he has obtained a decree for the price of the goods.

Let us explore the provisions on liens and their termination through the following cases.

Valpy v. *Gibson*

In this case, the seller had sent cloth in four cases to the shipping agents on the directions of the buyer, Brown.[1] Brown received the possession of the goods on 20 March. On 4 April, after the goods were loaded on a ship, Brown's agent asked that they be returned to Gibson to be repacked in eight cases instead of four. The price of the goods was payable on 24 April, but after the seller received the goods, Brown became insolvent. The question was if the seller could exercise the rights of unpaid seller. The court ruled:

The right which it was contended the defendants had, as vendors in the actual and lawful possession of the goods, on the insolvency of the vendee, cannot, we think, be sustained. The goods being sold on credit, and the complete property and possession having vested in Brown, they became his absolutely, without any lien or right of the vendors attaching to them, any more than on any other property of Brown; and their delivery to the defendants to be re-packed, could not have the effect of creating a lien for the price, without an agreement to that effect. We therefore think there must be judgment for the plaintiffs.

Thus, the seller was unpaid all along as he was yet to receive the price. Under the contract, he had given credit and an obligation to deliver before being paid. Once possession of the goods was given, there could be no lien over the goods.

Mordaunt Brothers v. *The British Oil and Cake Mills, Limited*

British Oils and Cakes Mill Limited were seed crushers and refiners. The Chrichton Brothers were oil merchants.[2] A third party, Mordaunt Brothers, were oil seed and tallow brokers. The parties had dealings with each other for some time. Chrichton Brothers would buy oil from British Oils and sub-sell

[1] *Valpy* v. *Gibson*, (1847) 4 CB 837.
[2] *Mordaunt Brothers* v. *The British Oil and Cake Mills, Limited*, (1910) 2 KB 502.

it to Mordaunt Brothers. Chrichton Brothers would issue a British Oils delivery order to this effect: 'Messrs. the British Oil and Cake Mills, Limited, Please deliver to Messrs. Mordaunt Brothers or order … tons boiled linseed oil in pipes ex our contract. (Signed) Crichton Brothers.'

We shall call the parties the seller, buyer, and sub-buyer. On receiving the delivery order, the sub-buyer would pay the buyer—Chrichton Brothers—90 per cent of the value of the oil named in the delivery order. On receiving the delivery order, the seller either sent word to Chrichton Brothers that the document was in order or retained it without comment. In either case, the name of the sub-buyer was entered into the books as the person to whom the goods were to be delivered. The parties successfully conducted business for several months. However, it ended when the buyer collected money from the sub-buyer but defaulted in paying it to the seller. The seller had received the delivery orders but refused to deliver the goods to the sub-buyer. The seller claimed a lien on the goods as an unpaid seller. The sub-buyer maintained that the lien was waived by the acceptance and acknowledgement of the delivery orders. Pickford J. delivered the following judgment:

It was next argued that the plaintiffs [sub-buyers] were entitled to succeed by virtue of s. 47 of the Sale of Goods Act, 1893, on the ground that the defendants [seller] had assented to the sales by Crichton Brothers to the plaintiffs. Several cases were cited in which it was held that unpaid vendors had assented to sub-sales so as to preclude themselves from asserting their right of lien. As a matter of fact all those cases related to sub-sales of specific goods. I am not, however, going to decide that s. 47 has no application to unascertained goods; but I wish to point out that such acts as presenting to an unpaid vendor delivery orders in favour of sub-purchasers and the entry accordingly of the names of the sub-purchasers in the books of the unpaid vendor may have a very different effect according as the goods are specific or unascertained. In the former case it may be more readily inferred that the unpaid vendor has assumed the position of an agent or bailee holding the goods for and on behalf of the sub-purchaser or holder of the delivery order, and the acceptance of the delivery order and entry of the holder's name in the books by the unpaid vendor might in the case of specific goods justify the inference that the unpaid vendor had accepted that position. No such inference could be drawn if the goods were not in existence, and it does not follow that because the inference may be drawn in the case of specific goods it will also be drawn in the case of goods in existence but unascertained. In my opinion the assent which affects the unpaid seller's right of lien must be such an assent as in the circumstances shows that the seller intends to renounce his rights against the goods. It is not enough to show that the fact of a sub-contract has been brought to his notice and that he has assented to it merely in the sense of acknowledging the receipt of the information. His assent to the sub-contract in that sense would simply mean that he acknowledged the right of the purchaser under the sub-contract to have the goods subject to his own paramount right under the contract with his original purchaser to hold the goods until he is paid the purchase-money. Such an assent would imply no intention of making delivery to a sub-purchaser until payment was made under the original contract. The assent contemplated by s. 47 of the Sale of Goods Act, 1893, means something more than that; it means an assent given in such circumstances as show that the unpaid seller intends that the sub-contract shall be carried out irrespective of the terms of the original contract.

Now in the circumstances of this case what was the effect of the inquiry by the plaintiffs [sub-buyers] whether the delivery orders of Crichton Brothers were 'in order' and the defendants' reply that they were? I think some light is thrown on the nature and purpose of this inquiry by the fact that the plaintiffs parted with their money before making the inquiry. Neither party regarded those inquiries as directed to the questions whether the defendants were to hold the oil as agents for the plaintiffs, renouncing any rights they might have to hold the goods till they were paid for by Crichton Brothers, and whether they were prepared to deliver to the plaintiffs and look elsewhere than to the goods themselves for any rights they might have in respect of them. Whatever might have been the effect of such an inquiry and answer in a case where specific goods were in question, I think in the present case where the goods were unascertained the inquiry and answer amounted to no more than this—that the defendants were ready to carry out the contract between themselves and Crichton Brothers with this modification, that delivery should be made to the plaintiffs instead of to Crichton Brothers, but that the delivery should be subject to all the other terms and incidents of the contract with Crichton Brothers.

Under the contract, the seller was under an obligation to give delivery of the goods to the buyer. Through the delivery order, the buyer assigned his rights to the sub-buyer. The seller acknowledged the sub-buyer's right. As the buyer had defaulted in paying the money, the unpaid seller had lien over the goods. The question was whether the seller had waived his lien by the acknowledgement of the delivery order. The communication from the seller must carry the intention to renounce the right for it to be a waiver. The seller had made no such communication; he only acknowledged that the sub-buyer was substituted to take delivery in place of the buyer.

D.F. Mount Ltd v. Jay & Jay (Provisions) Co. Ltd

Jay & Jay (Provisions) Co. Ltd, a merchant company, bought 500 cartons, each containing 48 tins of sliced peaches, from an importer.[3] This was a part of a consignment of 4,500 cartons that the trader had imported and stored in the warehouse of Delta Storage Ltd at Delta Wharf, Greenwich. Through two different contracts, Jay & Jay re-sold 250 cartons to a person named Merrick, who in turn intended to resell it too. It was agreed that Merrick would pay the price only on receiving it from his buyers. Further, the profit made by Merrick was to be equally shared between him and Jay & Jay.

Jay & Jay made two delivery orders on the wharfingers, instructing them to give a total of 250 cartons to Merrick. Merrick made an arrangement with D.F. Mount Ltd where Merrick would sell the cartons at a loss and buy them back a week later, leaving Mount a profit of £ 26. It was a falling market and the arrangement made sense. Merrick drew a delivery order on the wharfingers to deliver the cartons to D.F. Mount Ltd. and collected a cheque for £ 1,045 from the company. The next day, the company sent the delivery order it had received from Merrick to the wharf, and gave him a delivery order and collected a cheque for a higher price. The cheque was not realized and the company cancelled the delivery order made to Merrick. Jay & Jay in turn cancelled the contract with Merrick and requested the wharf to cancel the delivery orders given by them. Merrick was subsequently convicted for fraud. However, Jay & Jay and Mount were in dispute, with the former's claim of an unpaid seller contested by Mount. Salmon J. delivered the following judgment:

The case raises the familiar problem—which of two innocent persons, the plaintiffs or the defendants, shall suffer for the trickery of a rogue.

[3] *D.F. Mount Ltd* v. *Jay & Jay (Provisions) Co. Ltd,* (1960) 1 QB 159.

The plaintiffs contend that the defendants assented to the sale or disposition of the 250 cartons by Merrick to the plaintiffs, and thereby lost their right as unpaid sellers to the lien which they would otherwise have had upon the cartons. The defendants contend that if they assented to the sub-sale by Merrick, their assent was not an assent within the meaning of section 47, and rely upon Mordaunt Brothers v. British Oil and Cake Mills Ltd. It is clear from Pickford J.'s judgment in that case that the assent contemplated by section 47 means 'an assent given in such circumstances as show that the unpaid seller intends that the sub-contract shall be carried out irrespective of the terms of the original contract' and must be 'such an assent as in the circumstances shows that the seller intends to renounce his rights against the goods.' Pickford J. held that there had been no such assent on the part of the sellers.

The facts of that case are, however, very different from those of the present case. There the sellers had at no time any reason to doubt the buyer's ability to pay, and were not informed of the sub-sale until after the sale was effected. Pickford J. held that the sellers had assented to the sub-sale merely in the sense that they acknowledged its existence and the right of the sub-buyer to have the goods subject to their own paramount rights under the contract with the original buyer to hold the goods until paid the purchase price.

In the present case the defendants were anxious to get rid of the goods on a falling market. They knew that Merrick could only pay for them out of the money he obtained from his customers, and that he could only obtain the money from his customers against delivery orders in favour of those customers. In my view, the true inference is that the defendants assented to Merrick reselling the goods, in the sense that they intended to renounce their rights against the goods and to take the risk of Merrick's honesty. The defendants are reputable merchants and I am sure that it was not their intention to get rid of their goods on a falling market through Merrick on the basis that, if he defaulted, they could hold the goods against the customers from whom he obtained the money out of which they were to be paid.

…

The sale of the 250 cartons was a sale of unascertained goods. In my judgment, however, there is no reason why section 47 should not apply to unascertained goods, although I respectfully agree with Pickford J. that an inference can in some circumstances more readily be drawn against the seller in the case of a sale of specific goods than in the case of a sale of unascertained goods. I hold that the defendants assented to the sale of the cartons by Merrick within the meaning of section 47.

Ms Jain Mills and Electrical Stores v. State of Orissa

A seller who had delivered the goods through a carrier but remained unpaid raised an erroneous contention that the goods should be returned to him as there was a lien on the goods under Sections 46 and 47.[4] The High Court of Orissa responded:

On a perusal of the above quoted provisions it is seen that the lien is founded on possession and unless there is possession there is no lien. From S. 46(1)(a) it is seen that notwithstanding that the property in the goods has passed to the buyer, the unpaid seller of goods has, as such, by implication of law, a lien on the goods for the price while he is in possession of them. The unpaid seller has a right to detain the goods in his custody until the whole of the price is paid. A lien necessarily presupposes that the property in the goods has passed, as the seller cannot be said to possess a right of lien on his own property, which is in the nature of a right of distress over the property of another. The plaint 'A' schedule goods were despatched by rail to the defendants and the defendants received the same after 30-3-1973. The lien ceases to subsist the moment the seller loses possession of the goods.

[4] *Ms Jain Mills and Electrical Stores* v. *State of Orissa*, AIR (1991) Orissa 117.

So in the present case, in view of the admitted facts that the possession of the plaint 'A' schedule goods was delivered to the defendant on or about 30-3-1973, the plea of the appellants that they are entitled to the return of goods in exercise of their right of lien as unpaid sellers is without any basis and, therefore, merits no consideration.

SELLER'S RIGHT TO STOP GOODS IN TRANSIT

An unpaid seller loses lien if he delivers the goods to a carrier for the purpose of transmission to the buyer without reserving the right of disposal of the goods. However, if the buyer has turned insolvent, the unpaid seller has the right to stop the goods in transit, take possession of the goods, and regain the lien. Section 50 provides:

50. Right of stoppage in transit: Subject to the provisions of this Act, when the buyer of goods becomes insolvent, the unpaid seller who has parted with the possession of the goods has the right of stopping them in transit, that is to say, he may resume possession of the goods as long as they are in the course of transit, and may retain them until payment or tender of the price.

Section 51 specifies what constitutes goods being 'in the course of transit':

51. Duration of transit: (1) Goods are deemed to be in course of transit from the time when they are delivered to a carrier or other bailee for the purpose of transmission to the buyer, until the buyer or his agent in that behalf takes delivery of them from such carrier or other bailee.

(2) If the buyer or his agent in that behalf obtains delivery of the goods before their arrival at the appointed destination, the transit is at an end.

(3) If, after the arrival of the goods at the appointed destination, the carrier or other bailee acknowledges to the buyer or his agent that he holds the goods on his behalf and continues in possession of them as bailee for the buyer or his agent, the transit is at an end and it is immaterial that a further destination for the goods may have been indicated by the buyer.

(4) If the goods are rejected by the buyer and the carrier or other bailee continues in possession of them, the transit is not deemed to be at an end, even if the seller has refused to receive them back.

(5) When goods are delivered to a ship chartered by the buyer, it is a question depending on the circumstances of the particular case, whether they are in the possession of the master as a carrier or as agent of the buyer.

(6) Where the carrier or other bailee wrongfully refuses to deliver the goods to the buyer or his agent in that behalf, the transit is deemed to be at an end.

(7) Where part delivery of the goods has been made to the buyer or his agent in that behalf, the remainder of the goods may be stopped in transit, unless such part delivery has been given in such circumstances as to show an agreement to give up possession of the whole of the goods.

Let us note a few aspects of the provisions. The goods can be in transit through any means—rail, road, ship, air, or even a combination of these. The duration of the transit has the following elements:

1. The transit comes to an end when the carrier delivers the goods to the buyer or his agent. This can be before or after reaching the appointed destination.

2. After reaching the destination, even if the carrier does not deliver to the buyer but acknowledges that he is holding it on behalf of the buyer, the transit comes to an end.

3. The transit comes to an end if the carrier wrongfully refuses to deliver the goods to the buyer.

4. If part delivery of the goods is made, the remainder may be stopped in transit unless the agreement was that part delivery amounted to giving up possession of the whole.

5. If the buyer rejects the goods, and the carrier retains possession of the goods, the transit is deemed to continue.

Section 2(8) of the Act defines 'insolvent' as a person who 'has ceased to pay his debts in the ordinary course of business, or cannot pay his debts as they become due, whether he has committed an act of insolvency or not'. Insolvency refers to the person not having cash to pay and not to the assets of the person. The term is used here in the commercial sense of the buyer not having cash to pay. If the seller hands over the goods to the carrier and does not retain the right of disposal, he has no rights to receive the goods from the carrier or to interfere with the carriage. The carrier would be under a contract to deliver the goods to the buyer or his agent. How should the seller then go about getting possession of the goods from the carrier? Section 52 provides on this:

52. How stoppage in transit is effected: (1) The unpaid seller may exercise his right of stoppage in transit either by taking actual possession of the goods, or by giving notice of his claim to the carrier or other bailee in whose possession the goods are. Such notice may be given either to the person in actual possession of the goods or to his principal. In the latter case the notice, to be effectual, shall be given at such time and in such circumstances that the principal, by the exercise of reasonable diligence, may communicate it to his servant or agent in time to prevent a delivery to the buyer.

(2) When notice of stoppage in transit is given by the seller to the carrier or other bailee in possession of the goods, he shall re-deliver the goods to, or according to the directions of, the seller. The expenses of such re-delivery shall be borne by the seller.

The section requires the seller to give a 'notice of his claim' to the carrier. That is, the seller should inform the carrier that the buyer has turned insolvent, giving the seller the right to stop goods in transit and regain possession. What should the carrier do? On the one hand, he is under a contract to deliver the goods to the buyer. Failure to do so would be a breach of the contract. On the other hand, he is repossessing the goods. Section 52(2) resolves this conflict by requiring the carrier to re-deliver the goods to the seller on receiving the notice. Another section on the theme is Section 53:

53. Effect of subsale or pledge by buyer: (1) Subject to the provisions of this Act, the unpaid seller's right of lien or stoppage in transit is not affected by any sale or other disposition of the goods which the buyer may have made, unless the seller has assented thereto:

Provided that where a document of title to goods has been issued or lawfully transferred to any person as buyer or owner of the goods, and that person transfers the document to a person who takes the document in good faith and for consideration, then, if such last mentioned transfer was by way of sale, the unpaid seller's right of lien or stoppage in transit is defeated, and, if such last mentioned transfer was by way of pledge or other disposition for value, the unpaid seller's right of lien or stoppage in transit can only be exercised subject to the rights of the transferee.

(2) Where the transfer is by way of pledge, the unpaid seller may require the pledgee to have the amount secured by the pledge satisfied in the first instance, as far as possible, out of any other goods or securities of the buyer in the hands of the pledgee and available against the buyer.

The right of the seller to stop goods in transit is not affected by the buyer selling the goods further. However, if a document of title has been transferred by the seller to the buyer and the buyer in turn transfers it to the sub-buyer who takes it in good faith, the right of stoppage would not be available to the seller.

Let us explore the theme with a review of court cases. The first case is from before the codification of the law.

The Tigress

Lucy and Sons sold Bush wheat that was on a ship named Tigress.[5] One copy of the bill of lading was endorsed to Bush. Thus, Bush had the right to be delivered the goods on their arrival. However, the seller was not paid as yet and Bush became bankrupt while the wheat was still on board. The seller instructed the master of the ship to deliver the wheat and tendered the freight for the re-delivery. The master, however, refused to deliver the wheat without the seller establishing ownership over it. Lushington gave the following judgment:

All that is necessary is for the vendor to assert his claim as vendor and owner. Were the vendor, before he could exercise his right of stoppage *in transitu*, obliged formally to prove his title, that right would be worthless. The validity of a stoppage *in transitu* depends upon several conditions:—(1) The vendor must be unpaid. (2) The vendee must be insolvent. (3) The vendee must not have endorsed over for value. But for the vendor to prove to the master that all these conditions have been fulfilled would be always difficult, often impossible. For instance, whether the vendor is or is not unpaid may depend upon the balance of a current account; whether the vendee is insolvent may not transpire till afterwards (for it is, I conceive, clear law that the right to stop *in transitu* does not depend upon the vendee having been found insolvent); and lastly, whether the vendee has or has not endorsed the bill of lading over is a matter not within the cognisance of the vendor. The vendor exercises his right of stoppage *in transitu* at his own peril; and it is incumbent upon the master to give effect to that right so soon as he is satisfied that it is the vendor who claims the

goods, unless he (the master) is aware of a legal defeasance of the vendor's claim. The law is thus laid down by Lord Campbell in *Gurney* v. *Behrend* (3 Ell. & B. 622, 623): 'Prima facie the defendants had a right to stop the wheat, for it was still *in transitu*, and they were unpaid vendors. The onus lies on the plaintiffs to prove that they had become the owners, and that the right to stop *in transitu* was gone.' Moreover, I find that the indemnity offered by the plaintiffs to the master of the vessel, a copy of which is annexed to the petition, recites that Bush is the holder of the bill of lading, and claims the wheat under it; so that in fact the master had full knowledge of the circumstances.

Neither can I attach any weight to the further objection of the defendant, that, assuming that the plaintiffs had a right to stop *in transitu*, and that they duly asserted that right, yet the master was guilty of no breach of duty in refusing to deliver to them, inasmuch as he was simply retaining the custody of the wheat for the person entitled until it should appear who that person was. An abundance of cases shews that the right to stop *in transitu* means the right not only to countermand delivery to the vendee, but to order delivery to the vendor. Were it otherwise, the right to stop would be useless, and trade would be impeded. The refusal of the master to deliver upon demand is, in a case like the present, sufficient evidence of conversion: *Wilson* v. *Anderton* (1 B. & Ad. 450, 456). The master may indeed sometimes suffer for an innocent mistake; but he can always protect himself by filing a bill of interpleader in Chancery. ... I am therefore satisfied that the petition shows such a *prima facie* case of breach of duty as to render the vessel liable in this Court under the 6th and 35th sections of the statute. The motion to reject the petition must be rejected, with costs.

Thus, on receiving notice, the carrier is to re-deliver the goods to the vendor. If the direction of the vendor is unlawful or subsequently found to be unlawful, the vendor has to indemnify the carrier for the losses.

[5] *The Tigress*, (1863) 32 LJPM & A 97.

RESALE BY THE SELLER

What happens to the contract once the seller exercises lien over the goods or stops the goods in transit and regains possession? Does the contract come to an end? Does the property re-vest in the seller? Can the buyer pay the money and claim delivery of the goods? Section 54 deals with several of these issues that follow the exercise of a lien or stoppage in transit.

54. Sale not generally rescinded by lien or stoppage in transit: (1) Subject to the provisions of this section, a contract of sale is not rescinded by the mere exercise by an unpaid seller of his right of lien or stoppage in transit.

(2) Where the goods are of a perishable nature, or where the unpaid seller who has exercised his right of lien or stoppage in transit gives notice to the buyer of his intention to re-sell, the unpaid seller may, if the buyer does not within a reasonable time pay or tender the price, re-sell the goods within a reasonable time and recover from the original buyer damages for any loss occasioned by his breach of contract, but the buyer shall not be entitled to any profit which may occur on the re-sale. If such notice is not given, the unpaid seller shall not be entitled to recover such damages and the buyer shall be entitled to the profit, if any, on the re-sale.

(3) Where an unpaid seller who has exercised his right of lien or stoppage in transit re-sells the goods, the buyer acquires a good title thereto as against the original buyer, notwithstanding that no notice of the re-sale has been given to the original buyer.

(4) Where the seller expressly reserves a right of re-sale in case the buyer should make default, and, on the buyer making default, re-sells the goods, the original contract of sale is thereby rescinded, but without prejudice to any claim which the seller may have for damages.

Each of the four subsections deals with different aspects that may follow from the exercise of a lien or stoppage in transit. The term 'rescind' is used in contract law in relation to the innocent party bringing a voidable contract to an end. Section 54(1) states that the exercise of lien or stoppage in transit by itself brings the contract to an end and discharges the parties from their obligations under the contract.

Section 54(2) gives the seller the option to resell the goods and recover the price. He can give notice to the buyer of his intention to resell the goods. If the buyer pays the money within a reasonable period of time, the seller must give delivery of the goods. However, if the buyer fails to pay within a reasonable period of time, the seller can resell the goods. Consistent with the principles of the award of damages, the seller can recover a loss suffered due to the breach but not profit from the sale. In other words, if the sale proceeds are in excess of the loss suffered, he must return the balance to the buyer. Conversely, if the loss suffered is in excess of the sale proceeds, the seller can appropriate the entire amount and claim the rest as damages. The subsection gives the seller the freedom to resell the goods without giving notice. In this case, however, if the price realized on the second sale is less, the seller cannot claim the balance as damages. Further, the seller would not profit from the resale. The subsection does not explicitly mention that the act of resale by the seller rescinds the contract, but Subsections 1 and 2 do establish this.

The effect of resale is that the seller is selling to the second buyer goods whose ownership had been transferred to the first buyer. This will lead to conflict between the two potential owners. The seller has been given the remedy against the breach by the first buyer. Section 54(3) provides that the second buyer acquires a valid title against the original buyer.

Section 54(4) is not connected with the right of an unpaid seller; it relates to contracts that have an express term giving the right to the seller to resell in the case of default by the buyer. A term of this nature in a contract strengthens the general provisions on the rights of an unpaid seller. The contract comes to an end on the resale, leaving the rights of the seller intact so that damages may be claimed for the breach of the contract by the buyer. The reason the subsection mentions rescission is that the resale is within the contract itself. Thus, a resale would be considered as following through with the contract.

R. v. Ward Ltd v. Bignall

Ward Ltd put up an advertisement to sell two cars, a Vanguard Estate and a Ford Zodiac, for £ 395 and £ 490 respectively. On 6 May 1965, Bingall, a dealer in motor vehicles, saw the advertisement and visited Ward Ltd.[6] He examined both the cars and offered to pay a total of £ 850 for both. Ward agreed to this. Bingall paid £ 25 in cash and left to get the remaining £ 825 in cash from his bank, but then started to have second thoughts. He offered to pay £ 800 instead, which the seller declined. Through a solicitor, Ward wrote a letter to Bingall that quoted from the note Bingall had signed:

> A.M. Bignall—Purchase Vanguard estate—Ford Zodiac—for the sum of £ 850, signed 'A.M. Bignall'; £ 25 deposit paid as seen and approved.

The letter continued:

> In view of the foregoing it is our view that ownership of the said motor cars passed to yourself. ... and all that remains is for you to collect the same, and to pay to our clients the balance of the agreed purchase price. ... and that failure by you to take possession thereof, and to pay the balance of the

agreed purchase price, will place you in breach of the said agreement, and will entitle them to recover against you by way of damages such sum below the price agreed by you, should it be necessary to sell them elsewhere. In these circumstances please accept this letter as notice calling upon you to take delivery of the said cars and to pay the balance due of £ 825, on or before Tuesday next the 11th instant, failing which our clients will consider you in breach of the said agreement, will dispose of the said motor cars for the best price they can obtain, and in the event of them receiving a price below that agreed by yourself, will look to you for the difference after giving credit for the £ 25 already paid by you.

Bingall declined. Ward sold the Vanguard for £ 350 on 24 May but could not find a buyer for the Zodiac. On 12 October 1965, Ward's solicitors wrote to Bingall:

> In an effort to mitigate the damage following your client's repudiation our clients sold the said Vanguard for £ 350 but their efforts to procure a purchaser for the Zodiac have been completely fruitless. The Ford Zodiac is available for your client's collection against payment of the balance of £ 475, and if such is your client's desire arrangements can be made for payment of that sum in cash against delivery to your client of the car within seven days of this date, failing which we have advised our clients to institute proceedings for the said sum as the balance of money due and payable by your client for goods bargained and sold.

Ward moved court on 9 February 1966 claiming as damages the balance of the contract price, £ 825, minus the £ 350 received from the sale of the Vanguard, plus £ 22 10s advertising expenses in respect of the two cars since the date of the contract. This came to a total of £ 497 10s. The relevant provisions on the rights of the unpaid seller are in Section 48 of the Sale of Goods Act, 1893:

(1) Subject to the provisions of this section, a contract of sale is not rescinded by the mere

---

[6] R. v. *Ward Ltd* v. *Bignall*, (1967) 1 QB 534.

exercise by an unpaid seller of his right of lien ... or stoppage in transitu.

(2) Where an unpaid seller who has exercised his right of lien ... or stoppage in transitu re-sells the goods, the buyer acquires a good title thereto as against the original buyer.

(3) Where the goods are of a perishable nature, or where the unpaid seller gives notice to the buyer of his intention to re-sell, and the buyer does not within a reasonable time pay or tender the price, the unpaid seller may re-sell the goods and recover from the original buyer damages for any loss occasioned by his breach of contract.

(4) Where the seller expressly reserves a right of re-sale in case the buyer should make default, and on the buyer making default, re-sells the goods, the original contract of sale is thereby rescinded, but without prejudice to any claim the seller may have for damages.

Sellers L.J. delivered the following judgment:

The question on this part of the appeal is whether, if the property passed on the sale, the Zodiac car which has not been sold remains the buyer's property so that the action of the plaintiffs is for the price, or whether by the sale of the Vanguard the plaintiffs have rescinded the whole contract on the buyer's breach of it so that the ownership of the Zodiac reverted back to the plaintiffs and their remedy is in damages under the statute, or, in effect, damages for non-acceptance, giving credit for what they have received from the sale of the goods or part thereof.

Subsections (1) and (2) of section 48 speak clearly. Subsection (4) expressly provides: 'the original contract of sale is thereby rescinded.' That was necessary because, where the seller 'expressly reserves a right of re-sale in case the buyer should make default,' a seller who re-sold under such a contract would be applying and affirming the contract, and his action would be consistent with it. Under subsection (3) no such provision of rescission is necessary, for, if an unpaid seller re-sells, he puts it out of his power to perform his contract and his action is inconsistent with a subsisting sale to the original buyer. Once there is a re-sale

in accordance with section 48 by an unpaid seller in possession of the contractual goods the contract of sale is rescinded, whether the re-sale be of the whole of the goods or of part of them, and in this respect subsections (3) and (4) fall into line.

As the property in the goods reverts on such a re-sale, the seller retains the proceeds of sale whether they be greater or less than the contractual price. The probability in normal trade is that the price would be less, giving rise to a claim for damages, as for non-acceptance of the goods.

Finnemore J. has interpreted section 48 (3) in Gallagher v. Shilcock. [1949] 2 K.B. 765:

'Having regard to the express provision for rescission in section 48 (4) ... where the right of re-sale has been reserved in the contract of sale, the true construction of subsection (3) is that, where an unpaid seller, in the absence of such a reservation, exercises his right of resale under subsection (3), that exercise does not operate to rescind the contract, for the seller, in so acting, is affirming the contract and ensuring that he receives the contract price.'

With all respect to that learned and very experienced judge, I think the construction works the other way round. The express reservation in a contract would permit the unpaid seller to resell without acting inconsistently or in conflict with his obligations. His conduct would not evidence a rescission by him on the buyer's breach. Nevertheless, subsection (4) makes the resale operate as a rescission and leaves the remedy, if any loss ensues, in damages. That brings it into harmony with subsection (3), which also gives a claim for damages for any loss occasioned by the original buyer's breach of contract. If the unpaid seller resells the goods, he puts it out of his power to perform his obligation under the original contract, that is, to deliver the contractual goods to the buyer. By the notice to the buyer, the seller makes payment of the price 'of the essence of the contract,' as it is sometimes put. It requires the buyer to pay the price or tender it within a reasonable time.

If he fails to do so, the seller in possession of the goods may treat the bargain as rescinded and resell the goods. The suit for damages becomes comparable to a claim for damages for nonacceptance of the goods where the property never has passed. The property has reverted on the resale, and the second buyer gets a good title. The seller resells as owner. Subsection (2) expressly gives the buyer a good title thereto as against the original buyer.

On this view of the law the plaintiffs cannot recover the price of the Zodiac, which is in the circumstances their property. They can, however, recover any loss which they have sustained by the buyer's default. The parties have sensibly agreed that the value of the Zodiac in May, 1965, was £ 450. The total contract price was £ 850, against which the plaintiffs have received £ 25 in cash and £ 350 in respect of the Vanguard, and have to give credit for £ 450 for the Zodiac. To the loss of £ 25 must be added the sum for advertising, which was admittedly reasonably incurred—£ 22 10s. The plaintiffs' loss was, therefore, £ 47 10s.

I would allow the appeal and enter judgment for £ 47 10s.in favour of the plaintiffs in substitution for the award of the deputy judge.

Diplock L.J. delivered the following judgment:

Whether or not the property had passed on May 6, 1965, the seller was only liable to deliver upon payment or tender of the balance of the purchase price (see the Sale of Goods Act, s. 28 and was entitled until then to retain possession, either by virtue of his lien as an unpaid seller if the property had passed (Sale of Goods Act, s. 39 (1)), or by virtue of his right to withhold delivery if the property had not passed (subs. (2) of the same section). In either case, the unpaid seller has a right to resell the goods if he gives notice of his intention to do so and the buyer does not within a reasonable time pay or tender the price (Sale of Goods Act, s. 48 (3)). The note in the current edition of Chalmers that the right of resale only arises where the seller exercises his right of lien or stoppage in transitu, that is, where the property has passed to the buyer, is in my view wrong. This subsection enables a seller in possession of the goods to make time of payment of the purchase price of the essence of the contract whether the

property has passed or not. The seller cannot have greater rights of resale if the property has already passed to the buyer than those which he would have if the property had remained in him.

The letter of May 6, 1965, contained notice to resell on or after May 11. Whether that was a reasonable time or not does not matter. The buyer never tendered the price, and on or before May 24 the seller resold the Vanguard for £ 350. He advertised the Zodiac for sale, but failed to find a buyer at the advertised price, and on October 12, 1965, offered to deliver it to the buyer against payment of £ 475, being the balance of the original purchase price of £ 850 for the two cars less the deposit of £ 25 and the £ 350 received on resale of the Vanguard car.

The letter of October 12, 1965, in which that offer was made expressed the intention of the seller to institute proceedings against the buyer for the sum of £ 475 'as the balance of money due and payable … for goods bargained and sold.' When the writ was issued on February 9, 1966, however, the cause of action was not framed as an action for the balance of the purchase price under section 49 (1) of the Sale of Goods Act but as an action for damages for non-acceptance under section 50 (1), although the particulars of damage were inappropriate to an action for damages for non-acceptance. In the particulars of damage in the statement of claim credit was given, against the balance of the purchase price of £ 825, for the sum of £ 350 for which the Vanguard had been sold, but no credit was given for the market price of the Zodiac.

At the trial neither party, nor the judge, seems to have given his mind to the question of where the property in the Zodiac lay by that date. The only argument as to the quantum of damages was based on the contention that the seller ought to have mitigated his damage by accepting the buyer's offer to purchase the Zodiac alone for £ 500 on May 6, 1965. That contention was illfounded. At the date of that offer the contract of sale of the two cars was still in being. The offer to buy the Zodiac alone was a proposal by the buyer to rescind that contract by mutual consent coupled with an offer to enter into a fresh contract of sale of the Zodiac alone. The seller, as he was entitled to do, refused to rescind the existing contract of sale at that date, and no question of mitigating his damages then arose. The judge appears tacitly to have accepted the view that the seller was under a duty to mitigate his damage as soon as the buyer wrongfully repudiated the contract but to have taken the view that his rejection of the buyer's offer of £ 500 for the Zodiac was not a breach of that duty for the reason that the seller was entitled to test the market before accepting any offer to buy either or both of the cars. The judge awarded the seller the damages which he claimed and made no allowance for the value of the Zodiac, which the seller still retains.

If the seller, at the date of the issue of the writ, had been in a position to bring an action for the balance of the purchase price and had done so, the measure of damages awarded by the judge would have been correct and the seller would have been entitled to retain possession of the Zodiac by virtue of his unpaid seller's lien until the judgment was satisfied (Sale of Goods Act, s. 43 (2)). If, however, he were only in a position to claim damages for non-acceptance, which was what he did, the prima facie measure of his damages would be the difference between the contract price and the market price of the two cars (Sale of Goods Act, s. 50 (1) and (3)), and any reasonable costs, such as those of advertising, incurred by him in reselling the cars. The onus of proving the market price of both cars lay upon the seller. The evidence of the sale of the Vanguard at £ 350 on May 24, 1965, was evidence of the market price of the Vanguard. Evidence of the price at which he had advertised the Zodiac but failed to sell it was some evidence that its market price was less than those figures, which ranged from £ 490 on May 25, 1965, to £ 450 on July 1, 1965. The lowest figure at which it was offered was, however, rather late in date, and in order to avoid any necessity for a new trial the parties have very sensibly agreed on a figure of £ 450 as the market price of the Zodiac at about the end of May, 1965. If, therefore, the seller's only right at the date of the issue of the writ on February 9, 1966, was for damages for non-acceptance, the appeal must be allowed and

the damages awarded reduced by £ 450 from £ 497 10s. to £ 47 10s.

In this court it has been contended on behalf of the seller that, when an unpaid seller who retains possession of goods the property in which has passed to the buyer exercises his statutory right of resale under section 48 (3) of the Sale of Goods Act, he does not thereby elect to treat the contract as rescinded, but remains entitled to recover the purchase price from the buyer although he must give credit for the net proceeds of sale of any of the goods which he has sold. Authority for this proposition is to be found in the judgment of Finnemore J. in Gallagher v. Shilcock, and the question in this appeal is whether that judgment is right or not.

Finnemore J. based his conclusion on his view as to the construction of section 48 of the Sale of Goods Act, and in particular upon the contrast between the express reference in subsection (4) of section 48 to the contract being rescinded when goods are resold under an express right of resale and the absence of any reference to rescission in subsection (3) of section 48. With great respect, however, I think that that disregards basic principles of the law of contract, and that there is another explanation for the contrast between the two subsections.

Rescission of a contract discharges both parties from any further liability to perform their respective primary obligations under the contract, that is to say, to do thereafter those things which by their contract they had stipulated they would do. Where rescission occurs as a result of one party exercising his right to treat a breach by the other party of a stipulation in the contract as a repudiation of the contract, this gives rise to a secondary obligation of the party in breach to compensate the other party for the loss occasioned to him as a consequence of the rescission, and this secondary obligation is enforceable in an action for damages. Until, however, there is rescission by acceptance of the repudiation, the liability of both parties to perform their primary obligations under the contract continues. Thus, under a contract for the sale of goods which has not been rescinded, the seller remains liable to transfer the property in the goods to the buyer and to deliver possession of them to him until he has discharged those obligations by performing them, and the buyer remains correspondingly liable to pay for the goods and to accept possession of them.

The election by a party not in default to exercise his right of rescission by treating the contract as repudiated may be evinced by words or by conduct. Any act which puts it out of his power to perform thereafter his primary obligations under the contract, if it is an act which he is entitled to do without notice to the party in default, must amount to an election to rescind the contract. If it is an act which he is not entitled to do, it will amount to a wrongful repudiation of the contract on his part which the other party can in turn elect to treat as rescinding the contract.

Part IV of the Sale of Goods Act, sections 38 to 48, deals with the rights of an unpaid seller both before the property in the goods has passed to the buyer and after it has passed. The mere fact that a seller is unpaid does not necessarily mean that the buyer is in breach of the contract, or, if he is, that his breach is one which entitles the seller to exercise his right to treat the contract as repudiated. Section 39(1) and (2) states what the unpaid seller's rights are in relation to the possession of the goods before and after the property has passed to the buyer. Subsection (1) (c) provides that he shall have 'a right of resale as limited by this Act.' Sections 41 to 47 deal in greater detail with the exercise by the unpaid seller of his rights in relation to the possession of the goods after the property has passed to the buyer. Section 48 deals with several topics. Subsection (1) reads as follows: 'Subject to the provisions of this section, a contract of sale is not rescinded by the mere exercise by an unpaid seller of his right of lien ... or stoppage in transitu.'

If the contract provided for delivery upon a specified date, the seller's conduct in failing to deliver on that date would put it out of his power to perform one of his primary obligations under the contract if time were of the essence of the contract. It was, therefore, necessary, or at least prudent, to provide expressly that if his failure to deliver were in the mere exercise of a lien or

right of stoppage in transitu it did not discharge his liability to deliver the goods upon tender of the contract price, or the buyer's liability to accept the goods and to pay for them.

Subsection (2) deals with a different topic, videlicet, the title of a new buyer to whom the goods are resold by the seller. If the property in the goods at the time of the resale remained in the seller, the new buyer would obtain a good title at common law and would require no statutory protection. The subsection is, therefore, limited to cases where the property in the goods at the time of resale had already passed to the original buyer, and provides that, where the seller is in possession of the goods in the exercise of his unpaid seller's lien or right of stoppage in transitu, the new buyer shall acquire a good title, and this is so whether or not the seller had a right of resale as against the original buyer.

Subsection (3) reads as follows:

'Where the goods are of a perishable nature, or where the unpaid seller gives notice to the buyer of his intention to resell, and the buyer does not within a reasonable time pay or tender the price, the unpaid seller may resell the goods and recover from the original buyer damages for any loss occasioned by his breach of contract.'

This is the provision of the Act which confers 'a right of resale as limited by this Act,' referred to in section 39 (1) (c). The right dealt with in this subsection is a right as against the original buyer. As a stipulation as to time of payment is not deemed to be of the essence of a contract of sale unless a different intention appears from the terms of the contract (Sale of Goods Act, s. 10 (1)), failure by the buyer to pay on the stipulated date is not conduct by him which entitles the unpaid seller to treat the contract as repudiated. He remains liable to deliver the goods to the buyer upon tender of the contract price (Sale of Goods Act, s. 28). Apart from this subsection, if the unpaid seller resold the goods before or after the property had passed to the original buyer, he would remain liable to the original buyer for damages for non-delivery if the original buyer tendered the purchase price after the resale, and if the property had already passed to the original buyer at the time of the resale he would be liable to an alternative action by the original buyer for damages for conversion. The purpose of the subsection is to make time of payment of the essence of the contract whenever the goods are of a perishable nature, and to enable an unpaid seller, whatever the nature of the goods, to make payment within a reasonable time after notice of the essence of the contract. As already pointed out, an unpaid seller who resells the goods before the property has passed puts it out of his power to perform his primary obligation to the buyer to transfer the property in the goods to the buyer and, whether or not the property has already passed, to deliver up possession of the goods to the buyer. By making the act of resale one which the unpaid seller is entitled to perform, the subsection empowers the seller by his conduct in doing that act to exercise his right to treat the contract as repudiated by the buyer, that is, as rescinded, with the consequence that the buyer is discharged from any further liability to perform his primary obligation to pay the purchase price, and becomes subject to the secondary obligation to pay damages for non-acceptance of the goods. If the contract were not rescinded by the resale the seller would still be entitled to bring an action against the buyer for the price of the goods although, no doubt, he would have to credit the buyer with the proceeds of the resale. If that were the intention of the subsection one would have expected it to provide this in express terms. That it was not the intention is, however, apparent from the words used to define the remedy of the unpaid seller who has exercised his right of resale, videlicet, to 'recover from the original buyer damages for any loss occasioned by his breach of contract.' It is, of course, well-established that where a contract for the sale of goods is rescinded after the property in the goods has passed to the buyer the rescission divests the buyer of his property in the goods.

Subsection (4) deals with the consequences of a resale by a seller, not necessarily an 'unpaid seller' as defined in section 38, made in the exercise of an express right of resale reserved in the contract on the buyer making default. If such an express right were exercisable after the property in the goods

had passed to the buyer, its exercise might, on one view, be regarded as an alternative mode of performance of the seller's primary obligations under the contract, and the resale as being made by the seller as agent for the buyer. It was, therefore, necessary to provide expressly that the exercise of an express power of resale should rescind the original contract of sale. That is, in my view, the explanation of the express reference to rescission in subsection (4). The absence of a similar express reference to rescission in subsection (3) is no sufficient ground for ascribing to subsection (3) a meaning which the actual words of the subsection would appear to contradict and which would, in my view, conflict with the general principles of the law of contract.

In the present case the unpaid seller only resold part of the goods which he had contracted to sell to the original buyer. This makes no difference, however. His primary duty under the contract was to deliver both cars to the buyer. If he delivered only one, the buyer would be entitled to reject it (Sale of Goods Act, s. 30 (1)). By his conduct in selling the Vanguard on May 24, 1965, the unpaid seller put it out of his power to perform his primary obligation under the contract. He thereby elected to treat the contract as rescinded. The property in the Zodiac thereupon reverted to him, and his only remedy against the buyer after May 24, 1965, was for damages for non-acceptance of the two cars, of which the prima facie measure is the difference between the contract price and their market value on May 24, 1965.

I, too, would allow this appeal, and enter judgment for the plaintiffs for £ 47 10s. instead of £ 497 10s.

The common law court judgments have used the words 'repudiation', 'rescission' and 'termination' interchangeably. However, the settled outcome is the same irrespective of the terms, although the interchangeable usage does lead to confusion. For the breach of a condition of a contract, the innocent party can elect to terminate the contract. The termination will discharge the parties from subsequent obligations under the contract. The innocent party will receive damages for the loss suffered due to the breach. He can also nullify the voidable contract. In this case, the parties are restored to the position they were in before the contract was made. The innocent party is paid compensation for the damages suffered due to the misrepresentation. Nullifying a voidable contract is more appropriately called rescission. The measures of damages for termination and rescission are different. The interchangeable use of the terms can lead to doubts on the use of the term 'to rescind' in the Sale of Goods Act, 1893.

The judgment uses the term 'rescission' in both the senses to resolve different issues. The notice to resell makes time an essential part of the contract. The failure of the buyer to pay the price within a reasonable period becomes a repudiatory breach, giving the seller the right to terminate the contract by resale—in other words, rescission. However, the effect of this is that if the ownership is transferred, it reverts to the seller. This could happen in two ways. If the seller got the ownership of the goods at the point of resale (a position that is not consistent with the rest of the provisions), the sale made by the buyer in the interim would be valid. Only by putting the seller in the position he was in before the contract was made can this effect be neutralized. Thus, the effect is that the seller never lets go of the ownership. The judgment rightly uses rescission for this.

Section 30 also provides on the buyer remaining in possession of the goods and making a sale to another buyer. In this respect, there is an overlap between the two provisions. However, the scope of the two provisions is different. The first difference is obvious. Section 30 applies whether or not the seller is unpaid, but only if the second buyer is given delivery of the goods or a document of title. Under Section 54, this is not necessary. Section 30 requires the second buyer to be bona fide with no knowledge of prior sale. Under 54, this is not required. Section 30 not only protects the interests of sub-buyers but also other interests like pledges or other dispositions. The effect of Section 54, however, is limited to resale.

In this context, a curious implication seems to follow from Diplock's judgment. If the ownership is not transferred to the buyer, the seller is in any case free to sell the goods to the second buyer. The seller will pass a valid title by being the owner. Thus, Section 54 is not required to vest ownership in the sub-buyer. Further, where the ownership is not transferred, the seller can certainly maintain lien over the goods, refusing to deliver the goods till he is paid. However, as there has been no sale, there can be no resale. Thus, the provisions of Section 54 would not be available to the seller to sell the goods and rescind the contract. The contract would prevail on its terms. If the seller sells the goods, he may be liable to the buyer for breach of the contract. There is no court judgment on this startling implication of the section.

P.S.N.S. Ambalavana Chettiar and Company Limited v. Express Newspapers Limited, Bombay

In this case, the seller sold a stock of 415 tons of newsprint. The parties had not provided on the time of transfer of property.[7] As the goods were specific, the property passed when the contract was made. On 26 November 1951, the parties made a new arrangement that the

---

[7] *P.S.N.S. Ambalavana Chettiar and Company Limited v. Express Newspapers Limited, Bombay,* AIR (1968) SC 741.

buyer would buy only 300 tons. The Supreme Court thus interpreted the effect:

It is true that originally the property in the entire 415 tons had passed to the appellants. But the result of the variation of the contract was to annul the passing of property in the goods. The effect of the bargain on November 26, 1951 was that the respondent would sell and deliver to the appellants any 300 tons out of the larger stock of 415 tons. As from November 26, 1951, the property in the entire stock of 415 tons belonged to the respondent. The parties did not intend that as from November 26, 1951 the property in any individual portion of the stock of 415 tons would remain vested in the appellants.

The seller sold the goods to another buyer. The dispute was whether the right of an unpaid seller to sell goods would be available. The court noted:

The statutory power of resale under s. 54(2) arises if the property in the goods has passed to the buyer subject to the lien of the unpaid seller. Where the property in the goods has not passed to the buyer, the seller has no right of resale under s. 54(2). The question is whether the property in the 300 tons of newsprint in sheets had passed to the appellants before the resale.

No portion of 415 tons of the newsprint lying in the respondent's godown was appropriated to the contract by the respondent with the appellants's consent before the resale. On the date of the resale, property in the goods had not passed to the buyer Consequently, the respondent had no right to resell the goods under s. 54(2). The claim to recover the deficiency on resale is not suitable.

The remedy for the seller would be ordinary damages for breach of contract by the buyer.

The respondent to claim as damages the difference between the contract price and the market price on the date of the breach. Where no time is fixed under the contract of sale for acceptance of the goods, the measure of damages is prima facie the difference between the contract price and the market price on the date of the refusal by the buyer to accept the goods... In the present case, no time was fixed in the contract for acceptance of the goods. On March 29, 1952, the appellants refused to accept the goods. The respondent is entitled to the difference between the contract price and the market price on March 29, 1952.

Mysore Sugar Company Limited, Bangalore v. Manohar Metal Industries, Chikpet, Bangalore

Here, the seller had advertised to sell items like copper ingots, copper scraps, and brass tubes, but the bidders were not given access to examine the goods.[8] Manohar Metal Industries was awarded the tender. The buyer took certain items on a part-payment basis, and when it came to lifting of copper ingots, he asked for time to pay the balance and to separate them from other items with which it was mixed up. Later, the buyer disputed the percentage of copper content in the articles. Despite repeated reminders, the buyer failed to pay and take the remainder of the goods. The seller informed the buyer that if he failed to pay, he would resell the goods—which he did after three months of giving the notice of re-sell. By then the price of copper had fallen, and the seller claimed the loss from Manohar Metal Industries.

The court decided that as the sale was unconditional, the ownership passed to the buyer at the time of making of the contract. As the contract was also by description, the goods should have conformed to it. However, as the buyer had taken a part of the goods, he had accepted them. The court ruled:

[8] *Mysore Sugar Company Limited, Bangalore* v. *Manohar Metal Industries*, AIR (1982) Karnataka 283.

Therefore, there is an unconditional contract of sale and there were, no doubt, stipulations for payment of price and delivery of goods subsequently. In such a case, the property in the goods passes on to the buyer and hence Section 54 of the Act comes into play. It is in record that the plaintiff issued a notice to the defendant ... making his intention clear that the buyer must lift the goods on payment as otherwise he will have to resell the goods and the defendant shall be liable for any loss caused. ... Within a reasonable time thereafter the company should have resold the goods by advertising. But the evidence on record shows that the advertisement was inserted ... after nearly three months.

...

It is needless for me to point out that a duty lay on the plaintiff to mitigate the damages. Even in view of S. 54 (2), it was the duty of the plaintiff to see that re-sale was effected within a reasonable time especially so, when the prices were falling for the relevant material. Three months delay, therefore, on the facts of this case, is certainly inordinate and re-sale has not taken place within a reasonable time as contemplated in Section 54 (2).

...

As explained above, there has been unreasonable delay in re-selling, on the facts of the present case, when the market price was falling. Hence, the value realised on resale does not afford a good ground to fix the damages. There is no evidence on record placed by the plaintiff to show the ruling price of the commodity at the time when there was breach of contract. The plaintiff has come to Court. The burden is on him to prove the alleged damages and since he has not placed any material evidence to show that he has suffered damages, he has to fail ...

... the respondent-defendant submitted that S. 54 (2) of the Sale of Goods Act should be read with Section 73 of the Act. It may be stated in this context that Section 73 contains this general principle with regard to fixing up of damages, whereas Section 54 speaks of specific case of moveable property sold. Section 54 is more specific whereas Section 73 is general in nature. Therefore, Section 54 prevails over Section 73 though both the sections are based on the same general principles.

* * *

The common law courts developed special rights for an unpaid seller who had retained possession of the goods in which the ownership had passed to the buyer. The seller has a lien over the goods to refuse delivery till he is paid the price. The seller has a right to resell the goods, with or without notice to the buyer, to recover the unpaid amount. The remedy is of the nature of self-help. The lien ends if the buyer pays the price or the seller gives possession to the buyer.

12

Other Provisions

In this chapter, we will review miscellaneous provisions of the Sale of Goods Act, 1930. The first one we shall look at is the capacity of the parties to oust the implied terms and conditions. Section 62 provides:

62. Exclusion of implied terms and conditions: Where any right, duty or liability would arise under a contract of sale by implication of law, it may be negatived or varied by express agreement or by the course of dealing between the parties, or by usage, if the usage is such as to bind both parties to the contract.

The section establishes the consensual nature of a contract of sale. 'Implication of law' refers to the terms the law accords to the sale contract. The conditions and warranties in relation to the quality of goods are examples of this. The section makes it possible for it to be expunged by express agreement, usage, or the course of dealings. As we recall from our study of contract law, the best means of incorporating a term in a contract is by entering into a signed contract. The courts almost never allow the course of dealing or usage to incorporate terms in the contract. This leaves only express agreement to cancel the implications by law. An express

agreement can be oral or in writing. As the express terms supersede the law, the courts interpret the terms strictly. Sellers and service providers used the provision to incorporate terms that completely excluded them from liability. The British courts countered this with the doctrine of fundamental breach where an exclusion clause that exempted the party from a fundamental obligation was invalid. The Supply of Goods (Implied Terms) Act, 1973, limited the powers of the sellers to exclude liability in consumer sales. In the subsequent cases, the British Courts abandoned and questioned the doctrine of fundamental breach. In the absence of legislation, the provision applies in India, making it possible for the contracting parties to remove implied warranties and conditions by providing so in express terms. All sale contracts have such terms displacing implied conditions and warranties.

AUCTION SALE

Section 64 is on auction sale. It provides:

64. Auction sale: In the case of a sale by auction—
　(1) where goods are put up for sale in lots, each lot is prima facie deemed to be the subject of a separate contract of sale;

(2) the sale is complete when the auctioneer announces its completion by the fall of the hammer or in other customary manner; and, until such announcement is made, any bidder may retract his bid;

(3) a right to bid may be reserved expressly by or on behalf of the seller and, where such right is expressly so reserved, but not otherwise, the seller or any one person on his behalf may, subject to the provisions hereinafter contained, bid at the auction;

(4) where the sale is not notified to be subject to a right to bid on behalf of the seller, it shall not be lawful for the seller to bid himself or to employ any person to bid at such sale, or for the auctioneer knowingly to take any bid from the seller or any such person; and any sale contravening this rule may be treated as fraudulent by the buyer;

(5) the sale may be notified to be subject to a reserved or upset price;

(6) if the seller makes use of pretended bidding to raise the price, the sale is voidable at the option of the buyer.

The section expresses the principle that contract law has developed on formation of agreement in relation to auction. The section was included, presumably, as auctions were a particular means of getting in a sale contract. Section 64(2) states that the bidder is an offeror in an auction and the auctioneer traditionally closes with the striking of the hammer. *Warlow* v. *Harrison*,[1] established that the owner's bid in an auction is invalid. Section 64(3) and (4) makes it possible for the bidder to bid after notifying the other bidders; otherwise, it will be considered fraudulent. Section 64(5) states that the auctioneer may set a reserve price, and will hence be under an obligation to accept the highest bid above the reserve price. The following is a case related to the section.

Consolidated Coffee Ltd v. Coffee Board, Bangalore

We have reviewed this case in Chapter 2.[2] The question that interests us here is whether the conclusion of the auction constituted sale. This was relevant with regard to an exemption from sales tax. The Supreme Court noted:

Regarding Section 64(2) of the Sale of Goods Act, it seems to us that that provision does not deal with the question of the passing of the property in the goods sold at auction sale, but instead, it deals with the completion of the contract of sale. It is true that sub-section (2) says that 'the sale is complete' when the auctioneer announces its completion by the fall of the hammer or in other customary manner, but, the next following provision which says: 'and until such announcement is made any bidder may retract his bid' suggests that what is complete at the fall of the hammer or the announcement of closure in other customary manner is that the contract for sale is complete. It is well known that our Sale of Goods Act, 1930 is based upon and is largely a reproduction of the English Sale of Goods Act, 1893 and in principle as well as in most details, the law of sale of goods in both the countries is now the same and, therefore, English authorities on interpretation of different sections, although not technically binding in India, would have great persuasive value.

It will be pertinent to observe that our Section 64 is based upon Section 58 of the English Act … At foot-note (2), Section 58 (2) of the Sale of Goods Act, 1893 is the provision indicated in support of the aforesaid statement of law and it is further stated: 'In an unconditional sale the property in the goods passes on the fall of the hammer' … This would show that under Section 58 (2) of the English Sale of Goods Act, 1893, normally, in an auction sale, at the fall of the

---

[1] *Warlow* v. *Harrison*, (1859) 1 E&E 309.

[2] *Consolidated Coffee Ltd* v. *Coffee Board, Bangalore*, AIR (1980) SC 1468.

hammer, a completion of the contract of sale takes place and until such time, the bidder may retract his bid, but if the auction sale happens to be an unconditional sale in respect of specific and ascertained goods, the title to the property passes simultaneously at the fall of the hammer, not by virtue of Section 58 (2) but by reason of the operation of Section 18, Rule 1 of the English Act (which is equivalent to Section 20 of our Act).

The question then was whether the auction by the Coffee Board was a conditional or unconditional sale. Contracts are consensual. The parties are free to set their own terms. This basic concept cuts across all provisions in the Sale of Goods Act, 1930. The Supreme Court noted the incorporation of the principle in Section 62, which reads, 'Where any right, duty or liability would arise under a contract of sale by implication of law, it may be negatived or varied by express agreement or by the course of dealing between the parties or by usage.' Thus, a sale by auction can be conditional or unconditional, as the Supreme Court noted:

… once it is accepted that auction sales to which Section 64 applies could be unconditional or conditional and that the auctioneer can prescribe his own terms and conditions on the basis of which the property is exposed to sale by auction, it must be held that the acceptance of any bid as well as the passing of the property in the goods sold thereat would be governed by those terms and conditions.

Reviewing the numerous terms and conditions imposed by the Coffee Board, the Supreme Court ruled that the auction was subject to those numerous conditions. Thus, the auction itself could not be taken to be a penultimate sale to an export. The claim of the permit holders failed.

SALE AND TAXATION

Section 64A provides: In contracts of sale amount of increased or decreased duty to be added or deducted: In the event of any duty of customs or excise on any goods being imposed, increased, decreased or remitted after the making of any contract for the sale of such goods without stipulation as to the payment of duty where duty was not chargeable at the time of the making of the contract, or for the sale of such goods duty-paid where duty was chargeable at that time—

(a) if such imposition or increase so takes effect that the duty or increased duty, as the case may be, or any part thereof, is paid, the seller may add so much to the contract price as will be equivalent to the amount paid in respect of such duty or increase of duty, and he shall be entitled to be paid and to sue for and recover such addition, and

(b) if such decrease or remission so takes effect that the decreased duty only or no duty, as the case may be, is paid, the buyer may deduct so much from the contract price as will be equivalent to the decrease of duty or remitted duty and he shall not be liable to pay, or be sued for or in respect of, such deduction.

It is the seller who is entrusted to collect tax and pay the government. Taxation also applies on the performance of a sale. If there is a change in the incidence of taxation after the formation of the contract but before its performance, the change will reflect on the seller. If the contract has accounted for this, the intent of the parties will be given effect. If the parties have not provided for it, the section provides the mechanism for resolution. If the change has made an additional demand on the seller, the seller will be entitled to collect it from the buyer. Conversely, if the change has led to the reduction of taxation, the buyer can claim the benefit from the seller.

13

Emerging Themes
Taxation and Internet Sale

As we noted right at the beginning of this book, law has been evolving like any other field of knowledge. While most fields of knowledge develop by building on existing settled knowledge, there is a difference when it comes to law. Law is an interpretive field. Use of a term will always be subject to newer interpretive possibilities. Further, at times, the law maker may expand or modify the original concept. This happened to the use of the terms 'sale', 'goods', and 'sale goods' with respect to the laws on taxation. In fact, most of the cases on the sale of goods have been on taxation. In this chapter, we will review some of the emerging aspects in this area. The other emerging subject we will review is sale through the Internet. A sale through an e-store raises questions about the jurisdiction of the contract, the liability of the parties, and taxation. We begin with the development of the law on sales tax.

SALE AND SALES TAX

Under the Government of India Act, 1935, the Provincial Legislature could legislate on 'taxes on the sale of goods and on advertise-

ments'. Following this, the provinces had made legislation imposing sales tax. As we know, according to the Sale of Goods Act, 1930, a 'sale' is a contract. Thus, the sale must have all the features of a contractual relationship. Second, a 'sale' is different from 'agreement to sell'. A sale happens only when the property passes to the buyer. In everyday use, however, the word could also refer to an agreement to sell. Disputes on the scope of the term in relation to the taxation legislation were inevitable. We shall see some of them in the following review of cases.

State of Madras v. M/s Gannon Dunkerley and Co. (Madras) Ltd

Under the Government of India Act, 1935, the Provincial Legislature could legislate on the subject 'taxes on the sale of goods and on advertisements'.[1] Under this, the Provincial Legislature had passed the Madras General Sales Tax Act, 1939, imposing tax on the 'sale of goods'. Section 2(h) of the Act defined a

[1] *State of Madras* v. *M/s Gannon Dunkerley and Co. (Madras) Ltd*, AIR (1958) SC 560.

sale as meaning 'every transfer of the property in goods by one person to another in the course of trade or business for cash or for deferred payment or other valuable consideration'. The act was amended by the legislature through the Madras General Sales Tax (Amendment) Act, 1947. The amendment was intended to include work contracts within its purview. Towards this, the definition of goods was extended to include materials 'used in the construction, fitting out, improvement or repair of immovable property or in the fitting out, improvement or repair of movable property.' The definition of sale in Section 2(h) was enlarged to include 'a transfer of property in goods involved in the execution of a works contract'. Following the amendment, rules were made to give powers to the administration to work out the cost of material in a work contract for the application of the sales tax.

M/s Gannon Dunkerley and Co. was a company engaged in works contracts including the construction of buildings, roads, and bridges. Following the amendment, the state imposed taxes on materials used on construction work. The company contended that the Government of India authorized the legislature to make laws on 'taxes on the sale of goods'. As there is no transaction of sale in respect of those goods, this did not include imposing a tax on the value of materials used in works. Thus, the amendment was *ultra vires*. The question involved examining the scope of the term 'sale of goods' in the Government of India Act, 1935. The excerpts from the Supreme Court are as follows:

The entire controversy, it will be seen, hinges on the meaning of the words 'sale of goods' in Entry 48, and the point which we have now to decide is as to the correct interpretation to be put on them.

The contention of the appellant and of the State which have intervened is that the provisions of a Constitution which confer legislative powers should receive a liberal construction, and that, accordingly, the expression 'sale of goods' in Entry 48 should be interpreted not in the narrow and technical sense in which it is used in the Indian Sale of Goods Act, 1930, but in a broad sense.

...

On these authorities, the contention of the appellant is well-founded that as the words 'sale of goods' in Entry 48 occur in a Constitution Act and confer legislative powers on the State legislature in respect of a topic relating to taxation, they must be interpreted not in a restricted but broad sense. And that opens up questions as to what that sense is, whether popular or legal, and what its connotation is either in the one sense or the other.

The court examined several sources and concluded that the meaning of the term 'sale' in legal sense is always one arising from a contract leading to passing of the ownership. The state further argued that the word 'sale' is, in its popular sense, of wider import than in its legal sense, and that is the meaning which should be given to it. The Supreme Court noted on this contention:

Now, in its popular sense, a sale is said to take place when the bargain is settled between the parties, though property in the goods may not pass at that stage ... and it is that sense that the learned Judge would appear to have had in his mind when he spoke of a commercial or business sense. ... this Court has consistently held that though the word 'sale' in its popular sense is not restricted to passing of title, and has a wider connotation as meaning the transaction of sale, and that in that sense an agreement to sell would, as one of the essential ingredients of sale, furnish sufficient nexus for a State to impose a tax, such levy could, nevertheless, be made only when the transaction is one of sale, and it would be a sale only when it has resulted in the passing of property in the goods to the purchaser. ... It has also been held ... that the sale contemplated by Entry 48 of the Government of India Act was a transaction in which title to the goods passes and a mere executory agreement was not a sale within the Entry. We must accordingly hold that the expression 'sale of goods' in Entry 48 cannot be construed in its popular sense, and that it must be interpreted in its legal sense. What its connotation in that sense is, must now be ascertained. For a correct determination thereof, it is necessary to digress somewhat into the evolution of the law relating to sale of goods.

…

Thus, according to the law both of England and of India, in order to constitute a sale it is necessary that there should be an agreement between the parties for the purpose of transferring title to goods which of course presupposes capacity to contract, that it must be supported by money consideration, and that as a result of the transaction property must actually pass in the goods. Unless all these elements are present, there can be no sale. Thus, if merely title to the goods passes but not as a result of any contract between the parties, express or implied, there is no sale. So also if the consideration for the transfer was not money but other valuable consideration, it may then be exchange or barter but not a sale. And if under the contract of sale, title to the goods has not passed, then there is an agreement to sell and not a completed sale.

Thus, the term 'sale of goods' was to be interpreted with reference to the transfer of ownership in goods. A contract can be formed only between two distinct individuals. People cannot form a contract with themselves. A transaction of this nature would not be considered a sale, on which sales tax could be levied. This was the relevant point in the following case.

J.C. Tax Officer, Harbour Division II, Madras v. Young Men's Association (Regd) Madras

The definition of sale was challenged from another perspective.[2] Clubs and societies are

---

[2] *J.C. Tax Officer, Harbour Division II, Madras v. Young Men's Association (Regd.) Madras*, AIR (1970) SC 1212.

created for the benefit of their members. They may serve food and beverages to the members for a price. A sale, however, requires a contract between two distinct persons. Are the clubs and members two distinct persons or is a club only acting for the members? Under the Act, a dealer was required to pay sales tax. Explanation 1 to Section 2(g) provided that 'A Society including a co-operative society, club or firm or an association which, whether or not in the course of business, buys, sells or distributes goods from or to its members for cash or for deferred payment or for commission, remuneration or other valuable consideration, shall be deemed to be a dealer for the purpose of this Act'. The Supreme Court ruled:

The essential question, in the present case, is whether the supply of the various preparations by each club to its members involved a transaction of sale within the meaning of the Sale of Goods Act 1930. The State Legislature being competent to legislate only under Entry 54, List II of the 7th Schedule to the Constitution the expression 'sale of goods' bears the same meaning, which it has in the aforesaid Act. Thus in spite of the definition contained in Sec. 2 (n) read with Explanation I of the Act if there is no transfer of property from one to another there is no sale which would be eligible to tax. If the club even though a distinct legal entity is only acting as an agent for its members in the matter of supply of various preparations to them no sale would be involved as the element of transfer would be completely absent. This position has been rightly accepted even in the previous decision of this Court.

The final conclusion of the High Court in the judgment under appeal was that the case of each club was analogous to that of an agent or mandatory investing his own monies for preparing things for consumption of the principal, and later recouping himself for the expenses incurred. Once this conclusion on the facts relating to each club was reached it was unnecessary for the High Court to have expressed any view with regard to the vires of the Explanations to Sections 2 (g) and 2 (n) of the Act. As no transaction of sale was involved there could be no levy of tax under the provisions of the Act on the supply of refreshments and preparations by each one of the clubs to its members.

Thus, the Supreme Court did not declare the provision in the Act itself ultra vires but limited itself to the nature of activities of the parties before it, ruling that their activities were only as an agent for the members. In *K.L. Johar and Co., M/s* v. *Deputy Commercial Tax Officer, Coimbatore III*[3] it was stated that a hire purchase was not a sale and could not be taxed. As we saw in Chapter 2, in *State of HP* v. *M/s Associated Hotels of India Ltd*[4] and *Northern India Caterers* v. *Lt Governor of Delhi*,[5] the Supreme Court declared that food served in restaurants and hotels was not 'sale' and sales tax could not be imposed on it. The prevailing legal position was thus explained by the Supreme Court in a subsequent case, *Bharat Sanchar Nigam Ltd* v. *Union of India*.[6]

... composite contracts such as works contracts, hire-purchase contracts and catering contracts were not assessable as contracts for sale of goods. The locus classicus holding the field was State of Madras v. Gannon Dunkerley and Co. IX STC 353 (SC). There this Court held that the words 'sale of goods' in Entry 48 of List II, Schedule VII to the Government of India Act, 1935 did not cover the sale sought to be taxed by the State Government under the Madras General Tax Act, 1939. The classical concept of sale was held to apply to the entry in the legislative list in that there had to be three essential components to constitute a transaction of sale—namely, (i) an agreement to transfer title, (ii) supported by consideration, and (iii) an actual transfer of title in the goods. In the absence of any one of these elements it was held that there was no sale. Therefore, a contract under which a contractor agreed to set up a building would not be a contract for sale. It was one contract, entire and indivisible and there was no separate agreement for sale of goods justifying the levy of sales tax by the provincial legislatures. ... Parties could have provided for two independent agreements, one relating to the labour and work involved in the execution of the work and erection of the building and the second relating to the sale of the material used in the building in which case the latter would be an agreement to sell and the supply of materials thereunder, a sale. Where there was no such separation, the contract was a composite one. It was not classifiable as a sale.

The Court accepted ... that the expression 'sale of goods' was ... a term of well recognized legal import in the general law relating to sale of goods and must be interpreted in Entry 48 in List II of Schedule VII of the 1935 Act as having the same meaning as in the Sale of Goods Act, 1930. According to this decision if the words 'sale of goods' have to be interpreted in their legal sense, that sense can only be what it has in the law relating to sale of goods.

The government intended to have a much broader scope for sales tax than the one given by the Supreme Court. Parliament amended Article 366 of the Constitution of India through the 46th constitutional amendment to negative the court judgments. The amendment was as follows:

366. In this Constitution, unless the context otherwise requires, the following expressions have the meanings hereby respectively assigned to them, that is to say—

...

(29A) 'tax on the sale or purchase of goods' includes—

(*a*) a tax on the transfer, otherwise than in pursuance of a contract, of property in any goods

---

[3] *K.L. Johar and Co., M/s* v. *Deputy Commercial Tax Officer, Coimbatore III*, AIR (1965) SC 1082.

[4] *State of HP* v. *M/s Associated Hotels of India Ltd*, AIR (1972) SC 1131.

[5] *Northern India Caterers, M/s (India)* v. *Lt Governor of Delhi*, AIR (1978) SC 1591.

[6] *Bharat Sanchar Nigam Ltd* v. *Union of India*, AIR (2006) SC 1383.

for cash, deferred payment or other valuable consideration;

(*b*) a tax on the transfer of property in goods (whether as goods or in some other form) involved in the execution of a works contract;

(*c*) a tax on the delivery of goods on hire purchase or any system of payment by instalments;

(*d*) a tax on the transfer of the right to use any goods for any purpose (whether or not for a specified period) for cash, deferred payment or other valuable consideration;

(*e*) a tax on the supply of goods by any unincorporated association or body of persons to a member thereof for cash, deferred payment or other valuable consideration;

(*f*) a tax on the supply, by way of or as part of any service or in any other manner whatsoever, of goods, being food or any other article for human consumption or any drink (whether or not intoxicating), where such supply or service, is for cash, deferred payment or other valuable consideration,

and such transfer, delivery or supply of any goods shall be deemed to be a sale of those goods by the person making the transfer, delivery or supply and a purchase of those goods by the person to whom such transfer, delivery or supply is made.

Subclause (a) negates the decision in *Vishnu Agencies* v. *Commissioner of Sales tax*[7] that a sale contract is formed through voluntary consent of the parties; Subclause (b) judgment *State of Madras* v. *M/s Gannon Dunkerley and Co. (Madras) Ltd*; Subclause (c) judgment *K.L. Johar and Company* v. *CTO*;[8] Subclause (d) judgment *A.V. Meiyyappan* v. *CIT, 20 STC 115*; Subclause (e) judgment *Jt Commercial Tax Officer* v. *YMIA*;[9] and

Subclause (f) judgment *Northern India Caters (India) Ltd* v. *Lt Governor of Delhi*[10] and *State of H.P.* v. *Associated Hotels of India Ltd.*[11] The following is an important case exploring the scope of the amendment and the meaning of sale of goods since then.

Bharat Sanchar Nigam Ltd v. Union of India

Mobile phone service providers give SIM cards to mobile phone users on the formation of a contract with them.[12] The SIM card enables a subscriber to use the provider's telephony service. The Central Government considered the cost of the sim card as a contract for provision of service and imposed service tax on it. The state governments considered it to be the supply of goods, and imposed sales tax on it. The question before the court was, therefore, whether the contract was for sale of goods, provision of service, or both. The Supreme Court noted:

Gannon Dunkerley survived the 46th Constitutional Amendment in two respects. First with regard to the definition of 'sale' for the purposes of the Constitution in general and for the purposes of Entry 54 of List II in particular except to the extent that the clauses in Article 366(29A) operate. By introducing separate categories of 'deemed sales', the meaning of the word 'goods' was not altered. Thus the definitions of the composite elements of a sale such as intention of the parties, goods, delivery etc. would continue to be defined according to known legal connotations. This does not mean that the content of the concepts remain static. Courts must move with the times. But the 46th Amendment does not give a licence, for

---

[7] *Vishnu Agencies* v. *Commissioner of Sales Tax*, AIR (1978) SC 449.

[8] *K.L. Johar and Co., M/s* v. *Deputy Commercial Tax Officer, Coimbatore III*, AIR (1965) SC 1082.

[9] *J.C. Tax Officer, Harbour Division II, Madras* v. *Young Men's Association (Regd) Madras*, AIR (1970) SC 1212.

[10] *Northern India Caterers, M/s (India)* v. *Lt Governor of Delhi*, AIR (1978) SC 1591.

[11] *State of HP* v. *M/s Associated Hotels of India Ltd*, AIR (1972) SC 1131.

[12] *Bharat Sanchar Nigam Ltd* v. *Union of India*, AIR (2006) SC 1383.

example, to assume that a transaction is a sale and then to look around for what could be the goods. The word 'goods' has not been altered by the 46th Amendment. That ingredient of a sale continues to have the same definition. The second respect in which Gannon Dunkerley has survived is with reference to the dominant nature test to be applied to a composite transaction not covered by Article 366(29A). Transactions which are mutant sales are limited to the clauses of Article 366(29A). All other transactions would have to qualify as sales within the meaning of Sale of Goods Act, 1930 for the purpose of levy of sales tax.

Of all the different kinds of composite transactions the drafters of the 46th Amendment chose three specific situations, a works contract, a hire-purchase contract and a catering contract to bring within the fiction of a deemed sale. Of these three, the first and third involve a kind of service and sale at the same time. Apart from these two cases where splitting of the service and supply has been Constitutionally permitted in clauses (b) and (g) of Clause (29A) of Art. 366, there is no other service which has been permitted to be so split. For example, the clauses of Art. 366(29A) do not cover hospital services. Therefore, if during the treatment of a patient in a hospital, he or she is given a pill, can the sales tax authorities tax the transaction as a sale? Doctors, lawyers and other professionals render service in the course of which can it be said that there is a sale of goods when a doctor writes out and hands over a prescription or a lawyer drafts a document and delivers it to his/her client? Strictly speaking with the payment of fees, consideration does pass from the patient or client to the doctor or lawyer for the documents in both cases.

The reason why these services do not involve a sale for the purposes of Entry 54 of List II is, as we see it, for reasons ultimately attributable to the principles enunciated in Gannon Dunkerley's case, namely, if there is an instrument of contract which may be composite in form in any case other than the exceptions in Article 366(29A), unless the transaction in truth represents two distinct and separate contracts and is discernible as such, then the State would not have the power to

separate the agreement to sell from the agreement to render service, and impose tax on the sale. The test, therefore, for composite contracts other than those mentioned in Article 366 (29A) continues to be—did the parties have in mind or intend separate rights arising out of the sale of goods. If there was no such intention there is no sale even if the contract could be disintegrated. The test for deciding whether a contract falls into one category or the other is to as what is the substance of the contract. We will, for the want of a better phrase, call this the dominant nature test.

The meaning of the above passages is clear. If the intent of the parties was to have two separate contracts, one for the provision of service and the other for sale of goods, even if the two are combined, they will be taxed separately. However, if this was not the intent, the contract can be severed into two only for 'deemed sales' covered under Article 366 (29A)—work contracts and catering of food. In other cases, the contract will be taken as a whole and its dominant nature will decide whether it is a sale contract or service contract. As there was inadequate information before the court on the nature of the contract itself, the Supreme Court did not express a view on whether a sim card represented a sale or a service. It noted:

It is not possible for this Court to opine finally on the issue. What a SIM card represents is ultimately a question of fact as has been correctly submitted by the States. In determining the issue, however, the Assessing Authorities will have to keep in mind the following principles: If the SIM Card is not sold by the assessee to the subscribers but is merely part of the services rendered by the service providers, then a SIM card cannot be charged separately to sales tax. It would depend ultimately upon the intention of the parties. If the parties intended that the SIM card would be a separate object of sale, it would be open to the Sales Tax Authorities to levy sales tax thereon. There is insufficient material on the basis of which we can reach a decision. However, we emphasise that if the sale of a SIM card is merely incidental to the service being provided and only facilitates the identification of the subscribers, their credit and other details, it would not be assessable to sales tax.

With the introduction and expansion of service tax, distinguishing and delineating a service contract from a sale contract will continue to be contested before the courts. Through the Finance Acts, service tax was levied on banking and financial services, including 'financial leasing services including equipment leasing and hire-purchase.' The Association of Leasing and Financial Service Companies challenged the constitutional validity of the provision,[13] contending was that as a hire purchase was a 'deemed sale', it could not be subject to service tax. The Supreme Court noted the contention of the Central Government with approval:

The learned Attorney General drew our attention to the conceptual distinction between a service tax and a tax on hiring transaction. According to him, the business of banking or organizing financial services is an organized activity and service tax is imposed on that activity of financial leasing services ... That, service tax is not imposed on the hiring part of a hire-purchase transaction. According to the learned Attorney General, it is wrong to suggest that the whole 'field' is covered by Entry 54 of List II as is sought to be contended on behalf of the appellant(s) because Article 366(29A), by way of a legal fiction, deems a tax on the delivery of goods on hire purchase to be a sale. To interpret this fiction to mean that even a tax on financial leasing services is a tax on delivery of goods amounts to creating a fiction within a fiction, which is impermissible in law. Therefore, according to the learned Attorney General, there is no question of the impugned levy being a levy

of service tax on a hire-purchase transaction. Relying on the doctrine of pith and substance, it was submitted that the substance of the impugned law must be looked at in order to determine whether it is in pith and substance within a particular entry whatever its ancillary effect may be. Applying the said test, it was submitted that imposition of service tax on financial leasing services including equipment leasing and hire purchase does not, in pith and substance, fall within the scope of Entry 54 of List II as extended by Article 366(29A).

The Supreme Court distinguished a financing transaction from a hire-purchase transaction. It noted:

... if the intention of the financing party in obtaining the hire-purchase and the allied agreements is to secure the return of the loan advanced to its customer the transaction would be merely a financing transaction. The point which needs to be re-stated is that the funding activity undertaken by the financing party which could be in the form of loan or equipment leasing or hire-purchase financing, would be exigible to service tax if such activity falls in the category of 'banking and other financial services' under Section 65(12) of the Finance Act, 1994. The financial transaction was earlier out of the tax net. In the process there are two different and distinct transactions, viz., the financing transaction and the equipment leasing/hire-purchase transaction. The former is exigible to service tax under Section 66 of Finance Act, 1994 (as amended) whereas the latter would be exigible to local sales tax/VAT.

The service tax was applicable to banking companies and non-banking finance companies (NBFCs). The Supreme Court noted:

... NBFCs essentially are loan companies. They basically conduct their business as loan companies. They could be in addition thereto in the business of equipment leasing, hire purchase finance and investment. Because NBFCs are basically loan companies, they are required to show the assets

---

[13] *Association of Leasing and Financial Service Companies* v. *Union of India*, 2011 (2) SCC 352.

leased as 'receivables' in their balance sheets. That, the activities of hire-purchase finance/equipment leasing undertaken by NBFCs come under the category of 'para banking'. That, in substance a finance lease, unlike an operating lease, is a financial loan (assistance/facility) by the lessor to the lessee. That, in the bailment termed 'hire' the bailee receives both possession of the chattel and the right to use it in return for remuneration. On the other hand, equipment leasing is long term financing which helps the borrower to raise funds without outright payment in the first instance. Here the 'interest' element cannot be compared to consideration for lease/hire which is in the nature of remuneration (consideration) for hire. Thus, financing as an activity or business of NBFCs is different and distinct from operating lease/hire-purchase agreements in the classical sense. The elements of the finance lease or loan transaction are quite different from those in equipment leasing/hire-purchase agreements between owner (lessor) and the hirer (lessee). There are two independent transactions and what the impugned tax seeks to do is to tax the financial facilities extended to its customers by the NBFCs under Section 66 of the 1994 Act (as amended) as they come under 'banking and other financial services' under Section 65(12) of the said Act. 'The finance lease' and 'the hire-purchase finance' thus squarely come under the expression 'financial leasing services' in Section 65(12) of the Finance Act, 1994 (as amended).

The common law concepts of sale and agreement to sell had developed over centuries. It was codified in UK law, which was adopted by the Sale of Goods Act, 1930. The concept of the sale of goods was built on the foundation of contract law, and in turn became the foundation on which taxation laws were built. Foundations, however limiting, cannot be changed without collapsing the structure built on it. Thus, the taxation laws were changed to give a wider meaning to sale. The change expanded the scope but also continued to rest on the same foundation.

This case law is based on the earlier sales tax laws that are now repealed by the states. Under the direction of the Centre, the states have enacted value-added tax (VAT) acts. Consistent with constitutional provisions, the VAT acts are on the sale of goods only. The key concepts and categories are the same as the earlier law. The tax is also imposed on the sale consideration. The difference is that the seller gets an input rebate for the taxes collected and paid. This results in the seller effectively paying tax on net value of the transaction, hence the term value-added tax. The case law reviewed above will continue to be of value in relation to the VAT Acts.

EXPANDING SCOPE OF 'GOODS'
The sale must be of *goods* for the tax to apply. As we noted at the beginning of the book, the original meaning of goods was tangible movable property. Goods came to be formulated as 'every kind of movable property other than actionable claims and money'. New intangible forms of property that were movable property emerged over time, ostensibly qualifying as goods based on that definition. The dispute on the nature of these properties arose in relation to taxation.

A power company supplies electricity to the consumers who pay for it. Is electricity to be considered goods? It is the property of the company and is certainly not movable. It certainly seems to qualify according to the definition in the Sale of Goods Act, 1930. But it is not like most other goods; it cannot be seen or touched. Further, as storage, possession and delivery is an integral part of the law on the sale of goods, that law could not be applied meaningfully if the property was not amenable to this. Looking at the law as a whole, one could say that to qualify as goods, the property should be capable of possession and delivery. This is how the scope of the term has expanded to assimilate newer forms of property. Let us study this further with the following review of cases.

K.E.S. Corporation v. J.C.T. Officer

Kumbakonam Electric Supply Corporation Ltd purchased and distributed electricity to local consumers in a given area in Tamil Nadu.[14] The sales tax laws could apply to the Corporation only if it were a 'dealer' according to the Madras General Sales Tax Act, 1959, and the Central Sales Tax Act, 1956, and only if electricity qualified as 'goods' within the Acts. The latter question was brought before the high court, which noted:

These two petitions, in which the petitioner is the same, raise an interesting question as to whether electricity, is 'goods' for the purpose of the Madras General Sales Tax-Act, 1959 and the Central Sales Tax Act 1956. There appears to be no direct authority on the question, but I have come to the conclusion that the question should be answered in the affirmative.

...

Under the Sale of Goods Act, 'goods' means every kind of moveable property other than actionable claims and money, and includes stock and shares, growing crops, grass and things attached to or forming part of the land which are agreed to be served before sale or under the contract of sale. Under this definition 'goods' must be property and it must be moveable. The inclusive part of the definition would seem to indicate that the property contemplated is of a tangible character, which may be capable of possession and touch and that the things which would come within the expression 'goods' should be such as may be put to human or other use. The scheme of the Sale of Goods Act visualises delivery of possession, which again indicates that what is contemplated by 'goods' under its provisions is tangible property which can be transmitted from hand to hand by delivery.

But I think the first part of the definition of 'goods' should not be read as controlled in its scope by the inclusive part of the definition. Any kind of property which is moveable will, therefore, fall within the definition of 'goods' provided it is transmissible or transferable from hand to hand or capable of delivery, which to my mind, need not necessarily be in a tangible or physical sense. The General Clauses Act, 1897, defines 'moveable property' as property of every description, except immoveable property, and 'immoveable property' includes of course, land, benefits to arise out of land and things attached to the earth, or permanently fastened to the earth. Under this Act, therefore, property is divided into two broad categories as moveable, and immoveable, and that which is not immoveable is defined to be moveable. This is a wide description which does not appear to be of much assistance in deciding the instant question.

But having regard to the two fold division of property, if the property in question is not immoveable, it must necessarily be moveable. From these statutory definitions it is clear therefore, that if electricity is property and it is moveable it will be 'goods'. It may perhaps be that when the Sale of Goods Act or the General Clauses Act was enacted, electricity as property was not so much in the contemplation of the legislature. But, as it seems to me, both from the scientific as well as the economic point of view, electricity appears to be such property as gas or water which is subjected to a particular process, bottled up and sold for consumption.

After all what is property? I think anything which is of value in a commercial sense and is fit for use in any conceivable manner will be property, provided it is capable of possession and transfer, such possession or transfer not merely in the physical sense. Electricity answers that description. Every day it is sold, purchased and consumed, it is too late in the day to say that electricity is not capable of sale as property. Electricity seems to be also moveable property, because it can undoubtedly be transmitted, of course, through insulators or through conductors from place to

---

[14] *KES Corporation* v. *JCT Officer*, AIR (1964) Madras 477.

place. It is also capable of delivery in the same way for consumption though again subject to the protection which is required, having regard to the peculiar nature and quality of electricity. It may be that electricity cannot be possessed in a physical sense, like tangible goods. It may also be true partly that electricity cannot be stored except in the form of batteries and similar devices. If, therefore, electricity is property and is capable of movement and delivery in the sense I have mentioned, I do not see why it cannot be regarded as goods.

The reasoning of the court was that every immovable property is movable property and would be 'goods' if it can be stored, possessed, and delivered. In the following case, the Supreme Court fully accepted the formulation.

Commissioner of Sales Tax Madhya Pradesh, Indore v. Madhya Pradesh Electricity Board, Jabalpur

The Madhya Pradesh Electricity Board was engaged in the production, distribution, and sale of electricity.[15] The case is identical to *KES Corporation* v. *JCT Officer*, except that the act in question is the MP General Sales Tax Act, 1959. The Supreme Court noted:

What has essentially to be seen is whether electric energy is 'goods' within the meaning of the relevant provisions of the two Acts. The definition in terms is very wide according to which 'goods' means all kinds of movable property. Then certain items are specifically excluded or included and electric energy or electricity is not one of them. The term 'movable property' when considered with reference to 'goods' as defined for the purposes of sale tax cannot be taken in a narrow sense and merely because electric energy is not tangible or cannot be moved or touched like, for instance, a piece of wood or a book it cannot cease to be

movable property when it has all the attributes of such property. It is needless to repeat that it is capable of abstraction, consumption and use ... It can be transmitted, transferred, delivered, stored, possessed etc. in the same way as any other movable property. ... If there can be sale and purchase of electric energy like any other movable object we see no difficulty in holding that electric energy was intended to be covered by the definition of 'goods' in the two Acts.

The Supreme Court in *State of AP* v. *NTPC Ltd*[16] reiterated the view and made additional comments on the nature of goods and their consumption. It noted:

It is settled with the pronouncement of this Court in Commissioner of Sales Tax, Madhya Pradesh, Indore v. Madhya Pradesh Electricity Board, Jabalpur[17] that electricity is goods. ... However, A.N. Grover, J., speaking for three-Judge Bench of this Court went on to observe that electric energy 'can be transmitted, transferred, delivered, stored, possessed etc. in the same way as any other moveable property'. In this observation we agree with Grover, J., on all other characteristics of electric energy except that it can be 'stored' and to the extent that electric energy can be 'stored', the observation must be held to be erroneous or by oversight. The science and technology till this day have not been able to evolve any methodology by which electric energy can be preserved or stored.

Another significant characteristic of electric energy is that its generation or production coincides almost instantaneously with its consumption.

* * *

Sale, Goods, and Intellectual Property

Books are certainly goods. The paper and ink in one accounts for only part of the value;

---

[15] *Commissioner of Sales Tax Madhya Pradesh, Indore* v. *Madhya Pradesh Electricity Board, Jabalpur*, AIR (1970) SC 732.

[16] *State of AP* v. *NTPC Ltd*, AIR (2002) SC 1895.

[17] *Commissioner of Sales Tax Madhya Pradesh, Indore* v. *Madhya Pradesh Electricity Board, Jabalpur*, AIR (1970) SC 732.

most of it lies in the ideas it expresses. Are the ideas goods, or is it the paper? Similarly, the cost of a blank CD is a great deal less than a music CD. When one buys a music CD, one is buying the music. What then are the goods in such cases where intangible property is in a tangible medium? The Supreme Court deliberated this in the following case in relation to import of goods.

Associated Cement Companies Ltd, M/s v. Commr of Customs

The laws for imposing custom duties also define 'goods' as including all 'movable property'. This case was on the charge of customs duty on the import of drawings and designs relating to machinery or industrial technology.[18] Under the contracts, foreign collaborators were to supply the know-how and technology. This came as drawings, designs, and diskettes, which were sent by courier or brought by a bearer. The importers declared a nominal value for the goods and allowed them into the country. Subsequently, the government authorities gathered intelligence that substantial sums were paid to the foreign collaborators under the contracts. According to the custom officials, the value of the drawings and design was misreported. The importers contended that the contract was for provision of knowledge, which was intangible. The tangible part, the piece of paper, had no value. As the court put its argument, 'drawings by themselves have no value, since if the drawings are lost they could be replaced and the loss would merely be of the cost of paper.' Section 2(22) of the Customs Act defines 'goods' as:

(a) vessels, aircrafts and vehicles;
(b) stores;

---

[18] *Associated Cement Companies Ltd, M/s* v. *Commr of Customs*, AIR (2001) SC 862.

(c) baggage;
(d) currency and negotiable instruments; and
(e) any other kind of movable property

The Supreme Court noted:

According to Section 12 of the Customs Act, duty is payable on goods imported into India. The word 'goods' has been defined in Section 2(22) of the Customs Act and it includes in sub-clause (c) 'baggage' and sub-clause (e) 'any other kind of movable property'. It is clear from mere reading of the said provision that any immovable article brought into India by a passenger as part of his baggage can make him liable to pay customs duty as per the Customs Tariff Act. ... Whether movable article comes as a part of a baggage, or is imported into the country by any other manner, for the purpose of the Customs Act, the provision of Section 12 would be attracted. Any media whether in the form of books or computer disks or cassettes which contain information technology or ideas would necessarily be regarded as goods under the aforesaid provisions of the Customs Act. These items are moveable goods and would be covered by Section 2(22)(e) of the Customs Act.

The next question before the court was on valuation of the goods being imported. Section 14 of the Customs Act, Customs Tariff Act, 1975, and rules under the two Acts provide details for valuation of the goods. What is relevant for our discussion is that the cost of the material cannot be separated from the intangible asset. The Supreme Court noted:

It is true that what the appellants had wanted was technical advice or information technology. Payment was to be made for this intangible asset. But the moment the information or advice is put on a media, whether paper or diskettes or any other thing, that what is supplied becomes chattel. It is in respect of the drawings, designs etc. which are received that payment is made to the foreign collaborators. It is these papers or diskettes etc. containing the technological advice, which are paid for and used. The foreign collaborators part with them in lieu of money. It is, therefore, sold by them as chattel for use by the Indian importer. The drawings, designs, manuals etc. so received are goods on which customs duty could be levied.

...

Significantly Chapter 49 also includes items which have substantial intellectual value as opposed to the value of the paper on which it is put. Newspapers, periodicals, journals, dictionaries etc. are to be found in Chapter 49 wherein maps, plans and other similar items are also included, while Chapter 97 talks about original engravings. It is clear that intellectual property when put on a media would be regarded as an article on the total value of which customs duty is payable.

To put it differently, the legislative intent can easily be granted by reference to the Customs Valuation Rules and the specific entries in the Customs Tariff Act. The value of an encyclopaedia or a dictionary or a magazine is not only the value of the paper. The value of the paper is in fact negligible as compared to the value or price of an encyclopaedia. Therefore, the intellectual input in such items greatly enhance the value of the papers and ink in the aforesaid examples. This means that the charge of a duty is on the final product whether it be the encyclopaedia or the engineering or architectural drawings or any manual.

Similar would be the position in the case of a programme of any kind loaded on a disc or a floppy. For example in the case of music the value of a popular music cassette is several times more than the value of the blank cassette. However, if a pre-recorded music cassette or a popular film or a musical score is imported into India duty will necessarily have to be charged on the value of the final product. In this behalf we may note that in State Bank of India v. Collector of Customs, Bombay, 2000 (1) Scale 72: (2000 AIR SCW 125), the Bank had, under an agreement with the foreign company, imported a computer software and manuals, the total value of which was US $ 4,084,475. The bank filed an application for refund of customs duty on the ground that the basic cost of software was US $ 401, 047. While the rest of the amount of US $ 3,683,428 was payable only as a licence fee for its right to use the software for the bank countrywide. The claim for the refund of the customs duty paid on the aforesaid amount of US $ 3,683,428 was not accepted by this Court as in its opinion, on a correct interpretation of Section 14 read with the rules, duty was payable on the transaction value determined therein and as per Rule 9 in determining the transaction value there has to be added to the price actually paid or payable for the imported goods, royalties and the licence fee for which the buyer is required to pay, directly or indirectly as a condition of sale of goods to the extent that such royalties and fees are not included in the price actually paid or payable. This clearly goes to show that when technical material is supplied whether in the form of drawings or manuals the same are goods liable to customs duty on the transaction value in respect thereof.

It is [a] misconception to contend that what is being taxed is intellectual input. What is being taxed under the Customs Act read with Customs Tariff Act and the Customs Valuation Rules is not the input alone but goods whose value has been enhanced by the said inputs. The final product at the time of import is either the magazine or the encyclopaedia or the engineering drawings as the case may be. There is no scope for splitting the engineering drawing or the encyclopaedia into intellectual input on the one hand and the paper on which it is scribed on the other. For example, paintings are also to be taxed. Valuable paintings are worth millions. A painting or a portrait may be specifically commissioned or an article may be tailor made. This aspect is irrelevant since what is taxed is the final product as defined and it will be an absurdity to contend that the value for the purposes of duty ought to be the cost of the canvas and the oil paint even though the composite product, i.e., the painting is worth millions.

...

In the case of St Albans City and District Council v. International Computers Ltd., (1996) 4 All ER 481 Sir Iain Glidewell in relation to whether computer programme on a disc would be regarded as goods observed at page 493 as follows:

'Suppose I buy an instruction manual on the maintenance and repair of a particular make of car. The instructions are wrong in an important respect. Anybody who follows them is likely to cause serious damage to the engine of his car. In my view, the instructions are an integral part of the manual. The manual including the instructions, whether in a book or a video cassette, would in my opinion be 'goods' within the meaning of the 1979 Act, and the defective instructions would result in a breach of the implied terms in S. 14.

If this is correct, I can see no logical reason why it should not also be correct in relation to a computer disk onto which a program designed and intended to instruct or enable a computer to achieve particular junctions has been encoded. If the disk is sold or hired by the computer manufacturer, but the program is defective, in my opinion there would prima facie be a breach of the terms as to quality and fitness for purpose implied by the 1979 Act or the 1982 Act.'

The above view, in our view, appears to be logical and also in consonance with the Customs Act. Similarly in Advent Systems Limited v. UNISYS Corporation, 925 F 2d 670 (3d Cir 1991) it was contended before the Court in United States that software referred to in the agreement between the parties was a 'product' and not a 'good' but intellectual property outside the ambit of Uniform Commercial Code. In the said Code, goods were defined as 'all things (including specially manufactured goods) which are moveable at the time of the identification for sale'. Holding that computer software was 'goods' the Court held as follows:

'Computer programs are the product of an intellectual process, but once implanted in a medium are widely distributed to computer owners. An analogy can be drawn to a compact disc recording of an orchestral rendition. The music is produced by the artistry of musicians and in itself is not a "good", but when transferred to a laser-readable disc becomes a readily merchantable commodity. Similarly, when a professor delivers a lecture, it is not a good, but, when transcribed as a book, it becomes a good. That a computer program may be copyrightable as intellectual property does not alter the fact that once in the form of a floppy disc or other medium, the program is tangible,

moveable and available in the marketplace. The fact that some programs may be tailored for specific purposes need not alter their status as 'goods' because the Code definition includes 'specially manufactured goods'.

We are in agreement with the aforesaid observations and hold that the value of the goods imported would depend upon the quality of the same and would be represented by the transaction value in respect of the goods imported.

Tata Consultancy Services v. State of Andhra Pradesh

This Supreme Court case dealt with the issue of whether computer software should be considered goods according to the laws on sales tax. One of the areas that Tata Consultancy Services (TCS) specialized in was computers.[19] As a part of their business, they prepared and loaded custom-made software on customers' computers. The court referred to this as 'uncanned software'. It also sold computer software packages off the shelf, which the court referred to as 'canned software'. The Andhra Pradesh government levied sales tax on canned software, contending that it qualified as goods within the meaning of the sales tax laws of Andhra Pradesh. TCS's argument was that the term 'goods' only included tangible movable property; computer software was not tangible movable property, and thus, not taxable under the act. The Supreme Court relied on *Commissioner of Sales Tax Madhya Pradesh, Indore* v. *Madhya Pradesh Electricity Board, Jabalpur*, and noted:

Thus this Court has held that the term 'goods' for the purposes of sale tax, cannot be given a narrow meaning. It has been held that properties which are capable of being abstracted, consumed and used and/or transmitted, transferred, delivered, stored or possessed etc. are 'goods' for the purposes of

[19] *Tata Consultancy Services* v. *State of Andhra Pradesh*, AIR (2005) SC 371.

sales tax. ... In India the test to determine whether a property is 'goods', for purposes of sales tax, is not whether the property is tangible or intangible or incorporeal. The test is whether the concerned item is capable of abstraction, consumption and use and whether it can be transmitted, transferred, delivered, stored, possessed etc. Admittedly in the case of software, both canned and uncanned, all of these are possible.

...

In the case of Associated Cement Companies Ltd v. Commissioner of Customs[20] the question was whether customs duty was leviable on technical material supplied in the form of drawings, manuals and computer disc, etc. The further question was if customs duty was leviable how it was to be valued. In that case also it was inter alia argued that custom duty could not be levied as the drawings, designs, diskettes, etc. were not goods and that they only constituted ideas. It had been submitted that what was being transferred was technology, i.e., the knowledge or know-how and thus, even though this may be valuable, it was intangible property and not goods.

The court quoted extensively from the judgment and continued:

To be noted that this authority is directly dealing with the question in issue. Even though the definition of the term 'goods' in the Customs Act is not as wide or exhaustive as the definition of the term 'goods' in the said Act, it has still been held that the intellectual property when it is put on a media becomes goods.

...

In our view, the term 'goods' as used in Article 366(12) of the Constitution of India and as defined under the said Act is very wide and includes all types of movable properties, whether those properties be tangible or intangible. We are in complete agreement with the observations made by this Court in Associated Cement Companies Ltd. (supra). A software programme may consist

---

[20] *Associated Cement Companies Ltd* v. *Commissioner of Customs*, AIR (2001) SC 862.

of various commands which enable the computer to perform a designated task. The copyright in that programme may remain with the originator of the programme. But the moment copies are made and marketed, it becomes goods, which are susceptible to sales tax. Even intellectual property, once it is put on to a media, whether it be in the form of books or canvas (in case of painting) or computer discs or cassettes, and marketed would become 'goods'. We see no difference between a sale of a software programme on a CD/floppy disc from a sale of music on a cassette/CD or a sale of a film on a video cassette/CD. In all such cases, the intellectual property has been incorporated on a media for purposes of transfer. Sale is not just of the media which by itself has very little value. The software and the media cannot be split up. What the buyer purchases and pays for is not the disc or the CD. As in the case of paintings or books or music or films the buyer is purchasing the intellectual property and not the media i.e. the paper or cassette or disc or CD. Thus a transaction sale of computer software is clearly a sale of 'goods' within the meaning of the term as defined in the said Act. The term 'all materials, articles and commodities' includes both tangible and intangible/incorporeal property which is capable of abstraction, consumption and use and which can be transmitted, transferred, delivered, stored, possessed etc. The software programmes have all these attributes.

The question then is, if the software were not sold through a CD but downloaded through the Internet, would it be a sale of goods? The downloading of the software meets all the criteria. Software is an intellectual property whose copyright vests in the author. However, once the software is put on a server, the copyright has been put to use to produce a file that can be downloaded. The file is capable of being transmitted, possessed, stored, delivered, and used. Thus, it should not make any difference whether the software is sold on a CD or downloaded. As the question before the court was only on 'canned software', the court refrained from pronouncing on the general question. It noted:

In both cases, the software is capable of being abstracted, consumed and use. In both cases the software can be transmitted, transferred, delivered, stored, possessed etc. Thus even unbranded software, when it is marketed/sold, may be goods. We, however, are not dealing with this aspect and express no opinion thereon because in case of unbranded software other questions like situs of contract of sale and/or whether the contract is a service contract may arise.

The unbranded software mentioned above referred to software that was not sold off the shelf, but was developed specifically for a party. In this case, we would first need to resolve whether it is a service contract or a contract for the sale of goods. If it turns out to be the latter, we would then have to find out where the sale was made in order to decide whether it is in the jurisdiction of a particular state.

Since the dispute arose, information technology has rapidly expanded and transformed. Software, music, and information are now sold directly over the Internet. The Finance Act, 2012, has amended the law on service tax in the Finance Act, 1994, by declaring certain activities to be services. Section 66E(d) provides:

66E. The following shall constitute declared services, namely:

...

(d) development, design, programming, customisation, adaptation, upgradation, enhancement, implementation of information technology software;

The amendment has resolved the dispute only in relation to information technology software. For other sales, like music and information, disputes may arise on the application of sales tax.

INTERNET SALE

The Internet has transformed all spheres of life, including business, trade, and commerce. In some areas, century-old principles of contract law have been satisfactorily extended to explain business done through the Internet. In others, the Internet has posed newer problems that have required legislation. In yet others, the extension of the existing principles to the new medium has created even more challenges. The subject is vast and has numerous aspects. In this section, we will limit ourselves to the Internet and the law of sale of goods. There are three ways that the Internet is used in sale contracts. The contracting parties communicate through an electronic medium like email instead of by post. A customer may buy goods from an e-store using the billing software of the Webpage. In both these cases, the goods are delivered to the buyer through a carrier. Alternatively, there could be a sale of intangible goods by an e-store, where the buyer will download the goods to his computer. Let us begin with the first, where the contract is made through the Internet.

Before the Internet age, when contracting parties communicated orally, in writing, through the post, or over the phone, the principles of contract formation, were well settled. The Internet brought in a quicker and more efficient means of communication. Let us first note the spheres where the medium could not be adopted by existing principles. The Evidence Act, 1872, obviously makes no reference to the Internet, so it could be claimed that a communication made through the electronic medium could not be admissible before a court of law. This and other acts have been amended accordingly.

A written document on paper authenticated by a person's unique signature has become the communication of offer and acceptance. An electronic communication may be in writing, but it is not on paper and not signed in ink. Thus, there could be ambiguities on the validity of an electronic document. The Information Technology Act, 1999, with subsequent amendments, has fully addressed these issues. It recognizes several means of authenticating an electronic document. On the Internet, entering one's password for an account or transaction is taken as an electronic signature. Writing one's name at the end of an email or attaching a scan of one's signature helps in locating the origin and the author of the mail. In addition, the act makes provision for digital signatures. An electronic signature is usually an encrypted key generated by software designed for that purpose The sender attaches the digital signature to the electronic record. The software encrypts the document. Recipients can de-encrypt the document only if they have the key for de-encryption. This makes it possible for the parties to confirm that the data has not been tampered with. Electronic communication has thus acquired the same status as other forms of communication. To remove any doubt, Section 10A of the Information Technology Act, 1999, provides:

10A. Validity of contracts formed through electronic means: Where in a contract formation, the communication of proposals, the acceptance of proposals, the revocation of proposals and acceptances, as the case may be, are expressed in electronic form or by means of an electronic record, such contract shall not be deemed to be unenforceable solely on the ground that such electronic form or means was used for that purpose.

Most business contracts have a clause on jurisdiction that specifies the court that may be approached if there is a dispute about the contract. The time and place are especially important if the contract has not provided on this. The place of formation of a contract is governed by the means of communication between the parties. If the mode of communication between the parties is interactive, the contract is taken to have been made where the offeror received the communication of acceptance. If the mode of communication is post-like, the acceptance is taken to be made at the place where the acceptor had put the acceptance in the course of transmission. Among the electronic modes of communication, email and SMS are post-like, while video conferencing and phone conversations are interactive. With mobile phones, electronic communication can be made from anywhere. Section 13(3) of the Act has provided for situations where the parties have not settled on the jurisdiction of a court:

13. Time and place of despatch and receipt of electronic record. ... (3) Save as otherwise agreed to between the originator and the addressee, an electronic record is deemed to be dispatched at the place where the originator has his place of business, and is deemed to be received at the place where the addressee has his place of business.

The act establishes that the communication is made between the parties from their place of business. Section 13(5) explains the scope of place of business.

(5) For the purposes of this section—

(a) if the originator or the addressee has more than one place of business, the principal place of business, shall be the place of business;

(b) if the originator or the addressee does not have a place of business, his usual place of residence shall be deemed to be the place of business;

(c) 'usual place of residence', in relation to a body corporate, means the place where it is registered.

The electronic communication, thus, leads to the formation of a contract. From this point on, there is no difference from a contract formed through other means of communication.

A Webpage is only a platform for communication. It cannot intrinsically be considered an offer or invitation to offer. The communication has to be judged by the standard principles of contract law with regard to whether its content is an invitation to offer, offer, or acceptance. Thus, each Webpage is a separate study in itself as to how communication takes place between the parties. Having said this, we will examine the usual manner in which e-stores trade with the customers.

An e-store displays the products for sale. The display is an invitation to offer. The customer selects and puts items in a 'basket' and gives the address for the goods' despatch. The Webpage gives the final amount to be paid by the customer and requires the customer to enter the details for payment by credit or debit card. Till this stage, the customer is free to abandon the purchase. Once the customer submits the credit or debit card details, he has irrevocably committed himself to the communication—he has made an offer. The payment details are sent to the credit/debit card Webpage, which accepts the request and pays the merchant. On receiving the payment, the merchant generates a confirmation note for the customer that appears on the screen of the customer. This is the acceptance of the customer's offer. All this happens automatically through the software in the server that hosts the merchant's e-store. Before submitting the offer, the customer is required to tick on the checkbox signifying acceptance of the terms and conditions of sale. The terms are added to the offer and become the terms of the contract. The merchant has already been paid, and has only to do his duty under the contract to transfer ownership to the customer and deliver the goods.

There are variations of this basic arrangement. The Webpage may require a person to become a member and get a username and password. While opening the account, the customer will accept the terms and conditions for using the Webpage, which may be separate from the terms and conditions for the sale. The Webpage may only be a platform for the buyer and seller to come together. This is the equivalent of a mall, which only maintains the building and rents the premises for the sellers. In this case, the legal person owning the Webpage is not the seller, and the customer may have not rights against the Webpage. The Webpage could also be a disclosed agent of the seller. In this case, the law of agency will apply. The role of the agent is to make a contract between the customer and the principal and then 'drop out' for the contracting parties to perform the contract. All the rights and duties in relation to the quality of goods and delivery may be only between the principal and the customer. Finally, the legal person owning the Webpage may be the seller. In this case, there are only the two parties—the buyer and seller.

Whatever the arrangement, in most cases, the seller would receive the payment along with the offer. After formation of the contract, it is the seller who has to perform the duty of delivering the goods according to the terms of the contract. The e-store would have provided the terms for carriage and delivery. For example, an Indian retail e-store has set the following terms: 'All items purchased from are made pursuant to a shipment contract. This means that the risk of loss and title for such items pass to you upon our delivery to the carrier.' Thus, the ownership as well as risk pass to the buyer much before the goods reach him. The customer may only have rights against the courier company for loss or damage to the goods. If the Webpage does not provide the details of carriage and delivery, default options provided by the law would apply: the goods are considered as delivered to the customer on delivery to the carrier and the ownership transfers to the customer when the goods are appropriated to the contract. As there are no conditions on transfer of ownership, the appropriation happens on delivery. Thus, ownership in the goods passes to the customer on delivery to the carrier.

The retail e-stores in India also deal with the customers on a cash-on-delivery basis. The customer orders the goods at the e-store and gives the address of the place where the goods are to be delivered, but the payment is made only on delivery. In this transaction, the ownership is not transferred to the customer when the goods are delivered to the courier. The courier carries it to the customer as an agent of the seller with the instruction to deliver the goods only on payment of the amount. The courier has to bring back the goods if the customer fails to pay the amount. Thus, the ownership transfers to the customer only when the courier delivers the goods to him.

A sale through an e-store is a sale of goods, so there is no question of any exemption from sales tax. However, as we have noted earlier, sales tax is levied by the state for sale within it and by the Centre for inter-state sales. In a sale by an e-store, as a customer could be located anywhere, there may be doubts whether a sale is an export, a sale within the state, or an inter-state sale. The sale of goods in the course of inter-state trade and commerce is taxed under the Central Sales Tax Act, 1956. Section 3 of the Act provides as follows:

When is a sale or purchase of goods said to take place in the course of inter-State trade or commerce:

3. A sale or purchase of goods shall be deemed to take place in the course of inter-State trade or commerce if the sale or purchase—

(a) occasions the movement of goods from one State to another...

The Supreme Court has summarized the clause thus:[21]

It is well settled by a catena of decisions of this Court that a sale in the course of inter-State trade has three essential ingredients: (i) there must be a contract of sale, incorporating a stipulation, express or implied, regarding inter-State movement of goods; (ii) the goods must actually move from one State to another, pursuant to such contract of sale; the sale being the proximate cause of movement; and (iii) such movement of goods must be from one State to another State where the sale concludes.

The court elaborated:

It follows as a necessary corollary of these principles that a movement of goods which takes place independent of a contract of sale would not fall within the meaning of inter-state sale. In other words, if there is no contract of sale preceding the movement of goods, obviously the movement cannot be attributed to the contract of sale. Similarly, if the transaction of sale stands completed within the State and the movement of goods takes place thereafter, it would obviously be independently of the contract of sale and necessarily by or on behalf of the purchaser alone and, therefore, the transaction would not be having an inter-state element.

The court illustrated this with reference to prior court judgments:

... when the movement of the goods from one State to another is an incident of the contract it is a sale in the course of inter-State sale and it does not matter which is the State in which the property

---

[21] *State of AP* v. *NTPC Ltd*, AIR (2002) SC 1895.

passes. What is decisive is whether the sale is one which occasions the movement of goods from one State to another. ... a sale would be an inter-State sale even if the contract of sale does not itself provide for the movement of goods from one State to another provided, however, that such movement was the result of a covenant in the contract of sale or was an incident of the contract.

Thus, whether a sale is an inter-state sale is a question of both fact and law. If, as a result of a contract, goods move from one state to another and there is a sale, the sale is an inter-state one. The taxation of sale by an e-store would be based on these principles. In the case of sales by retail e-stores of music, videos, and e-books through digital-only copies, the customer pays for the items and downloads them from the Webpage. We have seen earlier in this chapter that an intangible property that can be stored, delivered, and possessed meets the definition of goods. The transaction, thus, would either be a sale of goods or services. If it is a sale of goods, it would necessitate taxation. The difficult question would be whether it is a sale within the state, an inter-state sale, or an import. The movement of the goods is in the electronic data moving from a server to the computer of the customer. The location of the server may be of vital interest. Retail sale through e-shops has begun in India, and as it expands and registers its presence, the basis for taxation of intangible goods will be challenged. The resolution could be in new legislation for the emerging issues or the courts' extension of existing principles to the sale of intangible goods.

Case Index

Index